DATE			
MAY 1 0 1996			
AUG 0 3 2005			

BOOMTOWN COMMUNITIES

ENVIRONMENTAL DESIGN SERIES

Series Editor: Richard P. Dober, AICP

I define the term "environmental design" as an art larger
than architecture, more comprehensive than planning,
more sensitive than engineering. An art pragmatic, one
that preempts traditional concerns. The practice of this
art is intimately connected with man's ability to function,
to bring visual order to his surroundings, to enhance and
embellish the territory he occupies.

Richard P. Dober
Environmental Design

BOOMTOWN COMMUNITIES c.1

Gary W. Malamud

 VAN NOSTRAND REINHOLD COMPANY
NEW YORK   CINCINNATI   TORONTO   LONDON   MELBOURNE

To Judy

Copyright © 1984 by **Van Nostrand Reinhold Company Inc.**
Environmental Design Series, Volume 5
Library of Congress Catalog Card Number: 83:18419
ISBN: 0-442-26399-6

Manufactured in the United States of America.

Published by Van Nostrand Reinhold Company Inc.
135 West 50th Street
New York, New York 10020

Van Nostrand Reinhold Company Limited
Molly Millars Lane
Wokingham, Berkshire RG11 2PY, England

Van Nostrand Reinhold
480 Latrobe Street
Melbourne, Victoria 3000, Australia

Macmillan of Canada
Division of Gage Publishing Limited
164 Commander Boulevard
Agincourt, Ontario MIS 3C7, Canada

15   14   13   12   11   9   8   7   6   5   4   3   2   1

Library of Congress Cataloging in Publication Data
Malamud, Gary W.
   Boomtown communities.
   (EDS; 5)
   Includes bibliographies and index.
   1. Cities and towns—Growth—Social aspects.   2. City planning.
I. Title.   II. Series: Environmental design series (Van Nostrand Reinhold
Company Inc.); v. 5.
HT119.M34   1984   307'.14   83-18419
ISBN 0-442-26399-6

Contents

Series Editor's Foreword

Gary Malamud has chosen to tackle a difficult subject—the rapid, unexpected, and often unplanned development that accompanies growth in previously underdeveloped areas. Using a historical perspective, Malamud suggests that such growth will continue to appear in certain countries and regions, stimulated by potential economic gain, exploitive or otherwise. By applying workable planning techniques, however, Malamud expects that the problems associated with such boomtowns can be ameliorated. *Ameliorated* is carefully chosen. It means to make better or more tolerable—a logical goal for environmental designers addressing seemingly intractable problems under boomtown conditions, usually with little governmental structures, policies, or guidelines. In these situations, *Boomtown Communities* is a reference book that can help practitioners and clients, as well as those with a general interest in boomtowns.

RICHARD P. DOBER, AICP

Preface

Rapid population growth in communities of all sizes takes place for a variety of reasons, such as the opening or closing of a military base, the start of a new resort, or a government decision to create a new community for military security or for other reasons. The best-known cause, however, is the opening up of new energy exploitation or mining projects in remote areas. Whatever the reasons may be, all these causes create a sudden change in the region's economic, social, political, and financial structures that can overwhelm the ability of the community leaders, planners, and residents to successfully deal with it.

Changes of this kind create the "boomtown syndrome," a volatile mix of problems as varied as the structures in the affected community. The town cannot obtain funds fast enough for construction of new housing, health care, educational and recreational infrastructure, and for professionals required to staff these services. The town takes on an unattractive appearance. Value conflicts break out between preboom and boom residents, and all the affected town's citizens suffer a variety of emotional and social problems.

Rapid population growth and the setting up of new communities have bedeviled urban planners for centuries. Unfortunately, the world population crisis makes the problem even more acute today than ever before, and planners in national, regional, and local government are often no better equipped to deal with the "syndrome" than those of years past.

This study makes clear the fact that urban planning alone cannot overcome the boomtown syndrome. Planners have a major role to play, as do lawyers, politicians, economists, sociologists, social workers, psychologists, psychiatrists, and representatives of whatever industry is causing the disruption to the particular town. Coordinated planning and execution of boom-related activities by these professionals, along with the proper flow of funds, enable the town's public sector to expand as its private sector grows rapidly. All this is necessary to reduce the uncertainty that makes intelligent planning all but impossible. Few radical alternatives to current professional practice are given in this book; however, literature relating to each of these fields is discussed and evaluated.

My involvement in this field began with my choice of an M.B.A. thesis at New York University. One of my instructors, Dr. Thomas Gladwin, professor of management and international business, was, at the time, director of the Energy-Environment Conflict Project at New York University. He and a number of students were investigating ways in which antagonism developed between environmentalist opponents of energy projects and the industry-wide supporters of energy development, and studying methods to reduce this conflict.

At the National Conference on the Management of Energy Conflict in May 1980, Dr. Gladwin covered a number of methods used to manage this type of conflict: public involvement, environmental impact evaluation, siting mechanisms, environmental regulation, permitting procedures, and conflict management procedures. Among the questions raised by Dr. Gladwin concerning siting mechanisms was to what extent are boomtown problems (e.g., social disruption, inadequacy of public services, shortages of private goods and services, inflation, revenue shortfalls, resource losses to other uses, aesthetic deterioration, and fundamental change) associated with energy facility development? How can the growth management capabilities of small rural communities be enhanced in order to better cope with these problems?

My M.B.A. thesis dealt with both questions, but basically as they concerned energy development as a cause. The thesis covered existing theories of boomtown growth, and surveyed literature covering boomtown growth in Scotland and the Rocky Mountains. It discussed current compensation and facility siting procedures in the United States and overseas, and covered various theories for improving them. It evaluated current taxing and disbursement systems affecting boomtown finances. The thesis also discussed approaches to government and industry planning in the United States and Britain, mentioned innovations in national, regional, and state planning, and in growth management at the local level. Several innovations by industry were also discussed. Based on these approaches, the thesis developed the boomtown's solution model discussed at greater length at the end of this book.

This expansion of a thesis into a book intends to offer a historical perspective of rapid population growth; to show that this growth affects not only tiny communities but also huge cities; to cover the wide variety of causes of the boomtown syndrome; to show that the problems involved are worldwide; and to integrate various professions in their solution.

Boomtown Communities does indeed cover all these topics, and goes on further to answer the questions raised at the May 1980 conference. While boomtown problems are heavily related to energy facility development, this is by no means the only cause. It is very difficult, especially for financial reasons, to enhance the growth management abilities of small towns without getting industry and other levels of government involved. Even the planners serving the world's largest cities cannot deal with the problem independently.

I wish to thank several people for their assistance. Dr. Thomas Gladwin of New York University first gave me the idea of examining boomtown growth, and assisted me with countless articles from the university's Conflict Project dealing with aspects of the problem I could never have addressed through library research alone. I also want to acknowledge the contributions of a former classmate, Rhoda Gaufin, whose work on growth management in the West produced a number of contacts whose information has also added valuable material to my own research. A former professional colleague, Jason Makansi, helped me obtain very useful information about new-town planning during construction of the Tennessee Valley Authority's dam projects in the South. For this insight, I'd also like to thank Jesse Mills, chief librarian for TVA. I wish to thank as well the large number of town organizations, especially in South Africa, who provided me with information about communities about which I would never have otherwise been aware: Richards Bay, Secunda, Lichtenburg, Sasolburg, Saldanha Bay, and Pilgrim's Rest. The Canadian and Australian Consulates also gave me information about similarly obscure towns in their countries.

Finally, and most of all, I want to thank my wife, Judy, for her patience and support, without which this book may never have been written.

GARY W. MALAMUD

BOOMTOWN COMMUNITIES

1

Introduction to the Boomtown Syndrome

Among the authors studying the social, physical and financial impacts of energy development are Finsterbusch (1980), Bates (1978), Little (1977), O'Hare and Sanderson (1977), Lee (1980), and Vander Muelen and Paananen (1977). By far the most frequently cited and thorough boomtown theory research is that of Gilmore (1976), who shows the integration of financial, psychological and political problems in the boomtown syndrome. This book weaves these diverse fields of study together to show common patterns that develop in boomtowns.

SOCIAL EFFECTS OF ENERGY DEVELOPMENT ON IMPACTED TOWNS

There is little doubt of the chief cause of boomtown formation today. Most energy development and nonenergy construction activities (e.g., dams) occur in sparsely populated areas, such as the Rocky Mountains, northern Scotland, and western Australia. Little (1977, 402) succinctly defines the chief boomtown syndrome occurrence:

> Besides increased economic activity, the most distinguishing characteristic of boomtowns is an accelerated population growth . . . [which] in turn leads to a breakdown in municipal services. . . . Planning lags behind needs, and control of the community seems to rest with forces outside the immediate environments.

Gilmore remarks that the typical boomtown suffered from declining population before the boom, from a lack of nearby metropolitan areas, and from residents' inability to adjust to rapid change. As a town's population increases 10 percent a year, "severe institutional malfunctioning has already begun or is about to begin" (Little, 1977, 402). Gilmore and other writers consider an impacted community a boomtown if it experiences a population growth rate exceeding 15 percent annually. Actual boomtown populations can often double or triple over that time.

Unable to shelter new workers in permanent dwellings, a boomtown has to put them in temporary dwellings such as trailers and mobile homes. The absence of lawns, trees, and paved streets makes the trailer camps eyesores on an otherwise empty landscape.

It is not only the number of new residents that add difficulty. The newcomers often come from large cities in other parts of the country, and have values much different from those of the long-time residents. The problems faced are the same for Easterners settling in rural Wyoming as for English workers settling in northern Scotland. The newcomers and permanent residents both feel alienated and wary of each other's intentions.

Few detailed studies of the boomtown syndrome's sociological and psychological elements exist. (For one such study see the Alberta Oil Sands Environmental Research Program's excellent 1980 report of Fort McMurray, Alberta.) Little suggests that the social impacts of boomtowns are so elusive that only trained social workers ever detect them, and then, only a sizable time interval after the new population arrives. For this reason, behavioral scientists know very little about the social problems in towns forced through boom and bust periods by energy development.

Little mentions five problems that trained workers must observe. The most significant of these is the residents' mental health. Husbands work long, stressful days often including weekends. Wives may spend boring days trapped in trailers, with few jobs or recreational opportunities available. Children play on unpaved streets, and the aged often cannot deal with the more rapid tempo of life or with rapid change. Crowded conditions of newcomers often produces family conflict, depression, child neglect, alcoholism, drug, venereal disease, attempted suicide, and truancy problems that overwhelm a town's limited resources.

Value conflicts break out between long-time residents and newcomers who know they will be staying only a short time. Both in places like the Rocky Mountains and in rural Scotland, long-time residents form a homogeneous group, having rural, religious upbringings, and traditional moralities favoring the political and social status quo. Since the towns' fading preboom economies have forced most younger people out,

preboom towns tend to have populations above the normal average age. Newcomers, however, come young and old, liberal and conservative. Nearly all are anxious to see new schools, playgrounds, and social centers that most long-time residents don't want or need. If the old-timers think these changes will only benefit the new workers, who won't be paying taxes on their upkeep in future years, they will not only resent the newcomers but will also resist paying their share of the upkeep. It is no wonder that the two groups so often dislike each other.

Both personal and institutional interaction patterns change among the old-timers.

Friends who disagree on the merits of energy developments, or on the means for overcoming the resultant local problems may become enemies. . . . Many individuals who have nothing in common prior to the boom may develop strong friendships. . . . It becomes difficult to participate in a bridge or literary club if past friendships with members of the group have vanished. (Little, 1977, 410-412)

An energy project itself often forges new interest groups among both long-time residents and newcomers who are either for or against development, changing many people's political loyalties in the process.

A final problem is that long-time residents often cannot accept the uncertainty caused by change, while newcomers can't accept the uncertainty their own transience causes and feel little identity with the town. Boomtowns have high crime rates typical of communities with transient populations. Once the townspeople find strangers in their midst, informal, social controls break down, and the town must use more bureaucratic, impersonal ways of dealing with local problems. As the population diversifies, old-timers know fewer of their neighbors. Traditional community roles (e.g., mayor, police chief) often are redefined, replaced, or eliminated while new positions are created. As a boomtown becomes more modern and urbanized, the residents face the choice of adapting to change, keeping the status quo, denying the inevitability of change, or getting out.

These five factors discusssed by Little are somewhat similar to Finsterbusch's belief that population growth, psychological and social problems, intergroup conflict, and institutional adaptations are four of the six boom-town problems. He elaborates on the boom's effects on the town's elderly, who, he claims, see their lifestyle crumbling—they often approve a project before the work starts, then become hostile to it once the work has begun. He also points out that the proximity of many Western boomtowns to highly conservative Mormon and Indian communities is particularly troublesome. Finsterbusch also provides data relating to the extent of differences among old-timers and newcomers about their long-term regard for the town.

THE BOOM'S IMPACT ON THE TOWN'S PHYSICAL RESOURCES

Boomtown theorists unanimously identify the strain on available infrastructure—schools, hospitals, housing, water, sewage, recreation—as the most publicized impact. There simply is not enough of any of these to accommodate the hordes of newcomers who are accustomed to taking these services for granted, and existing services break down.

Housing is the most visible physical resource put under severe strain. This book will show, in boomtown after boomtown, that incoming construction workers and their families must settle for trailers or mobile homes, or for anything serving as a roof over their heads. Local property owners have been known to rent out barns and other normally nonhuman dwellings to newcomers. Ironically, these workers are there to put up new housing, but they must make do, too. The housing squeeze creates jerry-built, unsightly trailer parks and campgrounds, blighting the landscape. One Scottish town even tried to use old steamships to shelter temporary workers, but even this proved to be inadequate. The shortage of permanent housing inevitably sends prices of existing dwellings skyrocketing, further adding to newcomers' woes.

Other public services become scarce. The unwillingness of many professionals to move to an unsophisticated, isolated area creates shortages in medical, legal, and social service personnel, at the exact moment that the new residents demand such services.

Public education also feels the squeeze. Since many incoming construction workers are apt to have young families, the present school system becomes swamped with new students. Often a student's records do not even arrive from the previous school until after the student has departed. School staffs often have to work double or even triple sessions, and to hold classes in trailers, mobile classrooms, or even in nearby shopping centers.

Other public infrastructure and services suffer the strain, too. The water supply, electricity, sewage removal, road, public transportation and telephone systems all become woefully inadequate. The main problem, to be addressed more fully later on, is the difficulty of accurately predicting the levels of infrastructure and services the town's new population will need. And the future population is hard to estimate. Moreover, local officials are afraid of having an infrastructure glut after the boom if they overbuild. This, of course, saddles the residents who remain, many, if not most, of whom are voters, with huge payments for empty schools and idle hospitals.

Scarcities in boomtowns aren't limited to capital resources such as power plants and schools. Retailers can't supply the town's swollen population with consumer goods. Inflation strikes the consumer products and housing markets with equal harshness. The town's overall cost of living soars, hurting the many retirees among the preboom residents and adding to the value conflicts already discussed. The only long-time residents sure to benefit are property owners and retailers, who gain from scarcity until the demand for scarce goods brings in outside competitors. Not all retailers benefit equally. Finsterbusch remarked that many of them, accustomed to a slow-paced, personal business style, cannot adjust to the more hectic, profit-minded approach of the boomtown economy and close down.

In nearly all boomtowns, far more businesses suffer than benefit for a very simple reason: Neither large industries (e.g., tourism, ranching, farming, logging) nor small businesses can offer their skilled workers a salary or wage even remotely competitive with the pay that cash-rich energy developers can provide. Workers desert their employers in droves to join the energy hunt, forcing more enterprises into the red or out of business.

In general, the overall public service sector lags behind the energy-related private sector. In a normal market system, the supply of housing, infrastructure, public services, and consumer goods eventually rises to meet the demand. Boomtowns, however, are such short-lived phenomena that a great deal of planning and growth management are inevitably required to provide an adequate quality of life. Both of these, however, require resources far beyond the capabilities of all but a lucky handful of boomtowns.

FINANCIAL ASPECTS OF THE BOOMTOWN SYNDROME

The preboom town's financial structure is often as precarious as its physical infrastructure and the boom overwhelms them both. Residents wonder where they will get the money to build new schools, hospitals, roads, and houses. Unaccustomed to coordination with the state, most towns traditionally rely on local taxes to supply development funds. Most residents prefer to live in a jurisdiction in which some industry is already operating (out of sight, if possible). The industry will then supply much of the tax base without physically disfiguring the town itself.

Towns soon to be hit by energy projects face a far grimmer situation. The industry there cannot supply tax revenue until the project begins to operate. The infrastructure buildup, however, is needed before operation begins, during construction of the mine or energy plant. Thus the classic "front-end financing" problem so common to boomtowns: how to get the money when the town needs it most. This book will refer time and again to this problem, the solution to which is critical to solving the overall boomtown syndrome.

"Front-end financing" is not the only financial problem for the boomtown. Energy development projects are often miles away from the affected towns, outside the towns' jurisdiction. Unless political boundaries are changed (an unlikely event) or a new revenue-sharing scheme takes shape (a very necessary event), the energy firm will not provide the town with a penny of badly needed tax revenue. Yet the boomtown is expected to shoulder the entire load of caring for all the new workers!

Unless the new industry pays taxes directly to the newly inundated town, the community has to raise property taxes to meet soaring payroll costs. These tax hikes tend to fall on the old-time residents, for most local tax codes do not assess mobile homes in the same category as permanent homes. The construction workers in their trailers end up paying far lower property taxes, but benefit far more from the energy boom, than their long-time resident neighbors, adding even more to local resentment of the new arrivals. Finally, such a town cannot raise capital funds by issuing long-term bonds or by bank borrowing, since neither lender can be sure of the pace of industrial development enabling the borrower to repay the loan.

Solving these financial problems becomes part of the need for intergovernmental planning. All levels of government must, with industry's cooperation, make the disbursement of impact aid a far more timely and efficient procedure than it generally is now.

THE BOOM'S IMPACT ON LOCAL POLITICAL STRUCTURES

Most local officials in small, isolated rural towns know, or need to know, very little about the outside world. One can imagine their despair, therefore, when a major resource boom suddenly confronts them. Gilmore has graphically described their plight:

The local elected officials and a good deal of the public have already experienced the four common phases of attitude toward this boom development. The first phase was enthusiasm, with anticipation of economic growth satisfying a classic ambition of a small, declining country town: keeping the young folks at home.

The second phase was uncertainty, particularly among the elected officials, as to what the demands for public services to meet the growth might be. The third phase was near panic over the gap between prospective revenues and prospective expenditures, coupled with the realization that [the town] and its school district have nowhere near the bonding capacity to build the facilities needed to accommodate the growth. Finally, there evolves a problem-solving attitude as the officials and the public start trying to understand what the problems are and how to find help for them. The more information that is available on prospective change, the sooner the fourth phase comes.

Upon realizing that they had neither the knowledge nor the resources to deal with the town's problems, decision-makers . . . first turned to the state and federal governments for help. The response was unsatisfactory, so money grants from the industry generating the growth were sought. This led to competition and confusion among town, school district, and county, all the different governmental agencies seeking support. This created uncertainty among the firms, which wondered what the priorities should be and who should set them.

The local officials are ambivalent about land use planning and zoning. Their ranching and landowning constituents are strongly opposed to any intervention with their sole control of their property. State planning legislation is weak. Many of the local leaders in government, business, and banking are wishfully doubtful about the continuity of [the] boom.

All are bewildered by the varied new parties-at-interest to community development and decision-making. They include mining companies, land speculators, the *New York Times* correspondent from Denver, consultants and researchers who may not even identify their clients, and numerous state and federal agencies whose existing programs do not quite fit the local needs. (Gilmore, 1976, 536)

Local governments must, therefore, learn to plan, zone, negotiate with industry, evaluate different people's needs for compensation, fight for special state laws and for state and federal aid, work out new local tax codes, and revamp their infrastructure and services. Local professionals must learn to work with new types of people. The local business structure either has to adjust to the newcomers or face insolvency. Presently, however, political difficulties prevent the imposition of higher taxes, while "parochialism" prevents the development of growth management ideas. The entire local power and service structure faces a huge task in dealing with boom conditions.

THE GILMORE BOOMTOWN MODEL

Gilmore's research offers perhaps the most coherent, thorough example of boomtown theory. Gilmore offered this explanation of the boomtown's plight in the Problem Triangle shown in Figure 1.1.

As population grows at boom rates, existing local services fall short of need. Schools, classrooms, retailing inventories, housing, and the number of physicians in the community do not grow as rapidly as the number of people increases. Many people's recreational requirements are not satisfied by the available opportunities. The quality of life in the community is degraded.

As a result, it is difficult to attract people to this isolated community which has no substantial indigenous labor force to service the economic growth. There is apt to be an inadequate supply of labor, which is unstable and dissatisfied at best. Workers and their families do not want to stay in the community and some of those who do stay are pirated back and forth among employers. Industrial employee turnover rates and absenteeism go up rapidly. It is difficult to attract and retain a satisfactory work force, whether it is a work force for building and operating a power plant or gasification plant, for operating a restaurant, or for maintaining the county's roads and bridges. Industrial productivity and profits drop.

Because of declining productivity, or at least the absence of expected increases in productivity and profits, there is less money coming in to support public sector activities. In addition, social malaise or chaos causes private investors to be skeptical and unwilling to invest in commercial facilities, housing, or the other private sector needs. Insurance companies even stop writing

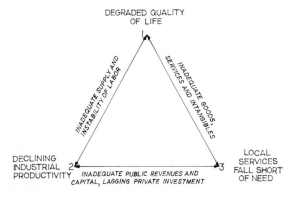

Figure 1.1
Gilmore's Problem Triangle (Gilmore, 1976).

casualty coverage in the boomtowns. Thus the situation is back where it started in the problem triangle, with local services and facilities finding it even harder to keep up with increasing population and demand. (Gilmore, 1976, 536)

Gilmore's boomtown model includes the local services (public) and the basic (private) sectors. They are in equilibrium before the boom. The community's residents determine the extent to which they are willing to pay for local services and, therefore, the quality of those services.

When the energy boom suddenly begins to pump vast sums of money into the basic service sector, the town's population must increase in order to fill the new jobs and the local service sector must expand as rapidly to keep the town's quality of life intact.

Gilmore, (1976, 538) offers these four techniques to help bring the public sector more rapidly into balance with the private sector, which together make up local growth management:

1. Balancing investment between the two sectors, involving the town and the energy firm setting up an investment strategy
2. "Affecting resource use and conservation" by zoning and other growth management techniques
3. "Developing the (local) labor force" by affirmative action and training programs to reduce the need for outside labor
4. "Accommodating and retaining" the old-timers, requiring an adequate quality of life, and having more comprehensive social service and adult education programs

REFERENCES

Alberta Oil Sands Environmental Research Program, 1980, *A Study of Human Adjustment in Fort McMurray,* Alberta Environment, Alberta, Canada, December.

Bates, V. E., 1978, "The Impact of Energy Boom-Town Growth on Rural Areas," *Social Casework* **59**(2):73-82.

Finsterbusch, Kurt, 1980, *Understanding Social Impacts,* Sage Publications, Beverly Hills.

Gilmore, J., 1976, "Boomtowns May Hinder Energy Resource Development," *Science* **191**:535-540.

Lee, Roger D., 1980, *Energy Development: Socio-Economic Impact Problems and Mitigation Strategies,* Utah State Department of Community and Economic Development, Salt Lake City.

Little, R. L., 1977, "Some Social Consequences of Boom Towns," *North Dakota Law Review* **53**(3):401-425.

O'Hare, M., and D. Sanderson, 1977, "Fair Compensation and the Boomtown Problem," *Urban Law Annual* **14**:101-133.

Vander Muelen, A., Jr., and O. H. Paananen, 1977, "Selected Welfare Implications of Rapid Energy-Related Development Impact," *Natural Resources Journal* **17**(2):301-323.

PART I

HISTORIC OVERVIEW OF BOOMTOWN GROWTH

2

Opening of the Western United States

Perhaps no other region witnessed such a proliferation of boomtowns in as short a time as the western half of the United States between 1850 and 1900. Boomtowns sprouted up for numerous reasons, but the two most common ones were the spread of the railroads across the prairies and mountains of the West, and the stampedes of gold and silver miners that began in California in 1848 and did not peter out until after the Klondike gold rush of 1898.

RAILROAD EXPANSION IN THE PRAIRIES AND ROCKIES

As railroads spread through the United States in the nineteenth century, cities and towns sprouted up along their routes. By 1850, several lines had reached the Mississippi River; a dozen years later they crossed the Great Plains and headed for the Rocky Mountains. Riegel (1926, 274-275) stated that:

The railroads did their part in helping to fill up the first tier of states[1] which became fairly well settled by the end of the fifties. At the same time a thin trickle of settlers pushed still further west—to Kansas and Nebraska and to the Pacific coast. The discovery of gold in California proved a very effective incentive, and was succeeded by the discovery of precious metals in Colorado, Utah and Nevada during the latter fifties and early sixties. The immigration of miners, traders and settlers soon became a steady stream across the plains.

By 1870, railroads were moving into sparsely populated areas. Their arrival hastened settlement along their routes in the traditional patterns: first animal trappers, then loggers and miners, and then settlers came. Not only did the railroad make it much safer for settlers to move West, but easier access to mail delivery reduced newcomers' isolation and their freight handling abilities decreased the frontier people's privation.

Although dozens of railroad lines were involved in Western settlement, this section focuses on three of them: the Union Pacific, Central Pacific, and Illinois Central.

McCague (1964) described the story of the Union Pacific as follows. Conceived in the 1850s, this line was to be half of the effort to link the Mississippi Valley with the Pacific coast (the Central Pacific was the other half). Figure 2.1 shows the route the Union Pacific took from Omaha through Nebraska and into Wyoming and Utah. The line was built from 1864 to 1869, and joined the Central Pacific at Promontory, Utah, in the famous driving of the "golden spike."

The figure only shows a few of the towns that sprouted along the Union Pacific's route. All suffered either from vice, land inflation, or flimsy building construction.

North Platte, Nebraska, was a typical boomtown. Such a place owed its existence largely to traders, who tended to move their posts from construction base to construction base. An alert businessman named John Burke appeared in North Platte with a log building dismantled after its service in Cottonwood Springs, hauled in fragments to the new site by ox teams, and reassembled at North Platte. It became a hotel—a single bleak room with rough bunks built around the walls. An otherwise unsung journalist by the name of Clark commandeered a boxcar, set up a small printing press in it and cranked out the town's first newspaper, *Pioneer on Wheels*. McCague describes North Platte's development as follows:

Canvas, raw lumber and cut sod blocks bloomed into homes and places of business along [the] brand-new streets. The population that winter [1866-1867] swelled from nothing to more than 2,000. Much of it was railroad [workers]. But a new element, too, was making its presence felt for the first time along the UP's trail. They came swarming in: drifters, saloonkeepers, gamblers, . . . all sorts and degrees of shady opportunists sniffing after the railroads' payroll dollars.

So North Platte was born and grew. (McCague, 1964, 139-140)

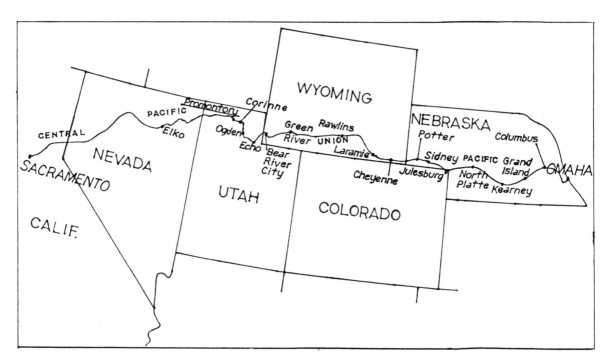

Figure 2.1
Route of the transcontinental railroad (McCague, 1964).

Unlike towns like Columbus, Nebraska,[2] that had existed before the Union Pacific and continued to grow, North Platte boomed only as long as it was the railroad's terminus. By Spring 1867:

North Platte had shriveled overnight to a rueful little railroad town of 300, its vaunted "Paris of Nebraska" dream buried in the debris of boom gone bust. The railroad terminal camp had moved a giant's stride further on, to raw, raucous Julesburg, which now roared more loudly and lawlessly than North Platte ever had. (McCague, 1964, 173)

By Spring 1868, Cheyenne, Wyoming, flourished as the new terminus. In time, Green River City also boomed, as did Beartown, near the Utah border.

As the Central Pacific headed east through eastern Nevada, it came upon Elko, booming even without the railroad, thanks to rich silver mines nearby. The railroad arrived in late December, 1868, and "found the place running wide-open, traders and land sharks reaping a boom-town harvest, streets a-boil with rough humanity, saloons and bawdyhouses busy around the clock; in short, the Central's sole authentic taste of 'Hell on Wheels,' UP style" (McCague, 1964, 315). The Central Pacific, however, never spawned as many boomtowns as the Union Pacific made famous.

Utah, the state in which the two lines met, had boomtowns of its own: Blue Creek and Corinne, near Promontory, were two of the better-known towns— places where "idle men [men left unemployed by the railroad's completion] . . . were met by eager gamblers, rotgut peddlers and bawdyhouse runners dedicated to prying loose the last remaining dollars in furious binges of farewell" (McCague, 1964, 315). These idle men spread crime throughout the railroad towns, especially in Utah.

McCague offered vivid descriptions of life in many of the railroad towns. One example was Cheyenne, which Grenville Dodge, the railroad's chief engineer, called the "gambling capital of the world," famous for its Headquarters Saloon, more than a dozen other saloons, and six theaters.

A local magistrate . . . was said to levy a ten-dollar fine on any man who drew a gun on another inside the city limits, "whether he

hit or missed" . . . But law enforcement was feeble, hardly existing in more than name only . . . .

After a while vigilante committees did spring up in an effort to keep crime from getting too blatant. An old log cabin was converted to a one-room jail. When it grew intolerably crowded, a semiofficial mob would release the occupants one at a time, ask each where he wished to go, point him in the indicated direction and send him on his way, frequently with a bull whip or a spray of six-gun slugs snapping at his heels if he loitered. Such methods disposed of the pettier criminals without much trouble. But . . . the worst of the real criminal leaders were scarcely interfered with. And the result was that Cheyenne's reputation spread far and wide, a stink in the nostrils of the godly . . . .

Yet under all the tawdry glitter, the evil and the drunken caperings, lived solid, sober citizens who has followed the Union Pacific into town, too. . . . On January 5, 1868, . . . Cheyenne's first public school building was dedicated. At the time the town was said to have two hundred children of school age. A little later this same spring a Rev. J. W. Cook organized an Episcopalian congregation to give Cheyenne its first church . . . .

So Cheyenne swaggered, worked, played and went about its affairs lawful and unlawful all through fall and winter and oncoming spring, the biggest, loudest, toughest—and most promising— terminal town the Union Pacific had spawned yet, or would spawn.

[Then, as the railroad moved inexorably westward,] Cheyenne had shrunk from a hot-blooded ten thousand people to a sober fifteen hundred and settled down, as the editor of the *Leader* wrote, "to be a quiet, moral burg." (McCague, 1964, 237-240)

Most of the Union and Central Pacific boomtowns were at one time or other terminus points, where the construction workers could relax before construction resumed. Gates (1934), in his discussion of the Illinois Central Railroad, showed the ways in which land speculation spawned towns throughout the railroad route, not just at the terminus.

Land speculation, then called "town-site promotion," was rife in Illinois before the Panic of 1837.

Optimistic promoters laid out towns anywhere and everywhere, without regard to their location, drainage, or transportation facilities. Having duly registered the plat they would proceed to advertise it in the local papers and in some cases would peddle the plat or the lots in the East, where gullible buyers could generally be secured. Lots were bought and immediately resold at increased prices. After the panic, many of the towns, were abandoned and their sites reverted to their original states. Such forgotten 'ghost' towns as Montezuma, Gloster, Moscow, Caledonia, Adamsburg, Presque Isle, and New Bedford bear witness to vanished dreams. (Gates, 1934, 121)

When the railroad came, towns in Illinois competed vigorously for the chance to become a transportation center. Since each town wanted such a role, town lot speculation began again. The railroad's charter forbade it to lay out towns, but its promoters made sure to cash in on lot sales. Four of them set up an unofficial group called "Associates" to buy the state government's land near the group's planned stations. So "the station sites were located by the directors of the IC on the Associates' land . . . ." (p. 124). Once construction of freight and passenger terminals ended, small storekeepers, innkeepers, and tradesmen followed.

Next would follow the construction of small flour mills, sawmills if there was timber in the vicinity, packing houses and grain elevators. Churches and school buildings were soon required, and their construction frequently led to the development of brick-making, quarrying and lumber yards. The retail business of the small tradesmen increased as the farming populace increased, and thus towns in the center of the more rapidly developing agricultural communities grew swiftly. (Gates, 1934, 124)

Before 1850, the Chicago branch route had 3 primitive towns (Bourbonnais, Urbana, and Spring Creek). By 1870, 28 new cities of considerable size had arisen: Kankakee, Mattoon, and Champaign led the list. "Manteno . . . may be considered as representative of these new station settlements" (p. 125). From nothing in October, 1854, it had grown in eight months to have 16 houses. Its 1860 population was 861, a figure that grew to 1,681 by 1870. The Associates and the railroad itself owned land upon which Manteno was built, and both competed in promoting town growth and selling lots. The Associates encouraged industries to move in and donated lots for schools, churches, and public buildings.

David Neal, leader of the Associates, used a standard plat to lay out their 33 towns. All had a grid and were laid out in blocks and lots, the prices of which rose as their distance to the station declined. They were the prototype of western railroads' "standardized townsite promotion."

Despite its own charter, the railroad itself became the biggest of the state's town-site promoters. Centralia was the most vital of the railroad's towns, among which were Tolono, Kinmundy and Elmwood. From a settlement of about 2,000 residents in 1855, Centralia grew to 3,190 in 1870; Kankakee sprouted from nothing to about 3,500 residents in 1858 (Gates, 1934, 127, 129). In other instances, the railroad sold town sites to promoters at a discount. This helped them set up "colonies" by selling lots faster than selling farmland. As chief carrier, the railroad could also offer reduced rates to manufacturers who agreed to set up plants such as lumbering and mining along its route.

Towns at junctions of east-west roads with the basically south-north Illinois Central line grew fastest. Freeport, Bloomington, Dixon, Mendota, La Salle, Decatur, and Mattoon all developed quickly by 1870. The last four of these didn't exist before the railroad was built. The fastest growing of all was Chicago, which had, by 1860, become the nation's largest railroad center. While Chicago could have grown as a port alone, "Chicago benefited more than any other city from the construction of railroads in the Old Northwest . . . . Produce which once had floated down the rivers to St. Louis and New Orleans was now carried by the iron horse to Chicago and eastern markets directly" (Gates, 1934, 139). Chicago, younger than either St. Louis or New Orleans, grew to be far larger than either of them. The Illinois Central helped Chicago more than almost any other railroad: from 30,000 residents in 1850, Chicago exploded—112,000 in 1860 and 299,000 in 1870 (p. 141). Housing became scarce and the usual boomtown land inflation followed.

The railroad had 10 towns along its route in 1850, 47 in 1860, and 81 in 1870. Their combined population, excluding Chicago, was about 12,000 in 1850, 70,000 in 1860, and 172,000 in 1870 (p. 147). "On the whole, the IC as well as the Associates made an excellent thing out of the town-site business

. . . . The towns helped to build up traffic for the line and their growth also served to increase the demand for agricultural lands . . . . Town development and rural development acted and interacted upon each other" (Gates, 1934, 148).

New Englanders began flooding into Illinois after 1850 on their way west. Rising farm prices, however, induced many of them to stay in Illinois. Most settled on farmland rather than in the towns. Post-Civil War prosperity attracted more Easterners and began to draw Europeans. "During this period, Illinois became the destination point of more immigrants from Europe than any other western state" (Gates, 1934, 252).[3]

Unlike the mining boomtowns, many of the railroad towns survived. Cheyenne is Wyoming's modern capital and Laramie is also a vibrant community. Most of the Illinois cities mentioned earlier also exist today. The main reason seems to be that the railroads went through potentially arable land near these towns. They brought thousands of farmers looking for a livelihood on the frontier. Once farming took hold, towns along the railroad became vital as markets and storage centers, both for farm produce and for goods shipped from the East.

CHICAGO: GROWTH OF THE MIDWEST'S GIANT

Few of the world's cities can rival Chicago's period of explosive growth in the nineteenth century. First incorporated in 1833 on the site of the destroyed Fort Dearborn, Chicago soon became a frontier town in spirit and body. "By the late 1830s, plank streets were in use downtown, but no one thought much of how the sewage and garbage were to be carried off. For the town was often below lake level and gravity couldn't do its drainage work" (Longstreet, 1973, 23). Chicago, in 1837, had about 4,000 people and probably as many land speculators. Three years later, people on wagon trains passing through but deciding to stay tripled the population.

The first railroad and the first ship both arrived in 1841. Ten railroads had their terminals there by 1855, "and eleven branch lines were active with pigs, grains, and home hunters in the West. The population was 80,000. There were 60 miles of sewers and more were needed" (Longstreet, 1973, 28). By 1860, when it hosted the convention where Abraham Lincoln was nominated President, Chicago had 60 hotels, 6 theaters, 80 ballrooms and dance halls, 40 newspapers and 93,000 people. It was also infested with crime.

Chicago grew rapidly also because it was the westernmost Great Lakes port for Easterners and foreigners passing through the Erie and other canals. From Chicago, they had to board wagon trains westward. Before the Civil War, Chicago also was a terminus for slaves fleeing the South along the underground railroad. "Wartime was boom time to Chicago —near the war's end, it had a population of nearly 170,000" (Longstreet, 1973, 39). It was becoming a huge transportation center for all the grains processed and grown on nearby farms and sent to the armies fighting in the South. Chicago had also become a hotbed of speculation in land and army supplies. Some speculators became wealthy, including Marshall Field, Philip Armour, Gustavus Swift, and Cyrus McCormick.

During the war, Chicago's population shot up by 70 percent, real estate values doubled, and city tax revenues mushroomed by 400 percent (p. 56). Chicago was by now the stockyard center of the Midwest: "The Union was fed its meat rations in large part by Chicago. One-third of all the hogs killed and processed into bacon, ham and lard in the West —nearly a million—was moved through Chicago in one three-month period" (p. 56). So were huge numbers of sheep, cattle, and horses.

Sewage treatment failed to keep up with the slaughterhouse wastes piling up during the war.

All this did not help the accumulation of bad smells in the city, or create a better system of sewerage. It merely added 75 miles of sewer lines of revolting slaughterhouse offal which poured their filth into the river which in turn poured into the lake from which the city drank its water from a wooden inlet just six feet from shore. Diseases of the alimentary canal killed off the weaker citizens and many babies . . . . The reek that came from such places as Garlic Creek was dreadful, and as the war produced more factories and killed off more pigs, when the wind was right, the odors of the stockyards and packinghouses could not be filtered out by scent held to noses or closed doors and windows. The position of health officer was invented, consisting merely of one appointed policeman, and most of his duties were collecting bribes from the worst offenders. (Longstreet, 1973, 59)

The opening of the Union Stockyards in 1865 confirmed Chicago's position as slaughterhouse of the United States. Four years later, the invention of the refrigerated railroad car gave a priceless lift to Chicago's transportation-hub status.

After the war, thousands of immigrants passed through every year, bound for iron mines, farms, or logging camps throughout the West. As Chicago's economy boomed, many of them stayed. This in turn lured many poor whites from the South. Chicago's population underwent an almost unbelievable expansion: from 300,000 in 1870, to 503,000 in 1880, 1.44 million in 1890, 1.7 million in 1900, 2.18 million in 1910, and 2.78 million in 1919 (Longstreet, 1973, 459). Probably no other American city has witnessed such a population explosion: 5.6 percent annual growth over a 60-year period.

TOWNS OF THE GOLD RUSH

If a person saw the fulfillment of his or her dreams in a faraway place, it was unnecessary to take a train to get there. So it was that, starting in 1848, long before the Union and Central Pacific linked the Midwest to the West Coast, spanning what was then called the Great American Desert, hordes of prospectors stampeded into the central California mountains searching for gold. The rush, of course, had begun with the inadvertent discovery of gold at Sutter's Mill. Before long, all of central California became a hotbed of frantic activity.

Although a railroad camp lasted only as long as the rail terminus was there, all its inhabitants knew how long they could live there. Few of them would have considered bringing their families to the camp. The California "Forty-Niners," however, brought incredible optimism to their camps, along with their picks and shovels. Many felt that they would be staying put for a long time, so the gold camps, unlike the railroad camps, went through several stages of evolution as the arrival of miners' wives and children brought social change to many mining camps. Smith (1967) gives a fascinating description of this evolution.

Eleven years after the 1848 Sutter's Mill strike, gold was found in Colorado, and silver in Nevada's huge Comstock Lode. Mining camps sprang up as soon as these areas opened up to the miners and quickly became miniature cities.

Urbanization meant that the problems which faced the more settled regions were transported to the frontier and placed in an entirely new environment. Such problems as municipal government, revenue and sanitation had to be faced and some attempts made to solve them before they got out of hand. Others such as law enforcement were magnified by the number and proximity of the people involved in the settlement. (Smith, 1967, 6)

The camps were isolated, yet they could not hope to be self-sufficient, especially for food. This attracted farmers to the mining areas, in turn creating demand for a means of transport back east for their produce. The advent of transportation—by road in the pre-railroad years—brought new merchants to the camps, all within a few years of the initial discovery. Those camps that lasted more than a year also developed theaters, schools, debating societies, literary clubs, churches, and public libraries. The miners, however, had very few ways of spending their money, a problem today's boomtown residents also have. In those days, the money inevitably went to brothels, gambling halls, and saloons.

Nearly all the camps were short-lived. As others sprouted with the word of rich new strikes in the nearby counties, settlers stampeded there and set up new camps. Since the mining camps depended on the local mine, few camps had the chance, as did the railroad towns, to become stable communities.

Unless the camps were lucky enough to be in the path of an oncoming railroad line, farmers had no easy way of shipping their produce. Most of the farmers could not have stayed long anyway, since most gold mining territory isn't suited to agriculture.

As gold mining declined in California, it boomed in Colorado. In 1859 nearly 100,000 prospectors[4] trekked to Colorado. By the 1860s miners with experience in these two states headed for Idaho, Montana, Utah, Wyoming, Arizona, and New Mexico.

Their attitudes, of course, went with them. Most of these people believed that there was no reason to stay put, that they would surely be successful the next time if they failed where they were. Such ideas made most miners uninterested in town planning, aesthetics, and camp safety. They were, however, quite attracted to the camp prostitutes, liquor salesmen, and gamblers, all of whom inevitably followed the miners from camp to camp. The lack of large numbers of wives, especially in a camp's early days, contributed to the miners' desire for drink, prostitutes, and gambling. The few women and children who did come west found their values changing quickly. With so many eligible men around, miners' wives often were far less reluctant to end a bad marriage than they would have been back east. Youngsters, especially the girls, grew up quickly—camp life offered little chance for a normal childhood. Ideas of neighborliness changed quickly, too. Although most residents were willing to cooperate to help build the town and help the needy and the sick, they did not interfere in each other's lives unless asked.

The high cost of travel and the hard life of the camp made for a homogeneous population; most camp residents had lived in other camps. Most were young, since older people were not as willing to chase elusive dreams or to put up with the rigors of frontier life. By the 1880s, however, mining camps showed a more mature population, both in terms of attitude and age. Their miners, after all, had spent twenty or more years drifting from camp to camp. As they aged, they took wives and fathered children;

this guaranteed a more diverse population for the newer camps.

The camp population, however, was racially homogeneous. Camps rarely allowed Hispanics, Chinese, blacks, or native Indians to live there without discriminating against them. The Chinese got the harshest treatment[5] because of language differences, customs, and their clannish nature, and especially for their willingness to work for less pay than the whites. Harassed, downgraded to "un-American" status, the Chinese became easy scapegoats "for the crime, vice and destitution of the country" (Smith, 1967, 31), and were isolated. The Chinese tended to search for gold in places where the less persistent miners believed that the mines were played out.

The camps at first were homogeneous in terms of class—everyone started out from scratch. As some miners struck gold, a wealthy class evolved, and as mining became big business, the gap between mine owner and miner grew wider.

The first campers to arrive slept on the ground until crude shelters became available. All these men had were pack animals, wagons, and supplies. As miners began settling into camp life, they realized (especially if they had lived in other camps) that some sort of government was necessary, mainly because of the lack of effective local or regional authority. The first rules often concerned street layout, taxation, the size of claims to land, and the procedures by which the claims were filed. Subsequent laws often set district borders and the procedures for appointing camp officials—president, recorder, sheriff, judge, miners' court. At first, nearly every able-bodied male 15 years or older could vote. Later on, residency, age, race, and possession of property became the voting criteria.

Although camps evolved over about a 10-year period from tents and wagons, their later appearance still shocked outsiders. Most miners by then lived not in the camp but closer to their claims. This may have contributed to their lack of concern for the camp itself. The lack of money, however, was the main problem. Without roads capable of supporting wagons with large loads of supplies, most towns suffered nearly complete isolation and could not easily develop a more civilized appearance. In the days before the federal government was ready to shoulder their financial burden, the camps could raise funds only by taxing their people, raising funds, or asking private contractors to build toll roads. Although huge maintenance problems ruined most purely speculative road projects, toll roads were used for a time in the Rockies and in California. The arrival of the railroad ended the toll road era.

The mining frontier presented a unique social situation: here were early Westerners forced to deal with all the urban problems in the wide-open West —problems that didn't confront the soldier, rancher or farmer. Although Smith did not cover mining in most of the West and failed to explain the effect of decline on people's values or the town's institutions, his account does offer an excellent way to monitor values and institutions in today's boomtowns as they go through the various stages of evolution.

Although the 1860s and 1880s mining camps were not identical with today's boomtowns, they had much in common with them as well as with today's financially strapped cities and states. All suffer from rapidly changing values and chronic financial problems. One can only hope that today's planners are more able to find answers than the leaders of the mining camps.

A TALE OF THREE CITIES

Few railroad and mining boomtowns evolved into large modern cities. However, the opening of the American West did spawn several boomtowns that grew tremendously despite their not being near a railroad or a mine. The three outstanding examples were San Francisco, Denver, and Los Angeles. The first two grew because of their indirect connection to the mining boom, and the third because of its marvelous climate and a spirit of self-confidence that few cities in the world have matched.

San Francisco

Although San Francisco began life in 1776 as a mission[6] and military post, the settlement barely grew until the late 1840s mining boom. San Francisco was so remote that few people had reason to go there.

Once gold was discovered at Sutter's Mill on January 24, 1848, both California and tiny San Francisco were in for boom times. On the day of the Sutter's Mill strike, only 1,000 people lived in San Francisco. As the mining boom progressed, it became evident that San Francisco and the mining camps needed each other badly. Even before the Panama Canal's construction, many people preferred the long sea voyage to California to traveling westward through the treacherous Rocky Mountains to the mines. San Francisco Bay is one of California's few natural harbors, so San Francisco quickly became the point of arrival for thousands of prospectors.

From July to December 1849, 805 ships entered the Bay with 30,920 passengers.[7] Most of these ships were left to rot at anchor, and many caught fire and sank unnoticed by their former crew or passengers. The city's permanent population had doubled to 2,000 by February 1849. But then, San Francisco really took off. In July 1849, it boasted 5,000 residents; this figure grew to 20,000 by December 1849 (McGloin, 1978, 32).

Even after most of the miners had passed through, San Francisco continued to grow for a far different reason: the enormous amounts of gold recovered from the central California mountains could not possibly be stored there safely. Wealthy prospectors soon realized that San Francisco was far more suitable for this purpose, so San Francisco quickly became a banking center.

By 1850 San Francisco was a full-fledged and somewhat sophisticated boomtown. Its first theatrical production took place in June 1849; by the early 1850s, it had a thriving cultural scene to accompany the saloons and brothels for which the town was far better known.

San Francisco, at that time, was a most unpleasant

place to live. A city made entirely of ramshackle wooden buildings, San Francisco had a volunteer fire department with only three engines and 90 men, plus a hook-and-ladder company with 40 men. This force was totally inadequate to deal with the series of six fires that broke out between December 1849 and June 1851. The 1851 blaze forced San Francisco to set up a regular fire department and to begin using brick construction and building water storage tanks.

Obtaining water for any purpose was a chronic problem in the 1850s. Stopgap measures preceded the operations of the San Francisco Water Works Company's system of flumes, tunnels, pumps, storage tanks, and pipes. San Francisco's sole source of fresh water was a lake 20 miles away.

San Francisco in its early days is best remembered for its vice. The town was so crime-ridden that vigilante groups formed as early as 1849, and again in 1851 and 1856. There were, however, about a thousand unsolved murders from 1849 to 1856, while corruption flourished in local government.[8] The most notorious section of town was the "Barbary Coast," an area full of whorehouses and saloons. Perhaps the most evil goings-on there involved the shanghaiing or kidnapping of merchant seamen onto ships.

Vice was by no means all there was to the boom atmosphere. Real estate values, prices, and wages soared. "Anyone who could saw wood [for houses] could earn $12 to $15 for a few hours work. Hack drivers called it a bad day if they didn't make at least $20, and even waterfront loafers sneered at anything less than $5 or $10 for an odd job" (O'Brien, 1948, 30).

San Francisco's growth continued unabated even after the California gold rush died down. The city benefited from the Nevada silver rush of the 1860s. Its connection to the transcontinental telegraph and railroad systems in the 1860s helped San Francisco grow to 150,000 residents by 1870 (McGloin, 1978, 87). By then, the city had developed a social upper crust of millionaires, most of whom owed their fortunes to the mining boom which by then had spread all over the West.

San Francisco continued to expand. Its 1880 population of about 240,000 grew to 300,000 by 1890 and 340,000 by 1900. Although the terrible 1906 earthquake interrupted this growth only briefly, its geographic isolation and watery surrounding limited population increases. Today, the city has only about twice its 1900 population. Nevertheless, San Francisco maintains its prominence among Western cities. It is as important a banking center as it was in its boom days, and it exerts as magnetic an appeal to Americans as its nearby mines did long ago.

Denver

Before 1858, no one cared much about the area between the hundredth meridian and the Rockies— The Great American Desert—even as settlers crossed it enroute to California and Oregon. That year, Denver was born when two groups of Indians and whites found small amounts of gold at the junction of several rivers.

As in the mining camps, Denver's first civic leader was a newspaper owner, William N. Byers, who led the effort to make Denver the regional center. More than anyone else, Byers is responsible for Denver's rapid growth in the nineteenth century.

Byers united the rival hamlets of Auraria and Denver City in 1860, but the new town failed to grow before 1870. Although millions of dollars worth of gold were extracted nearby and thousands of people passed through the settlement, few stayed there. Denver's 1870 census showed only about 4,700 residents. Although the area's miners helped Denver businessmen and speculators prosper, the miners owned no property and so could not be taxed to build public works. Nor did they volunteer to help the town grow.

As in all Western boomtowns, they preferred to spend their money on gambling, liquor, and prostitutes. Crime became rampant and vigilante groups were set up by 1860, as they were in early San Francisco. Few businessmen beside Byers cared much about Denver's interests, but Byers's efforts through his newspaper helped Denver obtain a jail, a sheriff and six policemen, plus laws against robbery, burglary, murder, and other offenses, all by 1862. Denver was developing a government without much help from federal or regional authorities.

Denver suffered from isolation as the mine camps did—nearly everything, especially food, had at first to be imported from the East. Since only locally grown produce could lower food prices enough to attract settlers, Byers's paper made an unsuccessful effort to attract farmers.

John Evans became Colorado's second territorial governor in 1862. He was, next to Byers, early Denver's most influential citizen. His wealth and status as a famous physician and scholar raised his image in Denver, and he helped Byers form the Colorado Agricultural Society, which in turn built a fairground displaying farm and mining equipment, goods, and extracted ores. Their most significant effort was to form a group of enthusiastic promoters—bankers, stagecoach line owners, and lawyers—who convinced the local and regional residents to raise funds to build a railroad to connect to the Union Pacific at Cheyenne. By 1870 Denver had become a key mountain railroad link to both coasts and to the Great Lakes. Denver owed its growth into a large city, if not its birth and infancy, to the railroads.

Denver was still a difficult place in which to live. Unlike most of the mining camps, Denver was situated on two streams, so it had to endure not only fires but floods. It was also "an exceedingly primitive town, consisting of numerous tents and numbers of crude and [badly] constructed cabins, with nearly as many rum shops and low saloons as cabins, where horses, cows and hogs roamed at will. . . ." (Dorsett, 1977, 28).

Denver had all the problems of a mining camp. The town had no churches, schools, hospitals, libraries, or banks in 1859. By 1860, however, it had 35 saloons for its 4,700 residents. Although a wild 1859-1861 crime spree had abated by 1862, animals continued to roam the streets and sickness was common. Denver, however, could not attract good doctors or nurses until the 1870s. Poor nutritional habits caused considerable illness until the arrival of the railroad

supplied the people with fresh produce at affordable prices.

Even as food prices moderated, the boom brought very high prices for lumber, nails, glass, and other nonfood goods. But most residents took these hardships in stride. As in San Francisco, a series of bad fires in the 1860s led to brick construction. Unlike San Francisco, Denver had to suffer a series of Indian raids in 1864-1865. It also had the problem of insolvent miners unable to obtain money to leave town, along with orphaned and deserted children. Imbued with the common "laissez-faire" attitude of the day, the town and county failed to raise enough money to help them.

As time passed, the area's fine climate attracted several wealthy Easterners who began to raise Denver's cultural life in the late 1860s. Women also began arriving in larger numbers after 1865. All this helped Denver develop a small middle class by 1870.

Between 1870 and 1900, Denver's population rose from 4,700 to 134,000, of which more than half were women (Dorsett, 1977, 57, 107). Early in this period dozens of civic leaders persuaded the state legislature to create a Board of Immigration to boost the state and city. This had the undesired effect with a few months of causing a labor glut, which the coming of the railroad helped create. From 1870 to 1890, the track mileage in Colorado rose from 157 to 4,176 (Dorsett, 1977, 60).

The impact of the railroads was monumental. Construction brought thousands of workers to Colorado, many of whom remained after the rails were laid. . . . As Denver became the hub of Colorado's rail network, wholesalers, warehousers and merchandisers congregated there. It was the easiest place from which to ship ores from nearby mining camps, smelters moved there from the camps, railroads could then ship out refined metals (gold, silver, copper). The railroads advertised the state all over the world, encouraged people to buy land the railroad companies owned along the tracks and to settle their towns, and urged tourists to come visit the area.

By 1890, however, nearly all the state's railroads were owned by outsiders, which was good in a way because Easterners still had far more money to spend on expansion and maintenance of the lines. Meanwhile, foreigners were speculating in mines and cattle ranches. All this activity and money helped Denver become a base for metallurgists and mining engineers by the late 1870s to serve these mostly British interests. This development in turn led to the formation in 1884 of the Denver Chamber of Commerce, whose main task it was to provide honest information of business activity to outsiders and to protect investors from swindlers.

More than 30 years after Denver's founding, William Byers and John Evans still led the local economy. They and about a dozen others made up Denver's business elite. These men invested their wealth, not in speculation, but in transportation, real estate, banking, utilities, and manufacturing, all of which helped Denver grow as their own fortunes prospered. These men created a power structure that controlled almost the entire city economy, building railroads, utilities, smelters, banks, industrial suburbs, and residential areas. Consequently, Denver sprawled from its 1874 area of 6 square miles to 59 by 1902.

After 1890, however, Denver's economy suffered from the imposition of the gold standard and the subsequent collapse of the silver market. The lean years forced civic leaders to work harder to attract tourists, agriculture, and industry. By 1900 Denver's leaders and citizens had a more realistic attitude toward its prospects as compared to the lofty optimism they had a decade earlier.

Denver's elite, as did San Francisco's, built huge mansions and expensive office buildings on land they owned. They built many large churches and private schools. The average citizen, though, had to endure streets that alternated between dust storms and mudholes, smoky air, terrible odors caused largely by untreated sewage, stray animals that often lay dead in the streets for days, and rising crime. As in all boomtowns, low salaries resulted in a shortage of policemen.[9]

Perhaps worst of all, the town suffered extensive poverty and destitution. The city leaders kept urging newcomers to arrive, then paid very low wages, practiced ethnic and racial discrimination, and cared nothing for the poor. While none of them actually wanted to exploit the poor, their focus on industry made them neglect the unskilled laborers and destitute women and children. People in the East suffering from lung disease heard about Denver's climate, but not about the money required to get adequate rest and proper food necessary for recovery. Italians, blacks, and Chinese suffered blatant discrimination. The Chinese suffered the worst treatment, and the native Indians were not far behind. Blacks were not treated as badly as the Chinese and native Indians. Their larger and more stable families helped the blacks deal with Denver society better than the other groups. Although small businesses, writing, and publishing were promising areas for women, hundreds of others, with no skills or education, were forced into prostitution.

Most citizens, however, lived between these extremes. The middle class became isolated from the rich, the poor, and the ethnic minorities. Denver spent little to care for its underclass, trying to get rid of them rather than looking for the causes of unemployment and destitution. Even those willing to help the poor selectively considered only those "worthy" of help. Poverty had barely been attacked by the end of the 1870-1900 boom. The city lacked a leader who knew all the interest groups' needs and could find areas of consensus.

And so, as the American frontier came to a close, Denver was a thriving, if still primitive city (by Eastern standards). It was the Rocky Mountain region's undisputed transportation and industrial center and its largest city, which it still is today. Chapter 9 will explore the boom that overtook Denver after World War II.

Los Angeles

Neither Denver nor Los Angeles owes its existence as a community to railroads, favorable climate, or farsighted, self-centered business leaders. Neither city, however, could have prospered as it has without them. Despite its being further away from the Eastern population centers than Denver and just as far as San Francisco, Los Angeles grew to become America's third largest city, having experienced a remarkable number of distinct booms to get there.

Though founded in the late eighteenth century by the same missionaries who founded San Francisco, Los Angeles did not start to boom until a hundred years later. When it did, it had nothing to do with the metals rushes that created Denver and San Francisco. Without a natural harbor, Los Angeles could not hope to rival San Francisco as a port of call for would-be miners, nor could Los Angeles match Denver's proximity to the mines. Nevertheless, its leaders knew how to take maximum advantage of Los Angeles's assets and turn them to their own benefit.

Oddly enough, Los Angeles first began growing as a cattle industry center, which nevertheless had many boomtown traits: The infant city soon became one of California's most notorious centers for gambling and vice. As in all boomtowns, inadequate law enforcement led most residents to obtain weapons. Los Angeles in 1850 had 3,500 residents, but few schools and churches. During the 1850s, Los Angeles's self-promotion campaign, unparalleled among American cities, began when the old Spanish culture had begun to vanish. The cattle industry also disappeared during a terrible 1862-1865 drought that plunged Los Angeles into depression.

A farm and real estate boom revived Los Angeles after 1867. Former cattle ranches were subdivided and sold to hordes of newcomers. By the early 1870s, irrigation and the digging of artesian wells had turned Los Angeles and southern California, formerly barley and corn farming areas, into a huge fruit-growing region. Los Angeles recovered its glow thanks to two commodities, land and water, one of which was always abundant, the other always scarce. Land and water together account for much of Los Angeles's turbulent history.

Los Angeles's first bank, set up in 1868, and those that followed it enabled newcomers to buy land and farm equipment on credit. The railroad arrived the next year. Not even Denver received as big a boost from the iron horse as Los Angeles did. The railroad not only helped thousands more Easterners visit the Los Angeles area, but also helped boost the Los Angeles agricultural industry by connecting it to the huge East Coast market—especially with the newly invented refrigerated railroad car.

No one took greater advantage of the railroad than Los Angeles's civic boosters. Starting in 1873, they began to advertise Los Angeles's climate nationwide, efforts they redoubled after a financial panic reduced Los Angeles's 1876 population of 16,000 to 11,000 four years later. Los Angeles in 1882 was "a dirty, sleepy country town of 5,000 . . . which did not seem to have a particularly bright future—it was a town without a port, it was not yet connected to the rest of America by any major spoke of transportation, its water supplies were limited" (Nadeau, 1960, 103).

When the Southern Pacific Railroad began offering Easterners a quicker rail trip to Los Angeles in 1881, that line and its competitors joined the civic boosters in getting westbound riders on its trains. Fare wars began bringing hordes of Easterners to the coast by 1886, and Los Angeles's population soared from 12,000 in 1882 to 100,000 in 1886 (Nadeau, 1960, 104).

Most of the new residents were families seeking to purchase land. One of these was 17-year-old Harry Chandler, a New Hampshire native who later made a giant impact on his adopted city. Chandler was one of the thousands who came West to recover his health, in his case from pneumonia that damaged his lungs. He eventually joined the staff of the *Los Angeles Times*. The owner was undoubtedly early Los Angeles's most remarkable citizen, Harrison Gray Otis, himself a transplanted Midwesterner, whose newspaper easily equalled Byers's for its impact on the city it served. Otis, who had an overpowering, warlike personality, made clear his idea of the perfect Angeleno:

Los Angeles wants no dudes, loafers, and paupers; people who have no means and trust to luck, cheap politicians, failures, bummers, scrubs, impecunious clerks, bookkeepers, lawyers, doctors. The market is overstocked already. We need workers! Hustlers! Men of brains, brawn and guts! Men who have a little capital and a good deal of energy—first-class men! (Halberstam, 1979, 99)

By mid-1886, the demand for housing forced land prices skyward. Prices in 1887 had reached five and six times the 1886 values.

In a city whose population could still be numbered in the tens of thousands, hundreds of real estate agents swarmed the streets. . . . Experiencing its first growing pains, the city was desperately short of sewers and other public facilities in the midst of enormous private expenditures on tract promotion. (Nadeau, 1960, 76)

Towns like Burbank, Whittier, and Hollywood were born. Los Angeles's major industry was real estate speculation, which caused an 1888 panic. "On bleak hills, the skeletons of luxury hotels were left like stranded driftwood, their windows broken, their grand ballrooms silent. Scores of ghost towns were created. . . ." (Nadeau, 1960, 80).

Around this time, Harrison Otis persuaded the city's main boosters to form the Chamber of Commerce, whose first task was to build a port at San Pedro, due south of Los Angeles. Once this was done, the harbor area residents voted to join Los Angeles, which today is nearly an hour's freeway drive away; the city limits had gone southward to the harbor in a mile-long corridor, surrounded by unincorporated areas.[10]

Few Americans today are aware that Los Angeles once had an unparalleled public transit system. Another of Los Angeles's giants, railroad magnate Henry E. Huntington, built an electric streetcar system on which a trip from downtown Los Angeles to Santa Monica took half an hour, and one from downtown to Redondo Beach took forty-five minutes. (Today these trips take far longer by bus.) The tracks even helped area real estate growth. Just as western cities sprang up near the Union and Central Pacific, so did southern California towns like Venice, set up in 1904, begin clustering along the streetcar lines. The population of existing communities such as Long Beach also soared. The trolleys cemented many isolated towns to Los Angeles as they became bedroom communities.

The streetcars, properly updated with the times, could have become a marvel of urban engineering. By the 1920s, however, automobiles and traffic lights had begun to reduce the trolley system's efficiency, doubling the travel time over most of the routes. The streetcars were doomed.[11]

While Harrison Otis was Los Angeles's best-known nineteenth and early twentieth-century civic booster, Frank Wiggins worked behind the scenes to turn the Chamber of Commerce into one of the world's most effective booster groups by 1890. He made sure that all Midwest trade fairs had the best California produce, and printed books and leaflets. It was "a fully organized, brilliantly conceived all-out propaganda effort that would make even the most modern huckster proud" (Halberstam, 1979, 107). The newly-invented refrigerator car made fresh oranges on Eastern breakfast tables a potent advertisement for California.

All this stimulated yet another population surge from 1893 to 1914. The Chamber's advertising found a ready market among the elderly and sick in the East who wanted to escape that area's severe winters.[12] As Los Angeles's population surged toward its 1910 count of 319,000 (Nadeau, 1960, 147), the new arrivals helped fuel another real estate boom, which World War I stopped temporarily[13] and the 1921 Midwest agricultural slump revived.

Promoters soon realized that the automobile removed the need to have shopping areas along streetcar lines. Many people, in fact, were now arriving in Los Angeles by car. New business centers sprang up overnight and people were buying land miles from the streetcar tracks. From 1922 to 1924, "the boom reached its peak, and Los Angeles became California's largest city. With capital gains taxes not yet enacted, lots were being sold and resold. The oil and motion picture booms brought new, enormous sums of money that fueled speculation still further. Among other effects, the twenties expansion doomed the streetcars and, by unrestricted land subdivision, ruined the shoreline of Santa Monica Bay from Redondo to

Ocean Park. Few public beaches remained for area residents.

Los Angeles was now moving out of its frontier period as a city ruled by men interested in unrestrained growth and rugged individualism. To a remarkable extent, as Chapter 9 will show, Los Angeles kept this ethic well into the twentieth century. As early as 1920, however, Los Angeles was a boomtown that had grown beyond the ability of its infrastructure to serve it; the symptoms that were to give Los Angeles a bad name throughout the United States—traffic congestion, sprawl, and air pollution—were already major problems for its citizens and evidence of that structural failure.

CONCLUDING REMARKS

Urban researcher Gunther Barth (1975) examined the development of what he called "instant cities," paying especially close attention to San Francisco and Denver. He makes clear that the people who created them did not in turn become "instant citizens." Even the miners interested in the towns' survival cared for them only as storehouses of mined gold.

Their citizens could not rely on the cities' momentum to lift them up financially, but had to hope they themselves could rise. Neither San Francisco nor Denver attracted people because of their level of urban amenities. "Overnight, they built cities on sites that had not demonstrated an ability to attract and sustain a population of urban density. The problems arising from the haphazard choice of locations threatened San Francisco and Denver with doom [if] they failed to continue to attract newcomers" (Barth, 1975, 132).

Their residents exploited the cities' opportunities especially if the gold fields were unkind to them. Most of them believed in chance and did not care about political, social, or cultural matters. The existence of those who did care, however, made the difference between future metropolises and future ghost towns.

Most of Barth's comments are also applicable to early Los Angeles. Without a natural port and with few fresh water sources, this site appeared to offer little hope of a large permanent settlement. The Midwest farmers who poured into Los Angeles also cared little for urban amenities, and most probably had had little contact with large Midwestern cities. This may account as much for Los Angeles's urban sprawl as did the civic boosters' huge interests in land ownership. Until the 1940s, Angelenos and rural Midwesterners shared many of the same traits: anti-labor unionism, rugged individualism, and lack of interest in a cultural establishment.

The only way any of these three cities could have grown was by the hope and faith of their residents and of their civic leaders and boosters.

NOTES

1. Louisiana, Arkansas, Missouri, Iowa, and Minnesota.
2. Columbus had been a stagecoach station.
3. Corliss (1950) offered more evidence about the Illinois Central's impact on the area's towns. West Urbana, now Champaign, was a station in 1854. One year later, it had 400-500 residents; its 1857 population was 1,500. Centralia, in July 1854, had one station. A few months later, it had 1,900 residents, almost 300 homes, 11 stores, 3 hotels, 2 churches, a flour mill, a school, and other structures (p. 87). Mattoon, nonexistent in April 1855, had by August a hotel, post office, dry goods store, and two groceries. A year later, it had 500 residents and 113 homes (p. 88). Before the railroad, Carbondale did not exist. By the opening of the Illinois Central, it had 300 inhabitants. In five years, the population rose fourfold. Between 1850 and 1860, Cairo's population went up tenfold and Richview grew elevenfold.
4. Called "fifty-niners," naturally.
5. Chinese suffered frequent lynchings in nineteenth-century Western cities just as blacks suffered them in the South.
6. A sort of school and church set up by Spanish missionaries.
7. All but 920 of whom were men.
8. Though now under American jurisdiction, San Francisco and much of California were geographically beyond Washington's effective control.

9. Denver in 1880 had one police officer for every 4,116 residents; the corresponding figures for New York and New Orleans were 1 per 400, and those for St. Louis and Cincinnati were 1 per 1,000 (Dorsett, 1977, 94).

10. Today's Los Angeles map still shows that umbilical cord to the harbor.

11. This is one more example of a booming city's growth outpacing its infrastructure. Today, of course, sprawling Los Angeles has virtually no mass transit system. High labor costs now doom any system on the scale of Huntington's streetcar system. Today's buses take twice as long to travel their route as cars do (Nadeau, 1960, 118). But the *Times,* ruled by the right-wing Chandler family, was always opposed to mass transit, especially city-owned and operated. As long as Los Angeles wants to finance a system by revenue bonds, it has to show investors that it can run a profit, something no American public rail system has done for years. While it would raise Los Angeles property values and save billions of dollars in road building and maintenance, a modern rail system seems doomed in Los Angeles. The major roadblock, however, is the insistence of the city's power structure that Angelenos will never accept an electric railroad. The public *did* accept Huntington's trolleys, and may well accept something like it today if the city elite can find a way to finance one.

12. Los Angeles's population doubled from 50,000 in 1890 to 102,000 in 1900, then tripled to 319,000 in 1910 (Nadeau, 1960, 147).

13. Laborers were needed in the Eastern armaments plants.

REFERENCES

Athearn, Robert G., 1971, *Union Pacific Country,* Rand McNally, Chicago.

Barth, Gunther, 1975, *Instant Cities,* Oxford University Press, New York.

Corliss, Carlton J., 1950, *Main Line of America,* Creative Age Press, New York.

Dorsett, Lyle W., 1977, *The Queen City—A History of Denver,* Pruett Publications, Boulder, Colo.

Gates, Paul W., 1934, *The Illinois Central Railroad and Its Colonization Work,* Harvard University Press, Cambridge, Mass.

Halberstam, David, 1979, *The Powers That Be,* Alfred A. Knopf, New York.

Longstreet, Stephen, 1973, *Chicago 1860-1919,* David McKay Co., New York.

McCague, James, 1964, *Moguls and Iron Men,* Harper & Row, New York.

McGloin, John B., 1978, *San Francisco: The Story of a City,* Presidio Press, San Rafael, Calif.

Nadeau, Remi, 1960, *Los Angeles—From Mission to Modern City,* Longmans, Green & Co., New York.

O'Brien, Robert, 1948, *This Is San Francisco,* McGraw-Hill, New York.

Riegel, Robert E., 1926, *The Story of the Western Railroads,* Macmillan, New York.

Smith, Duane A., 1967, *Rocky Mountain Mining Camps,* Indiana University Press, Bloomington, Ind.

3

Early Tourist Towns

A number of communities exist today only because they enjoy a nearly perfect climate, relative to nearby towns or cities. This chapter will show that, although these towns were capable of experiencing boom conditions, none of them could have grown to be cities the size of Los Angeles or San Francisco. They just did not have a diverse enough economy to attract people of varying occupations; today, they remain attractive places mainly to the sun-seeking tourist and elderly retiree.

MIAMI, MIAMI BEACH, AND THE FLORIDA LAND RUSH

In 1910, "Miami Beach was a swamp, a home for ferocious alligators, fierce snakes, witless rabbits, and other wildlife" (Mehling, 1960, 5). Most Miamians wanted no part of it, even with the long beach on the island's Atlantic side.

Miami Beach owes its very existence to four far-sighted people: Julia Tuttle, Henry Flagler, John Collins, and Carl Fisher. In 1895 Ms. Tuttle convinced Flagler to extend his Florida coast railroad down to Miami Beach. In the 1900s Collins began growing produce, bought up much of the island's beachfront, and decided to allow hotel construction, not only along the west side of what was to become Collins Avenue, but right on the ocean. There was to be no oceanfront promenade in Miami Beach.

None of these people had the impact of Carl Fisher, a most remarkable entrepreneur. It was he who "manufactured" Miami Beach in the 1920s. He had already acquired the reputation of an innovative businessmen. With construction of the Indianapolis Motor Speedway already part of his legend, he arrived in Miami Beach in 1912. He immediately lent Collins the money to finish the first causeway across Biscayne Bay between Miami Beach and Miami. When the bridge opened in 1913, Fisher was prepared to create a beach resort from this uninhabited island. He had already bought a large portion of Collins's land.

Fisher began to fill in huge areas of bayside swamp

with sand sucked up by huge dredges from the bottom of the bay. He then had topsoil brought in from the nearby Everglades and planted grass, trees, and shrubs. But Fisher was unable to attract his fellow Northern millionaires until he successfully completed two major projects in the late 1910s.

The first was the 4,000-mile Dixie Highway connecting Miami Beach to much of the Midwest and Northeast. The second was construction of a series of lavish hotels in nearby Palm Beach, enabling the rich to sample the Florida lifestyle he was forever trying to create.

What really created Miami Beach, however, was land speculation.

Northerners heard astonishing tales of real estate values rising 1,000 percent and more in one week. Some lots were quadrupling their prices between sunrise and sunset of the same day. Outlanders even came to hear of the charm of indigenous, exotic tropical life; one form was the "palmetto bug," which, anywhere else, was a cockroach. . . .

Florida also sold the exquisite concept of water front. It marketed all it had. Then it conceived more and sold that, too. Ditches were dug through land subdivisions and puddling streams became "canals at your back door. . . ." Northerners, who had always been vaguely intrigued by the place, didn't realize that Florida's natives had gone daft. So they fell in with the boom, and either hurried down to buy in person, or enclosed their checks with advertising coupons that appeared in Northern newspapers. (Mehling, 1960, 34)

As in Los Angeles, Miami Beach boosters knew how to exploit the emerging mass media to attract a faraway market. "In the early twenties, they came at a rate of one and a half million a year; two and a half million came in 1925" (Redford, 1970, 149).

All this was part of a great 1920s land boom that affected cities from Los Angeles to New York.[1] But nowhere else did it approach the mania of Florida, especially in the Miami-Miami Beach area. Among the hordes of newcomers were a reputed 25,000 real estate agents working out of 2,000 offices. As in Los Angeles, building efforts boomed beyond any possible population boom. Just as people bought desert land unseen in Los Angeles, so they bought swamp land unseen in Florida. " 'Manhattan Estates' was advertised as being 'not more than three-fourths of a mile from the prosperous and fast-growing city of Nettie'; there was no such city as Nettie, the name being that of an abandoned turpentine camp, yet people bought" (Allen, 1931, 195).

Miami was the center of the land speculators, who "sold whatever could be sold, wherever it happened to be, regardless of whether water was under it, around it, in it, or over it" (Mehling, 1960, p.36). As in Los Angeles, people bought land with a small down payment, waited for land values to soar, and sold out.[2] Those Northerners who did want to live there had to pitch tents on their land, creating instant boomtowns. Holllywood, Coral Gables, Boca Raton, and Fort Lauderdale also developed in the boom, and many people bought land along the Dixie Highway without ever reaching Miami. But it was Miami Beach that "became the playtime home of a new American royalty, the bootstrap millionaires of commerce" (Mehling, 1960, 48).

The boom broke in early 1926, and a hurricane that September shattered it. Banks began failing in Florida two years before they began failing nationwide. Primarily because of a shocking number of bad loans, 31 went under in 1928 and 57 in 1929.

During the Depression, Miami Beach survived on the business of wealthy tourists who came down during Christmas week and from the end of January through Easter. Miami Beach was not yet a year-long tourist mecca.

Far more than Los Angeles, San Francisco, or Denver, Miami Beach (and Miami to a lesser extent) was run by business for business, without any thought of town planning. Miami Beach did not have a zoning ordinance until 1933, but even that law allowed beachfront construction. About 50 hotels were built between 1930 to 1940, many of which for the first time were built between Collins Avenue and the ocean. Thirteen of these went up in 1939 alone.

World War II, of course, hurt the tourist industry; after 1945, however, the boom was to start.

"Miami Beach as we know it today—the world's

largest complex of hotels, motels, apartments, entertainment, and convention facilities—did not exist until the 1950s" (Redford, 1970, 230). But the growing popularity of air conditioning and the airlines' package tours and effort to attract Northerners who could stay a short time spurred the fifties boom.

By 1950 or 1951, many large hotels were open year-round. Having taken full advantage of air-conditioning, they found it cheaper, as the airlines did, to spread their overhead over a full year. Air-conditioning not only attracted Northerners for the summer but enabled builders to put up hotels with smaller rooms.

It was in the early fifties that the lavish Miami Beach hotels went up. Their names, such as Martinique and Deauville, always created a special, distinct image. The most famous hotel, the Fontainebleau, was built in 1954.

It was also in the fifties that

the most sexless rape in history was completed. A submissive city . . . allowed its ocean front to be violated. The submission was irrevocable, too; there is no way of getting these hotels down without dynamite. But no one seemed to care among those who could intervene. And to those who couldn't, no one listened. (Mehling, 1960, 57)

Developers jammed 72 motels into two and-a-half miles of ocean front on Collins Avenue that in 1960 still had no sewage line. The number of Miami Beach hotel and motel rooms shot up from 21,000 in 1945 to 57,000 in 1960 (Mehling, 1960, 59). Many of the visitors of those rooms have to make do sometimes with swimming pools, since the Miami Beach ocean-front has been vanishing for 30 years. At some hotels, the beach vanishes completely at high tide.

Then, as surely as it had risen for 15 years, Miami Beach began a perhaps inexorable decline, caused by the same technological and social forces that had created its biggest boom. As American cultural standards began to rise, people realized that Miami Beach's leaders had created a cultural as well as an environmental wasteland. Once the jet airliner had brought relatively unspoiled Caribbean and European vacation spots within easy reach of the masses, they began abandoning Miami Beach in droves. Even the rich, for whom Carl Fisher had created Miami Beach, now wanted more culture and less forced formality than Miami Beach offered, as well as the chance to use the beach.

Hemmed in by water, Miami Beach has not shared in the phenomenal growth Florida has seen in the last 20 years, some of which even neighboring Miami is enjoying. Today, Miami Beach is known more as a retirement haven than as a vacationland. No one really knows what will happen to Miami Beach when its elderly begin to die out.[3] Already one of the few major Florida cities without population growth, Miami Beach appears destined for further decline.

THE FRENCH RIVIERA

The Riviera offers further evidence that towns relying on tourism alone are destined to remain fairly small. The towns along the Mediterranean coast never developed the diversified economic base to attract large numbers of people, and their terrain would have made large population centers difficult anyway.

Just as Miami Beach did not thrive as a resort until Northerners began discovering it with the help of jet airliners and air conditioning, so it took the British, Germans, Scandinavians, and, finally, the Americans, to put the Riviera on the tourist's map.

The towns of the Riviera are strung out along a narrow strip of coastline hemmed in by the Alps (see Fig. 3.1). The mountains effectively prevented Europeans from discovering the Riviera until the last two centuries. Roads were impassable in the winter and dangerous the rest of the year, and the railroad did not reach Nice, the Riviera's largest city, until about 1860.

When an early visitor, Englishman Tobias Smollett, visited in 1763, only Nice, with a population of 12,000, was a true city.

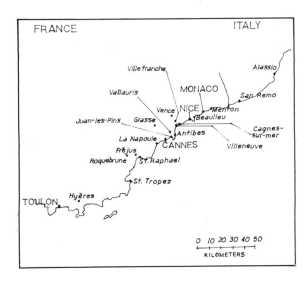

Figure 3.1
Towns of the French Riviera.

Cannes was still a fishing village . . . in 1834. Antibes had some standing as a garrison town in the eighteenth century, but it seems to have had limited attractions. Monaco had an old established harbor and fortress, but Monte Carlo did not exist even in name until the second half of the nineteenth century. Menton, until comparatively recently, was considered primarily as a source of lemons. . . . Towns in what is now regarded as the hinterland of the Riviera, such as Grasse and Vence, were relatively of more commercial importance in the eighteenth century than they are today. (Howarth, 1977, 5)

From 1763 to 1765, Smollett began arousing British interest in the Riviera. He and other prominent English travelers helped the Riviera's economy and population expand. Cannes's population rose from 3,000 in 1834 to 10,000 in 1868 (Howarth, 1977, 20). This city was "more or less invented" in 1834 by Lord Brougham, a leading English politician, who stayed at this little seaport for 35 winters and talked about it to all his prominent and powerful British friends. "The Riviera of . . . Brougham was a lazy, sun-splashed, mutually inaccessible litter of fishing villages, each in its own pocket of mountain; one big city, Nice; an impoverished port, Saint-Tropez; and independent but threadbare principality, Monaco" (Bocca, 1962,

98). The railroad arrived in 1863, and wealthy Russian and English families began coming to the Riviera, especially to Nice. The railroad also helped Menton grow as a health spa beginning in 1861. Fourteen years later, Menton had become a major winter resort with many hotels, more than a hundred villas, and a largely foreign population exceeding 1,600, according to the writings of the Englishman, Dr. James Bennet.

Dr. Bennet, who suffered from tuberculosis, found in his studies that asthmatics, consumptives, and bronchitis sufferers all benefited from wintering at Menton. Publicizing this, he encouraged many other ailing Englishmen to come down. "As a result, Menton developed to a considerable extent into a kind of winter sanitorium for the British, giving rise to the well-known saying that Cannes was for living, Monte Carlo for gambling, and Menton for dying" (Howarth, 1977, 51).

Monaco benefited the most rapidly from the railroad. Its government helped a French company headed by M. Francois Blanc build Monaco's first profitable casino and an opera house. When Blanc bought the casino concession, first granted in 1856, the railroad had reached Cannes. The line from Nice through Monaco to Menton was opened in 1868. The next year, its Prince announced the abolition of taxes. Monaco had 2 hotels in 1868, and 48 in 1900; 2 jewelers in 1878, and 15 in 1900.

In the years immediately following the coming of the railway to Monaco a new kind of sovereign state was in effect coming into being, a state based on the profits derived from allowing visitors to gamble. In time, citizenship of that state was to become one of the most sought after of any in the world; to millions who never saw the inside of either, the terms "Monte Carlo" and "casino" were to become almost synonymous. (Howarth, 1977, 37)

Other developments helped bring British residents to the Riviera: the end of French requirements for passports and an express train with sleeping cars from Calais to the Riviera that began service in 1883. This train became almost as opulent as the famous Orient Express.

Hyères, Beaulieu, St. Raphael, and Antibes also

lured British invalids, and English doctors were soon serving them. Anglican churches were built. Cannes in 1890 had 19,000 residents, and five English or Scottish churches;[4] St. Raphael then had a population of 3,500 and a resident English chaplain, and Cannes had 36 hotels and 14 pensions,[5] 700 to 800 villas, and an economy dependent primarily on British tourists. Nice in 1880 had about 65,000 inhabitants, with 25,000 additional visitors arriving in the winter. The British brought a problem upon themselves, as the cost of living on the Riviera doubled in 15 years.

The British rarely stayed during the summer because sanitary conditions, worsened by the heat, led to typhoid outbreaks in many areas (British doctors and sanitary engineers soon reduced this problem.) The English also wanted to be in London during the summer's social season.

Few members of royalty visited the Riviera until the nineteenth century. By the 1890s, however, Queen Victoria was a regular visitor,[6] preferring to visit Hyères, Cimiez, and Grasse when she was not seeing her hemophiliac son at Menton. In her last ten years, she spent seven winters there. The Queen's children suffered from rheumatism, hemophilia, and other illnesses, and spent much of their time on the Riviera. Russian nobles and other European royalty also began visiting. Despite Howarth's concentration on the English, Bocca claims that the Russians, more than any other foreigners, became the Riviera's economic foundation, teaching the local residents how to make vodka and losing huge sums in the casinos.

Many other foreign royal figures soon visited the Riviera, as did British prime ministers and other foreign politicians.[7] The "rich and the pleasure-loving" had by 1900 made the Riviera their own playground. Many fortunes were lost at the casino, and much more was spent on villas. The Riviera had become a rich man's society.

The Riviera, however, changed drastically after 1918. World War I brought much of European royalty and the Riviera's "belle époque" to an end. Since the Bolshevik Revolution decimated the Russian upper classes, it was left largely to the British to keep the

Riviera going. Now, however, Englishmen of more modest means began going there, both to visit and to live. Even those who visited after the war, however, avoided the Riviera in summer. In addition to old habits dying hard, unsanitary waste disposal procedures hindered the Riviera towns' development into summer resorts. By 1939, however, Americans and British— though still not the French—had turned the Riviera into a year-long resort, and not just because of their social lives. Air conditioning, refrigeration, and insecticides—three things vital to making summer in hot climates more tolerable—were still in early stages of development in the 1920s.

The Riviera also began attracting artists and writers.[8] St. Tropez became especially well-known in the 1920s and 1930s as a "colony" for intellectuals, especially Americans lured perhaps more by French liquor than by French ambience.

In the 1930s, the summer movement to the Riviera became a stampede

and with the introduction of the paid holiday in 1936 in France, the middle classes began coming down. World War II dealt the Riviera a blow from which it almost failed to recover. The specter of Hitler to the north and Mussolini to the east sent many millionaires packing. But many wealthy Frenchmen from Nazi-occupied France found the Riviera a relatively safe haven. The hotels and casinos had never had it so good. (Bocca, 1962)

A "mad Riviera spree" lasted from 1940 to 1942, but the poorer farmers suffered greatly and some nearly starved. The spree ended with the Nazi occupation of southern France, and all the ugly variations on the Gestapo-vs-Resistance fight occurring all over France came south.

The war itself arrived in July 1944. When the Allies invaded southern France, bombs and land and naval shells hit many Riviera towns heavily.[9] By war's end, "along the broken Riviera, there bubbled like some foul brew all the excesses, humiliations, and brutalities that mark a community at the end of its physical and moral tether" (Bocca, 1962, 132).

World War II greatly reduced British influence in the Riviera as the American presence grew. The early postwar years, however, offered few attractions for Americans.

Except for the battlefields of Normandy, the Riviera had taken the worst beating of any area of France. Saint-Raphael and Saint-Tropez were rubble. Menton . . . had been fought over twice, in 1940 and 1944, and was a wreck. . . . The entire Riviera was crumbling into a dust that was no less melancholy for the fact that the dust was in pastels of pink and blue. (Bocca, 1962, 134).

The Allied military occupation did little for the tourist business. A London newspaper called the Riviera "Europe's deserted playground" in 1948.

Bocca claims that "quite literally, the bikini saved the Riviera." The two-piece swimsuit became popular just after World War II. Soon, the image of bikini-clad beauties began bringing the rich and famous back to the Riviera.

Monte Carlo came back to life. Cannes became a year-round traffic jam, a nightmare for claustrophobes. Juan-les-Pins . . . exploded into the most garish community on the Cote d'Azur. And the bikini had come to stay. . . . From the starvation and depression days of 1946 to the booming Riviera of today, the bikini has led the way, the itsy-bitsy-teeny-weeny banner and symbol of the Cote d'Azur. (Bocca, 1962, 140)

The recovery of Monaco was especially spectacular. From 1945 to 1955,

Monaco appeared to be on the point of death, a slowly expiring community of retired generals, drab gamblers and stray cats . . . [at the same time that] Nice was a torrent of life. All the old atmosphere of sin and voluptuousness had gone, but nothing had taken its place. To the immediate postwar generation, Monte Carlo seemed—was—dull and stuffy. (Bocca, 1962, 150)

It offered neither film festivals nor a health spa to compete with other gambling resorts.

And then, *boom!* Monaco became a boomtown. [By 1961] all three communes of the principality—Monte Carlo, Monaco-Ville and the port area of La Condamine—[were] throbbing with energy, prosperity and people. Everywhere . . . one sees new buildings under construction until one wonders dizzily where space can be found for more. . . . The population, 41,000 to the square mile, is the densest in the world outside the Vatican. (Bocca, 1962, 150)

Bocca claims that Monaco's new excitement owes nothing to its tax-sheltered status, which it already had for a long time, but instead to the marriage of Grace Kelly to the then relatively unknown Prince Rainier.[10]

As Monaco boomed, so did the entire Riviera in the sixties and early seventies. Many apartment houses, highways, marinas, motels, and large stores went up. Nevertheless, few Riviera communities ever were really boomtowns, for even in the nineteenth century, the local infrastructure was able to match the area's business cycle. Hotels and restaurants either closed or cut back in summer, as did the railroads. Tourist towns like these suffer only when travelling to them becomes too expensive or when foreign exchange fluctuations or restrictions work against foreign travelers wishing to visit. Perhaps the physical and economic integration of the Riviera with the rest of France will help it surmount the periodic crises of the energy problem better than the Florida and Caribbean resorts that are much further from their largest tourist markets. Despite its notorious traffic jams, occasional fouled water, and overcrowding, its pleasant climate will no doubt continue to draw millions of tourists.

NOTES

1. During the 1920s, New York's borough of Queens doubled its population to one million, and all of Long Island was to show Florida-style real estate speculation as did suburbs in Chicago, Los Angeles, and Detroit. By 1928 and 1929, many suburbs were overbuilt and people did not begin filling them in until World War II.
2. What they actually sold were the "binders" on their land. Binders were sold more often than were first installments. Binders were 10 percent cash deposits that held purchases of land for a 30-day title transfer period. Carl Fisher's ownership of the only large parcels of developed land prevented this madness from engulfing Miami Beach. Fisher insisted on 25 percent down, the remainder to be paid off in three years; he also offered a 10 percent discount on all cash sales (Redford, 1970, 152). But Fisher participated in

the boom anyway. His companies sold more than $6 million of new land in 1923, more than $8 million in 1924, and $23.4 million in 1925 "as more and more islands, waterways, streets and subdivisions filled the bald plain Carl had dredged up from Biscayne Bay" (Redford, 1970, 154).

3. Miami Beach has perhaps the highest average age of any American city.

4. This brought more and more British churchmen, many of whom denounced Monte Carlo's "wickedness." By the 1920s, however, this sentiment had faded.

5. A pension is a small European hotel.

6. This was regardless of the fact that she linked Cannes to her son Edward's hedonistic lifestyle and disliked Monte Carlo.

7. Winston Churchill spent his last years painting there.

8. These included such writers as Robert Louis Stevenson, D. H. Lawrence, Rudyard Kipling, Alfred Lord Tennyson, and H. G. Wells.

9. Much of the action was centered around St. Tropez. Just as it was becoming "the undisputed intellectual and artistic heart of the Riviera" (Bocca, 1962, 46), the fighting reduced it to rubble. Although it was quickly rebuilt, the artists never came back. Not until the 1950s did St. Tropez again become an artistic center, now largely of the French film industry.

10. The impact of Princess Grace's death in September 1982 on Monaco's luster remains to be seen.

REFERENCES

Allen, Frederick L., 1931, *Only Yesterday,* Bantam Books, New York.

Bocca, Geoffrey, 1962, *Bikini Beach,* McGraw-Hill, New York.

Howarth, Patrick, 1977, *When the Riviera Was Ours,* Routledge and Kegan Paul, London.

Mehling, Harold, 1960, *The Most of Everything,* Harcourt Brace and Co., New York.

Redford, Polly, 1970, *Billion Dollar Sandbar,* E. P. Dutton and Co., New York.

4

Resource Development

SOUTH AFRICA: THE DIAMOND AND GOLD BOOMS

South Africa is blessed with a variety of natural resources that, perhaps, are unmatched anywhere else: coal, diamonds, gold, uranium, and many rare "strategic minerals." Exploitation of each of these has during the country's history produced a spectacular boom as wild as any the United States ever witnessed. Nowhere else did these booms create as severe a newcomer-old-timer value conflict as in South Africa.

Diamonds and gold are by far the country's best-known resources, and each of these is associated with one particular boomtown—diamonds with Kimberley and gold with Johannesburg (refer to Fig. 4.1). Kimberley, though, stopped growing after its initial boom, while Johannesburg is still expanding. Johannesburg is perhaps the world's only metropolis that grew out of a mining boomtown. This section

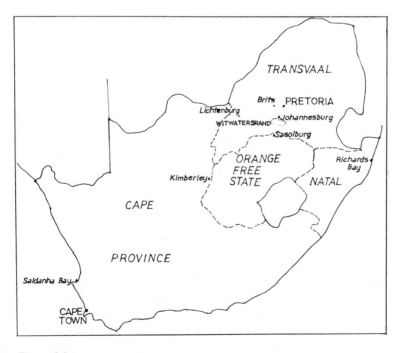

Figure 4.1
The boomtowns of South Africa.

illustrates the contrasting nineteenth-century booms of Kimberley and Johannesburg.

Kimberley

In 1867 surveys first indicated the presence of diamonds in the area of the Vaal River about 200 miles southwest of present day Johannesburg. Within two years, "South Africa's first diamond rush was under way" (Roberts, 1976, 15), and by 1870, thousands of prospectors from all over the world had arrived. All along the Vaal, instant tent cities sprang up, covering a hundred miles of riverbank by 1871. Thousands also headed for the nearby hills, one of them being Colesberg Kopje on the farm of the De Beer brothers.

One of the camps there was named New Rush, which at this time was a jumble of tents, wagons, dirt paths, and saloons, and

a complete absence of any sanitary arrangements . . . due, almost entirely, to the hasty way in which the camps had been established. Thousands of diggers had flocked there and gaily settled around the mines without giving a thought to the necessities of everyday living. . . . Closepacked and overcrowded, [the camps] festered in the sun and stank to high heaven. Drainage was impossible and no attempt was made to dispose of even the most foul-smelling rubbish; the carcasses of slaughtered oxen, sheep and goats were left to rot outside tents, and the only lavatories were huge open trenches, often dug within the camp itself. (Roberts, 1976, 74)

Flies were everywhere, water was always in short supply; diarrhea, dysentery, malaria, and typhoid (called enteric or camp fever) were common ailments. The lack of water and medical care made hygiene almost impossible.

The camps were highly susceptible to dust storms, with howling winds capable of overturning heavy wagons. The heat of the semiarid area was merciless. Severe rainstorms were a mixed blessing. The women, barred from the saloons and limited to taking care of families, had a difficult existence. Even nonminers suffered scurvy from the lack of fresh vegetables.

Nevertheless, these diggers, like the miners in the United States of years before, were optimists. They were also rowdy, young, brash, noisy, and hotheaded, and New Rush, "the most crowded and turbulent of the camps, had a population younger, brasher, noisier, and more hotheaded than their neighbors" (Roberts, 1976, 79). The Old De Beers camp was much more sedate. The Dutoitspan camp, on the other hand, was near the veins considered the most promising, so it had most of the Colesberg Kopje's offices, stores, and hotels, and the local newspaper. By the end of 1872, Dutoitspan had become as lively and sophisticated as any other South African town. The future, however, was not to be kind to this camp.

Sunday church services were common in Dutoitspan and New Rush, but so were prostitutes, who were mostly black girls. Liquor was readily available, as were opportunities to gamble. Organized dances, theaters, and other types of entertainment offered more sedate amusement. By and large, the miners at Dutoitspan and Old De Beers, and many of those at New Rush, tried to live less riotously than those who were making headlines.

On July 5, 1873, the area's British overlords changed the name New Rush to Kimberley, in honor of Lord Kimberley, Britain's Secretary of State of the Colonies. Renaming did not change the power structure of the town that never really controlled its own affairs in those days but was under British rule. The miners had even less control over the price received for their diamonds, which plummeted as the Kopje yielded more and more stones. Neither the government nor any powerful company was in a position to control output and prices.

To make matters worse, despite the passage of several years, Kimberley was a disorderly, overcrowded, and filthy town. Landslides began striking the mines too, and water seepage into the mines became severe. Yet by 1875, the camps were quickly becoming districts. Kimberley had absorbed the Old De Beers camp. Iron houses were replacing tents and wagons. More wives and families were joining the miners. Street watering reduced the dust problems, and the government provided enough money to build a hospital on

Kimberley's main street. By 1875 Kimberley had Catholic, Protestant, and Jewish houses of worship, a Masonic lodge, a theater, a social club, and a public library. Cricket and rugby matches, prize fights, and cockfights drew large crowds. Kimberley was by now far more sedate than most contemporary American or Australian mining camps.

Roberts (1978) provided a uniquely detailed examination of the ways in which Kiberley's government evolved during the mid-1870s. It was a combination of outside edicts and self-governance (see Roberts, 1978, 3-6). The first town council, elected on December 11, 1877, nominated and elected Kimberley's first mayor two weeks later. The council's major tasks during its first term of office were setting property tax rates, and appointing appraisers, auditors, and town officials. This was much easier to debate than to implement.

Kimberley was linked to the South African railroad network in February 1876, and the telegraph arrived at that time as well. Despite this and other material signs of progress,

no control had been exercised over the town's development. Corrugated-iron houses (better, to be sure, than tents) had sprung up haphazardly; the streets were still little more than footpaths.... The main thoroughfares were, if anything, in a worse condition.... Bumpy, dusty, strewn with stones and full of holes, [they] often became unusable in the rainy season.... In the townships sanitation remained very much a matter of chance. (Roberts, 1976, 146).

Kimberley suffered as much from fire as any American mining camp. By 1877 the legislative council had purchased three fire engines and set up a volunteer firefighting force. When these efforts proved inadequate, the council bought a larger engine in 1879. Not even this prevented Kimberley from being ravaged by major fires.

As occurred in the U.S. camps, company mining began to take over from individual prospectors in Kimberley around 1880. Deeper mining required money only a company could provide. This need brought banks, foreign investors, and speculators to the town as well. The population also increased at this time. By 1877—nearly a decade before the founding of Johannesburg—Kimberley was South Africa's second largest town, with about 13,000 residents. It grew far faster than neighboring Dutoitspan because its mine was more productive.

In the early 1880s, Kimberley solved some vexing problems. In late 1882, construction of a pipeline from a nearby reservoir to Kimberley was completed. In the same year, Kimberley was lit at night by electric lamps. Roberts (1978) states that these events made 1882 the year in which Kimberley's growth really began. But Kimberley still could not create an effective force to combat devastating fires until well into the twentieth century.

Kimberley suffered throughout its history from a problem far beyond its control. Unlike Johannesburg, Kimberley's prosperity depended on a commodity whose price gyrated wildly. The Kimberley of 1883 had already endured a number of diamond price slumps. Unlike gold, which major governments use as a financial standard, diamond prices depend on consumers' changing tastes and incomes, and governments have few ways to stabilize diamond prices. Price plunges produced massive unemployment in Kimberley. The solution was to attract other industries to Kimberley, something that it has to this day not really achieved. This dearth of other industries has severely limited the growth of Kimberley's population.

Perhaps history's cruelest trick on Kimberley was that, just as railroad connections with the rest of the country were completed around 1886, major gold discoveries were announced on the Witwatersrand—the "Rand"—200 miles northeast of Kimberley. The railroad that Kimberley leaders had hoped would bring new businesses to town carried instead many miners and company officials out to the Rand and the infant town of Johannesburg.

Men who had become moderately rich in Kimberley went on to become the multi-millionaires of Johannesburg, [which] quickly eclipsed Kimberley as South Africa's foremost industrial town. [Yet] Kimberley men and Kimberley money supplied the knowledge and materials necessary to develop the gold mines. (Roberts, 1976, 244)

Some of the wealthy diamond merchants, however, did do something about the periodic diamond market depressions: they "amalgamated" or unified the mines' operating companies. Cecil Rhodes emerged as the head of De Beers Consolidated Mines, which even today runs the huge South African diamond industry. Amalgamation meant the end of competition among rival firms and the control of prices and output. But it also meant the shutdown of the famous Dutoitspan mine, with bankruptcies and unemployment following it.

Once Kimberley mines were controlled, much of the turbulence went out of the town. Strangely, a new building boom hit Kimberley; with Rhodes's prodding, "more substantial shops and offices" arose, and wealthy suburbs were built, one of which was Kenilworth, a tidy village built especially for De Beers employees.

None of these events alleviated the unemployment problem. The worst off were the young men who had been well-paid miners or young mine executives, unwilling to take whatever jobs were offered. Kimberley's unemployment problem, coinciding with the Rand gold boom resulted in a decline in its population by half from 1888 to 1891 (Roberts, 1976, 281). Many of the young jobless men went to the Rand, joining those Kimberley residents already there since 1886.

Despite all the problems, Kimberley had finally begun developing into a modern city. Now largely a company town of De Beers, Kimberley received a new theater, mining school, and town hall, all built in 1899, just in time for the famous siege of Kimberley during the 1899-1902 Boer War. (The next section, covering Johannesburg, will closely examine the war as the most vivid evidence of newcomer-old-timer value conflicts that exist in boomtowns.) For exactly four months, the town, now swollen with refugees from the nearby countryside, endured shortages and shelling. Disease and malnutrition, especially among the black refugees, took more lives than the 8,500 shells lobbed into Kimberley.

Kimberley survived the war as a mature town, seemingly long past its 1870 mine camp days. But it was still susceptible to changes in the world diamond market and suffered yet another diamond depression in 1906-1908. Since no cartel (even OPEC) can set both a commodity's price and output arbitrarily, the slump in demand forced De Beers to stop buying raw diamonds in order to keep up the price. Hundreds of miners were laid off.

Kimberley officially became a city in 1912, when it finally absorbed Dutoitspan, then named Beaconsfield. The city enjoyed several fruitful years before World War I. "The diamond industry, always vulnerable to international crises, was paralyzed by the war. Mining ground to a halt. . . . [Kimberley's largest mine] was put permanently out of action. . . . The effect on Kimberley was catastrophic" (Roberts, 1976, 361). So were the effects of the postwar influenza epidemic that killed nearly 10 percent of Kimberley's 50,000 residents.

Kimberley survived these traumas, but still faced many problems. Although all but the largest of its mines reopened in 1919, the discovery of large diamond deposits in German Southwest Africa before the war threatened De Beers's control of the world market (the new mines were not, of course, amalgamated with theirs until Germany's defeat). Once accomplished, this plunged Kimberley into still another depression in 1921.

At this point Kimberley really tasted the bitter lessons of its inability for 50 years to attract other industries. The Great Depression brought the diamond industry to a total halt. Kimberley's population decreased, and it became a very quiet place. By this time, the elderly and those rich enough to settle on the coast had forsaken Kimberley's relatively unhealthy climate and by the onset of World War II, Kimberley's economy appeared near collapse.

Finally, a group of planners realized that Kimberley could prosper as the center of the newly named Northern Cape region. Irrigation projects after the war boosted area farming. A regional development association of area businessmen and politicians spurred railroad electrification, and new road and railroad building. The area's population rose by 50 percent during the 1960s. Thanks to De Beers, Kimberley is still the center of the country's diamond industry and the company's headquarters. Four of its mines are still operating. During these years, Kimberley developed socially, culturally, and architecturally. As can be expected, post-war Kimberley lost much of its mining camp atmosphere and charm, and it resembles any other small city. Although it looks rather ordinary, it looks back on an extraordinary past.

The lesson learned from Kimberley is that no town can develop into a major city based on one industry, despite the best efforts of area leaders and planners. Kimberley still cannot completely protect itself from diamond prices, which have gyrated these past few years as wildly as ever. Until it attracts completely new industries, Kimberley will remain a pleasant but small city, dwarfed by nearby Johannesburg.

Johannesburg

South Africa's key gold mining area is the Witwatersrand, normally called the "Rand." Today, one city dominates not only the Rand but all of South Africa. This city, Johannesburg, is the country's unquestioned commercial center and by far its largest city. Its growth in less than a century from a mining camp rivals that of any other world city (Letcher, 1936, 287).[1]

Throughout the 1850's, South Africa was rumored to have gold. Diamonds were found in the then independent Boer-ruled[2] Orange Free State around 1870, when Kimberley began as a tent-filled camp. The diamond fields of Kimberley, however, were only the prelude to the Rand goldfields.

The Rand is a 60-mile-long ridge running roughly east and west, its center about 30 miles south of Pretoria. It was, and is, the largest gold field in the world. The uncovering of its buried riches solved the financial difficulties of the [Transvaal] Republic, but it created tragic problems of is own, and no one foresaw this more clearly than President Paul Kruger, who told his countrymen in a prophetic statement: "Instead of rejoicing you would do better to weep, for this gold will cause our country to be soaked in blood." (Farwell, 1976, 21)

Gold was first found in the other independent Boer republic, the Transvaal, in 1870, but mining did not become intense until the mid-1880s. The Transvaal government proclaimed the Rand goldfield, to be operated under its jurisdiction, in September 1886, at which time a government land surveyor decided on the location of the area's population center. On October 3, 1886, the still unborn town was called Johannesburg. Two months later, the first property auction was held, and a diggers' committee formed. Within a few weeks, the camp had a coffeehouse, two drugstores, a bank, a club, and many saloons.

Unlike American mining camps, Johannesburg's history illustrates the powerful influence of a central government. (Kimberley's history also shows this very clearly.) The government selected a "Sanitary Board" in 1887 to run the town's affairs. Perhaps the Transvaal government was more influential in Johannesburg than the British territorial rulers were in Kimberley, for

unlike most other mining settlements, that on the Witwatersrand changed from canvas to brick in a surprisingly short time. By the middle of 1887, [the] original camp had already been abandoned, mainly owing to the gold finds beneath it, most of its buildings being moved a few hundred yards to Johannesburg proper. (Rosenthal, 1970, 169)

Inflation was rampant. Fifty-dollar lots were selling for up to $3,750. From the beginning, the private sector outpaced the public. While large, multistoried commercial buildings went up, the post office was far too small, the telegraphers were swamped with work, and the courthouse could not have more than one trial simultaneously. Far worse, the water supply was impure and streets were dark at night. The infant city nevertheless had a theater, a billiard room, churches, "two or three small private schools," and a market — where prices were higher than in the surrounding Transvaal, so it received much of the area's produce. As in other modern resource boomtowns, Johannesburg attracted Transvaalers to work in construction, transportation, and other mining-related activites. By 1890, Johannesburg had its first rail link, electricity, and, in 1894, a telephone exchange. At that time, however, gold began to be harder to find, so banks cut back their loans and the gold boom halted all over the Rand. To make things worse, a drought hit the area, forcing the government to ship in extra food. Johannesburg was fortunate, however, for another gold boom was to leave the city with more than 80,000 residents by 1895.

No gold rush in history attracted such numbers. During its prime in the 1870s, Virginia City, in Nevada, touched 25,000. Ballarat [Australia] during the 1850s numbered over 40,000, . . . Bendigo perhaps 30,000, while Leadville in Colorado once housed a similar number. Neither had Helena, Montana ever more than 10,000, nor any of the camps in British Columbia with a total of 25,000, nor the Yukon. The Klondike Rush, still in the future, did not draw more than about 25,000. (Rosenthal, 1970, 193)

The mere size of the Rand fields must account for such an inaccessible place giving rise to a city like Johannesburg, which could not even be reached from the coast until 1892. As Johannesburg, grew, the gold mining companies helped turn it into a modern city.

Many had huge amounts of land outside the fields and began to build suburbs, with cottages, gardens and tree-lined avenues. One of these became the wealthy section of Johannesburg. Owner companies adopted a not unsuccessful form of early town-planning, specifying that plots must be of a minimum quarter-acre size, by demanding that a minimum sum be expended on the house itself, that not more than one residence should occupy a single plot, that neither subdivisions nor shops and business premises be allowed (Rosenthal, 1970, 236).

However, water supply problems and the lack of transportation out to these areas limited expansion for some time.

In 1890 the boom picked up steam again as gold production rose, hitting feverish proportions by 1894. Another railroad link, to the east coast, helped too. In October 1895, the mines' yield exceeded a then unheard of 203,500 ounces.

The outside world was now about to encroach on Johannesburg and the Rand, for perhaps nowhere else did outsider-native tension in a boom condition reach such a peak as on the Rand. Unlike other areas of gold digging (e.g., Pilgrim's Rest and De Kaap), the Rand had given rise to a larger city than any other in the Transvaal, populated largely by Americans, and Englishmen, whom the Boers called "uitlanders."

These gold seekers, many of them footloose adventurers, were a different breed of men from the farmers and small tradesmen who had previously been drawn to the Transvaal, and the government was ill-prepared to cope with them. Less than 15 percent were married men who had brought their families with them and intended to settle. The rest were either single or men who had left their families in their home countries and intended to go back as soon as they had made their fortunes. They congregated in and around Johannesburg, where John Merriman, a [South African] politician, described them as "a loafing, drinking, scheming lot" who would, he said, "corrupt an archangel, or at any rate knock a good deal of bloom off its wings."

The Transvaal government tried to be helpful, but the size of the uitlander population increased so rapidly that it was frightening: they were fast outnumbering the Boers themselves, and they made little or no effort to settle into Boer ways; they were, in fact, strident in their demands for concessions, changes in the laws, even, as they were the most heavily taxed, the right to vote. Most of all, they wanted things done the right way. Their way. (Farwell, 1976, 21)

At first, these problems only briefly halted the massive Rand gold mining and Johannesburg's explosive growth. As the city's population grew towards the 200,000 mark by 1900, a Town Council assumed limited power with actions such as taking over gas and electricity supplies from private firms. Even the outset of the Boer War itself in 1899 did not affect Johannesburg much. "The gold output was steadily rising, and the shafts going deeper; new companies were being floated . . . , sporting events were in progress, and in the theaters and music halls attendances were as good as ever" (Rosenthal, 1970, 327).

People, however, began leaving in August 1899; 26,000 went to Britain's coastal Natal and Cape Colonies (Rosenthal, 1970, 328). By October, the stock exchange, courts, shops, warehouses, and markets closed down. The city's capture by the British in May 1900 (followed closely by that of Transvaal's capital, Pretoria) merely led to two years of guerrilla war, though the British won it in 1902. After the British takeover, Johannesburg began opening the mines, which had been closed with the 1899 uitlander exodus. On December 17, 1901, the stock exchange reopened after most of the uitlanders returned.

Perhaps Johannesburg and the Transvaal had the perfect British overlord at this crucial time: Alfred Milner, formerly governor of British-ruled Cape Colony and high commissioner for South Africa. As head of the new Transvaal government, he brought in talented Englishmen to staff the civil service. They enlarged Johannesburg's boundaries and replaced its "antiquated administration" with an English-style town council in 1903.[3]

The town council had its work cut out for it; Johannesburg was still a primitive, disease-ridden city with inadequate roads, lighting, water supply, and sewage disposal. The council quickly reorganized the courts, police, schools, upgraded Johannesburg's water supply and electricity services, and opened a streetcar system in 1906. More suburbs sprang up. Such development was possible because Milner had access to all the money he needed.

When the Union of South Africa was proclaimed in 1910, among its most valuable resources were the more than half a million population of the Rand's gold fields. By 1924, the Rand accounted for half the world's yearly gold output, and Johannesburg boasted a university, many garden suburbs, a modern sewage system, large parks, paved streets, and good bus service.

The Great Depression failed to dampen Johannesburg's prosperity. During the early 1930s, new searching technology found gold veins more than a mile underground as rich as those found half a century before. In 1936, Johannesburg's population surpassed half a million. During the Nazi era, South Africa, and Johannesburg in particular, acquired a sizable Jewish population.

Then, as the atomic age opened up, searchers found vast amounts of uranium in the Rand's gold fields. Uranium extraction and refining began there in 1952. Another huge gold vein was discovered in 1946 south of Johannesburg, in the former Orange Free State. Though 200 miles away, their operation came under the same Johannesburg-based firms. Three large towns, Welkom with a population now above 100,000), Virginia, and Allanridge came into being as gold extraction from the new fields began in 1951.

The Rand is still the free world's leading source of gold; it is also South Africa's largest industrial complex, and home for more than three million people, half of whom live in the Johannesburg area. (Rosenthal, 1970, 353) Furthermore,

despite the gradual exhaustion of the older mines, the metropolis continues to grow faster than ever. Beyond the vast white dumps of crushed ore, some a mile long and hundreds of feet high, the emphasis is moving more and more towards manufacturing, particularly since the establishment of a steel industry nearby. . . . Great coal deposits have made possible not only an electricity grid to meet the needs of the Rand, but serving points in other provinces. . . . (Rosenthal, 1970, 353)

EARLY TEXAS OIL BOOMTOWNS

The prominence of Texas as an oil-producing state began with the spectacular Spindletop gusher on January 10, 1901, which made nearby Beaumont boom from a population of 9,000 to 50,000 in three months (see Fig. 4.2) as the town filled with speculators, oilfield workers, and spectators.

Pig wallows sold for $35,000 and cow pastures for $100,000. Land 150 miles from Beaumont sold for $1,000 per acre and land within the proven Spindletop field sold for $900,000 an acre. . . . The development of the field was likewise frenzied, with wells being drilled as close together as physically possible. . . . Accompanying the feverish drilling at Spindletop came construction of storage, refining and transportation facilities. . . . Many workers slept in tents, paying 50 cents a night, with no charges for hordes of malaria-bearing mosquitoes. Ramshackle huts sprang up, and the settlement of Gladys City, adjacent to Spindletop, overflowed with roughnecks. Saloons, whorehouses, and gambling parlors flourished, ready to relieve the farm boys who flocked to the oil fields of their hard-earned wages. (Rundell, 1977, 38-39).

The Spindletop strike touched off frantic drilling throughout southeast Texas. The Humble field was such an area, 20 miles north of Houston, where

Figure 4.2
The oil boomtowns of Texas (Rundell, 1977).

large-scale production began in 1905.[4] Humble was larger than most Gulf Coast fields.

Social conditions in Humble resembled those elsewhere along the Gulf coast. Oil-field toughs and sharpies quickly turned callow farm boys into wary, self-sufficient men. Fighting and killing were frequent, with the dead usually getting summary oilfield burials. Sanitation facilities did not exist, but hordes of mosquitoes did. Workers drew wages of $3 for a 12-hour day. Their expenses included 15 cents for a drink of whiskey or a bottle of beer, 25 cents per haircut, 15 cents for a shave, 50 cents each for trousers and shirt, 25 cents per bath, a dollar a day for room and board. Saloons, gambling houses and bawdyhouses eagerly fleeced roughnecks of

their hard-earned money. A Humble saloon, constructed of slabs from a nearby sawmill, offended particularly. If workers did not spend freely, the bartender would get them drunk, haul them to the back room, and lift their wallets. (Rundell, 1977, 82)

Other oil discoveries near the Texas-Oklahoma border also created boomtowns. Electra, for instance, began when a nearby field gushed in 1911, and a "tent city mushroomed." Burkburnett, 12 miles north of Wichita Falls, boomed for similar reasons. However, even a slight rain turned the town's unpaved streets into mudholes.

The Goose Creek field began heavy production in 1916, and Humble Oil and Refining Company built a huge refinery there. Three separate towns sprouted nearby: Goose Creek, Pelly, and Baytown. Only Goose Creek had existed in the pre-oil days, and Pelly—the closest town to the field—was not such a good place to live. Baytown was closest to the refinery.[5] In 1948, the area's residents voted to live in Baytown.

Following the tradition of oil companies, Humble provided housing and community facilities for its workers. This tradition began in oil fields distant from towns or where towns did not furnish sufficient housing. If a field was to be developed, a labor force was required, and workers had to have some place to live, with company camps or towns resulting. Humble had previously built camps in the Goose Creek, West Columbia and Ranger fields. The development of Baytown as a company town proceeded haphazardly. When construction got under way in 1919, Humble's first move was to provide World War I army barracks and tents near the refinery. The company could sleep and feed 1,000 workers in barracks and mess halls by January 1920. It furnished small houses only for married supervisors and skilled hands. Then in 1922 it constructed dozens of one- and two-room rental dwellings for the unskilled. . . . The company built schools for white and Mexican children. . . . In 1923, Humble altered its policy by assisting employees to build homes in Baytown rather than building homes itself. The company laid out tracts, built sidewalks and streets, provided utilities, and offered home loans. (Rundell, 1977, 125)

Baytown is this book's first discussion of a company town, one way in which companies today attempt to avoid uncontrolled boomtown growth. The company went through several different levels of involvement in town planning. While not interested in aesthetic appeal, Humble nevertheless made a greater effort than most companies in those days to prevent social chaos in its community.

Houston had no role as a producing or refining city, but it joined Corpus Christi and Beaumont-Port Arthur as the Texas Gulf Coast's focal points for corporate or regional headquarters. Houston became the main oilfield equipment supply center. Houston's growth was led by "shrewd planners and promoters" like Joseph S. Cullinan, Patrick Calhoun, John Henry Kirby, and Jesse J. Jones, who also encouraged the setting up of refineries along the Houston Ship Channel. Houston's growth will be discussed in detail later on.

By Spring 1918, an oilfield boom raised the town of Ranger's population from 1,000 in 1916 to 6,000. The year 1919 brought 20,000 more to town (Rundell, 1977, 154). In the town, unskilled clerks in stores made $60 per week, and teamsters got $7 per day. New stores, hotels, offices, and supply houses sprang up. Incoming trains were crammed with equipment and new workers. Ranger had its share of gambling, prostitution, and murder, but the town's police did not try hard to crack down on vice. Ranger's boom subsided by 1922. Desdemona also boomed briefly in 1919, but today it is a village of 100.

Such Texas booms generally faded quickly because the fields could produce only so long as underground pressure on the oil remained high enough to avoid the need for expensive pumps.

The subsequent East Texas oil boom in the early 1930s helped Dallas become a boomtown.

It was started, fittingly enough, by a land developer. In 1841, John Neely Bryan laid claim to a square mile of land near an easily fordable point on the Trinity River. Bryan sold some lots and gave others away, particularly to young married couples. By 1872 he had attracted 1,900 people to his settlement.

The town changed dramatically with the coming of the railroad. Dallas' population soared to 38,000 by the 1890s as trains made the city the prime distribution center for both the state and the region. . . . The boom continued after World Was II, when the population more than doubled from about 400,000 to 900,000. . . . There is more construction in Dallas now than in almost all the major cities in the U.S. Only Houston and Los Angeles have outpaced Dallas in recent years. (Bancroft, 1982, 12)

RUHR VALLEY COAL TOWNS

The area in western Germany surrounding the Ruhr Valley, near that river's merging with the Rhine, is today western Europe's best-known industrial zone, and has been for centuries. It developed as an industrial area long before South Africa's Rand and any other region except the central English Midlands.

As early as 1800, the Ruhr was a key iron-making

center, an area in which large-scale farming had by then all but disappeared, but the region was by no means heavily urbanized. The Ruhr Valley's towns were still largely medieval in layout and population.[6] Many restrictions to Rhine river transport combined with river tolls to prevent Ruhr development until the late nineteenth century.

After 50 years, the Ruhr began to come into its own. Coal mining had spread over a wider area and the coal was now being used more than before for steelmaking. The iron, steel, and coal mining industries worked closer together than before as the area's iron and steel mills were beginning to use large amounts of Ruhr coal. From 1851 to 1856, coal output doubled while the iron and steel industries' share of coal consumption rose from 6.8 to 17 percent (Pounds, 1952, 67). Despite this industrial growth, the Ruhr remained a relatively backward, underpopulated agricultural area. Even as foreigners began investing in fledgling Ruhr enterprises, the area was still largely rural, and its population growth reflected that of Germany in general, indicating that no migration of workers to the Ruhr had yet occurred.[7] Not until after 1870 did the Ruhr's population increase greatly exceed that of Germany as a whole.

There were several reasons for this. The coal mines were scattered, generally at a distance from the towns. The miners, of course, had to live near the mines, so their growing communities became equally scattered, preventing city growth.

It is not surprising, then, that the cities remained small. [They] had expanded but little beyond their ancient walls. Dortmund had no more than 13,000 people at the mid-century, Essen only 10,000. Duisburg probably had 20,000 inhabitants and Ruhrort a mere 5,000. Hagen, despite its many steel works, contained only some 8,000 people. Bochum was but little larger, and the future cities of Gelsenkirchen and Castrop-Rauxel were now only small clusters of cottages. The . . . cities were still, as they had been for centuries, small and walled, as much agricultural as industrial in their interests. The greatest urban development, in fact, was marginal to the Ruhr and derived from the textile rather than metallurgical industries. (Pounds, 1952, 90)

From 1850 to 1900, the Ruhr made its principal stride toward its present state. The whole area became

industrialized, and small towns and villages became large cities. Among them were Dusseldorf, Essen, and Dortmund.

Villages like Gelsenkirchen, Wanne-Eickel, . . . and Castrop had grown into ugly sprawling towns (and Essen grew 150 percent from 1860 to 1870). Ribbon development enclosed . . . fragments of rural Westphalia, and were in the process of absorbing them into an unplanned, semi-urbanized sprawl. . . . [While] the older cities retained some character. . . in the newer cities was displayed nineteenth century industrialization at its worst. (Pounds, 1952, 127)

When coal mines, requiring towns to be small and scattered, dominated the Ruhr, these communities remained small and had considerable green spaces in between. Some coal companies built their own towns, many of which were well designed and laid out.

Steel mills, however, used thousands of workers in a small space, so their cities had to be large and close together. By 1900, the core city of Essen had 200,000 people, most of whom either worked for the giant Krupp steel and armaments works or were in Krupp workers' families. Krupp erected and owned much of the desirable housing. By 1893 Essen was the Ruhr's largest city, completely under Krupp's control. In addition to the shops covering 127 acres, owner Fritz Krupp also controlled Essen's school system, police and firefighting forces, communications system, and shops (Manchester, 1968, 236).

Other steel mills controlled their cities as completely.[8] Under Thyssen's control, for instance, Hamborn exploded to 102,800 inhabitants in 1900 from only 5,270 residents in 1885. Other cities like Dusseldorf and Duisburg, in the "greater Ruhr" though not in the "inner Ruhr," also grew rapidly, although they did not depend so much on one firm or even on one industry. Dusseldorf, for instance, used its position directly on the Rhine to become a transportation center.

This, then, was the region that became Germany's arms manufacturing center during the two world wars and that benefited the most from Hitler's arms buildup between the wars. Before heavy Allied bombing began in March 1943, the "greater Ruhr" had six cities of more than 250,000 persons.[9] Of these, only

Gelsenkirchen was not in existence before the nineteenth century. Compared to the others, which kept their medieval identity even during the war, Gelsenkirchen was "lacking in dignity and character . . . 'Gelsenkirchener Barock' is a German synonym for hideous taste" (Manchester, 1968, 19). This description also applies to Oberhausen, Hamborn, Bottrop, Ruhrort, and other smaller cities.

Nevertheless, Ruhr workers are so used to paternalistic treatment that few of them would ever consider leaving this region even if similar work were freely available elsewhere in Germany. It remains to be seen, however, whether such cities can remain under one company's control as West Germany's economy falters and companies have to lay off workers.

AUSTRALIA'S EARLY RESOURCE RUSHES

Geology and geography have too often conspired against easy resource exploitation since resources frequently are in remote areas. Nowhere has this proven more true than in Australia. This vast continent has been blessed with incredible mineral riches that rival South Africa's, and cursed with few good natural harbors near these riches. Most of Australia's wealth in uranium, gold, and countless other minerals are centered in the north and northwest, thousands of miles from ports and population centers (the two being synonymous in Australia— see Fig. 4.3).

Nevertheless, Australia has experienced a number of mining booms. Gold, for instance, was first dis-

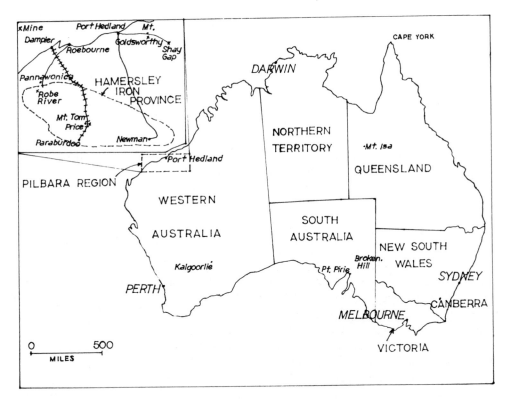

Figure 4.3
Australia's principal energy and mining boomtowns (Wilson, 1980).

covered in New South Wales and Victoria states in 1851. Two distinct waves of prospectors (the first were native Australians and the second were mostly Chinese) swelled Melbourne's population. "In Melbourne and on the [gold] fields, tents and makeshift dwellings housed the swollen population, fortunate as they were that the relative mildness of the . . . climate permitted year-round living in such conditions" (Wilson, 1980, 37). Victoria's agriculture industry predictably lost laborers and suffered from an overall increase in area wages. The gold rush, however, did not last long, and farmers exploited the new demand for meat and other foodstuffs. Within Victoria, a group of gold boomtowns continued to flourish in the 1860s. As professional, organized mining inevitably replaced the prospectors, industry developed in "the more durable mining locations." These areas suffered from primitive transportation that prevented their towns from diversifying their economies from gold, meat, and wool.

A depression hit eastern Australia in the 1890s. Melbourne was saddled with a surplus of private housing and it ceased to grow rapidly. Both New South Wales and Queensland had an overcapacity of railroad lines. Drought was the major cause of the depression. A drop in wool prices quickly followed the collapse of Melbourne's building boom.

Then, in 1891, rich goldfields opened up in Kalgoorlie and Coolgardie in southwest Western Australia. Demand in this booming area for consumer and capital goods helped the eastern economy recover (Wilson, 1980, 55). Perth, on the west coast, grew faster than any other Australian state capital from 1891 to 1901. A water pipeline and a railroad were laid out to the fields, and port improvements were made. From 1901 to 1911, Sydney grew much faster than either Melbourne or Brisbane up the coast, and Wilson has been unable to give any reason for this.

From 1920 to 1945 Australia stagnated. Not even World War II succeeded in helping the mostly rural economy, whose wool and wheat could not be exported because of a lack in shipping ability. The postwar period revived both mining and agriculture.

The mining boom included further exploitation of old fields and exploration for the first time for bauxite in the Cape York Peninsula, uranium in the Northern Territory, iron ore and natural gas in the northwest Pilbara region, natural gas in the Cooper Basin, and offshore oil and gas.

Australia thus experienced several booms, none of which lasted long. Not until the mid-1970s did a sustained mining boom begin that doubled mining's contribution to the economy. (Chapters 13 and 17 will discuss this boom and its boomtowns in detail.)

HOW MOST EARLY ENERGY BOOMTOWNS WENT BUST

Nearly all of the early American, Australian, and South African mining boomtowns were doomed to decay. Once the nearby mines were played out beyond the ability of existing technology to exploit them, miners had no choice but to move on to newer mines. Since many miners were dreamers, the mere mention of a strike nearby was enough to send them packing, even if steady work were available where they were. Most miners dreamed of making it big on their own. And so mine camps declined and rotted away to nothing in a surprisingly short time, unmourned by their former occupants. Even those camps that had matured enough to have a stable society fell apart. Silverberg vividly described the process:

When the gold gave out, the town died. The yellow metal no longer came forth, and the miners drifted away, off to seek treasure in more likely quarters. The population dropped slowly, but steadily, until only the diehards remained. . . . A hundred and fifty people hung on in what had been a town of thousands. Windows broke and never were repaned. Wild creatures moved into the abandoned cabins. The gravestones of heroes toppled in the town cemetery, and the names of the heroes were forgotten. In time the hard core of settlers also moved away, leaving just the dead husk of the town. (Silverberg, 1968, 2)

Today's American West considers ghost towns as one of its biggest tourist draws. The most fortunate of the mining camps were restored to mint condition.

Most of them are today little more than one or two abandoned buildings chewed to bits by the relentless wind and winter snows. Some vanished without a trace, and even people familiar with an area have trouble finding their former sites.

Jenkinson (1967) explored the ghost towns of New Mexico (see Fig. 4.4). He stated that the first American gold rush of any importance may have occurred in the Ortiz Mountains in 1828. Numerous rushes since then created towns such as White Oaks. Once considered the territory's most bustling com-munity (p. 42), it died when demand for gold and silver fell off. The railroad bypassed the town, and the demand for minerals shifted to molybdenum and manganese. Now only tourists on their way to the site of the first atomic bomb test ever see the remains of White Oaks, which was quite a town in its brief heyday. It was founded in 1879 and reached its peak 14 years later. Its main street was 100 feet wide and half a mile long. It had a large schoolhouse, two saloons, and 4,000 people at its peak. White Oaks figured promi-nently in the adventures of Pat Garrett and Billy the

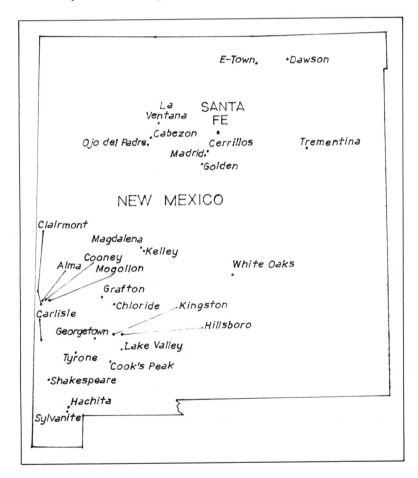

Figure 4.4
Ghost towns of New Mexico (Jenkinson, 1967).

Kid. By the 1880s, however, the Santa Fe and White Oaks Railroads decided to run their lines through nearby Carrizozo. Rising wages and the lack of profitable mining opportunities ended White Oaks' growth period. White Oaks never got the chance to become a railroad town and quickly declined.

Silverberg (1968) investigated ghost towns throughout the West. Arizona, Oregon, California, the Dakotas, and Nevada have ghost towns, as does New Mexico. Most of their mine camps lasted no longer than 20 years. Mining still keeps some camps going (e.g., Butte, Montana), tourism sustains others (Virginia City, Nevada, and Tombstone, Arizona), and farming, cattle raising, and lumbering support still others. But many more are true ghosts, with only a few wretched shacks (e.g., Bodie, California, and Bullfrog, Nevada), and other ghost towns have just vanished (e.g., Silver Reef, Utah, and Charleston, Arizona).

Some of them went through silver or copper booms after their gold boom, then they faded. As early as the end of 1850, California already had ghost towns, such as Washington.

Word came late of the famous gold strike at Sutter's Mill. San Francisco learned of it only in May, and the East took nearly a year to find out. As they arrived, prospectors set up camps named Coffee Gulch, Hog Eye, Hangtown, You Bet, Cut Throat, Boomo Flat, Fleatown, Whiskey Gulch, Poison Switch, and Shirttail Canyon, all of which died when the gold was played out. By 1860, less than one-fourth as much gold was extracted yearly as miners had taken out in 1852 alone. California's Sacramento Valley area is filled with camps that died in the 1850s.

Many California ghost towns were abandoned to nature, but others have been preserved. One example is Columbia, which became a state park. In 1853, perhaps only San Francisco had more people than this three-year-old camp. Water for either drinking or mining was scarce, and the camp suffered several fires. Although its population held steady at about 5,000 in the mid-1850s, it began to die in 1857. Now it is a tourist center, with art galleries, museums, and souvenir shops.

Still another unusual story surrounds Timbuctoo,

California. Only a ruined Wells Fargo building remains of this 1860s gold mining camp. It is likely to be consumed someday by fires like those that destroyed the church, two hotels, six inns, eight saloons, and other buildings after its decline in the 1870s. The site was recently purchased; the new owners hope to restore the Wells Fargo building and put up replicas of others long gone. The town is just east of Marysville.

After California's "Mother Lode" gold vein became impossible to exploit without heavy equipment, many prospectors headed for Oregon, Washington, and Canada, and then to Idaho, Montana, and the Dakotas by the 1870s. Others touched off the 1858 Colorado gold rush in which Denver was founded. Nevada, however, had the wildest stampede in 1859, when the silver-laden Comstock Lode gave birth to Virginia City, now a thriving tourist center. From 1860's "muddy, shabby collection of shacks," it grew in two years into a town of more than 15,000. In 1864, however, the mines began closing down after having produced $45 million in silver.

The years 1865-1872 were a time of depression in the area, although a great deal of ore was available and undiscovered. The boom came back in 1873, and Virginia City soon had a Millionaires' Row, with mansions, an opera house, and a five-story brick and stone hotel. A terrible fire in 1875 forced complete rebuilding of the town. However, the boom did not last for long. By 1881 the town's population had dwindled to below 400, never to rise again. Today Virginia City is a very successful tourist site, with saloons, hotels, restaurants, and even a weekly newspaper very much in business.

Other Nevada towns did not fare as well. Places such as Austin, White Pine, Hamilton, Treasure City, and Aurora all became little more than piles of rubble.

Colorado too has its ghost towns. Central City, for example, boomed several times between 1859 and 1914, thanks to gold and silver. It is today, as is Virginia City, a thriving summer tourist center.

Utah witnessed a mining rush beginning in 1863. Silver Reef in the southwest was a thriving town in 1877, complete with hotels, restaurants, stores, banks, and churches. Bad times began in 1881, and the last mine closed in 1891. This town never revived in any form.

Idaho had a short boom in the 1860s and became a steady producer of minerals. Silver City, Pierce City, and Ruby City all died quickly as Idaho's first boom ended by 1870. The state proved more fertile for farmers than other western states. Then the willingness of San Francisco bankers to finance more expensive mining with new technology heated up Idaho's mining boom again in the 1880s. The last mine, however, closed for good after years of decline. Though no longer booming, Idaho still remains an important mining state.

Wyoming also had an 1860s gold rush. South Pass City had 4,000 residents, 5 hotels, 4 law offices, and 13 taverns by 1869. Atlantic City and Miners' Delight were also born. This boom ended in 1872.

The discovery of gold in South Dakota's Black Hills in 1874 gave rise to Deadwood, one of the West's most notorious towns. In July 1876 it had 25,000 residents, but it became a ghost town two years later. Deadwood, with only 100 people, is today a thriving tourist center with some mining still going on nearby.

Few mine camps were as lawless, brutal, or disorderly as myth would have people believe. Montana's, however, were. Its gold rush came in the 1860s, as did the Idaho, Utah, and Wyoming stampedes. "But for some reason, Montana tended to attract men who had had no luck in the neighboring states, and some who had been floating around for 10 or 15 years or more with nothing to show for their adventures" (Silverberg, 1968, 208). Western Montana had some of the West's toughest towns. Bannack thrived until 1865, then fell apart in 1880. Nevada City was a flourishing boomtown in late 1863 and is today only a few rundown shacks. Virginia City thrived then, too, complete with a theater, lecture hall, and other businesses. Its population, however, dwindled from 10,000 in 1865 to 2,500 in 1870, and below 1,250 by 1880. Now it is a tourist "ghost town."

Arizona and New Mexico experienced booms later on. Cerrillos, Elizabethtown (see Jenkinson) and many other lonely towns are scattered throughout New Mexico. Gila City, La Paz, and Boothill all fell into disuse. Tombstone was more fortunate. It peaked in the early 1880s; mining ended in 1911 and never again flourished. Revival began as the town was proclaimed a historic site in 1925, and it speeded up in 1964. "Tombstone today glitters with renewed splendor" (Silverberg, 1968, 262). Charleston and Contention City nearby were its contemporaries, but no one cared to revive them.

The last old-time Western mining boom took place in Nevada in 1900. Tonopah, Goldfield, Bullfrog, and Rhyolite thrived from 1900 to 1910 and all died afterward.

Many accounts exist of ghost towns, but for sheer detail, few can match the story of Meadow Lake, California, told by Fatout (1969). He wrote of such towns as Dry Diggings, Nevada City, and Rough and Ready. Meadow Lake, however, lasted for almost a hundred years, and it suffered a gap between hope and reality that made its destiny spectacular even for a mining camp. Its fate was crueler than that of camps that lasted for a shorter time—Meadow Lake has completely vanished without leaving even crumbling ruins behind. "Nothing stands to tell the visitor that here thousands of people swarmed and labored, stubbornly pitted themselves against wilderness and hard Sierra (Nevada Mountains) winter, assailed the grim granite ridges, and built what they firmly believed would become a metropolis, long-lived and lusty" (Fatout, 1969, xii).

The Pacific Northwest has its share of ghost towns. Weis (1971) explored many of them, often having to rely on the memories of old-timer residents to find town sites not shown on any map. He found and described 15 of them in Oregon, 10 in Washington, 12 in Idaho, 10 in Wyoming, and 14 in Montana (Fig. 4.5 through 4.9 show their locations). Perhaps the region's moist climate and relative isolation account for the lack of life being shown in Northwest ghost towns. Almost without exception, they are lucky to survive with a few battered old buildings. Many have simply vanished.

Mining knew no national boundaries, so the mountains of British Columbia province in Canada hide a huge number of ghost towns, a subject studied

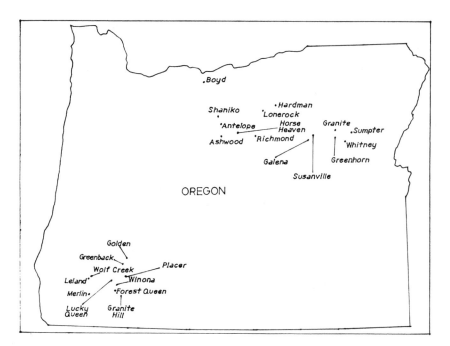

Figure 4.5
Ghost towns of Oregon (Weis, 1971).

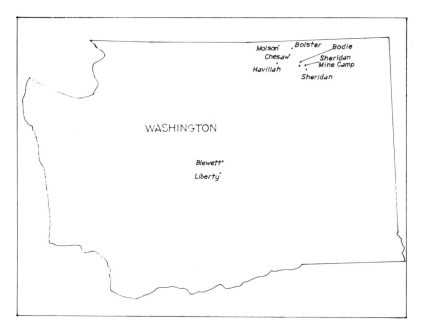

Figure 4.6
Ghost towns of Washington (Weis, 1971).

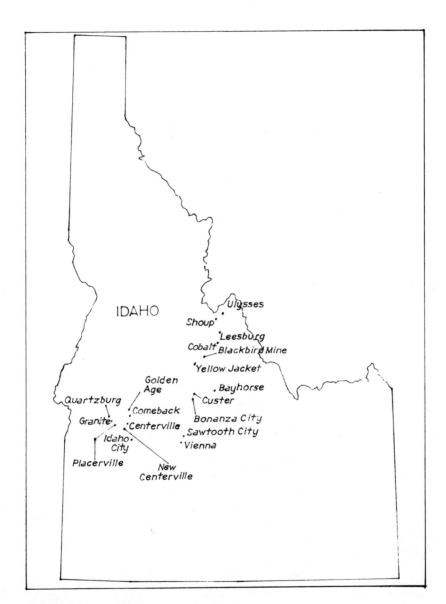

Figure 4.7
Ghost towns of Idaho (Weis, 1971).

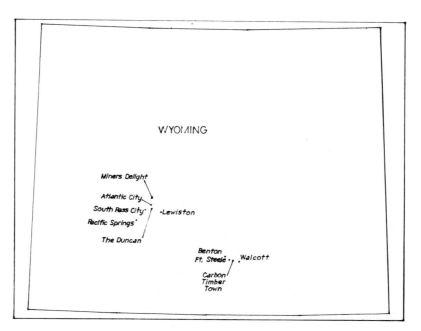

Figure 4.8
Ghost towns of Wyoming (Weis, 1971).

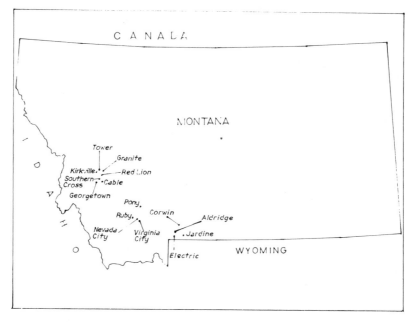

Figure 4.9
Ghost towns of Montana (after Weis, 1971).

by Ramsey (1963). His findings almost match those of Fatout—few traces of any of British Columbia's ghost towns exist. Most of them are in the Harrison Lake and Fraser River areas, active when British Columbia's role as a Hudson's Bay Company fur trading outpost was ending and the 1860s gold rush was underway (see Fig. 4.10).

The area attracted the usual boom population—gold-seekers, traders, soldiers, politicians, prostitutes, and criminals. The scattered remains of their stampede stretch up the province's rocky spine all the way to the Yukon border. These northern towns, such as Bennett City and Discovery, owed their brief existence to the 1898 Klondike gold rush.

Like fossils, these ghost towns scattered throughout western North America bear silent witness to a bygone era. There is always the danger that many of today's resource towns in the United States, Canada, Australia, Scotland, and elsewhere will end up as fossils, too, unless government and industry leaders

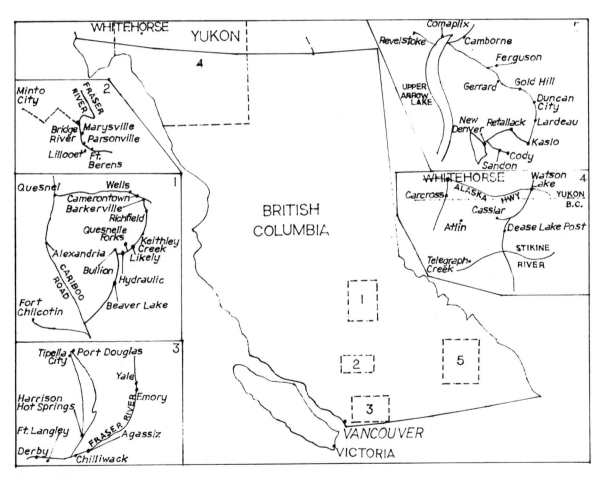

Figure 4.10
Ghost towns of British Columbia (after Ramsey, 1963).

and planners show more concern for their future than those of a century ago.

NOTES

1. Letcher (1936) offered these statistics to compare with Johannesburg's explosive growth: Chicago had 4,000 residents in 1837; 395,000 in 1874; 420,000 in 1876; and 3.4 million in 1930. Buenos Aires grew from 220,000 residents in 1876 to 2.2 million in 1936. Sydney's population went up from 95,000 in 1861 to 237,000 in 1881; 400,000 in 1891; 488,000 in 1901; and 1.2 million in 1933. Melbourne grew from 283,000 in 1881 to 1 million in 1933. This means that these cities' annual growth rates during the indicated time period were: 7.52% for Chicago, 3.9% for Buenos Aires, 3.58% for Sydney, and 2.46% for Melbourne. Letcher compares these examples to Johannesburg's growth, which is as follows: 17,300 residents in 1890; 109,000 in 1902; 237,000 in 1911; 288,000 in 1921; 377,000 in 1931; 400,000 in 1933; and 485,000 in 1936. These figures average 7.52% from 1890 to 1936, matching the highest rate of the other cities mentioned. Such explosive growth is now overwhelming many large Third World cities. These rates, though, are still far below the 15% yearly growth that Gilmore defines as boomtown expansion. If huge cities, with their large and relatively sophisticated governments and planners, cannot deal with growth rates below 15%, then small cities do not have much hope of dealing with growth rates above 15%.
2. The Boers are the descendants of Dutch and other Europeans who settled in South Africa several centuries ago. Until the 1899-1902 Boer War, the Boers were almost all farmers. They practiced a very rigid form of Protestantism (the Dutch Reformed Church still dominates their thinking, especially on racial segregation). The descendants of these Boers still dominate South African politics and agriculture.
3. This is the same type of local government that Kimberley, originally part of the British-ruled Cape Colony, had almost from its beginning.
4. The local justice of the peace, Pleasant Humble, gave his name to a village of 700 people. The oilfield then took its name from the town, and the Humble Oil Company took its name from the field.
5. Its Main Street brothels had attracted the world's sailors for years.
6. The area's largest city, Cologne (actually outside today's Ruhr), had about 50,000 people in 1800. Nearby Dusseldorf grew much more slowly. Essen in 1823 still had room in which to expand within its ancient walls, and counted only 4,000 residents. Soest had about 5,000 inhabitants in 1800, Dortmund about 4,000, Bochum 2,000, Elberfeld more than 20,000, Barmen 19,000, and Recklinghausen 2,000 (Pounds, 1952, 43).
7. The Ruhr's province of Rhineland-Westphalia grew by 63% from 1816 to 1861; Germany's other major region, Prussia, expanded 66%; all of Germany grew 53% (Pounds, 1952, 80).
8. The cities of Hamborn and Muelheim (controlled by Thyssen), Dortmund (Hoesch and Dortmunder Union), and Bochum (Bochumer Verein) are other examples.
9. These cities are Dusseldorf, Essen, Duisburg, Dortmund, Wuppertal, and Gelsenkirchen.

REFERENCES

Bancroft, Bill, 1982, "The Night the Hunt Brothers Pushed Dallas Too Far," *Historic Preservation* **34**(3):10-15.

Farwell, Byron, 1976, *The Great Anglo-Boer War,* Harper & Row, New York.

Fatout, Paul, 1969, *Meadow Lake—Gold Town,* Indiana University Press, Bloomington, Ind.

Jenkinson, Michael, 1967, *Playthings of the Wind—Ghost Towns of New Mexico,* University of New Mexico Press, Albuquerque.

Letcher, Owen, 1936, *The Gold Mines of Southern Africa,* Arno Press, New York.

Manchester, William, 1968, *The Arms of Krupp,* Little, Brown & Co., Boston.

Pounds, Norman J. G., 1952, *The Ruhr,* Indiana University Press, Bloomington, Ind.

Ramsey, Bruce, 1963, *Ghost Towns of British Columbia,* Mitchell Press, Ltd., Vancouver, B.C.

Roberts, Brian, 1976, *Kimberley: Turbulent City,* David Philip, Cape Town, South Africa.

Roberts, Brian, 1978, *Civic Century,* Northern Cape Printers, Kimberley, South Africa.

Rosenthal, Eric, 1970, *Gold! Gold! Gold!,* Collier-Macmillan, Ltd., London.

Rundell, Walter, Jr., 1977, *Early Texas Oil,* Texas A & M University Press, College Station, Tex.

Silverberg, Robert, 1968, *Ghost Towns of the American West,* Thomas Y. Crowell Co., New York.

Weis, Norman D., 1971, *Ghost Towns of the Northwest,* Caxton Printers, Ltd., Caldwell, Idaho.

Wilson, R. K., 1980, *Australia's Resources and Their Development,* University of Sydney, Department of Adult Education, Sydney, Australia.

5

Towns of the Trans-Siberian

So far, this section has explored the variety of ways in which boomtowns were born as America and Canada looked west for new territories and resources, dotting a vast landscape with mining and railroad camps. A similar epic has been going on in Russia for the last century, but the Russians have had to look to the east for land and riches—to Siberia.

Any attempt to exploit the riches of Siberia faced as daunting an array of obstacles as ever faced the Americans and Canadians. These obstacles include land as mountainous, swampy, bandit-ridden, and fraught with terrible weather as anything the American railroad builders or miners had to conquer.

THE RAILROAD

The building of the Trans-Siberian railroad from the Ural Mountains to the Pacific (see Figure 5.1) was a stupefying undertaking. Achieved at about the same time as the great American railroad boom, its builders had to deal with red tape unimaginable to the American bureaucrat and some of the harshest climate on this planet. It was also at least twice as long as the transcontinental American railroad and built with far more primitive equipment. As in the United States, the Trans-Siberian spawned numerous boomtowns.

That is not the entire story, though. No country has ever had to dismantle its industrial base and move it thousands of miles the way the Russians did during World War II to keep it safe from the advancing Germans. It is as if all the industry from Chicago to Pittsburgh were dismantled and moved to the Rockies in a few months. The unbelievable feat of moving hundreds of factories from western Russia beyond the Ural Mountains into Siberia could not have been done without the iron will of the Russian government and people—and an available railroad. As Russian industry moved east, communities that had been little more than boomtowns when the railroad was built—and were even less than that before the railroad—exploded into great cities rivaling those of western Russia.

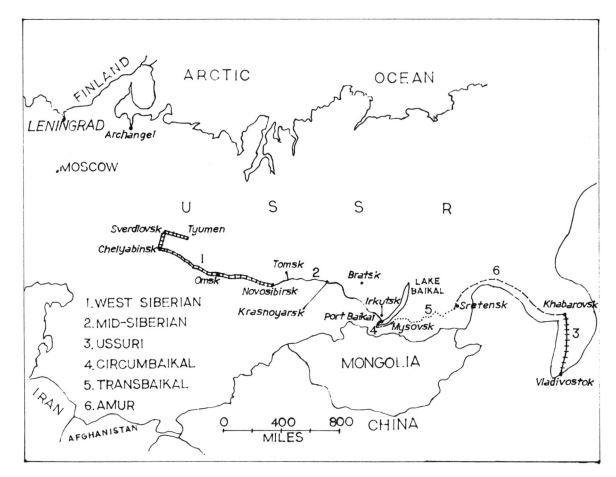

Figure 5.1
Key cities along the Trans-Siberian railroad (Tupper, 1965).

In 1890, however, most Siberian towns had a mining-camp flavor. Omsk was a particularly inhospitable city. Tomsk was somewhat more cultivated. Krasnoyarsk was uninteresting to tourists, who normally went on to Irkutsk. During the summer, Irkutsk's citizens took advantage of traveling circuses, concerts, horse races, fishing on the Angara River, and boat rides on Lake Baikal.

As for Sretensk, "It is possible but unlikely that someone in a moment of aberration has said a good word for [it] as it appeared in summer" (Tupper, 1965, 308).

Construction of the railroad came in spurts, covering the years 1891 to 1916. Russia already had railroads connecting European Russia to the Urals at Tyumen, so Czar Alexander III decided in 1891 to do more or less what the Union and Central Pacific's originators did—build one line from Vladivostok on the Pacific coast to link up in central Siberia with another line going east from Tyumen through Chelyabinsk.

Construction of track east of Chelyabinsk began in 1892, reaching Omsk two years later. This city desperately needed a railroad to help it grow. While some hide-clad herdsmen from the [nearby countryside] may have regarded Omsk with wide-eyed enchantment . . . more sophisticated visitors detested the place: in summer, they sweltered in temperatures that soared into the high nineties; in winter, they were numbed by cold that touched 42 below. In all seasons, winds swept through the unpaved streets — treeless because of the barren, saline soil — and raised storms of acrid dust or piled snowdrifts high against the dismal houses and buildings, almost all of which were wooden. . . . The city's medical institutions for a civilian population of more than 30,000 comprised exactly one lunatic asylum, one lying-in hospital, and one municipal hospital with only 25 beds. The importance of Omsk as an administrative, military, trading and shipping center was belied by its atrocious inns (carpetless rooms, avaricious owners, high rates, bugs and vermin). (Tupper, 1965, 109)

Because of the railroad, "by 1899, the value of the city's industrial output had increased by nearly 60 percent, its population soared from some 37,000 to more than 50,000 in . . . 1897-1899 alone" (Tupper, 1965, 112).

Construction of the line east from Omsk to the Ob River lasted from 1893 to 1897; at about the same time, the Ob River-to-Irkutsk section was built.

As in the United States, political considerations influenced the track's route. For instance, the city of Tomsk came out on the short end of the stick. Second only to Irkutsk as Siberia's largest city, Tomsk eagerly looked forward to being on the main Ob-Irkutsk railroad. The planners' decision to bypass Tomsk for two years instead helped a "miserable settlement" called Novonikolayevsk grow into today's Novosibirsk, "the Chicago of the Soviet Union" and modern Siberia's largest city. Figure 5.1 shows that Tomsk had to settle for a branch line.

Housing for workers was less of a concern for the planners and builders of the Trans-Siberian than it was for their counterparts in the United States. Siberia had long been a dreaded place of exile and imprisonment during the czarist regimes. Many of the railroad laborers were convicts and exiles, and most of the others were from the primitive countryside. Laborers working on the track were not about to complain about whatever housing or food they were given.

The railroad reached Irkutsk in 1899. Irkutsk, the so-called "Paris of Siberia,"

was not only eastern Siberia's most important administrative, transportation and commercial center, but was also a magnet to throngs of gold miners, fur traders, tea merchants, Chinese gold smugglers, exiles and ex-convicts, footpads, prostitutes and occasional foreign travelers eager to see the remote city with its "civilized savages" so luridly described by [various journalists]. (Tupper, 1965, 195-197)

Although the city had telegraph service to the west by the 1860s, it sometimes took six weeks for ordinary telegrams to go there. The telephone arrived in 1891, followed several years later by electric lighting on a few streets. As in all towns in the early boom stage, the darkened streets were a haven for violent criminals. Since Irkutsk was still a gold prospecting center in 1902, the miners took advantage of the available forms of vice and became easy prey for various criminals. As in Denver, rich mine owners built lavish mansions that would have impressed European Russian aristocrats, but they were very philanthropic to local churches and schools; some wealthy women worked on behalf of orphans and poor families.

As the railroad wound through Siberia, it became lined with new towns and existing communities in the throes of expansion. These places usually had a church, homes, and warehouses.

While all this activity was going on in the west, the line from Vladivostok to the Ussuri River at Khabarovsk was built. Vladivostok, today the headquarters of the Soviet Pacific Fleet, was in 1891 "a slatternly town of muddy, unpaved streets, open sewers, grim military barracks and warehouses, unpainted wooden houses, and hundreds of mud-plastered straw huts of the Chinese and Korean settlers who comprised about a third of the port's 14,000 inhabitants" (Tupper, 1965, 83). In 1891, the building of the railroad north and west from this point began. Vladivostok during the next five years had all the troubles of the Union Pacific towns; it suffered from marauding bands of convict laborers who killed and robbed its citizens. Unlike the Chinese workers on the American railroad, those on the Vladivostok-Khabarovsk run were difficult to supervise; they were unfamiliar with shovels and wheelbarrows and refused to work in the rain. Regularly scheduled service on this easternmost link of the Trans-Siberian began in 1896.

By 1900 the only incomplete sections of track were those around the south end of Lake Baikal and the long Sretensk-Khabarovsk "Amur run." Geography hampered the first of these; the mountains around Lake Baikal made the construction there extremely slow and dangerous. It was not completed until 1904. Red tape hampered the other line. Not until 1907 did the new Parliament approve the "Amur run," which took another nine years to build. On the eve of World War I, the Trans-Siberian railroad was complete.

Its effect on Russia was as profound as the transcontinental railroad was on the United States. The Trans-Siberian helped transform Siberia by enabling millions of peasants to live on the unsettled "virgin" land.

Settlers were willing to go to Siberia, but they tended to scatter throughout Siberia until the railroad arrived. By 1900, however, the peasants could ride in boxcars as far as Sretensk. The railroad gave the migrants not only direction but safety. By 1898 their mortality rate had fallen from 20 percent to 0.2 percent. Government facilities sprouted along the line to feed, shelter, and give medical aid to passengers.

INDUSTRY

Peasants alone could not make Siberia boom, however. Not until the Soviet government began to build massive industrial complexes (mainly iron and steel) in the Urals near the new city of Magnitogorsk did Siberian growth really take off. The Urals have vast quantities of iron ore but little coking coal as the Ruhr has, so planners had to search for coal in the Kuznetsk basin south of Tomsk. Without the railroad to carry prodigious amounts of coal to the Urals, no iron and steel industry could have developed there.

Sverdlovsk became the center of huge machinery plants. It and other Siberian cities boomed during the 1930s. From 1926 to 1939,

the population more than tripled in Novosibirsk and Sverdlovsk, and quadrupled in Chelyabinsk. Novokuznetsk, the heart of the Kuznetsk coalfields, developed from a community with about 3,900 inhabitants to a city of almost 170,000, while the combined population of Irkutsk, Ulan-Ude, Chita, and Khabarovsk increased by 269 percent. (Tupper, 1965, 414)

Such population increases were helped largely by legions of free workers going to make a better living, by uprooted peasant farmers, and by millions of slave laborers.

Farm equipment, produce, grain, timber, and oil shipments overwhelmed the Trans-Siberian. Thanks to extensive modernization in the 1930s, the railroad was able to carry entire industries east of the Urals and away from the invading Nazis several years later.

The postwar government's insistence on heavy industry has proved a boon to the Siberian cities along the Trans-Siberian. Omsk, directly on the line, is now twice as large as Tomsk, lying on a branch line. Novosibirsk had about 900,000 people in 1959 and has well over a million today. Remote Khabarovsk has 320,000 residents, and equally distant Irkutsk has 370,000, with little evidence of its 1890s raw boomtown atmosphere.

Even today, new Siberian cities are arising. Bratsk began life in 1954 as a classic Soviet effort to exploit Siberian wealth by building a hydroelectric power plant able to supply power to new industrial plants and the new city to house the workers and their families. A village of 3,000 in 1954, Bratsk grew to 165,000 by 1972, the period in which its frontier atmosphere faded.

Soviet planners, however, did no better with Bratsk than they have anywhere else in the country's economy. Bratsk's planners were admitting by 1972 that the power plant had been completed years before most of the region's planned industries were available to use its electric power. As has occurred in many booming towns in the United States, nearly half of the 54,000 workers who built Bratsk departed after completion of the job. It took either high pay or a sense of adventure or patriotism for them to come at all. A spur of the railroad had to be built nearby.

Bratsk, however, suffered from the usual boomtown problems: shortages of consumer goods, lack of cultural facilities, and the difficulty of attracting, training, and holding a modern work force in a region with eight months of winter weather. The cold also cut off supplies of fresh produce.

Bratsk still suffers aesthetically, too. It has a "stamped from the mold quality. . . . Even now it is less a city than eight Siberian Levittowns . . . without any metropolitan center . . . A sprawling collage of large concrete dormitories facelessly lining spacious avenues almost entirely bereft of trees," (Smith, 1972, 2), an appearance that reportedly dismayed the late Soviet Premier Aleksei Kosygin. Many residents, however, are far more content with the place. They enjoy the relative lack of hustle and bustle so common in European Russia.

As time passes, the Soviets will undoubtedly begin to tap the incredible mineral wealth of Siberia. The process will be slow in this coldest of inhabited regions, but progress will be made. Much of it will be due to the existence of the Trans-Siberian railroad.

REFERENCES

Smith, Hedrick, 1972, "New Siberian City Leaves Raw Past Behind," *New York Times,* April 22, p. 2.

Tupper, Harmon, 1965. *To the Great Ocean—Siberia and the Trans-Siberian Railway,* Little, Brown & Co., Boston.

6

Early Government Towns

This book has so far looked at communities that either boomed or sprang up from nothing because of individual decisions to exploit the potential for wealth, or at least for making a better living. Later on, it will explore communities that were created by the companies that employed most of their residents. Still others owe their existence to a national government that, either for strategic or national-security reasons, preferred to isolate certain of its citizens.

Governments are today creating entirely new cities primarily to exploit regions that have until now been neglected. Cities such as Brasilia will be examined later on. But new government cities are not new to this century. Two of the world's best-known cities got their start as planned communities and national capitals more than a century ago. Yet, neither Washington, D.C., nor Leningrad could possibly have grown as they did without government involvement; society's inertia would have otherwise combined with these cities' poor geography to nip them in the bud.

LENINGRAD

The City of Lenin owes its existence to Peter the Great. Constantly at war with his European neighbors (especially the Swedes), obsessed with Western culture and technology, Peter was determined to build a city—his city—on the shores of the Baltic Sea (see Fig. 5.1, in the previous chapter) to serve as Russia's window to the west and as a western fortress.

A military leader, Peter wanted the fort built first, then the city. He could not have picked a poorer location in that area. He built St. Petersburg on a "wild, flat, empty marsh . . . , a bog, soggy with water. In the spring, thick mists from melting ice and snow hung over it. When strong southwest winds blew in from the Gulf of Finland, the [Neva] river backed up and many of the islands simply disappeared underwater" (Massie, 1980, 355). No traders had ever built so much as a village here. To the neighboring Finns, "neva" means "swamp." No one but a Russian czar would ever have dared to build anything on such a site, let alone a capital city. Peter, however, was one of Russia's most autocratic, stubborn czars. His city was built on that spot.

After seizing the mouth of the Neva from the Swedes, Peter began building the fortress of St. Peter and St. Paul on May 16, 1703. With only pickaxes and shovels, laborers actually had to carry in dirt in small bags to raise the level of Hare Island above possible flood levels.

Peter diverted much of Russia's trade from Archangel to St. Petersburg, set up shipyards there, and encouraged foreign ships to come in. To attract the Russian nobility, Peter brought in an Italian architect to begin putting up public buildings and palaces. With his absolute powers, Peter could call in craftspeople and unskilled laborers from all over Russia to

drive the piles into the marshes, hew and haul the timbers, drag the stones, clear the forests, level the hills, lay out the streets, build docks and wharves, erect the fortress, houses and shipyards, dig the canals.

The hardships were frightful. Workers lived on damp ground in rough, crowded, filthy huts. Scurvy, dysentery, malaria and other diseases scythed them down in droves. Wages were not paid regularly and desertion was chronic. (Massie, 1980, 360)

Thousands of workers died, many no doubt from the backbreaking task of bringing in almost all the required rock and wood.

Peter also had to force many hundreds of aristocrats, government officials, and merchants to move from Moscow to St. Petersburg.

They were now obliged to build new houses at great expense in a Baltic marsh. They had to pay exorbitant prices for food imported from hundreds of miles away. . . . They hated the water on which the Tsar doted, and none set foot in a boat except by compulsion. Nevertheless, having no choice, they came. The merchants and shopkeepers came with them and found solace in the fact that they could charge outrageous prices for their goods. (Massie, 1980, 361)

Many laborers stayed on after working for the time period set by Peter; they could not afford to go home. As occurred in all wooden towns, St. Petersburg suffered from frequent fires. Peter gave every civilian

and military officer, including himself, a firefighting assignment for extra pay. Unlike most boomtowns, St. Petersburg had no water in winter with which to fight fires. When the Neva and the Baltic froze, only hatchets and axes were useful, and then, of course, burning buildings had to be demolished.

Early St. Petersburg also suffered repeated floods. And "even 15 years after its founding," as fancy palaces and gardens were going up regularly,

daily life in St. Petersburg remained, in one foreigner's description, a 'hazardous hand-to-mouth bivouacking.' One problem was that the region simply could not feed itself. . . . St. Petersburg would have starved without provisions sent from outside. Thousands of carts traveled from Novgorod and even from Moscow during the warmer months bringing food to the city; in winter, the lifeline was maintained on a stream of sleds. If these supplies were even slightly delayed along the way, prices immediately soared in St. Petersburg. (Massie, 1980, 364)

Although many resident aristocrats and foreign ambassadors joined countless humble residents in hating the place, Peter loved it. And after Peter's death, his successors transformed the primitive town into a city so breathtaking in its beauty it would be called the Babylon of the Snows and the Venice of the North. This construction accelerated after several military victories secured the land to the southwest.

This new city became Russia's capital in 1712, and ministries had to move from Moscow on Peter's orders. After the Swedish threat to the area disappeared in 1709, the city spread rapidly, and more palaces, churches, and government buildings went up.

By 1722 Peter's efforts to attract trade finally made his city Russia's leading port. Late in his rule, which ended with his death in 1725, Peter concentrated on making St. Petersburg a cultural center. Peter must have been pleased with his efforts in his last days.

He would have been horrified by events after his death. Nothing could make up for St. Petersburg's bleak winter or its location as the world's most northerly major metropolis. Russia's westernmost city was acutely vulnerable to attack from the west. Renamed Leningrad after the Bolshevik Revolution, the city ceased being the capital as Moscow grew to become the Soviet

Union's largest city. Its climate contributed greatly to the city's misery during the brutal German siege of World War II, and Leningrad was the last major Russian city to be repaired after the war.

Peter, however, would be greatly pleased by today's Leningrad. It is a great tourist attraction, with its multicolored palaces, its network of canals, and the variety and richness of its cultural life. Most of all, it is the most gracefully European and the least monotonous of all Russian cities. This city still bears Peter's stamp after 300 years.

WASHINGTON, D.C

Leningrad's evolution was relatively straightforward: A series of rulers was determined to make it the center of Russia's government, commerce, and culture. In such a society, they could demand anything and everything necessary of their people to make the city a metropolis. No other kind of ruler could have willed Leningrad to grow. This is the problem that has bedeviled Washington, D.C.: The capital of the United States never attained Leningrad's commercial or cultural status, and so never attained Leningrad's population. At least ten American cities outrank Washington in size. Yet, its comparatively small population is the source of Washington's charm, especially compared to crowded, hectic New York, or sprawling Los Angeles.

Every American learns in school that Washington originated as the design of Frenchman Pierre L'Enfant, who decided that the new capital of the infant American republic was to have the boulevards and plazas of Paris. Its location, however, was purely political. No planner would have willingly selected "a spot where tidal swamplands yearly bred fevers and oppressive damp heat blankets the city every summer" (Green, 1962a, 12).

Washington nevertheless began its existence as a boomtown under federal control. It resembled mining camps in outward appearance, "unformed streets, roofless houses, and the clutter of stone, lumber, and debris about the unfinished government buildings. Not until the November winds stripped the trees bare would the rawness and untidiness of the new capital afflict men fresh from the elegance and comforts of Philadelphia" (Green, 1962a, 14).

Alexandria, Virginia and Georgetown, Maryland immediately began competing with Washington as the area's commercial center. As government workers began moving in after 1800, land speculation became rampant in all three towns. Unlike Leningrad, Washington's resident government was far from pleased with having to do its business there. In its early years in Washington, Congress often had ideas about relocating. All this prevented industrial growth in the new District of Columbia. Once companies began setting up in Washington, Alexandria and Georgetown opened competing firms, which, in a small market, could only hurt each other. Only the Navy Yard provided much industrial work. Moreover, their far inland location prevented any of the three towns from becoming the huge port that Peter was able to make out of Leningrad.

Government neglect of Washington became evident as the agrarian-minded Jefferson administration took power, and the Congress began its chronic neglect of the city's needs, refusing to allocate taxpayer funds to modernize a city few of their constituents would ever see. Most of the valuable real estate was government-owned and beyond property taxation. Washington suffered the common boomtown problem of an insufficient, poorly paid police force, and a large poverty-stricken population. The problem in Washington was especially acute: workers coming to Washington to work on government buildings were often left bankrupt when Congress failed to vote funds to complete them. In 1802, about 42 percent of Washington's revenues were spent on relief of the poor (Green, 1962a, 42). Congressional miserliness also hampered the growth of public education.

Wartime proved Washington to be just as vulnerable to attack as Leningrad, as the invading British drove President Madison out of Washington and burned the capital's major buildings during the War of 1812. Only southern congressional pressure and a huge bank loan for rebuilding may have kept people's fears of a permanent government pullout from being realized.

The postwar period witnessed the first of several building and land speculation booms that periodically swept Washington, after which an 1818 collapse became the first of several to hit the capital.

None of the booms helped Washington's sanitation problem of inadequate garbage disposal and the spreading tidal swamps. For 40 years, summertime fever epidemics were to plague Washington. A city of scattered buildings like Washington suffered few fires. In all other respects, however, especially aesthetic, Washington resembled a boomtown:

The city L'Enfant had laid out on a scale to represent the genius of the new republic had in fact attained little aesthetic distinction. Partial execution of the plan left large areas untouched, which spoiled the effect.... Most of the Mall (between the Capitol and the Potomac River) was a wasteland of swamps dotted with clusters of sheds along the canal. Vacant lots occupied much of the city . . . and the streets connecting one village with the others that together comprised the capital were still little more than rutted paths. . . . (Green, 1962a, 106)

Only with Congress's help could Washington become a more aesthetically or culturally attractive city.

Even that was not enough to make Washington boom as a commercial center. The small regional population living nearby in a "relatively unfertile" area and the lack of local manufacturing hampered its growth. Because communication and sources of supply were inadequate, banks were not interested in building branches. Without bank credit, large industrial growth in Washington was impossible. City services also suffered from insufficient funds. In the mid-1850s, the educational, police, and firefighting systems all deteriorated. Local taxpayers were not willing to fund better city services, but were in fact willing, as late as the 1850s, to accept animals wandering through the streets.

While Northern industry boomed in the 1850s, Washington's faltered. "Whether because of insufficient capital, too small a skilled labor force, a limited market,

or inadequate shipping facilities, the District could claim scant industrial progress. . . . (Green, 1962a, 192). Only the Civil War forced Congress to approve the laying of railroads to the south. The war accelerated the steady expansion of government, which more than made up for industrial stagnation in raising Washington's population.[1]

The city was unprepared, however, for the great Civil War boom. Although the city finally had a modern water supply system and gas lamps lined the main avenues, sanitation in 1860 was still terrible. The dumping of waste into alleys, the stray animals, the mosquitoes breeding in stagnant ponds, and "appalling" infant mortality all continued unabated as did arson, prostitution, and thievery.

Washington's population doubled from 1861 to 1863. Several thousand Union soldiers helped keep the resulting crime wave under some semblance of control, but prison space was hopelessly inadequate. As smallpox epidemics hit the city several times, disease proved a more formidable menace to the city than the Confederate armies.

The war only worsened sanitary problems since the Army needed corrals and slaughterhouses for its mules, cattle, and horses. "The [water supply] aqueduct, however, saved the . . . civilian community from untold misery in the last summer of the war. . . . " Nothing prevented the war's traffic of wagon trains, horses, mules, and cattle from tearing up the streets.

Along with its nearly 200,000 civilians, wartime Washington also had as many as 50,000 soldiers in military hospitals; in addition,

the demand for food, lodging, household wares, and clothes sent prices skyrocketing ... and the war was enriching tailors, stationers, blacksmiths. . . . Skilled workmen commanded unheard-of wages . . ., merchants with stock bought cheap could sell at huge markups, and people with real estate to dispose of made killings, but petty tradesmen without the credit to purchase goods at the right moment, common laborers and people on salaries suffered. (Green, 1962a, 263-264)

Another 40,000 fugitive slaves flooded into Washington by the end of the war; ignorant of hygiene, they worsened the city's health problems.

The wartime boom inevitably ended with the war. As the 1870s went on, however, Washington began to emerge as a cultural center, especially as Northern views of Washington as a pro-slavery Southern city faded. Nothing had reduced Congressional apathy toward the city, particularly as a series of local financial crises convinced the lawmakers that Washingtonians were financially irresponsible. After 1878 Congress therefore took full control of Washington's government, but also guaranteed its solvency. Having given up on the idea of becoming a major transportation and commercial center, Washington instead underwent a series of building and real estate booms that benefited speculators far more than the average citizen.

Infrastructure development toward the turn of the century did help the average Washingtonian, however. It now had telegraph and telephone services, electric street lights, and trolleys. The city, though, was still grappling with an inadequate water supply, inadequate sewage and drainage systems, and poorly graded and unpaved streets. The citizens seethed with resentment at Congressional neglect. One possible reason for their failure to demand self-government was that they feared Negro influence or even domination. Even the few middle-class blacks feared that poor Negroes would elect city leaders who favored the poor.

The Washington of 1900 was a cultural center receptive to art and literature, but one where most cultural attractions came from outside the city.[2]

Washington escaped the hordes of European immigrants that strained other cities' infrastructure to the breaking point. In fact, from 1901 to 1916 Washington underwent extensive beautification as numerous public buildings went up. Much less was done about the shanties and tenements with no sanitary facilities where thousands lived and fell ill.

World War I again turned Washington into a military boomtown as "people eager to be useful poured into Washington during the first week of the war and the flow did not lessen until the Armistice in November 1918" (Green, 1962b, 237). Most of the 130,000 soldiers stationed near Washington spent their leave times there. Washington had about 525,000 people by 1918, and they stretched the city's services almost to the breaking point. Most of the wartime jobs went to out-of-towners, straining local housing even further. Not until January 1918 did the federal government get involved in finding shelter for its new workers.

This time, the boom did not end with the war. Washington's population grew 25 percent from 1917 to 1920 (Green, 1962b, 273). The 1920s prosperity and Congress's upbeat mood helped improve Washington's police force, school system, water supply, and sewage system.

The New Deal and World War II had a profound effect on Washington. In the last 50 years, Washington lost much of its provincial image and its lightweight status among world capitals as the United States grew into one of the world's leading powers. Now a magnet for millions of tourists and a source of jokes throughout the nation, Washington has come a long way since its founding. Of course, it has never grown large enough to challenge New York or Chicago as a large American metropolis the way Leningrad challenges Moscow. To this day, Washington remains a company town; even if that company is the United States government. And, a lack of diverse industry will continue to hold down population growth.

NOTES

1. Green (1962, Vol. 1, 183) provides the following population figures, taken from the U.S. Census: 3,210 (1800); 8,208 (1810); 13,247 (1820); 18,827 (1830); 23,364 (1840); 40,001 (1850); 61,122 (1860); 109,199 (1870).
2. Washington did not have a major performing arts center until 1971, and even then it had difficulty generating local talent.

REFERENCES

Green, Constance M., 1962a, *Washington: Village and Capital, 1800-1878,* Vol. 1, Princeton Univeristy Press, Princeton, N.J.

Green, Constance M., 1962b, *Washington: Capital City,* Vol. 2, Princeton University Press, Princeton, N.J.

Massie, Robert K., 1980, *Peter the Great,* Alfred A. Knopf, New York.

7

Early Company Towns

More common than the government-built and owned town is a community owing its existence to a single company that may have either built the town or employed most of its residents. Newly built company towns are becoming popular alternatives to having small existing communities undergo overwhelming changes in population and local values.

Companies have been building their own communities for centuries. The more successful include Gary, Indiana; Nowa Huta, Poland; and Wolfsburg, Germany.

The major town-forming types of industry are iron and steel mills (Gary, Indiana; Rourkela, India; Ciudad Guyana, Venezuela), aluminum smelting (Kitimat, Canada; Sabned, Guinea), heavy machine building and armaments works (Salzgitter, Germany; Magnitogorsk and Volgograd, USSR), petrochemical works (El Tablazo, Venezuela; Aliaga, Turkey) and automobile plants (Wolfsburg, Germany; Togliatti, USSR). (Galantay, 1975, 39)

In most, if not all of these, the needs of the industry came before the design of attractive living environments, and private infrastructure always came before public infrastructure.

Since many nineteenth-century company towns failed, Galantay stated that private industry is not the best at developing and operating new towns.

Firms considering setting up their own towns have to keep one eye on past experiments that failed, usually because of the company's lack of concern for the residents in the town's design. No better example exists of this myopia than the failed town of Pullman, Illinois.

PULLMAN

Pullman was at one time America's best-known company town. In 1880, railroad car millionaire George Pullman had an architect and landscape designer plan and built "a model town and factory" eight miles south of Chicago. Pullman was a capitalist idealogue who "hoped that an 'ordered and beautiful' environment complemented by public and community facilities would 'uplift' its residents and solve the company's employee problems" (Buder, 1967, 2).

Pullman's dream failed when the company was   *61*

forced to sell the town to its residents after his death in 1897. Today's company town planners must look at the reasons for this community's failure.

Pullman paid close attention to the ideas of the Model Tenement Movement, which in the 1870s "assumed that American workers could afford adequate housing provided that site selection, design and all phases of construction were...planned in advance. Rents would be charged returning seven percent on investment but would still be reasonable for tenants" (Buder, 1967, 2). Aesthetics would raise the investment price and were thus considered unnecessary.

Using his ideas of mass production—which were far more common in industry than in construction in those days—Pullman built his town between 1880 to 1884. The factories were grouped together, separated by broad streets and green spaces from the residences, and spread out on a grid. The residential areas had their own lawns and tree-lined streets. A railroad station was the heart of the civic-center.

The town, however, looked monotonous, especially during the long winters. The housing appeared "machine-made" or barracks-like. Most unfortunately, Pullman left no doubt that he controlled all aspects of town life. He refused to allow saloons, his agents ran town affairs closely connected to company affairs, and the town itself was isolated from surrounding towns by a belt of company-owned land. Pullman had Victorian ideas about proper behavior and appearance of his employees, even in their own apartments, and his agents constantly snooped and informed on them if they didn't conform. Few elections were held, and the residents had just as little to say about town affairs, especially their rents, as they had about company affairs, especially wages. Pullman was notoriously antagonistic to labor unions.

Pullman's workers soon rebelled against his ideas. They kept the saloons and brothels of neighboring communities very busy. Many also resented his behavioral and appearance codes. The company, of course, ran the town's basic services, and its banks, hotels, and the theater, making many residents feel alienated from their own town; they were willing to

live in Pullman's town only if they were content as Pullman's employees.

When the company suffered downturns, people were often anxious to relocate. The depression of 1893 led Pullman to cut wages without cutting rents. The factory's workers walked out, and the strike soon spread to the railroads carrying George Pullman's cars. While they criticized his town, Pullman's detractors overlooked its basic flaw:

He erected his community because of a conviction that workers could afford superior homes when built with the economies of mass production. This went beyond the Model Tenement Movement's intention to erect decent housing renting for less than ten dollars a month. (Buder, 1967, 8)

This conviction led Pullman to raise rents to a maximum $14 a month, too high during slow times at the factory. Rents exceeded those in Chicago by 20 to 25 percent. Pullman could not expect his residents to pay for the town's parks and other nonnecessity items.

Once the town was sold in 1899 and Chicago took over city services, decline set in. Today, Pullman is just another Chicago neighborhood.

What went wrong? Pullman's plan neither offered guidelines for growth nor allowed room for change. Businessmen argued that Pullman had assumed too much responsibility for the town's welfare, while urban reformers criticized the fact that he imposed his total control over town life. Both sets of critics agreed on the town's being too dependent on the Pullman Palace Car Company.

KOHLER

Alanen and Peltin (1978) trace the development of Kohler, Wisconsin, a town four miles west of Sheboygan, and the change in relationships among the Kohler Company, its workers, and the town's residents.

The Kohler Company produces plumbing fixtures, electric plants, engines, and precision controls. Walter J. Kohler, Sr., who ran the family-owned firm from

1905 to 1940, had the greatest impact on the firm's labor relations and on the town of Kohler. Several years after Walter Kohler's father, John, moved the plant from Sheboygan to Kohler, Walter Sr. began examining various town planning ideas in pre-World War I Europe and America. Kohler had much the same ideas as Pullman did 30 years before: "To attract and maintain a stable group of employees; to increase worker morale and productivity; to regulate the morals and deportment of community residents by prohibiting such activities as gambling, prostitution, and the sale of alcoholic beverages" (Alanen and Peltin, 1978, 146). Pullman had based his town, on the Krupp-Essen relationship, which didn't allow workers to buy their homes. Kohler based his on the English garden city concept, which did. When Walter Kohler began building the town in 1916, he encircled it with a green belt, as Pullman did.

The town of Kohler received mostly favorable comments after its completion in the late 1920s, largely because the company treated its workers far more generously during the Great Depression than Pullman treated his in 1894. Therefore, when Kohler employees struck in 1934, there was a reaction of surprise. The firm, just as anti-union as Pullman's was, refused to allow a local union to represent all its workers. As the Depression cut Kohler sales, the firm started laying off workers, starting with those living outside the town of Kohler. The Kohler Building and Loan Association, closely linked to the Kohler Co., required all mortgage payments to be deducted from worker paychecks; foreclosures began in 1930. During the strike 2 men were killed and 47 hurt, but the workers won their major demand even though they had to join a company union.

The strike's outcome brought calm to the town until 1954 when the union called a walkout, again demanding affiliation with a larger union, this time the United Auto Workers. The strike lasted five disastrous years, tearing the town apart by setting friends and family members against each other. Conditions grew worse when a surveillance network similar to Pullman's was revealed. Not until 1965 did strike-related court proceedings end, with each side winning something.

The town of Kohler survives today, itself quite an accomplishment compared to Pullman's fate. Recent surveys show most residents are satisfied with the town's planning and with its company ties. Alanen and Peltin feel that town life is far more democratic today than in the 1930s, although the Kohler Co. is still the community's principal employer and one of the region's major landowners.

Alanen and Peltin do not think that future company towns will develop as Kohler did, and doubt that most Americans will accept the paternalism of a Kohler. Their conclusion on the Kohler experiment offers both praise and criticism:

The population and economic pressures which several resource-rich areas of the United States are currently encountering . . . have forced planners, corporation executives and public officials to consider again the problem of how to provide adequate housing and community services for workers and their families. Guiding and managing boom town growth, not to mention the decline or bust which often follows such rapid and exploitative development activities, would appear to call for the forging of new linkages between government and industry. . . . Adequate and meaningful contingency plans should be developed for communities which face serious social and economic disruption because of resource depletion or the phasing out of a major industry. Perhaps the real challenge these new community endeavors face is that of developing physical environments which are the qualitative equal of Kohler, while . . . providing opportunities for those participatory activities . . . characteristic of an independent and democratic polity. (Alanen and Peltin, 1979, 158)

LAKE SUPERIOR MINING COMMUNITIES

For more than a century, companies in the upper Midwest have sponsored town planning. Though most provided housing and basic services, their intent has still been to raise worker productivity. Alanen (1979) claimed that

Corporate sponsored town planning in the Lake Superior region produced a variety of benefits, but the expectations were exaggerated and many of the idealized goals brought in from outside and forced onto unwilling or disinterested workers often detracted from the projects and hastened their demise. (Alanen, 1979, 257)

Among these communities, those numbering more than 5,000 residents are Grand Rapids, Hibbing, Chisholm, and Virginia (all in Minnesota), and Ironwood, Bessemer, Wakefield, Ishpenning, Brainerd, Negaunee, and Iron Mountain (all in Michigan). Dozens of smaller planned communities also dot the area.

Ever since the 1840s, the Lake Superior area has been a center of copper and iron mining booms and busts. Early towns from this period showed the highest paternalism level, especially in northern Michigan's Copper Country. A reporter pointed out in 1911 that paternalism killed the desire for unions among town workers. When they wanted higher wages, strikes were common.

The mining companies exerted no greater unilateral control over all facets of community existence than in their management of the regional housing supply. Employees who lived in company houses were not allowed to transfer or assign their leases without company consent, and many residents faced the possibility of eviction with no more than fifteen days notice. (Alanen, 1979, 264)

Not until 1942 were Copper Country miners able to affiliate with a national union; the closure of most of the mines over less than a 20-year period made this academic.

Iron companies also built their own towns, such as Gwinn, Michigan, and Coleraine and Morgan Park, Minnesota. Applicants for Coleraine housing were thoroughly screened. John Greenway of the Oliver Iron Mining Co. planned Coleraine,[1] limiting the townspeople to those born in North America and western Europe. U.S. Steel sponsored Morgan Park, near Duluth, in 1913. Iron firms, however, were generally less paternalistic than those in copper.

As labor problems and costs rose in the 1930s and 1940s, many Lake Superior mining companies began to sell off their houses. They then went through a "severe recession" from 1947 into the early 1950s. Four new towns went up then: Babbitt, Hoyt Lakes and Silver Bay, Minnesota, and White Pine, Michigan.

Though coming closer to planners' goals than earlier towns, none of the four ever achieved all of these objectives especially those involving creation of enough housing. Alanen makes clear that the high-quality housing, recreational and cultural aspects of these towns

often were exchanged for basic democratic rights, privileges, and opportunities, and constituted an affront to the dignity and intelligence of the persons being served. The planning policies developed in executive suites . . . sought to impose corporate standards for efficiency, health, morality, and behavior upon employees; few attempts were made . . . to incorporate the views and expressions of the very people for whom planning efforts were intended. (Alanen, 1979, 273-274)

All this helped aggravate the usual labor-management tensions. The towns built in the 1950s showed attempts to comprehend the future residents' attitudes, but "short-term economic objectives continued to prevail over community planning goals. Human health and environmental quality . . . were hardly considered," and the towns' future was not considered. "Until the long term social, economic, and environmental consequences of human needs, depleted resources, obsolete factories . . . are somehow accommodated within the planning process, boom and bust cycles of activity will continue to plague these communities. . . ." (Alanen, 1979, 274).

EARLY SWEDISH COMPANY TOWNS

Although the modern Swedish welfare state is well-known for town planning innovations, nineteenth-century Swedish industry developed its own communities with all the social myopia of Pullman and Kohler. Johansson (1975), for example, describes the development of Sandviken in north-central Sweden, designed in 1862 around a new steel mill. In three years, it had 1,600 people living very primitively. The company controlled the activities that could take place in the town itself.

As in the United States and Russia, railroads also spawned new towns in Sweden.

The station building with its monumental architecture and frontal area, usually provided a starting-point for the main street, which was drawn from the station at right angles to the railway line. Around the station square and the main street [were] shops, the railway hotel . . . the post office, the . . . bank, the municipal offices or town hall, etc., plus the houses of the well-to-do. On the other side of the track, along various sidings, were . . . workshops, timber yards, etc., together with the less controlled residential construction. It was largely in communities like this, of which there are [about] a thousand throughout the country, that Swedish industrialization took place. (Johansson, 1975, 30)

Mines, glass factories, and sawmills also provided the impetus to build new towns.

IMPLICATIONS FOR FUTURE COMPANY TOWNS

Alanen pointed to the 1975 contention of W. S. Wikstrom of the Conference Board that federal fair housing laws could require industry to become more involved in guaranteeing all workers an opportunity for decent housing. Alanen also made clear that new answers must be thought out for towns located in resource areas, possibly joint funding of town development projects by business and government or the joint establishment of community development corporations. It may be necessary to include elected town representatives on the boards of directors of participating companies.

Such actions might have avoided much of the tension now afflicting Manville, New Jersey (Freedman, 1982). The company best known for asbestos production created the town after the turn of the century. It provided the land for the high school football field, money for the town's ambulances, and the materials required for its town hall, water supply system, and two fire houses. Manville now has about 11,000 people. The company's 1982 bankruptcy, to avoid ruinous losses from disease-plagued asbestos workers' lawsuits, has divided the community, with workers suing for damages bitter about the move, and merchants and

other workers agreeing with it since it might save the company and their jobs.

Even bleaker evidence of past planning failures is the present condition of those Lake Superior mining communities. Hibbing, Minnesota, may be merely the best-known hardship case among them.

Hibbing . . . was once so extravagantly rich that the police and fire chiefs made their rounds in Rolls-Royces, and the town fathers imported elegant chandeliers from Belgium to gussy up the high-school auditorium. Today the iron range is an economic moonscape. Unemployment is as high as 80 percent in some communities [as of December 1982], and only one of eight major iron-ore mines has avoided a lengthy shutdown [in 1982]. . . . Authorities report a sharp rise in the number of problems related to alcohol, the child-abuse caseload has more than doubled and home-mortgage foreclosures are running at twice the rate of 1981—itself a bad year. . . . Many younger people are simply pulling out. (McCormick, 1982, 115-116)

NOTE

1. John Greenway later planned the company town of Ajo, Arizona.

REFERENCES

Alanen, Arnold R., 1979, "The Planning of Company Communities in the Lake Superior Mining Region," *Journal of the American Planning Association* **45**(3):256-278.

Alanen, Arnold R., and Peltin, Thomas J., 1978, "Kohler, Wisconsin: Planning and Paternalism in a Modern Industrial Village," *Journal of the American Institute of Planners* **44**(2):145-159.

Buder, Stanley, 1967, "The Model Town of Pullman: Town Planning and Social Control in the Gilded Age," *Journal of the American Institute of Planners* **33**(1):2-10.

Freedman, Samuel G., 1982, "The Town That Manville Built Has Mixed Feelings," *New York Times,* September 1, p. B-1.

Galantay, Ervin Y., 1975, *New Towns: Antiquity to the Present,* G. Braziller, New York.

Johansson, Bengt O. H., 1975, "From Agrarian to Industrial State," in Hans-Erland Heineman, ed., *New Towns and Old,* The Swedish Institute, Stockholm, Sweden.

McCormick, John, 1982, "The Mesabi: A Bleak Winter," *Newsweek,* December 6, pp. 115-116.

PART II

BOOMTOWN GROWTH IN THE MID-TWENTIETH CENTURY

8

Modern Government Towns

As population growth overwhelms established third world cities from Sao Paulo to Lagos, governments have increasingly followed the examples of czarist Russia and early America by building new capitals from scratch. Just as Leningrad and Washington carried the burden of poor planning and site selection long into their histories, so have more recently built cities been plagued by poor selection either of their site or of the architectural style for their buildings.

Among the world's large government-built cities are New Delhi (India), Canberra (Australia), Brasilia, Chandigarh (India), and Islamabad (Pakistan). Galantay (1975) claims that most suffer from a contradiction between their purpose and their design. While those government cities in less developed countries attract the poor (because of their superior welfare services) and minority groups hopeful of escaping persecution in more established areas, the cities' physical structure and housing patterns based on income level guarantee segregation.

Companies or governments building new towns for energy projects do not have to concern themselves with the scale of these new cities, but should instead pay close attention to the planning deficiencies apparent in most of them, since a badly planned large city is just as difficult to live in as a badly planned small town.

BRASILIA

The first of today's government cities to come to most people's minds is Brasilia. The man most responsible for putting this long-delayed dream of Brazil's economic planners into effect was Juscelino Kubitschek, the Brazilian President in the 1950s, who saw that coastal cities, particularly Rio de Janeiro and Sao Paulo, were becoming hopelessly overcrowded. He also realized that only the government could induce or, if necessary, force large numbers of Brazil's coastal dwellers into the country's vast hinterlands. Only in this way could Brazil hope to tap the immense mineral riches of the area lying south of the Amazon basin and north of Rio and Sao Paulo (see Fig. 8.1).

Kubitschek's idea was hardly new. As early as 1891, shortly after Brazil's independence from Portugal, the country's republican constitution called for setting aside about 6,000 square miles for a new capital. The 1946 constitution set a 2,000-square-mile site on the inland Goias plateau and the actual site was chosen in 1954. President Kubitschek set up a development corporation called NOVACAP two years later and

Figure 8.1
New towns and boomtowns of Brazil.

approved urban planner Lucio Costa's design in 1957. He gave the city its unique bird-shaped design, surrounding an 11-mile-long north-south axis and a long east-west axis.

Given almost a blank check by NOVACAP, the planners let their imaginations soar, and Brasilia's cost went the same way. NOVACAP's deadline for completing the entire project was April 21, 1960—the date set by the Brazilian Congress for the transfer of the capital from Rio. The problems to overcome were immense:

In the beginning, NOVACAP had to fly almost everything into the site.... It offered Brazilians three-year, tax-free lots in a "free city" if they would come to work there, and it gave them wood to build houses. (Giles, 1960,1)

[But] as workers poured into Brasilia, they spilled out of the "free city" area and built their wooden shacks and tents on the slopes of the plateau [surrounding the city. Although the creation of an artificial lake would literally drown those shacks,] less simple to cope with, however, is the future of the "free city," an incredibly ramshackle town where some 70,000 workers and their families stay. The mud-packed, sloping central avenue—"just like the old Western towns in the United States," a Brazilian guide is fond of saying—is lined with small stores and markets.... When the need for labor ends, the authorities say they expect that the city will be destroyed. (p. 23)

The government hoped to avoid the example of this "free city" during the remaining phases of construction by preparing "reception areas," satellite towns betwen 15 and 45 miles from Brasilia's center. This meant that the towns were to have mostly lower-income workers, and that per-capita income would decline as the distance from Brasilia rose.

The government wanted to bring as many single men as possible in the first group of government officials to move in, which they hoped would relieve the anticipated housing crunch. It did far less, however, to stop the project's ballooning cost. These officials began moving in in 1960, the city's inaugural year.

As the city grew in the next decade,[1] flaws in Costa's layout and in the architecture of Oscar Niemeyer became apparent. As the government expected, many

foreign diplomats and their families had to be forced to move from comfortable Rio to the raw frontier and to a city that "is not the poetic, functional city of egalitarianism dreamed of by the original planners. In many ways it has gone wrong" (Howe, 1972, 12).

Housing prices rose so quickly that Brasilia, like all modern cities, developed large slums and small wealthy districts. Most of the slums (as previously mentioned) are in the satellite cities. Traffic problems became a nightmare in a city which was actually designed for the automobile. The pedestrian in Brasilia was no better off; Brasilia was designed without traffic lights and with few sidewalks. Howe wondered whether the problem lay with the deviation of Brazil's military government from the original designs, or whether Kubitschek, Costa, and Niemeyer were guilty of naiveté. Howe concluded that both were partially to blame.

Its residents, numbering a million by 1979, developed the conflict in values present in all boomtowns. The original residents, migrant workers, and younger members of the new residents seem to like the city, while visiting business people, unmarried diplomats not fluent in Portuguese, and people transplanted from Rio do not.

Brasilia suffers from all the same isolation of a western American boomtown. It's far too distant from the coast (540 miles) to drive, and air transportation there is limited. Telephone links to the rest of Brazil are relatively poor.

When the reluctant diplomats arrived in the early 1970s, housing prices soared. By 1972, it took $500 to $750 a month to rent an apartment, 40 percent more than in Rio. After these reluctant transplantees recovered from the housing price shock, they learned that Brasilia lacked Rio's pulsating cultural life.

Brasilia's residents can expect little relief from high prices until goods are produced locally and do not have to be flown in from the coast. As of 1976, however, no significant amount of industry or commerce had moved in.

Brasilia's civil servants and politicians often fly out on weekends, and "with its wide, empty concrete avenues, it looks like, and seems to function as, an airport" (*Economist*, 1976), an ironic comment for a city that looks from above like an airplane.

Brasilia today is thus an anomaly, a city with more than a million people but with "no visible pollution, about 200,000 cars but hardly any traffic lights or intersections, neighborhoods that with few exceptions look like each other, no distinctive accent, no elective politics, a dozen or so paved walkways, and almost nothing to do on weekends" (Hoge, 1979, 12).

Ironically enough, the city is being modified by its own residents, who number far more than the original designers or planners had expected. Restaurants and other establishments have clustered in shopping centers, digressing from the old neighborhood-store idea of the planners, and in areas designed for public buildings. The designers certainly did not anticipate the satellite cities that replaced the poor workers' settlements closer to the city, and from which the workers now commute to the center—an idea especially abhorrent to Costa. Perhaps worst of all, the area's dry climate guarantees that Brasilia will always have to bring in much of its food from the coast.

Thus, Brasilia is a prime example of incomplete and hasty planning, the evidence of which is being broken down by the residents who have to cope daily with a city not designed for them. Nearly every other modern government city shares its problems; perhaps no planner however visionary, can expect his or her creation to turn out any better than Brasilia has.

CHANDIGARH AND ISLAMABAD

In addition to creating two countries, the partition of India in 1947 was responsible for creating two new cities. One of the regions divided between India and Pakistan was the Punjab, India's most fertile agricultural region. The Indian government needed a new regional capital for its portion of the Punjab after its old capital, Lahore, became part of Pakistan. The Pakistani government later decided that the country's post-1947 capital, Karachi, was becoming

overcrowded and that it, too, wanted to exploit the interior and spread out a burgeoning population. At the same time, the Pakistanis decided that neither Karachi, on the populated coast, nor Lahore, too near the Indian border, was suitable for modern Pakistan's capital. Pakistan decided to build a new city in the Punjab. Two new cities thus emerged within a short distance of each other: Chandigarh, India and Islamabad, Pakistan.

Chandigarh

Just as Brasilia bears the stamp of Lucio Costa and Oscar Niemeyer, Chandigarh today is undeniably a creation of the famous Swiss architect Le Corbusier. Unfortunately for its residents, it's more a Corbusian than an Indian city. It was poorly designed, since the government centers, employing half the city's labor force, are far from the workers' homes. Most of them have to ride bicycles to work. By 1968, industry employed only nine percent of the work force, a problem identical to Brasilia's.

Chandigarh is a city strictly divided by function, with specific areas of the city dedicated to private housing, universities, industries, and commercial areas. This division guarantees that certain areas are deserted by day, others by night. The residential areas themselves are strictly segregated by income. (Crossette, 1982, ix-21). Such planning invites many questions. One wonders, for example, whether or not an area's schools and shops will be able to change with the neighborhood's demographic makeup.

As simple a thing as a resident's driving from his area to the home of a friend could be most difficult in Chandigarh's streets, which apparently act as spokes of a wheel connecting neighborhoods to the downtown, but not to each other.

Chandigarh now has about 250,000 residents. Most of its poorer citizens prefer the city to their ancestral villages in the far more poverty-stricken countryside, where their homes would not have electricity, gas, and running water. Most of Chandigarh's more fortunate residents have mixed feelings.

The city has achieved some importance as an educational and cultural center. It is less successful as a commercial center and its regional impact has been negligible. . . . Chandigarh suffers from overplanning and strict controls. It has no self-government and is considered by Indians to be an expensive city to live in. Little attempt has been made to make it attractive for marginal population groups. . . . [The city] is a mirage which does not quite fit in with Indian reality. (Galantay, 1975, 17)

Islamabad

By 1959 Pakistan's new strongman, President Ayub Khan, decided to create a new capital at Islamabad. Unlike Le Corbusier, the designers of Islamabad knew that Islamabad had to become the focal point of economic growth throughout northern Pakistan if it were ever to justify the huge expense of its construction.

Islamabad's design is generally considered far more "rational" than Chandigarh's or Brasilia's. It looks more like a city, and less like artwork made of steel and concrete. Unlike Brasilia, Islamabad is fairly close to an existing industrial center: Rawalpindi. The two cities combine to offer the kind of diverse economic base that can attract Pakistanis from Karachi and other coastal cities.

Kraft's impression was somewhat less agreeable:

Like Brasilia—and, to some extent, Washington—the capital of Pakistan bears many telltale signs of an artificially created town. It has broad streets, square blocks, modern buildings by such architects as Doxiadis, Ponti, and Edward Durrell Stone, and functionally separated sections—one section for government buildings, another for embassies, a third for government housing, and several shopping centers. Abundant parks and other bits of greenery assure roominess: Islamabad, with a population of a hundred and ten thousand, spreads out over an area of three hundred and fifty-one square miles, whereas Rawalpindi . . . has a population of more than a million in an area of fifty-five square miles. By Asian standards, pedestrians are few in Islamabad, and automobiles plentiful. There is an absence of the usual smells and sounds. The capital seems detached from the pulsing life of the country. (Kraft, 1981, 67)

Perhaps Kraft should have considered Islamabad as half of the population center of the area. Islamabad's future ability to develop its own industry to become a well-rounded town bears watching.

OTHER MODERN GOVERNMENT TOWNS

In 1910, the ruling British decided to move India's capital from Delhi (now Old Delhi) to a new city separated from it by parkland. When the city was inaugurated in 1929, it was to have no more than 57,000 people. It took only ten years to show the inadequacy of the British plans. By 1971, the Delhi-New Delhi metropolis had 3.6 million residents, then exceeded in population only by the Calcutta metropolitan area and the city of Bombay.

In the 1910s a Chicago architect, Walter Burley Griffin, designed Canberra, Australia. The Australian parliament moved there in 1921, but it was another 30 years before the city itself began to take shape (exactly as Washington, D.C. took decades to grow after the U.S. government moved in). After 7 years of construction, work on the city was completed in 1964. Canberra has a more homogeneous and wealthier population than most of the other new capitals and probably will not experience a huge population growth as they did—all this thanks only to the homogeneous population of Australia and its slow growth rate.

Australia's constitution requires the seat of government to be within government-owned land, so the entire city has developed without land speculation. Government here is both planner and developer. Although Canberra's slow growth in the 1940s and 1950s cut into government land revenues' abilities to make up development costs, Canberra still benefits from the close coordination of planning and development activities. Since a building has to be erected before a site is sold, no speculation in raw or developed land exists. This reduces the pressure on prices, since the National Capital Development Commission "has complete control over the supply of sites and, as long as it estimates future demand [based largely on government staffing policy] correctly, can maintain supply at a level to meet it, at prices equal to the cost of subdivision" (Neutze, 1978, 194).

Perhaps no other country has built as many new cities as the USSR. The Soviets began modern town planning largely as a result of Stalin's insistence on heavy industrial growth. Among those built during Stalin's rule were Karaganda, Magnitogorsk, Zaporozhe, and Stalingrad.[2]

From 1928 to 1932 [Stalin's first five year plan] sixty new cities were set up. Sixty-seven more were built during World War II, mostly to locate Soviet industry beyond the reach of the German army. Growth of these cities did not stop with the war. Karaganda, for instance, had 116 residents in 1926, 164,000 in 1939, and 460,000 in 1972 (Galantay, 1975, 44).

After the Soviets overran the nations of eastern Europe, they spread the idea of new "socialist towns" to their new satellite countries. But these countries' high population densities did not justify the construction of new towns as Siberia's sparse population did. The Soviets' apparent purpose, then, was to distribute "socialist" workers among the conservative rural people. Most east European new towns were poorly planned, plagued by uneven flows of funds and inadequate infrastructure provision. Galantay believes that most governments there no longer believe in new industrial towns.

One problem for these large cities stands out as crucial to town planners at the local level. It is the need to consider plans for the future of the new city after the energy project or the current source of local revenues should stop operating. Only a diverse economic base will guarantee any town or city long-term survival and prosperity.

NOTES

1. By 1970 Brasilia had half a million total population, including all the government agencies' workers.
2. Karaganda was built in 1926 and Magnitogorsk in 1929, both as coal centers. Zaporozhe began in 1930 as a hydroelectric power center. Stalingrad—as the Nazis later realized—was both a key industrial center and strategic location.

REFERENCES

Crossette, Barbara, 1982, "Le Corbusier's Chandigarh," *New York Times,* April 25, pp. X-21.

Economist, "An Airport, Not a City," July 31, 1976, pp. 26-28.

Galantay, Ervin, Y., 1975, "New Towns: Antiquity to the Present," G. Braziller, New York.

Giles, William E., 1960, "Brazil Welcomes Ike to Its Controversial New Capital Today,"*Wall Street Journal,* February 23, pp. 1ff.

Hoge, Warren, 1979, "Capital of Brazil, All Grown Up But With No Place to Go," *New York Times,* March 17, pp. 2ff.

Howe, Marvine, 1972, "Brasilia . . . Has Emerged as a Real Capital," *New York Times,* November 2, p. 12.

Kraft, Joseph, 1981, "Letter from Pakistan," *New Yorker,* August 10, pp. 53-75.

Neutze, Max, 1978, *Australian Urban Policy,* George Allen & Unwin, Sydney, Australia.

9

Modern Tourist, Retirement, and Business Boomtowns

Towns in many different sections of the United States are booming today for a variety of reasons: some have become retirement havens, others are a great place to do business, while still others are fun to visit. This chapter examines the ways in which a boomtown atmosphere can be generated without the presence of the fully diverse economic base one normally expects of a thriving community.

TOURIST BOOMTOWN: ORLANDO, FLORIDA

The land booms of Miami and the surrounding areas in southern Florida did not touch the central part of the state. As late as the 1960s, the area around Orlando seemed to be good only for agriculture.

In 1967 Walt Disney Productions began accumulating 27,500 acres southwest of Orlando. Disney World's opening in late 1971 touched off a boom similar to the frenzy of the 1920s. Seldom has a region undergone the explosive growth that Orlando has seen in the last decade. By early 1973 land prices had skyrocketed "from 4 to 20 times in a radius of 50 miles." Traffic patterns in the area had to be altered, and new roads had to be built. The capacities of the area schools, hospitals, and clinics doubled in a few years.

The millions of visitors required gas stations, banks, restaurants, motels, and hotels. Most Orlando bankers and businesspeople must have realized that many of these facilities were to undergo seasonal variations in business, just as those in the Miami area have. To reduce the impact of these fluctuations, Orlando faced the challenge of attracting a far more diversified economic base than Miami and Miami Beach ever had.

From the outset, Disney World was expected to add thousands of new residents to the Orlando area. The metropolitan population, for example, was considered likely to grow from 428,000 in 1970 to 561,000 in 1975. The local officials did not plan well to accomodate this growth and had allowed the area to expand unchecked until the 1980s. Water supply and waste disposal, as vital to Orlando as to cities in the arid Southwest, have so far failed to keep up.[1] Surrounding Orange County is also "wracked" by housing and traffic problems.

Most of the new jobs created by Disney World are in the low-paying trades and services. These workers cannot afford the detached housing that developers find profitable, and the apartments they can afford are unprofitable to build. Homebuilders must therefore hope for new industries to attract better-paid workers. The local and state governments may have to build apartments for the service workers if they want Disney World, Sea World, Epcot, and all the other central Florida theme parks to thrive and spawn new attractions.

Orlando began addressing its infrastructural inadequacy in the late 1970s and early 1980s. It began building a new airport in 1978 and deregulation increased the number of airlines wanting to use it. The subsequent upward revision of the airport's size delayed its opening until September 1981.

Orlando recently set up a crime prevention commission to fight the lawlessness that made Orlando's crime rate the sixth highest in 1980 (according to the FBI). The city is in need of more police officers and prison space. In an effort to fight traffic congestion, Orlando is trying out shuttle buses, and may start building underground garages and clustered housing.

Orlando drew up a state-mandated growth management plan in 1980. This plan avoids zoning but encourages multifamily housing, plans most sewer lines for downtown areas, rewards developers for using water-saving techniques, encourages high-rise construction downtown, and has raised sewer hookup prices 400 percent to make developers pay more of the infrastructure cost. It is questionable, however, whether or not the county will be willing to spend $350 million for new infrastructure to meet the growth management plan for the year 2000.

By 1982 Orlando was becoming the high-technology center of Florida. Dozens of electronics and computer companies have begun taking advantage of Orlando's climate and cluster of theme parks nearby to attract young engineers. These industries may make it profitable for builders to increase the supply of apartments that many of these young engineers want. The new apartments will also be a boon to the ever-increasing number of service workers at the expanding number of local theme parks.

Many retirees are also moving to the Orlando area. They are attracted to what they claim is a slower-paced and less pseudo-friendly lifestyle than that available in southern Florida. Those senior citizens not staying in Orlando move to places like Vero Beach, where speculators have helped double the price of oceanfront condominiums (Harrigan, 1979).

Recently, Orlando has developed a cultural life: ballet, music, and theater. This will help attract industrial workers accustomed to these urban amenities. These new residents will swell the Orlando metropolitan area's 1.3 million population recorded in 1980 to an expected 1.65 million by 1985. (*Advertising Age*, 1975, 101-102.)

RETIREMENT BOOMTOWNS

By offering their bone-dry climate to the elderly, either to live in retirement or to recover from illness, Phoenix and Tuscon, Arizona, have absorbed huge numbers of senior citizens, many of whom cannot afford to enter the hyperinflated California real estate market. With a relatively small, affluent population, Arizona's state government has not been forced into large social expenditures, and so can offer a low-tax, relatively cheap life in the sun for these retirees. Its urban leaders, however, must soon decide whether or not they want increasingly elderly populations, and to what extent they will allow industry to enter the region to attract younger residents. Since the elderly require a high level of medical care but cannot contribute nearly enough toward its provision in this time of skyrocketing medical costs, the state and its major cities may have to sacrifice some of the regional environment's purity by attracting new industry capable of supporting a more stable population—one that won't decline drastically in the next two decades.

Phoenix's 1945 population of 65,000 boomed to more than 670,000 in 1976, with another half million residents in the outlying suburbs. Most of the newcomers arrived from the Northeast and Midwest, but a surprising number have been coming from California to avoid that state's higher taxes. More than 400 people moved into Phoenix every day during 1979 (Lindsey, 1979, 6). Just as newcomers do everywhere else, they brought along air pollution, traffic, inflation well above the national average, suburban sprawl as aesthetically displeasing as anything in Los Angeles, and "overburdened utilities."[2] No one expects future growth to diverge from the automobile and the single-family house, but many Phoenix leaders wonder whether energy and water supplies can sustain such growth for long.

Most important to Phoenix's expansion is the availability of cheap land, which encouraged developers to skip over large areas near the city center, despite the rising cost of supplying utilities and city services as the distance from downtown rises. City planners have been trying to get builders to fill in these vacant areas before going fare out of town. The state, which owns much of the land on the outskirts of Phoenix (and Tucson, too), has the capability of helping Phoenix grow in a more sensible, cost-efficient manner.

Phoenix's growth will have to be more rational in other aspects, too. Since the region's average age is rising, it will be necessary to create mass-transit system almost from scratch. Few taxis and virtually no buses are available in Phoenix (Hardt, 1980, X-7). The city must expand its freeway system, which covered only 18 miles in 1975 (Kaufman, 1975), and consider the need to have more sidewalks for elderly pedestrians. Flood-control measures and central city redevelopment are also crucial to Phoenix's future.

Resistance to organized planning, however, is strong in this bastion of free enterprise. Phoenix residents, especially those from Los Angeles, regularly reject freeway bond issues. Without the means to cover the increasingly long distances from their homes to downtown, Phoenix's inhabitants will not help revive the city center by demanding cultural and entertainment centers there, and will instead have to develop their own regional centers. Worst of all, their insistence on the free use of their cars has given Phoenix some of the West's worst smog.

Tucson's growth has certainly kept up with that of Phoenix, having increased its population from 50,000 to 500,000 in 30 years (Tinker, 1981, X-13). Here, too, growth was strictly outward, and downtown Tucson was badly neglected and abused.

During the great boom of the past three decades, much of the old central area was bulldozed and given over to a complex of high-rise government buildings, a community center and a charming but barely half-filled shopping village. . . . But the commercial life has moved out, leaving the downtown area a lunching site for government workers by day, a deserted park by night, except for the theater sections of the commercial center. Tucson has [grown] via suburban sprawl like Los Angeles and Phoenix, so buses are rare and taxis are very expensive to ride. (Tinker, 1981, X-13)

This situation has hardly kept newcomers away: New residents arrived at 1,200 per month (*Advertising Age*, 1975, 106-107), not as many as Phoenix received, but still a substantial number for a smaller city. This figure applied during a national recession—before then, it was 2,000 per month. Tucson in the 1970s was the fastest-growing American city of under 500,000 residents.[3]

Not until 1972 was all this growth subject to any kind of comprehensive planning. During the early 1970s Tucson lost its Spanish-style architecture to new office and government buildings; spending went out of control then, too, as the operating budget shot up from $40 million to $100 million. Although Tucson is a major military city,[4] it depends to a large extent on the shifting fortunes of the copper industry.[5]

Tucson's leaders face other problems. The city depends on a constantly dwindling groundwater supply, a fact forcing Tucson to consider tapping the Colorado River for additional supplies.[6]

Not all newly-retired Southwest residents live in Phoenix or Tucson. Consider the example of Truth or

Consequences, a small New Mexico community along the Rio Grande.

Though T or C, as it's called, is part of the only county in the state where deaths exceed births, so many pensioners have come here in recent years that the town's allotment of cheap federal electricity is almost exhausted: it will have to pay six times as much for private power, if it can get any. (Blundell, 1980, 1)

T or C is one example of many small towns in American rural areas that began growing rapidly in the 1970s, part of a so-called "rural renaissance." But overheated growth can also bring bulging schools, unpaved streets, strained services, community conflict, and erosion of the country lifestyle that attracted these people in the first place. All these symptoms are on display in the rural Southwest. Towns there are being deluged by retirees from all sections of the country who want to live far from the cities. These towns also serve as escape hatches for disenchanted Western city dwellers fleeing smog, crowding, and crime. T or C's population has shot up by one-third since 1970, to about 7,000 residents, but the retirees' fears of pollution have kept industry at bay. Town officials are equally frustrated in their attempts to get money from the state, county, or the residents themselves. The town manager claimed that "They want everything they had where they came from, but they don't want to pay for it." The elderly's attitudes toward financing new schools will not help the town attract younger residents to help boost the tax base. Towns like T or C almost certainly will be in for rough times when this generation of retirees is gone.

MODERN BUSINESS BOOMTOWNS

Chapter 2 illustrates the factors helping Los Angeles and Denver to experience their nineteenth and early twentieth century booms. Their headlong growth did not stop then, however, and they remain two of America's most dynamic cities today. Other communities have begun to boom in the 1970s for similar reasons. One outstanding example is Stamford,

Connecticut. Without the climate of Los Angeles or the landscape of Denver, Stamford nevertheless has a business and political elite that use the city's advantages to create a business boom rivaling any in the Rockies or on the West Coast. But Stamford also confronts may of the boomtown problems that still bedevil Los Angeles and Denver.

Denver

As the twentieth century proceeded onward, Denver's earlier boom ebbed somewhat, but men such as Robert Speer, mayor from 1904 to 1918, promoted steady growth all the same. During and somewhat after his term in office, Denver's population rose from 134,000 in 1904, to 213,000 in 1910, to 256,000 in 1920, and Colorado doubled its population to nearly a million. Denver was riding an energy boom, as coal production soared from 437,000 tons in 1880, to 3 million in 1900, and 12 million in 1920 (Dorsett, 1977, 122, 129).

Speer became mayor of a badly organized and operated city, one that was clearly becoming too diversified and large for the old business elite to run. Speer "launched a city beautiful movement, expanded public services, and declared war on poverty, [reducing] class tensions and conflict [by making] the city's wealthiest citizens aware of ways in which they could contribute to the . . . needy" (Dorsett, 1977, 137). By the time of Speer's death in 1918, the city had joined the American urban mainstream.

Just as Denver was in need of new leadership, Benjamin Stapleton became mayor in 1923. As the city's chief executive from 1923 to 1931 and from 1935 to 1947, Stapleton led Denver through the World War II boom. He also continued Speer's beautification program to such an extent that Denver reached its peak of beauty and quality of life during the war (Dorsett, 1977, 244).

However, a new postwar boom replaced the steady urban growth of the Speer and Stapleton regimes. As was true in the 1880s, the city's business leadership encouraged growth regardless of the cost. Denver mushroomed from 322,000 residents in 1940 to 416,000 in 1950 and 500,000 in 1960.

Denver was now becoming a huge center of petroleum firms and federal government activities. The armed forces, in the midst of their Cold War expansion, centered many of their activities there. Chemical and electronics companies grew as government contractors. During the 1950s and 1960s, the territory near Denver became a huge complex of medical laboratories, resource development activity, and aerospace companies.

Skyscrapers began rising as construction rode the boom. The expressway boom of the 1960s helped bring in more tourists, skiers, and industries. By the 1970s, however, this growth had become so chaotic that Denver's power brokers no longer held complete control of city affairs. Progrowth sentiment declined in Denver during the 1970s, but the antigrowth movement has so far been unable to produce leaders capable of moving Denver in a clearly different direction.

If Denver is to continue to use its nearby mountains to attract new residents, its leaders will have to show more foresight in planning orderly, environmentally compatible growth than they have in the past.

Los Angeles

Los Angeles was basically a frontier city until the Great Depression, and remained one in the outlook and sentiment of its leaders well into the 1960s. Chapter 2 discusses Harrison Gray Otis and his son-in-law, Harry Chandler, who led the city's business elite in the early twentieth century. Harry and his son, Norman, wanted the city to continue growing outward, rather than upward, because the absorption of land—owned mainly by the Chandlers and their business allies—was good for them. It is not surprising that the Chandlers believed in the invincibility of property rights and the un-Americanism of zoning and urban planning. Even as late as 1950, the Los

Angeles *Times* represented "a small group of men who controlled the community and who knew what was good for the community because in their own eyes they *were* the community" (Halberstam, 1979, 102). By the end of the 1920s,

[their] accumulated work . . . was beginning to tell upon the face of southern California. They had created a traffic problem in downtown Los Angeles that has never been solved. They had committed gross blunders in community planning that would take decades to undo. Some of them had vandalized a beautiful coastline. (Nadeau, 1960, 166).

During the 1930s, Los Angeles was one of the American cities hardest hit by the Depression. In 1930 southern California showed a very high bankruptcy rate by national standards. For the first time, Los Angeles attracted hordes of poor people, and the city tried for the first time to prevent certain types of people from settling. Los Angeles channeled its energies into attracting industry.

To do so, Los Angeles needed vast amounts of water and electric power. Through a series of controversial actions (e.g., the famous "water wars"[7]), its business elite, led in this case by water superintendent William Mulholland, secured both. The careful planning shown then has enabled the electricity and water supply systems to keep up with Los Angeles's explosive growth far better than any other city service. Their leaders' close ties to the political power structure guaranteed their ability to get far greater funding than the other infrastructural components.

Los Angeles's aerospace and motion picture booms began in the 1910s and 1920s, thanks largely to Harry Chandler. New aircraft factories sprouted through the 1930s, and World War II and subsequent wars spurred growth. The technological revolution in the aerospace industry led to Los Angeles's becoming a huge electronics industry center. The city today is also the center of a huge federal defense establishment.

Los Angeles's sunshine had as much to do with the transfer of the movie industry from the East Coast as Harry Chandler did. Despite the occasional scandals of the film industry, Los Angeles came to accept its presence once it realized the industry's ability to attract thousands of hopeful stars and starlets, raise real estate prices, and bring in vast new wealth.

Los Angeles's final boom began after World War II, as thousands of veterans working there or passing through the area moved into new tract housing. The San Fernando Valley also grew rapidly from 170,000 in 1944 to 850,000 in 1960. As in all the other booms, much of the area's infrastructure failed to grow with the population increases. The Valley's sewers, street curbs, storm drains, and sidewalks in 1960 bore no resemblance to those elsewhere in Los Angeles.

Los Angeles, in 1982, is in the ironic position of fighting desperately to hold on to its people. Many senior citizens have found Arizona a healthier and cheaper place to live. As the next section will show, Orange County, just to its southeast, has attracted huge numbers of people. It is unlikely that Los Angeles will continue to grow as it has throughout its history unless the city improves its air and develops some sort of mass transit system (see Chapter 2).

Orange County

This area, touching the southeast corner of Los Angeles, has become the center of southern California's urban growth. It grew at a very hectic pace in the 1950s and 1960s, and at a steadier rate in the 1970s.

Much of the county's explosive growth was unplanned and unusually rapid, even for southern California. It began after World War II, being immensely helped by Disneyland and Knotts Berry Farm, and within 20 years it transformed agricultural land to residential, then to commercial, and finally to industrial land. Its industry was, in 1977, almost entirely professional and white-collar. Few heavy industries came in because raw materials, cheap transportation, energy sources, and an available blue-collar labor pool were all scarce. Such industries as computers, electronics, medical equipment, drug research, and

other "high-technology" companies have reduced the county's dependence on aerospace and other defense industries. These firms can use the area's superb climate not only to lure workers but to develop work-enhancing job environments.

Orange County has been among the leaders in designing industrial parks, where a variety of companies can take advantage of multi-user buildings, off-street parking, and landscaping on sites ranging in size from 10 to 400 acres. By far the largest of these is the 6,000-acre Irvine Industrial Complex, which by 1977 had 800 industrial tenants, employing more than 40,000 workers, and taking up a reported 7.2 million square feet of office space, up from 1.5 million square feet in 1970 (*Business Week,* 1977, 76-77).

Ironically, the northwest section of Orange County, nearest to the city of Los Angeles, has not shared in the county's overall growth (exactly the situation occurring in Phoenix). Towns such as Buena Park, Garden Grove, and Los Alamitos have begun to decline in relation to those in the expanding southeast. Officials in the declining towns are trying to lure new industries, taking advantage of their large, skilled labor pools.

In raw dollars, Orange County underwent the most frenzied real estate boom in American history; between 1975 and 1978, $13 billion was added to housing values. In early 1975, the average single-family home was valued at about $40,000. Three years later, that figure had more than doubled.

Yet Orange County has grown in unexpected ways, dissimilar perhaps to any other booming American city. People living there say that it is a kind of "urbanized space . . . more dense than a suburb and more sprawling than a city" (*Business Week,* 1977, 76-77). Within its boundaries are four cities of more than 100,000 people.

The county was fourth in population growth from 1970 to 1976 among counties with more than half a million people. Retailers, real estate developers, and bankers sprouted there. However, county officials are concerned that the building of roads and waste treatment plants in the southern half of the county is way behind schedule. Freeways are inadequate to handle existing traffic loads. Even the large number of planned communities cannot go up fast enough to meet the demand. Many commuters now have to travel long distances from homes in neighboring Los Angeles or Riverside County. Some officials now fear that a shortage of affordable housing may curb new business growth.

Stamford

This Fairfield County, Connecticut, town owes its boomtown stature to the state's desire to attract new industry. Connecticut offers a much more favorable tax structure than neighboring New York City and State. Cities all over southwestern Connecticut, including Darien, Norwalk, Greenwich, and Fairfield have benefited from industries moving their headquarters out of New York, but Stamford is the area's unquestioned business capital. Few boomtowns better illustrate the effect of rapid growth on the area's price and population structure. Despite the construction of numerous office towers in recent years, Stamford still does not have enough blue-collar jobs and is losing middle-income people. It also suffers from arson and congested traffic. Blue-collar employees out of work can no longer afford to stay in the area around Stamford nor can anyone making less than executive-level salaries or paying off a mortgage. By 1982 nearly one-fifth of Stamford's municipal workers lived outside the city.

For all its new resources, Stamford appears hard pressed to soften the adverse effects of the boom. . . . Agencies responsible for growth—from building inspection to the Fair Rent Commission to the Zoning Board—are not required to work together, and that legislative power is too thinly spread between two elected bodies, the Board of Representatives and the Board of Finance, and [the mayor]. (Freedman, 1982, E-7)

Stamford shows that cities smaller than Denver and larger than the tiny energy boomtowns can experience the entire spectrum of boomtown problems.

NOTES

1. The entire ecological balance of Florida is precarious. When rainfall is below normal, Orlando has to pump water from underground reservoirs called aquifers. Repeated droughts in the 1970s forced Orlando to pump excessive amounts of water. The increased rate of depletion of the aquifers helped create huge "sinkholes," including a famous one in suburban Winter Park. The spurting population created increasing demand for food in the area, so huge amounts of water also had to be pumped to farmers. As new industry comes in, it too will require water. The aquifers will continue to be depleted unless rainfall returns to normal. The increasing urbanization has covered over areas that used to absorb rainwater. Now rain is evaporating more than before, adding even more to aquifer depletion. If this continues unchecked, the swampy Florida environment will dry out. This is a challenge for planners and for hydrological engineers.

2. By 1979 Phoenix had 745,000 residents, 28% more than in 1970; its metropolitan area doubled in population to 1.5 million from 1963 to 1979 (Lindsey, 1979, 6).

3. Tucson's annual growth rate declined from 8% to 4% in early 1975, then went back up to 7.5%. One forecast had the city's metropolitan area growing from 452,000 in 1974 to 743,000 in 1980 and 1.14 million in 1990 (Advertising Age, 1975, 106-107).

4. Tucson is headquarters to the Army's communications command and an Air Force base.

5. Copper mining provided 17% of the Tucson metropolitan area's payroll. The Amax Company predicted two or three new mines opening up between 1975 and 1980. One wonders about the effect of the disastrous 1980s copper industry slump on Tucson.

6. Figure 15. 1 shows that Tucson is both further south and further east, away from the Colorado River, than is Phoenix. So many users take water from the river further upstream that it is barely a trickle by the time it reaches southern Arizona. It may not provide the increased water supply that Tucson (and perhaps Phoenix) will require in the years ahead.

7. These "water wars" were the inspiration for the 1974 movie "Chinatown."

REFERENCES

Advertising Age, 1975, "Orlando 1975: A Whole New (Disney) World," December 15, pp. 101-102.

Advertising Age, 1975, "Tucson: Climate Lures Tourism and Industry," December 15, pp. 106-107.

Advertising Age, 1978, "Growth Makes Phoenix Area Anything But Empty Desert," December 15, pp. 132-138.

Blundell, William E., 1980, "New Rural Migration Overburdens and Alters Once-Sleepy Hamlets," *Wall Street Journal,* July 3, pp. 1-11.

Business Week, 1977, "More Than a Suburb, Less Than a City," September 5, pp. 76-77.

Dorsett, Lyle W., 1977, *The Queen City: A History of Denver,* Pruett Publishing, Boulder, Colo.

Forbes, 1972, "What Walt Hath Wrought," June 1, pp. 221-22.

Freedman, Samuel G., 1982, "Can Stamford Afford to Be So Rich?" *New York Times,* November 14, p. E-7.

Halberstam, David, 1979, *The Powers That Be,* Alfred A. Knopf, New York.

Hardt, Athia, 1980, "What's Doing in Phoenix," *New York Times,* November 23, p. X-7.

Harrigan, Susan, 1979, "The Bloom is Back in Central Florida, But it Isn't All Roses," *Wall Street Journal,* July 21, pp. 1ff.

Jaynes, Gregory, 1981, "Booming Orlando Wondering if Growth is Worth the Trouble," *New York Times,* September 19, p. 8

Kaufman, Michael T., 1975, "In Era of Urban Decline, One City Rises: Phoenix," *New York Times,* April 5, p. 31

Lindsey, Robert, 1979, "Phoenix Getting Problems Its New Residents Fled," *New York Times,* May 19, p. 6

Mayer, Martin, 1978, "Tremor in Orange County," *Barron's,* January 16, pp. 11-16.

Miller, Tom, 1982, "What's Doing in Tucson," *New York Times,* February 14, p. X-10.

Nadeau, Remi, 1960, *Los Angeles—From Mission to Modern City,* Longmans, Green & Co., New York.

Nation's Business, 1976, "Growth Through Vision and Leadership," May, pp. 53-62.

Nation's Business, 1973, "On Top of the (Disney) World," February, pp. 64-66.

Schaaf, Dick, 1977, "Orange County: Tidal Wave of the Future, *MBA* **11**(4): 15-18.

Scherer, Ron, 1982, "Cities on the Rise—Orlando," *Christian Science Monitor,* February 23, pp. B1-8.

Singer, Glenn, 1982, "What's Doing in Orlando, *New York Times,* March 14, p. X-10.

Tinker, Frank A., 1981, "What's Doing in Tucson," *New York Times,* February 1, p. X-13.

10

Examples of Wartime Boomtowns

One of the ways in which wars fracture societies is by causing the population of select cities to swell. This can occur for several reasons. Civilians often consider certain cities to be safe havens from the fighting, especially during guerrilla wars, which are fought largely in the countryside. Merchants and businesspeople flock in to take advantage of the black markets wars usually spawn by reducing the supply of consumer goods on the open market. Chapter 6 shows how the population of Washington, D.C., became swollen with soldiers during the Civil War, and with civilian workers during the two world wars.

This century has introduced another type of wartime boomtown. As wars become more scientific, governments demand total secrecy for their military research. This desire for secrecy has created the need, as seen during World War II, either to build entirely new communities or expand existing ones to handle the necessary scientists, top military personnel, and hordes of civilian technical workers.

This chapter provides examples of the various types of communities affected by recent wars. In each of them, planning constantly lagged behind the urgencies of the moment, and occupants at all levels of society became victims of circumstances beyond their control.

WARTIME SAIGON AND PHNOM PENH

History has seen many guerrilla wars, from the Boer War to Algeria in the 1950s. None, however, offers the evidence of such a war's effect on large cities as the Indochina war of the 1960s and 1970s, which quickly engulfed the region's two major cities, Saigon and Phnom Penh. From 1960 to 1970, 1.3 million refugees poured into Saigon (Smith, 1970, 1). It was not the fighting alone that drove all these people out of villages where their families had lived for centuries. Even the slums of Saigon offered a far greater supply of goods and services (especially electricity) than were available in many villages.

Government officials at first expected most of these

refugees to return home after the fighting. If the outside world had not impinged on the war, they might have done so. The Saigon of 1975, however, barely resembled the Saigon of 1960. The city was deluged with American cigarettes, television sets, and other commodities easily available to the Saigon populace on the black market. These attractions helped swell Saigon's population, and the former peasants availing themselves of these unheard-of luxuries were not likely to return to their old villages after the war.

One resident American said that Saigon's population had soared from its intended population of 300,000 to more than 3 million. The city clearly was not equipped to handle them. Smith cited one family that had to "pirate" electricity from a private line. Refugees clustered in a belt of shacks and shantytowns surrounding Saigon. One can only wonder how a victorious South Vietnamese government would have handled these people.

Saigon suffered sharp environmental deterioration that had nothing to do with bombing or shellfire. Traffic congestion became chronic, as the booming wartime economy slaked residents' thirst for motor vehicles, especially the ubiquitous Honda motorbike. The government estimated Saigon to contain 600,000 vehicles ranging in size from bicycles to automobiles, or 2,770 for each mile of street (Roberts, June 23, 1968, 6). This vehicular explosion created a pall of smog that by 1970 was reportedly reducing the city's famous trees to skeletons.

Prices in Vietnam skyrocketed—two-bedroom apartments, for example, were going to Americans for up to $700 a month in 1968. The medical community in Saigon was unable to deal with the huge number of shantytown residents, especially children, who fell ill and flooded the hospitals. Some observers believed that far more Vietnamese doctors were working in France than in South Vietnam.

Peace brought little relief to Saigon, renamed Ho Chi Minh City by the victorious North Vietnamese. Few jobs were available, and most residents could no longer afford the American-made goods hawked in the streets. These streets were also full of children, either orphaned by war or turned out from the shantytowns by parents unable to afford their care. The Communist officials, however, were able to keep telephone, electricity, and refuse-collection services going fairly smoothly.

One Westerner estimated that the Communist takeover reduced the city's population to about 2 million (Hersh, 1979, 10). Among the vanished are most of wartime Saigon's beggars and vagrants, along with nearly all the owners of its private establishments, bars, and clubs, all closed by the Communists. Ho Chi Minh City is probably quieter now than it was before the war.

A far ghastlier fate awaited Phnom Penh. Its authorities were even less capable of dealing with hordes of refugees than were those in Saigon. The war boosted its population from 600,000 to 2 million in about four years,[1] making every third Cambodian a Phnom Penh resident (Schanberg, 1974, 2). Once the refugees were unable to get shelter and money from relatives already set up there, they hit the streets, building shacks and even cruder leantos wherever they found space. Phnom Penh had thousands of street people, who were hard hit by worsening food shortages and contracted tuberculosis, dysentery, and other diseases. As in Saigon, many of Phnom Penh's street people were children, who begged and stole to survive. The numbers of refugees overwhelmed the government, so international relief agencies had to shoulder much of the load of helping the refugees. Tragically few of the street people were within reach of the agencies' provisions.

When the Communist Khmer Rouge forces over-ran the city (just days before the North Vietnamese rolled into Saigon), they ordered the complete evacuation of Phnom Penh and all other Cambodian cities. The Khmer Rouge, with far more radical social policies than the North Vietnamese, wanted to set up a rural society, in which cities had no importance. Millions of city dwellers died in the government's rural labor camps, and Phnom Penh still had not recovered its vitality by 1982, three years after the fall of the Khmer Rouge government.

LOS ALAMOS: THE SECRET BOOMTOWN

Wars spawn boomtowns in far less direct ways. Perhaps no other boomtown posed as many problems for its residents as Los Alamos, located in the rugged countryside of north-central New Mexico (refer to Fig. 15.1 in Chapter 15). Many homesteaders had moved into the area by 1900, but few towns were set up. In 1916, a wealthy Detroit businessman, Ashley Pond, set up a boys' school in Los Alamos. The school resembled a Boy Scout camp and was run almost in a military fashion.[2] By 1942, the school had more than 40 students. Its isolation and fine climate suited Ashley Pond just as it was to suit the United States government.

America was not only at war then but also well into its attempt to overtake Germany in the development of atomic weapons. That year, Army Chief of Staff George Marshall chose General Leslie Groves of the Army Corps of Engineers to direct the Manhattan District Project, a joint effort of the Army and several university laboratories to make large amounts of uranium-235 and plutonium-239, both necessary for nuclear bomb detonation, and to determine a feasible method of manufacturing nuclear explosives. Research had already been under way at schools such as the University of Chicago, where in 1942 Enrico Fermi supervised the world's first controlled chain fission reaction. By 1943, microscopic amounts of the two substances were available, not nearly enough to explode a bomb.

Noted physicist J. Robert Oppenheimer, then a professor at the University of California at Berkeley, convinced Groves that both theoretical and applied work required to produce an atomic bomb should go into one laboratory. They knew that the breakneck pace at which they were to work required a year-round

work environment. Groves regarded scientists as "eccentric children" (Kunetka, 1978, 16), and did not want the distractions of large cities near their work. A site chosen for their research had to have buildings suitable for conversion into laboratories and living quarters, along with adequate rail and air transportation. The government controlled about 90 percent of the 54,000 acres of land required for the laboratory, and Groves noticed that several large and many smaller structures of the type deemed necessary for the scientists were already there. But Oppenheimer badly misjudged the funds required; having estimated perhaps 100 scientists and their families as residents. The eventual size was in the thousands. Needless to say, the students, faculty, and leaders of the boys' school had little choice but to sell out to the federal government, for about $400,000. After buying the land, Groves ordered a military post with 254 Army personnel to be set up at Los Alamos.

In a fateful decision, General Groves appointed Oppenheimer director of the new weapons center, which formally opened on April 15, 1943. Though run under Army control, Los Alamos was operated under the auspices of Oppenheimer's old school, Cal-Berkeley, to make it easier for him to attract his colleagues. The vastly different personalities of Oppenheimer and Groves would have produced clashes in any case, but the formal operating structure of the lab made arguments even more frequent. Groves objected to Oppenheimer's insistence on the scientists' families joining them at Los Alamos, but eventually gave in. Other issues, however, were never fully resolved.

Thanks to the boys' school, Los Alamos did not start from scratch. Fuller Lodge, the school's largest building, was to become a dining room and guest-house. But many new buildings had to go up; by the end of 1943, Los Alamos had become a sprawling laboratory surrounded by barbed wire and patrolled constantly by guards.

Most people would have expected Los Alamos, of all wartime boomtowns, to have been thoroughly planned. Other than the buildings strictly for research purposes, however, the opposite was true:

During construction of the Technical Area [the lab facilities] . . . it was suddenly realized that housing for expected staff was almost nonexistent. . . . Both [the lab's planner] and Oppenheimer had seriously underestimated the housing needed. Some personnel were taken off Technical Area construction and set to building houses.

[For the first few months in 1943], staff members and their families had to be located at scattered dude ranches in the area. Once arrived in Santa Fe (the nearby capital of New Mexico), everyone had to make the tortuous 35-mile trip to Los Alamos by car or truck. The roads to the guest ranches were even more frightful, and living conditions were rustic. . . . It was cold until late April, and few buildings were heated. Not even the commissary was open, and box lunches had to be imported from Santa Fe every day.

Most of the technical buildings were rather flat, prefabricated structures in what was called modified mobilization style. Each one contained drab exteriors of clapboard sidings with simple pitched roofs of asphalt or wood shingles. Only a few of the Technical Area buildings had air conditioning and dustproof construction. . . . Buildings for the Army personnel were even less attractive.

Most new families . . . suffered some form of cultural shock. . . . As they made the initial drive through the beautiful New Mexico scenery, there quickly came the appalling realization that the squalid military town they were seeing was actually Los Alamos. They were even more appalled when they were shuttled off to live in rustic ranches, leaving their furnishings en route or in storage for the moment. . . . The ambiance of Los Alamos had become military. . . .

The original assessment of Los Alamos by Oppenheimer and Groves seemed fated to be wrong at every turn. No sooner had men and machines begun to arrive that the water supply ran short. Teams were sent to tap water in Los Alamos Canyon [and elsewhere]. The reservoir on the Hill grew algae. Winter weather froze and shattered pipelines. One huge water tank, then another, was finally built.

Oppenheimer and his advanced guard arrived [in March 1943] to find that Los Alamos now needed to provide the arriving hordes with sewerage systems, schools, stores, laundry, post office, telephones, garbage disposal, medical services and some police protection. As soon as scientists arrived and began work, they began their building requests. Everybody needed something. [To avoid costly delays,] Oppenheimer's solution was to spend more money and hire more contractors. . . . [When the lab] opened, it was a hell of a mess: few buildings were completed, and there was mud everywhere. (Kunetka, 1978, 45-47)

Groves and Oppenheimer appear to have had their problems as planners, a role for which at least Oppenheimer was not well prepared, having been a researcher and then a professor. But Oppenheimer proved to be an outstanding administrator, helping to keep an open scientific-inquiry atmosphere and mediating problems between Groves and his civilian scientists. He eventually became equally skilled as a project manager, responsible for infrastructure provision, supply deliveries, and related concerns. He was perhaps best at keeping down the squabbling among his staff, which included "a galaxy of eminent names and Nobel Prize winners," many of whom were foreign-born and resented living in such a primitive place. Yet Oppenheimer himself had not yet turned 40 when he took over Los Alamos. He was neither a Nobel Prize winner nor as high-ranking a scientist as some under his supervision. While Oppenheimer was able to avoid a rigid military administrative style, the lab still was located on a military post and he still reported to General Groves.

Kunetka offers one of the most complete descriptions of life under boomtown conditions (1978, 91-102). The place looked as shabby to its new residents as any other military post would have, the organization of housing was chaotic, most newcomers suffered intense culture shock, and they had no clear idea how long they would be asked to live there. For young couples, this made family planning that much more difficult.

The boomtown effect in Los Alamos was not limited to its residents. The contrast between them and the outside world also created the effect's complement of value conflicts. The region's Indians and the new Los Alamos residents looked at each other with sometimes condescending curiosity, but with neither great warmth nor hostility. But

the reaction in Santa Fe was somewhat different. Residents of that ancient city were at first amused with the new arrivals and considered them, as did the Indians, as merely tourists. . . . As Los Alamos grew, however, so did the demand on Santa Fe for gasoline, food, home items, and the like. The money Hill people [lab scientists and their families] spent barely offset the invasion of Laboratory buses that congested the archaic streets and the speeders and other wrong-doers that always seemed above the law. (Kunetka, 1978, 105)

Perhaps the biggest challenge in Oppenheimer's life lay outside his research. This scientist, who until his middle years was so immersed in scientific endeavors that he never read a newspaper or magazine, nor owned a telephone or radio, had to master in several months all the intricacies of business and personnel management. He generally did an outstanding job at Los Alamos. Yet despite his best efforts, the workload in 1944 became so heavy at the Lab that it overwhelmed even his efforts.

By 1944, there were over 2,000 scientists and technicians at the Lab, most of them with families. Everything was hard pressed: housing, laundry, water, and most home amenities. The Lab was suffering too, with an antiquated wage and salary plan, poor procurement, waiting lists for critically needed staff, and poor management within groups of staff members. . . . Community problems remained, despite Oppenheimer's administrative juggling. Housing, for example, was one of Oppenheimer's most frustrating and seemingly unresolvable headaches. . . . At least part of Oppenheimer's headache was caused by military perceptions of Los Alamos as a purely temporary effort. Housing was a major investment, and the Army was reluctant to spend more money than necessary. Groves continually dragged his feet on Los Alamos requests for more housing appropriations. . . . Oppenheimer was never able to resolve the housing problem satisfactorily. (Kunetka, 1978, 114-115)

The housing problem had a predictably bad effect on morale. Of the 200 men recruited in November and December 1944, one-third had quit by January 1945. Most of these were technicians, many of whom must have become disillusioned with the blatant caste system at Los Alamos. Scientists, considered more essential workers, usually received better housing than the technicians, although they did not always have larger families.

By the summer of 1945, when all Los Alamos's work culminated in the first atomic bomb test in southern New Mexico, the Technical Area had itself mushroomed into 37 buildings, and the entire laboratory into about 250 structures. There were 300

apartment buildings, 200 trailers, and 52 dormitories housing more than 4,000 civilian and 2,000 military personnel.

Immediately after the war, when America seemed intent on dismantling its entire military establishment, peace meant that unemployment was likely, in Los Alamos for all but military people and senior scientists. This, plus the lack of urgency and the heightened awareness of the Lab's lack of comfort, led many others to leave voluntarily. The size of the staff had fallen to only 1,000 employees by October 1945, fewer than ever before. On October 16, 1945, Oppenheimer himself resigned.

Los Alamos's tasks by no means ended with the war and Oppenheimer's reign. After the war Los Alamos continued to build nuclear weapons to be stockpiled elsewhere, and to perfect its research methods. It became a civilian laboratory in 1957, when the surrounding fences came down.

Los Alamos today has a population of 13,000. Washington still funds much of the Laboratory's work, half of which deals with weapons research, and half (at least in the late 1970s) with solar and nuclear-fusion energy research. It has undergone a good deal of physical change, too. Permanent concrete buildings have replaced most of the prefabricated wartime structures; and a motel, restaurants, and community center have replaced Oppenheimer's Technical Area.

Los Alamos still suffers boomtown problems.

The rapid growth of the staff of the lab in the 1970s increased the demand for houses and sent prices up. Total population of Los Alamos and nearby White Rock, which started out as a wartime construction camp, now totals about 20,000. . . .

The town has not quite cut the federal silver cord. The fire department, which after all might need a security clearance to answer an alarm, is paid for by the Department of Energy. The federal government also pays the local government $850,000 a year in lieu of the taxes the lab does not pay. . . . The schools receive $3.5 million from the federal government under the law that provides subsidies to schools with high enrollments of children of people employed on federal work. (Walsh, 1980, 1212)

The most significant boomtown problem Los Alamos faces, however, is that

The prospects for new sources of tax revenue are not encouraging since Los Alamos has only a small commercial district with retail stores, fast-food franchises, and a couple of motels, usually booked up with earnest-looking visitors in East Coast or West Coast attire. There has been no growth of spin-off industries to help the tax base. The second industry in Los Alamos is real estate. (Walsh, 1980, 1212)

These days, laboratory workers are not the only people raising the demand for housing. Many Laboratory retirees, and even some of their parents and relatives, live there. Some of Oppenheimer's wartime colleagues now have sons or daughters working at Los Alamos. They are attracted by the open Western lifestyle and an array of cultural attractions that Oppenheimer could only have dreamed of. Los Alamos's public schools are among New Mexico's best.

Even today, not everyone cares for the necessarily artificial aspects of Los Alamos life. Walsh (1980, 1212) cited housing prices, isolation from both urban and country life, lack of rewarding jobs for women, divorce, alcoholism, drug abuse, and racial homogeneity as problems confronting today's Los Alamos.

Los Alamos has, nevertheless, survived the wartime boom that created a research center and weapons lab from a boys' school almost overnight. It is far from certain, however, whether it can avoid becoming a bust town, particularly in these days of Federal fund cutbacks. The current Administration's emphasis on military research should help Los Alamos continue as a weapons center, but future presidents may not be so generous. Los Alamos's future is, at best, unclear.

OAK RIDGE: TVA'S STEPCHILD

The uranium production work at Oak Ridge, Tennessee, was as vital to the Manhattan Project as the weapons laboratory at Los Alamos. Yet Oak Ridge owed its role in wartime research to a set of circumstances totally different from that influencing Los Alamos.

The Oak Ridge facility was an offspring of the massive federal effort during the 1930s and 1940s to bring electricity to a huge area of the southeastern United States. (Chapter 13 covers TVA in detail.) The electric power provided by the Tennessee Valley Authority was essential to Oak Ridge's mere existence, let alone its top-secret activities.

Construction of both the plant and the city began in 1942. Three uranium purification plants were to be the heart of the production center. At one point in the spring of 1944, 47,000 construction workers were on the site; the full-time operating force was to be only a few thousand workers less than that a year later. On February 20, 1945, the first uranium-235 production units began operating, and were followed shortly by the gaseous diffusion plant, the electromagnetic plant, and the Oak Ridge National Laboratory containing the plutonium-producing reactor. As in Los Alamos, Oak Ridge underwent the full boomtown formation process: "With the surge of people into the new area, stores, shops and various other commercial enterprises moved into hastily assembled structures—awaiting the building of more permanent facilities—to serve the needs of the newcomers" (Robinson, 1950, 47).

In early 1943, planners intended to handle 13,000 residents, but more than three times that number were expected less than a year later. By the spring of 1945, the number had reached 66,000, and rose to 75,000 in September, "occupying 10,000 family dwelling units, 13,000 dormitory spaces, 5,000 trailers and more than 16,000 . . . barracks accommodations" (Robinson, 1950, 49). Almost overnight, Oak Ridge had sprung up to become Tennessee's fifth largest city. When the first estimate proved wrong, prefabricated houses had to be brought in, "clogging the highways for months," and schools and other infrastructure had to be built.

All these problems had a predictable adverse effect on the early residents, the first of whom moved into their trailers in July 1943. Even the first residents of "semi-permanent-type" housing had their difficulties (Robinson, 1950, 51-60).

Oak Ridge was administered in quite a different manner from that of Los Alamos. On September 23, 1943, the Roane-Anderson Company, a subsidiary of New York City's Turner Construction Co., contracted with the Manhattan Project to perform a large variety of activities there. Roane-Anderson "collected the rent, delivered the coal, picked up the garbage, fixed the faucet, replaced the fuses," operated 800 buses, 17 cafeterias and food dispensaries, ran a sizable dairy and poultry farm nearby, operated a small railroad line, ran a large laundry business, was landlord for more than 35,000 dwellings, ran the area's police and fire departments, maintained 300 miles of roads, ran the area's schools and hospitals, and employed roughly 10,000 people.

After the war, Roane-Anderson turned over many of its functions to other private firms when the government relinquished its total control of Oak Ridge. At this time, the University of Chicago's Metallurgical Laboratory turned over control of the research center to Monsanto and Union Carbide. As of 1950, it had three chemistry buildings, a technical area, a uranium reactor building, a physics laboratory, and supporting buildings. Their peacetime activities involved the manufacture and distribution of radioactive materials to hospitals, farms, and industry. The surrounding city had hundreds of new permanent homes and apartment buildings, a daily newspaper, a radio station, a country club, a Chamber of Commerce, several new schools, and other public buildings.

The stories of Oak Ridge and Los Alamos show that even the federal government has proven to be an indifferent and careless boomtown planner, particularly at times in which the nature of the projects being done in these communities called for quick decisions and decisive project management. The government's insistence on isolation and secrecy forced massive construction efforts in regions ill-prepared to accommodate them. Many people accustomed to a well-to-do lifestyle were thrown together, equally ill-prepared, under all the emotional and social strains of the boomtown syndrome. Perhaps the government could not have done any better under these frantic conditions; only a similar emergency in the future will tell.

NOTES

1. This corresponded to a 35% annual increase. Even Gilmore would have considered this a full-fledged boomtown.
2. The school's graduates included such notables as author Gore Vidal, Arthur Wood, president of Sears, Roebuck & Co., and sports mogul Bill Veeck.

REFERENCES

Hersh, Seymour M., 1979, "Black Market Makes Ho Chi Minh City Run," *New York Times,* August 10, p. 6.

Kunetka, James W., 1978, *City of Fire,* Prentice-Hall, Inc., Englewood Cliffs, N.J.

Roberts, Gene, 1968*a*, "Saigon is a Vehicular Jungle . . ." *New York Times,* June 23, p. 6.

Roberts, Gene, 1968*b*, "Waif in Saigon: Symbol of a City," *New York Times,* October 5, p. 3.

Robinson, George O., Jr., 1950, *The Oak Ridge Story,* Southern Publishers, Inc., Kingsport, Tenn.

Schanberg, Sydney H., 1974, "Phnom Penh Streets Home for Thousands," *New York Times,* July 29, p. 2.

Shipler, David K., 1973, "Saigon Throbs With Life, But Scars Go Deep," *New York Times,* July 25, p. 3.

Smith, Terence, 1970, "Refugees Pose Urban Crisis in Saigon," *New York Times,* February 16, pp. 1ff.

Walsh, John, 1980, "Los Alamos—Coming to Terms With the 1980s," *Science* **209**:1211-1215.

11

Current Examples of Nonenergy Boom and Bust Towns

NONENERGY BOOMTOWNS

Not all boomtowns or newly formed towns are creations of the energy or mining industry, either in the United States or abroad. In America, industries in Connecticut, Florida, Maryland, Wisconsin, and Oregon have all spawned boomtowns or new communities. One foreign company town anxiously awaiting its fate is Wolfsburg, home of West Germany's Volkswagen corporation.

Calvert Cliffs, Maryland, is one American non-energy boomtown (Finsterbusch, 1980); construction of a nuclear power plant brought sharp changes to the regional labor market. Tobacco and lumber workers joined the construction force, and several lumber mills closed. Unlike many boomtowns, Calvert County did not increase public service spending sharply for Calvert Cliffs. While school enrollment rose by 1,300 in seven years, school spending as a fraction of the county budget stayed constant. Perhaps the increased rate of settlement of Washington, D.C. professionals in Calvert County reduced the need to raise utility tax payments. These new residents built many summer homes, providing tax dollars without creating new demands on services, especially those for children.

Waterford, Connecticut, is an even more unlikely boomtown. As in the Calvert Cliffs' example, Waterford is close to several nuclear plants (*U.S. News and World Report*, 1975, 70-74). Their operating utility pays 60 percent of Waterford's taxes, reducing the town's property tax rate by 25 percent. Since the plants had been running for several years by 1975, the town's economy was able to record a budget surplus. Residents worry about thermal and radioactive pollution, but are generally content with the plant's impact.

Dam-building activities made the population of Sweet Home, Oregon, rise by 21 percent in five years (Finsterbusch, 1980, 146). Crime and alcoholism grew worse during construction, but declined afterward nearly to preboom levels. The natives were pleased with the improved town services the "miniboom" created.

Nuclear plant construction created another boomtown in Skagit County, Washington, to the surprise of none of its residents. Most of them favored the project, but forced the utility to agree to local zoning rules and prepayment of taxes as requirements for plant construction.

The Levitt brothers managed to avoid boomtown conditions in Bucks County, Pennsylvania, when they decided to build Levittown to satisfy the needs of workers at the new Fairless Steel Works. The brothers made all the major development decisions, eliminating the "knowledge time lag" common to boomtowns (where those involved do not know until too late the decisions to be made or the manner of implementing them). Since the Levitts knew that the townspeople were not in an economic boom, they did not have to risk losing their money if the town busted. Many such boomtowns, including some famous ones discussed later in this chapter, have busted. Fear of their community's becoming a bust town propels many opponents of energy development.

Seneca, Illinois, is a classic boomtown that later busted. World War II revived the nearby shipyard for several years. Acute shortages of private capital and the lack of local government's willingness to pay for the infrastructure for its temporary population—all of whom were to leave when the war ended—were problems peculiar to Seneca and plagued other war-created boomtowns that weren't to become postwar research centers (e.g., Los Alamos and Oak Ridge). Newcomers rarely felt welcome, resented old-time resident hostility, and avoided involvement in local affairs.

Fairbanks, Alaska, served as the management, transportation, supply, labor market, and supply service center for the trans-Alaska oil pipeline. The area's population jumped from 45,000 in 1973 to 63,000 in 1975. While natives left other preboom jobs to work on the pipeline, newcomers also wanted pipeline jobs. The cost of living was too high for newcomers working anywhere except on the pipeline, so local jobs often went begging. This led to abnormally high job turnover in these other industries. The state had to impose rent controls to prevent huge rent hikes. The vacancy shortage became severe. Fairbanks had

anticipated a pipeline building boom in 1970; delays led its leaders to limit future civic development, leaving the city unprepared for the late 1970s boom. It is indeed very difficult to predict the future well enough to use investment money wisely (Finsterbusch, 1980, 155-159).

Page, Arizona, was conceived in 1957 by the federal Bureau of Reclamation, which also planned and operated the town until 1975 (Little, 1977, 416). Within these 18 years, a huge hydroelectric power plant and another huge coal-fired plant were erected. Page experienced annual population changes ranging from +153 percent to −42 percent. Page, however, did not suffer much from these changes because the federal government operated everything there except the schools until 1975. Federal funds went into planning and building all the town services, but they did not insulate Page from social problems despite all its residents having been newcomers. After the 18-year period, tension had appeared between new residents and the original residents who had arrived in 1957.

One prominent European company town is concerned about becoming a bust town, courtesy of the Japanese auto industry. Wolfsburg, West Germany, was designed in the late 1930s, most likely by the Nazis, from the design of Hitler's architect, later his Armaments Minister, Albert Speer (Geddes, 1979, III-7). Speer called the new city the "Town of the Strength-Through-Joy Cars." The city's sole industry was the production of the Fuehrer's idea of the People's Car—in German, "volkswagen" (Geddes, 1979, III-7). The town was renamed Wolfsburg, after a nearby castle, in 1945.

[It] is dotted with white-stucco high rises and row houses separated by patches of woods and man-made lakes. Concert halls, theaters, parks and swimming pools are scattered throughout the community for its 130,000 citizens. The streets are spotless. . . . But despite the passage of four decades it has remained a company town. (Geddes, 1979, III-7)

One-fourth of its residents work for Volkswagen, which owns two-thirds of the apartment houses directly or indirectly. In 1948 planners had intended Wolfsburg to have 35,000 residents, but the figure had to be raised to 100,000 in 1955. Wolfsburg's location near the East German border, and its small, highly paid labor force have deterred other companies from investing there. The town therefore relies on Volkswagen for 90 percent of its tax revenue. It is easy to imagine the nervous state of its leaders and residents as Volkswagen sales slump amidst worldwide economic recession and relentless competition from the Japanese automakers.

BUST TOWNS

What Wolfsburg and all other company towns and present-day boomtowns fear most is a rapid decline leading to a bust. Decline can take place gradually or suddenly (a bust). It can occur after a boom or a long, stable period, and can result from a decision to build, or not to build something. The ghost towns discussed in Chapter 4 are only the most vivid and extreme examples of bust towns. Communities can go into even a severe economic downturn without literally crumbling away, as did some of the Wild West ghost towns.

Construction projects typify a boom-bust situation, while military bases create stable-bust towns. Stable-bust is often worse than boom-bust, since the newly unemployed are old-time residents, not former newcomers who knew their work was going to end. Few studies are available of bust towns, and only slightly more studies exist of declining towns.

Seneca, Illinois, was shown in this chapter to have been a boomtown that suffered less than others have when its boom ended and its shipyard ceased operation. The situation in other stable-bust towns are often far worse; in addition to the unemployment of long-time residents, the specter of old businesses going bankrupt, people unable to sell their homes rendered nearly worthless, collapsing schools, and emigrating young people is especially difficult to accept.

Seneca went bust between March and July 1945 as shipyard employment shrank from 9,000 to nothing.

Although nearly all the boom's employees, housing, and businesses vanished, the boom did create a community club and several other new businesses that stayed after the boom ended. By 1950 Seneca had improved its appearance and self-image.

Sweet Home, Oregon, also saw a mini-boom followed by a bust. Sweet Home is a classic example of the way in which a development project, in this case dam construction, was "expected by local residents to spur population and economic growth, but instead stimulated the community to overextend its school and municipal services" (Malamud, 1981, 72). The $80 million project was taking place near a town of 4,000 residents. The community did benefit from increased educational and other town services, but owed these benefits not to regional growth but to an influx of construction workers, requiring service expansions supported with local tax dollars. The dam construction did help the previously sagging lumber industry revive. After the boom, the former construction workers could go back to the logging industry.

Local planners had expected more immigration after the dam's completion than they received, so the town's per capita municipal service expenses were extremely high. Very little assistance came from any higher level of government.

The original residents willingly allowed the newcomers to direct community redevelopment programs in a way that was sure to benefit the newcomers more than themselves. Yet the old-timers had to shoulder the load after the newcomers had departed.

Caliente, a southwestern town, provides the best history of a bust-town situation (Cottrell, 1951, 358-365). Caliente was a steam-locomotive servicing center for a major railroad. Few resources were available nearby to support the town in any other way. The residents, unaware of change in the offing, built permanent homes, water systems, businesses, four churches, and extensive educational and recreation systems (Malamud, 1981, 73-74). So long as the steam locomotive was in use, Caliente was a necessity. With the adoption of the diesel, it became obsolescent. Probably the greatest losses were suffered by the older nonoperating employees, not by the railroad, the general public, or the more skilled mobile workers. Local merchants, operating employees, bondholders, churches, and homeowners all paid heavily for their shortsightedness.

Presque Isle, Maine, became a stable-bust town when a military base closed down in 1961, costing the city a $2.5 million payroll. The local Chamber of Commerce, however, had begun an industrial development program that helped persuade a potato processor to set up a plant there. The Chamber of Commerce and the local government, working together, persuaded the Air Force to leave most of its equipment in place after the city bought the base for a "modest" price, so that the city could set up an airport and industrial zone there. By 1968 the zone included wood processing, leather goods, paper and rubber plants, a publishing firm, a vocational school, plus the potato processor. The town now has more business activity than it did while the Air Force base was operating.

Edgemont, South Dakota, also suffered a military base closure, an Army facility, but this town had only partially recovered by 1970. Moses Lake, Washington, suffered an air base closing, but recovered very rapidly. When typically self-sufficient military bases shut down, the military often sells them to local residents for a small price, as occurred in Presque Isle, so that the impacted town does not suffer too badly.

During the Carter Administration, William J. Sheehan, head of the Defense Department's Office of Economic Adjustment, ordered a study of the ways in which communities adapt to military base closings. Of 77 bases closed from 1961 to 1977, 72 had been put to industrial, educational, recreational, commercial, or aviation use. There are now more than 40 industrial parks, 7 four-year colleges and 26 postsecondary vocational schools. But nearly all such affected towns underwent a depressed condition followed by readjustment, and nearly all recovered fairly well after one to four years. Herbers (1979) described the efforts made by Mobile, Alabama, after Brookley Air Force Base was closed in 1969. Helped substantially by the Defense Department's having left

all the streets, water, and sewer systems intact, the area became a "bustling subcity," with many industries represented. The city had obtained the land for a pittance, knowing that "old bases attract industry because their new owners, usually some level of government, are frequently able to make better deals than the owners of private property" (Herbers, 1979, B-9).

Still another bust-town story with an apparently happy ending is Portland, Maine (Butterfield, 1982, A-16). This decaying port city is to be boosted by construction of the Bath Iron Works' ship overhauling and repair yard near the famous shipyard up the coast. Since 1970 Portland has been putting up highways, office buildings, new restaurants and shops as it reverses a 25-year decline since World War II. The shipyard itself has never been busier, with a billion-dollar backlog in orders, nor has it ever been more efficient. The first 8 of 21 guided missile frigate-class ships ordered by the Navy were delivered a total of 116 weeks early, and all under budget. The state's largest employer, the Bath shipyard, has 6,700 workers, more than at any time since the war. The firm invested more than $16 million for the Portland yard, while the state and city each approved the raising of $15 million in bonds. The federal General Services Administration helped the situation even further by approving Maine's request to take over an abandoned federal drydock. The Bath shipyard's repeatedly having been cited even by critics of the defense establishment as a model of efficiency can only help Portland's recovery in the years ahead.

At the other end of the spectrum is the sad tale of Black's Harbor, in Canada's New Brunswick province. It was controlled by Connors Brothers, Ltd., a sardine-packing and fish-processing concern. Connors provided free water, waste disposal, police, and fire protection services to its 1,700 employee-residents. Then the firm sold these services to the new village council for $3, after 80 years of ownership. Since the company refused to sell either the houses it owned or much of its land, Black's Harbor cannot attract new industry. But Connors thinks that partial independence will help the village get more provincial aid.

Company towns . . . have been phasing out all over North America, either because of the exhaustion of the minerals or other natural resources around which the towns were built, or because companies have discovered that the paternalism inherent in such communities is unpopular or impossibly expensive or both. (Churcher, 1974, 18)

Connors still owns the local cannery and fish-meal plant, supermarket, laundromat, gas station, three-fourths of the vacant land, and 80 percent of all housing units. "Gone are the free clothes that some of the employees' children once received, as well as discount milk from a company farm and free credit at the hardware store for all Connors employees" (Churcher, 1974, 18).

Part of Connors's decision may have stemmed from its purchase in 1967 by George Weston, Ltd., a large grocery and food-processing firm based in Toronto. Connors itself, rather than the villagers, turns out to have had most to do with the turnover of the village services. At any rate, Black's Harbor is getting substantial help from the province, which funds 70 percent of its operating budget. The town is also trying to get New Brunswick to pay for rebuilding the water system.

Churcher cited a 1966 study of isolated company communities built in the western U.S. More than 150 of the 190 towns had been either abandoned by the companies or sold to private owners. Although the German system may function in a different fashion from the American, Wolfsburg may have to undergo drastic changes in its socio-economic structure if Volkswagen cannot continue to shoulder its traditional burden of providing for the town. Bust towns offer the lesson that a boomtown must consider bringing in new industry (or, as in Portland's case, hoping that its mainstay will remain profitable) to avoid having the same problems that Caliente did.

REFERENCES

Butterfield, Fox, 1982, "Bath Shipyard's Success a Boon for Portland, Maine," *New York Times,* February 17, p. A-16.

Churcher, Sharon, 1974, "In One Ex-Company Town, Some Yearn for the 'Good Old Days' of Paternalism," *Wall Street Journal,* December 31, p. 18.

Cottrell, W. F., 1951, "Death By Dieselization," *American Sociological Review* **16:**358-365.

Finsterbusch, Kurt, 1980, *Understanding Social Impacts,* Sage Publications, Beverly Hills, Calif.

Geddes John, 1979, "Wolfsburg: A One-Company Town," *New York Times,* May 27, p. III-7.

Herbers, John, 1979, "Cities Find Conversion for Old Military Bases a Boon to Economies," *New York Times,* April 26, pp. 1ff.

Little, R. L., 1977, "Some Social Consequences of Boom Towns," *North Dakota Law Review* **53:**401-425.

Malamud, Gary, 1981, "A Comprehensive Solution to the Boomtown Syndrome," master's thesis, New York University.

U.S. News and World Report, 1975, "New Boom Towns Across U.S.," November 10, pp. 70-74.

12

The World's Exploding Cities

Officials in tiny communities undergoing population growth so rapid that it overwhelms their infrastructure can take heart from the fact that they are not alone. Even with their legions of well-paid professional planners, many of the world's largest cities are proving incapable of dealing with annual growth rates well below the 15 percent that Gilmore (1976) defined as boomtown expansion.

Mexico City, Djakarta, Teheran, and Caracas are the capitals of nations so endowed with oil that one can hope that an efficient government will be able to provide the funds to sustain orderly growth.

Most countries, especially those in the debt-ridden, oil-poor Third World, are far less fortunate. The rush to the cities is afflicting countries rich and poor. Cities of 100,000 or more have absorbed about 577 million new residents in the last 15 years, out of a world population below 4 billion, through birth or migration (Wilsher, 1975, IV-3). Another 1.4 billion are expected to join them by the year 2000. There will then be at least 25 cities with more than 12.5 million residents, at least 18 of which will be in the Third World. By 1975 only New York City and Tokyo-Yokohama had reached that status. The first new members of the club will be Mexico City, Sao Paulo, and Shanghai, with Peking, Bombay, Calcutta, Seoul, Buenos Aires, Rio de Janeiro, Cairo, Karachi (Pakistan), Teheran, New Delhi, Bangkok, Manila, Lima, Bogota, and Djakarta to follow. Figure 12.1 shows the astonishing growth rate of some of these cities. As rapid as their growth may be, however, none have expanded more than 6 percent annually in the time shown by the graph.

MEXICO AND NIGERIA

Few Third World countries today have expanding economies able to employ most of their new urban residents. Even the oil-rich Mexican economy has fallen on hard times, and is incapable of employing Mexico's poor either in the countryside or in the cities to which they are migrating. In any country, urban

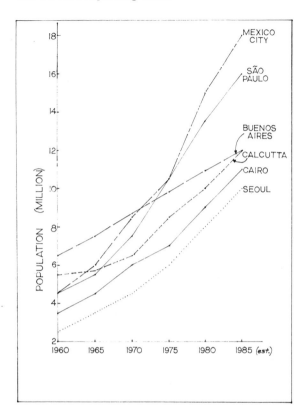

Figure 12.1
The world's fastest-growing cities (Wilsher, 1975).

facing the poor of Mexico City and Lagos, (Nigeria), yet most of these people willingly put up with them. Their national government cannot blame colonial rule as the reason for their lack of preparation for the urban explosion. It is true that the British did not upgrade the infrastructure of Lagos during their rule, but

the postcolonial government has built no underground drainage, sewerage, or storm drains, so that the stench has to be smelled to be believed. . . . Traffic is the most intractable headache, worse even than housing, where every program put forward is made obsolete by increased migration before it leaves the planner's desk. So tightly packed is the population that any attempt to widen or straighten a street, let alone perform major works . . . sets off social tensions that can last for years. (Wilsher, 1975, IV-3)

Many Third World governments would have been corrupt and inefficient even without colonial rule. Those newly independent states do have one handicap; they tend to rely on Western consultants for planning and building major projects. These consultants rarely take complex social matters into account and usually ignore the people's most basic needs—jobs and housing. Most Third World governments would rather build large showcase projects to enhance their own reputation than begin national growth in the countryside, where most of their people live and where poverty is normally the worst.

INDIA

The most famous advocate of rural development, at the expense of urban growth and heavy industry, was India's Mahatma Gandhi. Yet nowhere else has runaway urban growth been so obvious for so long. Calcutta, India's largest city, has been synonymous for a century with urban wretchedness. Half of the area of the city, which has 8 million residents, has no sewers. Many city services are collapsing, including streetcar services, sewage disposal, sanitation, and shelter provision. The knowledge that "cities, even in India, do not starve" drives thousands of Bengali villagers there each year.[1] However,

poverty is much more concentrated, and therefore much more visible than rural poverty, although it is often less brutal to its victims. The problem urban planners face in these exploding cities is that most of the new urban poor are very content not to be among the rural poor any longer, and will not leave the slums their huge numbers have made inevitable.

These new urban poor willingly endure conditions that the urban middle and upper classes deplore. Sao Paulo is among the richest of the urban giants, yet "infant mortality is higher than it was ten years ago; the average journey to work is over three hours, and 73 percent of the people are officially stated to be suffering from deficient diet" (Wilsher, 1975, IV-3). Chapters 16 and 18 illustrate the brutal conditions

[Cities] do die . . . from water-borne diseases and inadequate sanitation. . . . In the meantime, seven million tons of silt have accumulated in the sewers, cutting the drainage capacity by half. Uncollected "night-soil" from the city's 40,000 public privies pollutes the air and frequently overflows into the public water supply. Overstretched pumping machines often break down for 48 hours at a time. The threat of breakdown of essential services is constant but despite it, the new arrivals pour in. (Wilsher, 1975, IV-3)

By no means is Calcutta alone in its predicament, even among Indian cities. Bombay's status as India's richest city has made it a mecca for millions of rural poor. City leaders worry that these migrants will soon overwhelm the city and brings its infrastructure crashing down. Housing is, as always, the first infrastructural component to go. As many as half of Bombay's people live in slums ranging from vile to all but uninhabitable. Up to a million people live in the streets. Other Bombay infrastructure is in equally sad shape. "Garbage stands uncollected. Pavements crumble and buildings fall down. The incidence of water-borne diseases increases as sanitation facilities are overtaxed. And everywhere, it seems, there are people" (Stevens, 1982, 2). As they enter this most westernized of Indian cities, they are perhaps losing some of their rural Hindu ways. While the city tries to deal with the crisis, some observers feel that only a national effort to attack rapid birth rates and dire rural poverty can reduce Bombay's woes.

EGYPT

Egypt's capital city also suffers from overpopulation, as a result of which

Cairo, a city designed for two million people, now accommodates three or four times that number, yet in 20 years hardly a penny has been spent on expanding its basic services. Buses, trains, power, telephones, sewage, water supplies, taxis, hospitals—all have been strained to the very limits of capacity. (Holden, 1975, VI-13)

All this is but a reflection of Egypt's unparalleled birth rate, which has doubled its population in 20 years to about 40 million. Smog obscures the Pyramids,

potholes not even a New Yorker can imagine are everywhere, and "Cairo is in a straitjacket of rationing or perennial shortages of most staple items" (Howe, 1977a, 2). The city suffers from inadequate housing,

garbage heaps, sewer overflows in the streets . . . and broken sidewalks . . . congested schools and clinics, frequent electricity cuts, and telephones that consistently ring the wrong number if they ring at all. . . . Greater Cairo has one of the highest population densities in the world and at present has more than 8.7 million inhabitants. The annual growth rate exceeds 4 percent. Projections range from 16 million to 20 million . . . by the year 2000. . . . Large areas of central Cairo are overcrowded and deteriorating, with limited sanitary services. And huge squatter settlements have grown up on the fringes of the city, completely without sanitary services. (Howe, 1977a, 2)

The sewers, built in 1914, were meant for 960,000 people. The city is short 750,000 housing units. Cairo's main cemetery is home for 20,000 to 100,000 people. Population growth far outpaces the government's efforts to revamp the city's infrastructure through dealings with many foreign companies and government agencies.

A vivid reminder of Cairo's crisis took place on December 6, 1982, when a huge sewer main burst beneath a densely populated neighborhood in western Cairo. "Foul-smelling black water . . . gushed through main avenues and streets where more than 60,000 people live" (Farrell, 1982, A-14). The broken main is part of a sewage system built as far back as 1910. The foul flood has affected rich and poor Cairenes alike.

Among the more elaborate of the government's efforts to relieve the mess in Cairo is its plan to build a ring of cities 30 to 40 miles from Cairo. One city, The Tenth of Ramadan, was to have 150,000 residents by 1982. Trying to reduce speculation, the government decreed that only it could buy land, and at the price the original landowner had paid for it; this rule, sensible as it may have been theoretically, merely slowed down the pace of construction. Huge problems confront the government. Water supply to many of the new cities will be difficult. Planners argue the relative merits of first selling the land or first planning the economic base to support the cities (Howe, 1977b, 2).

TURKEY

Along the crossroads of European and Asian civilizations, Istanbul has experienced its share of chaotic growth. It has grown from 1 million people in 1950 to 5.5 or 6 million today (Morgenthaler, 1980, 1). Its population growth rate of 70,000 per year makes Istanbul fortunate among Third World cities. Although Istanbul's problems are not quite as severe as those in other Third World cities Istanbul suffers from rural depopulation, resulting in urban income inequality, unrealistic expectations of rural people of opportunities in the city, rising birth rates, lack of decent housing, and the abundance of shantytowns called "gecekondus" in Istanbul. Here, too, these settlements slowly develop basic services along with social tensions.

LATIN AMERICA

In no other region is urban overpopulation such a crisis as in Latin America.

An amber corona of pollutants shroud the Andean peaks rimming the Chilean capital of Santiago. The narrow streets of the white-washed colonial city center in the Ecuadorean capital of Quito awake to shimmery clear mountain mornings but are soon engulfed in smoky, caterwauling traffic jams.

Mexico City, home of 131,000 factories as well as 14 million people, and Sao Paulo, center of nearly half the entire production of Brazil, live in a permanent silvery haze. The leafy valley in which the Venezuelans built their capital city of Caracas has become a sooty basin of carbon monoxide in quantities more than 15 times the danger level established by the World Health Organization.

The Bolivian river that runs through the middle of La Paz . . . is so filled with garbage that people in nearby offices get nauseated from the odor. And the Brazilian city of Cubatao has become so polluted that its mayor refuses to live there and state officials moved out when their request for gas masks was turned down. (Hoge, 1981, 22)

The United Nations predicts that by the year 2000, six Latin American cities will have at least 10 million people.[2] An urban economist stated that "some cities are . . . reaching population levels new to urban policy making" (Hoge, 1981, 22). As these cities expand, their lack of an industrial base (relative to American cities) drive down their people's chance for employment. Until recently, national planning and fund disbursement in Latin America had favored urban over rural.

In these exploding cities, even the wealthy suffer the effects. All electricity users in Bogota must cut power off for two hours every day. Affluent neighborhoods of Rio de Janeiro such as Copacabana have the same noise levels from traffic as the slums near the airport. Acoustics experts, in fact, consider Rio the world's noisiest city, due largely to the city's topography[3] and Brazil's status as the Third World's largest automobile producer.

Sao Paulo was the world's leading symbol of the urban population explosion before Mexico City captured its attention. Although Sao Paulo has grown rapidly since World War II, its "industrial sector has been able to absorb only a fraction of the growing labor force. . . . Rapid migration to the metropolitan area during the past two decades has not only aggravated the problems of urban services and housing, but has also had a significant impact on employment" (Schaefer, 1976, 1). From 1935 to 1970, migration swelled the city's population a remarkable 7.7 percent a year, from 600,000 to more than 8 million residents. Half these people had no running water or drainage system in their homes.

The city's development during this time into Brazil's industrial center did little to alleviate its people's poverty. Not only did Sao Paulo have a nine percent unemployment rate in 1970, but at least one-third of the working population of the city and its suburbs had wages at or below the national minimum wage; they suffered from the decline of that wage from an index of 112 in 1962 to 82 in 1971.

In a single 20-year period, 1950-1979, Greater Sao Paulo's population tripled from 2.7 to 8.1 million (Schaefer, 1976, 20). Most of the new Paulistas were absorbed into the service sector, not the capital-intensive basic industrial sector. No one can say for sure whether the lack of skilled labor, the lack of educational chances for the poor, or government industrialization policies were most responsible for the concentration of income in the hands of the wealthy few. As the income pyramid expanded at the bottom, of course, wages for the unskilled masses declined even further.

The response of Sao Paulo's officials since 1970 to all this growth is not encouraging. "The quality of life in Greater Sao Paulo seems to have worsened over the years as a result of rapidly increasing population pressures and relatively low levels of urban development and expenditure. The Sao Paulo budget provided only $28 a person in public services in 1968, vs. New York's $750" (Schaefer, 1976, 81). The city's mayor in 1971 said that Sao Paulo's growth had to be stopped for a while to prevent it from going beyond anyone's control.

One reason for the difficulty of controlling Sao Paulo's growth is that no effective metropolitan government exists. Sao Paulo instead has 37 administrative units (municipalities) that are largely autonomous. "Sao Paulo's planning is still diffuse, located in the various [municipality] planning agencies, state secretariats and federal ministries. Clearly, without some form of metropolitan government, it has been difficult, if not impossible, to make co-ordinated, city-wide decisions..." (Schaefer, 1976, 83). Schaefer

concluded that urban infrastructure projects can reduce unemployment—an idea now hotly controversial in the U.S.—and that Brasilia has to provide a good deal of the money to fund them. Brazil is not Mexico, however. Though both countries have abnormally high foreign debt levels, Brazil lacks Mexico's energy resources to provide future sources of urban growth-control funding. The least Sao Paulo can do is to streamline local and regional government planning and administration to avoid wastefully duplicative efforts.

Brazil's urban explosion has spread beyond Rio and Sao Paulo. In 1972, 59 percent of Brazilians lived in cities, compared to 46 percent in 1962 (*Economist*, 1972, 16), and the figure was no doubt higher in 1982. Massive migrations from the chronically impoverished northeast region and from defunct coffee plantations in the interior have swelled all the coastal cities of Brazil (see Fig. 8.1 in Chapter 8). However, few of these migrants find meaningful jobs, and most find housing only in the "favelas," the Brazilian version of the shantytowns found all over the urban Third World.

The 1970 census showed that only half of Brazil's urban dwellers had a steady piped water supply, and only one-fourth had connections to urban sewer systems. Table 12.1 shows the extent to which

Table 12.1
The Rush to the Cities

	1950 Population (millions)	% Growth 1950-1960	% Growth 1960-1970	1970 Population (millions)
Belem	0.23	60	57	0.57
Fortaleza	0.21	73	46	0.52
Recife	0.51	54	33	1.05
Salvador (Bahia)	0.39	62	58	1.00
Greater Rio de Janeiro	3.10	52	53	7.20
Greater Sao Paulo	2.40	88	87	8.40
Brasilia	0.09	203		0.27
Belo Horizonte	0.34	90	72	1.11
Campinas	0.10	81	84	0.33
Curitiba	0.14	150	40	0.48
Porto Alegre	0.38	65	41	0.87

Source: Economist, 1972, "Brazil Survey," September 2, pp. 16-19.

population increase strained the infrastructure of Brazil's cities.

By 1980 at least 70 percent of Latin Amercia's population lived in cities of 20,000 or more residents. Six cities held 80 percent of Brazil's urban population in 1970 (Wagner and Ward, 1980, 250). Since structural changes in the Brazilian economy created this movement to the cities, structural changes may be the only way to stop it.

ITALY

Not all of the world's desperately overcrowded cities are in the Third World. Nowhere is this more evident than in Naples, a city whose people have become ingenious practitioners in the art of getting by.

Like an elegant old invalid somewhat overdressed in the glorious rags and tatters of a colorful past, Naples appears to bask in its history, content, as always, simply to survive. Seen through the haze that shimmers on the deep-blue water of the gulf, the city seems as reassuringly eternal as the familiar local songs that for centuries have celebrated its immortality. . . .

. . . Something drastic had [recently] happened . . . just below the surface of life here, some profound change had taken place from which the elegant old invalid might not recover. (Murray, 1981, 144)

That event was the devastating southern Italian earthquake of November 23, 1980. As many as 3,000 people died in the poor villages in the mountains beyond Naples.

The earthquake of 1980 served to exacerbate and also to focus attention on the related problems that for many decades have afflicted the Mezzogiorno . . . : what to do about the underpopulated, depressed areas, where even in the best of times the living is precarious, and about the overpopulated coastal cities like Naples that lack any means to provide permanent employment for their slum dwellers, at least a quarter of whom are always without work. (Murray, 1981, 145)

Murray stated that the effects of the tremor on Naples were not as severe as those inland, but it nevertheless "threatens to bring about the complete dissolution of a social structure that has for many years survived on the edge of an abyss by its wits and by all sorts of peculiar expedients" (p. 145). Even in Italy, Naples has become notorious for the amount of petty crime in its streets. Many of its residents admit that living there is becoming intolerable, and that too many Neapolitans have given up hope for a better life.

CONCLUSION

This despair is the major predicament for all governments dealing with swollen cities. They must fight years of inertia and neglect, convince their citizens who live in the countryside that they need not move to the major cities to improve their lives, and make it economically and physically attractive for them to stay. A depopulated countryside cannot feed the cities' teeming masses, so national planners must strike the right combination of emphases on rural and urban development. These steps, like the equally necessary imposition of birth control, will take decades to become effective. City planners must realize that these new city dwellers understand poverty in relative terms: As long as the countryside offers them even less comfort than the cities, they will endure even the vilest of urban slums.

NOTES

1. The plight of Calcutta and the surrounding Bengali territory *is* a direct result of a decision made by the British during their rule. Compelled by Moslem leaders to partition the Indian subcontinent into Hindu and Moslem states, the British had to split the region of Bengal into what was to become Moslem East Pakistan and the Indian region of Bengal. Until partition, Bengal was a thriving, although storm- and flood-wracked region, in which jute was produced in the east and shipped to factories in Calcutta to the west, from which it was exported. Cut off from Calcutta by the partition, the jute growers of East Pakistan (today, Bangladesh) were doomed to economic strangulation, while Calcutta itself was deprived of one if its largest industries that could today have helped sustain the hordes of Hindus now migrating into the city.

2. These cities are Mexico City, Sao Paulo, Rio de Janeiro, Buenos Aires, Lima, and Bogota.

3. Rio is hemmed in between hills and the ocean.

REFERENCES

Economist, 1972, "The Urban Explosion," September 2 (Brazil Survey), pp. 16-19.

Farrell, William E., 1982, "Burst Sewer Floods Area of Cairo and Imperils Health of Residents," *New York Times,* Dec. 17, p. A-14.

Hoge, Warren, 1981, "Unchecked Urbanization Clogs Latin America," *New York Times,* Oct. 18, p. 22.

Holden, David, 1975, " 'Hero of the Crossing,' They Shout, 'Where is Our Breakfast?' " *New York Times,* June 1, p. VI-13.

Howe, Marvine, 1977a, "In Cairo, Houses Fall and Services Fail, But People Stay," *New York Times,* Sept. 13, p. 2.

Howe, Marvine, 1977b, "Egypt's Plan for Desert Cities Stirs Much Debate But Little Building, *New York Times,* Oct. 20, p. 2.

Morgenthaler, Eric, 1980, "Ancient Istanbul Feels Strain of Fast Growth as Throngs Crowd In," *Wall Street Journal,* Oct. 21, p. 1.

Murray, William, 1981, "Letter From Naples," *New Yorker,* Dec. 14, p. 144ff.

New York Times, 1977, "Squalor and Pollution Afflict the Growing Cities," January 30, p. XII-20.

Schaefer, Kalmann, 1976, *Sao Paulo—Urban Development and Employment,* International Labor Office, Geneva, Switzerland.

Stevens, William K., 1982, "Bombay is Now Home of the Elite and the Hopeless," *New York Times,* Sept. 7, p. 2.

Wagner, F. E., and Ward, John O., 1980, "Urbanization and Migration in Brazil," *American Journal of Economics and Sociology* **39**(3):249-259.

Wilsher, Peter, 1975, "Everyone, Everywhere, is Moving to the Cities," *New York Times,* June 22, p. IV-3.

13

Resource Towns Outside the Fossil Fuel Boom

THE TENNESSEE VALLEY

In the current worldwide rush for energy supplies, one source is being all but ignored — the power of the world's mighty rivers. Many of these, unfortunately, are in areas so hostile to life that they may never be tapped, in areas such as northern Russia and Canada, which, despite impressive efforts so far (see Bratsk, Chapter 5), remain only partially exploited.

There are areas, however, especially in poor countries, in which hydroelectric power is being boldly exploited. The standard by which such projects may be measured is the Tennessee Valley Authority, the earliest and probably the most controversial electrification project ever undertaken. Figure 13.1 shows a few of the dams TVA built in 20 years.

On May 18, 1933, Franklin Roosevelt signed the act creating the TVA. However, southern congressmen who agreed with the plan expected the U.S. government merely to build the dams, not to sell power and thereby compete with private utilities. Neither they nor their constituents really knew what they were voting for, nor did anyone know the extent to which TVA would have authority over the valley residents' lives. The public had little idea what a government corporation (as opposed to a government bureau or agency) was. But the three people heading it, of whom David E. Lilienthal was to become the best known, had enormous power to change the lives of all the Tennessee Valley's residents. They did not have to answer to Congress, either in considering plans or in building dams, and had the funds of the U.S. Treasury at their disposal.

Just after TVA was set up, it began building the Cove Creek Dam on the Clinch River, renamed later after Senator George Norris, one of TVA's most powerful boosters. Near the dam was Norris Village,

the model town, or ideal town, of the Tennessee Valley, as the authority conceived a rural town. It had grown out of Chairman Morgan's belief that money ought not to be wasted on ugly temporary shacks of the "shotgun" type that usually housed a construction force. Why not make the workers' village into something permanent that would serve the community when the dam building was

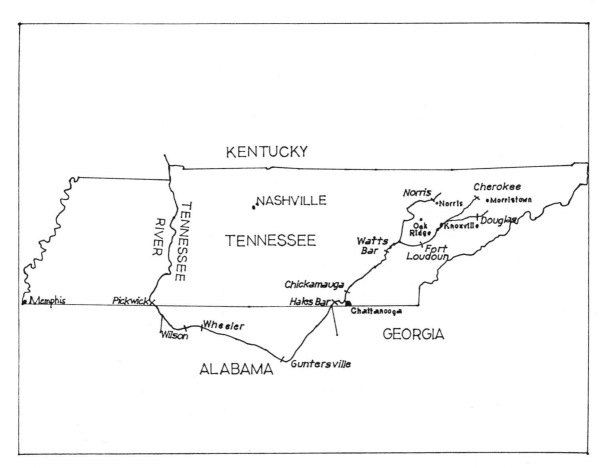

Figure 13.1
The region affected by the TVA (Davidson, 1948).

over—something like a "resettlement" or a "subsistence homestead" project?" . . . [But] country folks could not live in a park, away from means of subsistence. And anyway, in those rather small houses, just what would you do with a pack of children and a lot of kinfolks? But Norris Village did very well for people who had few children and perhaps no nearby kinfolks—namely, the staff and office force of TVA itself. It speedily became, therefore, their suburban residence, and served very well for that. (Davidson, 1948, 229-230)

At about the same time, in 1934, Wheeler Dam was also built, 15 miles upstream from Wilson Dam. Early on, TVA decided to build a so-called high-dam system, with maximum power output the first priority and navigation second. To assure adequate flood control the high-dam system would also require storage dams on the tributary rivers united with the main river's high dams in a single system. All these dams would transform the river into a chain of placid lakes. The planners failed to realize that the loss of large areas of good farmland through inundations of the high-dam system might anger the people of Tennessee and Alabama more than flood control and cheap power might please them. Many families would have to be evicted from their homes, but few industrial plants, towns, railroads, or highways would be affected.

By the end of 1945, almost every one of TVA's planned dams was either up or going up. At these projects, TVA converted the remains of the construction workers' villages into recreation centers, unlike Norris Village. Also, "by June 1946, the authority had removed 13,499 families from . . . reservoir areas, and there were still about one thousand families to be removed. Of the 13,499 families, 4,578 were owners of their land" (Davidson, 1948, 255). At least 72,000 people were removed.[1]

By 1945, TVA had achieved a monopoly of Tennessee Valley electricity sales: a navigable 9-foot channel from Paducah, Kentucky to Knoxville, Tennessee; a trebling since 1940 of available kilowatt-hours of electricity; and power provision to nearby Oak Ridge's atomic research facilities. Twenty-six dams went up in four states: Tennessee, North Carolina, Alabama, and Kentucky.

Chapter 10 shows that Oak Ridge was the best-known of the communities made possible by TVA. The Authority, however, was not directly involved in building or operating Oak Ridge. First a center for atom bomb research, it became a nuclear power research center after the war, during which time the city lost many of its boomtown traits as the gates of secrecy came down. Only the plants and laboratories remained closed. In 1955 the United States gave up management and ownership of the city, whose residents then set up a town government. All of its facilities became theirs in June 1960.[2]

TVA also spurred the development of the Arnold Engineering Development Center, a kind of Oak Ridge for aerospace research and development in the Tullahoma area, along with the George C. Marshall Space Flight Center in Huntsville, Alabama and the nearby Army Ordnance Missile Command. From 1950 to 1962, Huntsville's population rose from 16,000 to about 85,000.

Norris today is a

bedroom suburb of Knoxville and Oak Ridge with very strict standards for who can live there. It is composed almost entirely of people who work for either TVA or Oak Ridge and who have moved into the town from outside the region. The Norrisites and their Anderson County neighbors, even including Oak Ridge, do not get along at all. . . . It has no industry other than TVA. (Jesse C. Mills, 1982, personal correspondence)

Mills (1982) also offers the example of Morristown, Tennessee. Once a railroad boomtown in the 1880s, it boomed again when furniture producers began building their plants in the Southeast.

Today, other countries imitate TVA's procedures and intentions. One outstanding example is Itaipu Dam, connecting Paraguay and Brazil across the Parana River, and its associated boomtown, Puerto Stroessner, Paraguay (see Fig. 8.1 in Chapter 8).[3] This community, created 25 years ago, grew rapidly from 15,000 residents in 1975 to more than 90,000 in 1982. In 1975 construction on the dam began; it was to begin operation by the end of 1982. Although six more years of work are forecast on projects upstream of the dam, the maximum labor force of 39,000 had been cut in half, and layoffs continued at 100 per day in 1983.

The boom continues, meanwhile, at gaudy stores to which Brazilians flock by bus and car to buy cheap contraband imports, ranging from Scotch whisky to Japanese video recorders. Black market money exchangers carrying leather pouches circulate the streets.

Smuggling is so prevalent that once a year the Government declares an amnesty on tax evasion. Tax collectors then bargain individually with businessmen over what the tax might have been if the business were legal. The businessmen "donate" about 20 percent of that to the Government.

The Mayor said that plans were under way to build an airport and a railroad to the capital [Asuncion, Paraguay], and that cheap electricity from the dam would attract industry and jobs—but all in the future. (Schumacher, 1982, 8)

One wonders, though, whether these plans can be made economically feasible once the six years of construction along the river are complete and only the dam's operating workers remain.

Another area slated for enormous hydroelectric power projects is northern Quebec province, Canada, an area remote even from most Montrealers. Still another is Siberia. New boomtowns will certainly arise in these areas and will have the same problems as

Norris, Tennessee, and Puerto Stroessner, Paraguay —how to attract enough industry to lure prospective residents once construction ends.

SOUTH AFRICA: LICHTENBURG AND SALDANHA BAY

This section examines two South African towns that have grown tremendously in recent years due to the country's huge metals mining industry: Lichtenburg and Saldanha Bay.

Lichtenburg, in the western Transvaal region (see Fig. 4.1 in Chapter 4), was established in 1873 and quickly grew as a farming village. In 1925 diamonds were discovered nearby, and roughly 100,000 people quickly converged on the area. During the next quarter-century, "the Lichtenburg diggings produced 7,220,846 carats" of diamonds (A. D. Bosman, 1982, personal correspondence). Today, long after the diamond boom, Lichtenburg's population has receded to about 20,000, most of whom are engaged in agriculture and cement manufacturing.

Saldanha Bay has a far more colorful past. On the Atlantic coast just northwest of Cape Town, it was a relatively small settlement best known as a site of naval battles and a haven for pirates and murderers for about its first 175 years. Then it became the site of an 1844 stampede—not for gold or silver, but for guano, bird droppings, then a valuable fertilizer.

In 1832 Captain Benjamin Morrell published his account of a trip to Saldanha Bay four years before. He related how he found the surface of an island in the bay to be covered with guano to a depth of 25 feet (Burman and Levin, 1974, 92-93). The guano layer was actually about three times the thickness that Morrell had estimated.

Morrell's findings set off a "guano rush." At its height in 1844, the crews of about 400 vessels were digging up the guano on Ichaboe Island. Nearby Malagas Island was about equally rich in guano. A "shanty city" rose on Malagas Island and another on the shoreline. A dispute among the hunters regarding the right of some of them to use Indian laborers led to a "drunken orgy" that did not end until a British warship with marines arrived to restore order.

Within months, all the thousands of tons of guano were gone. The site was completely abandoned. In later years, Saldanha Bay was used as a quarantine station to take advantage of its isolation and lack of water and railroad connections, which also discouraged any permanent settlement there. The Boer War brought about the rail link and an expanded port to help unclog the Cape Town facilities of arriving British ships. The railroad finally reached Saldanha Bay in 1913, but it thrived only as a whaling center and fishing-industry village until World War II.

Saldanha Bay always was best known as a safe haven for ships negotiating the Cape of Good Hope, and has seen many wrecks just offshore. Nonetheless, an adequate water supply impeded Saldanha Bay's growth until World War II.

The Nazi presence in North Africa early in the war meant the closing of the Suez Canal. The Allies' only alternative supply route to the North African battlefields was around the Cape. Cape Town could not handle the entire shipping load alone now any better than it could in the Boer War. The Allies again took note of nearby Saldanha Bay. Before long, the presence of contractors, British military personnel, and engineers had strained Saldanha Bay's water supplies. A pipeline to the nearby Berg River was furnishing badly needed water by early 1943. Docks, oil storage tanks, anti-submarine boats, aircraft, a weather station, an airfield, minelayers, and a field telephone system all appeared quickly, swamping the countyside's ability to provide food to all the new area personnel.

The move paid off handsomely for the Allies, however, as more than 200 ships found safety at Saldanha Bay from submarine attack during 1942 alone. Convoys to Britain and the battle areas began forming there.

When the war ended, Saldanha stagnated, its population falling to 2,200 by 1965. Then in the mid-1970s, it became an export harbor for the steel industry based on the Western Cape's expanding iron mines at Sishen, about 500 miles away. By 1974 a steel mill was scheduled to go up there, a step likely to raise the area's population to 42,000 (Burman and Levin, 1974, 157). A dry dock, another railroad line, port expansion, and a new water-supply dam were also planned.

The first iron-ore train arrived at Saldanha on May 14, 1976, and the first ore-laden ship departed from its docks on September 27 of that year. Five years later, separate docks and storage areas were handling the Western Cape's copper, lead, and zinc.

"Saldanha, therefore, is in a state of flux. The pattern of growth, the way of life which has developed over three centuries, is on the point of changing dramatically" (Burman and Levin, 1974, 158).

BRAZIL'S NEW BOOMTOWNS

Desperate to reduce its dependence on imported oil, Brazil is turning more and more to its vast interior, rich in timber, numerous minerals, and perhaps even oil. For example, the Brazilian government, hoping to attract people and businesses to the Amazon basin (see Fig. 8.1 in Chapter 8), set up the Manaus Free Trade Zone in 1967. The act creating the Zone includes provisions for duty-free imports for its industries, exemptions from federal and state value-added taxes on its goods, and low interest loans. Businesses responded, as light industry followed merchants into the Zone. Suframa, the national agency overseeing the Zone, built a large industrial area east of Manaus, in which both Brazilian and foreign companies participate. Manaus itself has developed a skyline and a trained labor force, and its population has risen from 250,000 in 1967 to 600,000 in 1978 (Bareau, 1978, 154-155).

However, only the 6,200-square-mile area of the Zone itself is benefiting, at the expense of the vast Amazon basin itself. The basin's resource-extraction industries are losing skilled workers. To deal with this, the government will probably try to reward Zone firms that invest profits in the interior rather than take them out.

Other towns are sprouting in Brazil's vast jungle-covered interior. The forest near Santarem has been a gold prospector's mecca since the mid-1950s. The city was founded after the American Civil War by Confederates fleeing the occupying Union troops. Santarem's population was then about 5,000. The gold bug raised this to 30,000 in 1962, and about 150,000 in 1977 (McDowell, 1977, 20). The small city has all the boomtown headaches.

Illiteracy, disease and poverty abound. Naked children frolic outside palm-thatched huts and wooden shacks. . . . Women wash clothes in the Tapajos (river) or in nearby creeks. The 'sewage disposal' system remains the river and a squadron of . . . large, ugly vultures that perch defiantly on nearby rooftops . . . Distended human bellies still bespeak disease and malnutrition. (McDowell, 1977, 20)

Santarem is as isolated as any American gold camp; the closest communications media are 500 miles away. The town is nevertheless attracting doctors and other professionals. By 1977 it also had one paved street, four largely ignored traffic lights, and an up-to-date hotel and airport.

In few other places in the world is there more of a value conflict between residents and prospectors. Brazilians took little notice of the Amazon basin until the middle of this century. Now, its minerals are drawing new construction, the building of highways, and other forms of development to the area. In bringing the twentieth century to the area, these projects may be destroying an ancient culture:

Highways have sliced across Indian reservations, followed by swarms of settlers bringing disease and a frontier determination to displace 'aborigines' by any means necessary. . . .

The Transamazon Highway, the 3,100-mile stretch that parallels the Amazon River from the Andes to the Atlantic, has created serious social problems by giving rise to brawling, crime-ridden boom towns. The highway was a bold concept but it was also hastily and poorly planned. (McDowell, 1977, 20)

The story sounds identical to that of the American West a century ago, and there is little reason to suspect that the outcome in Brazil will be any different.

AUSTRALIA'S NEW METALS-MINING TOWNS

As Brazil has done, Australia is awakening—again —to its vast mineral riches. By 1980 its top 15 resource projects included seven metals extraction schemes scattered throughout the country.

Much of Australia's iron ore comes from Western and South Australia. Most new iron ore export projects involve new port construction and new towns, especially in the west (see Fig. 4.3 in Chapter 4).

Four . . . projects emerged in a large half-circle through the Pilbara. From east to west they were Goldsworthy, Mt. Newman, Mt. Tom Price and Robe River. The Mt. Goldsworthy project built a port near Port Hedland and towns at Mt. Goldsworthy and Shay Gap. The Mt. Newman project shares the new port at Port Hedland with Goldsworthy . . . [and] built the town of Newman. The Hamersley project built a port at Dampier . . . [and] towns at Mt. Tom Price and Paraburdoo. The Robe River project has a . . . town at Pannawonica. (Wilson, 1980, 205)

Australians extract their copper mostly at Queensland's Mt. Isa mine. New South Wales, Queensland, and Tasmania also produce lead, zinc, and silver. Australia has one-fifth of the world's bauxite reserves, much of which is in the Cape York Peninsula. Alumina production from bauxite is significant in Australia because its customers do not want the pollution problems involved in smelting. New plants in Australia, however, will "involve difficult questions of Aboriginal land rights and intrusion on Aboriginal society" (Wilson, 1980, 208).

Australia has had numerous "natural resource towns" (Wilson, 1980, 395), many of which died when their resource base dried up years ago. Others go through a brief boom in population and production, then employment stops rising as the provision of services and goods becomes more efficient. Most of the new natural resource towns, including Mt. Isa, Broken Hill, Pt. Pirie, and Kalgoorlie-Boulder, are now troubled by rising capital investment that reduces the need for workers. A large number of even smaller towns now exists, including nickel towns around Kalgoorlie, Pilbara iron ore towns in the northwest, and bauxite towns in the north. Some of these are so small that

the workers are flown in for a few weeks at a time, and then returned to the (nearby) capital city for a rest period. But some of the other centers with more permanent infrastructure have almost as high a turnover of labor and population. Levels of 100 percent turnover per annum are found in newer and smaller centers, while 50 percent is commonplace. (Wilson, 1980, 397)

This system raises worker transportation and settling and training costs for companies, and lowers work force morale. "Three adverse factors have been identified by social surveys—isolation, climate and a low level of provision of amenities and services. . . . Critics of the latest wave of settlement in the inland and north maintain that much of the process has been misconceived" (Wilson, 1980, 397). Since Australia's state governments are reluctant to build up the mine projects' infrastructure, each mining company ended up putting in its own towns.

Thus near Dampier in the Pibara, there are five separate jurisdictions and special-purpose urban units which could have been planned as a whole. This separate development deprived the centers of . . . economies of scale in the provision of services and amenities. . . . Three new towns may be developed in a radius of 30 kilometers at Yeelirrie, Mt. Keith and Leinster by separate mining companies. . . . In the current boom stage in the North and West, regional planning has been neglected. . . . The typical company mining town therefore exhibits social disequilibrium and high turnover—circulation without settlement—suggesting we have not yet found a strategy for permanent settlement of the north. (Wilson, 1980, 397-399)

When R. H. Arnot in 1974 attempted to show where Australian climate and soil conditions could support planned new towns, he realized that most of these areas were along the coast and largely in the east, where there already were large towns and cities. Nevertheless, the lure of precious metals will keep the Australian outback an active prospecting and boomtown region.

Kalgoorlie, for example, was founded in the 1890s gold rush. Nickel, however, kept the town going in the 1960s until the massive gold price run-up in the early 1980s. Since 1979 "the town . . . has gone gold-mad, and tourists are flocking in from all over Australia in the hope of becoming rich. Spurred by highly publicized finds of chunky nuggets, they are spending their vacations or weekends around this remote town looking for gold" (Kamm, 1980*a*, 2). The hotel and six new motels are jammed, as is Australia's "only open red-light district," as busy now as it was in the 1890s.

Another outback boomtown is Darwin, on the northern coast, so remote that it is closer to Indonesia than to any other sizable Australian city. Darwin has thrived despite its having been demolished twice, by the Japanese air force in World War II, and by a 1974 cyclone. Eighty percent of its residents are under 35 years of age. It is a classic modern boomtown, the heart of a huge mineral deposit. Its suicide, rape, and alcoholism levels are all above the national average. Drug addiction is also a problem. Darwin's remoteness makes almost all consumer goods very expensive. Miners come in from the nearby outback to spend their earnings, up to $800 a week. A former town official said that "They play hell when they come to town. The pub becomes home" (Kamm, 1980*b*, 10). So do the casino, hotels, motels, discotheques, and brothels.

If there are problems with the native aborigines on the Australian mainland, they are even more severe in the southwest Pacific islands where there is mining. An example is Bougainville Island, where a huge copper mine has thrust the society into modern times. The islanders, including the Nasioi living near the mine itself, had lived in ways unchanged since the Stone Age. Living in the island's southeast, the Nasioi remained out of contact with Western civilization until 1901. Australia took over the island in 1949, but cared little about enriching the lives of groups such as the Nasioi, either by educating their children or improving the techniques of their farmers.

It was in this climate of growing tension that the great copper project began in 1964.

Even if the representatives of the mining company had been aware of the existing social situation and had been prepared from the first to cope with it, they would have experienced difficulties in their dealings with the Nasioi. In fact, early contacts between company and villager were deeply flawed by ignorance on both sides, and the subsequent record of the company has been characterized by frantic efforts to fill the vast gaps in its knowledge of the local scene, and to reduce the social tension which the company inherited and further aggravated. (Morris and Ogan, 1972, 109)

Australia's Mining Ordinance, giving the government title to all mineral rights underground conflicted with age-old Nasioi ideas about land ownership. Australia's administrators overruled the majority of the Nasioi who opposed the mine.

Because their wishes had been ignored, many Nasioi today suffer . . . even greater feelings of intimidation, inadequacy to adjust to modern conditions, betrayal, and even fear for their physical and spiritual safety than they did in 1962, when some of them demanded a change of administration. (Morris and Ogan, 1972, 110)

Local landowners received as royalties only about 6 cents for every $100 of copper concentrate sold. Only upper level employees were eligible for married housing at the mine, and most native workers were young, single men. Like the majority of Nasioi, they lacked specific skills and education, and had never been gainfully employed. The mine was to pay compensation to villagers, but only a fraction of it was in cash, the remainder in goods or in village rebuilding efforts, and villagers were either unable or unwilling to put the cash into more development. Compensation was unevenly distributed, most of it going to natives near the mine and its ports. But the mine did generate a market for the natives' produce. The company also tried to start new Nasioi businesses, but the mine never benefited many villagers who had lost their farms.

Morris and Ogan (1972) offer substantial evidence of the mine's harmful social effects on the Nasioi. Although the Nasioi population in the 6- to 15-year old age group may have risen as much as 25 percent from 1964 to 1970, primary school population declined almost 20 percent, mainly because the social tension created a deteriorating attitude among the Nasioi toward Western-style education. Most of the new medical workers serve the "urban sector," not the mostly rural Nasioi. As in boomtowns everywhere,

the influx of single transient male workers to the [mine area] caused a sharp rise in vagrancy, prowling and burglary, and crimes associated with drunkenness. European construction and mining employees . . . can, and do, enter villages accessible by vehicle, offer liquor to Nasioi regardless of age or sex, and invite Nasioi girls on "picnics." "Wet canteens," operating under special regulations and free of licensing laws which govern hotels, exist in each of the mining and construction camps. Whole parties of village men drink to stupefaction in the canteens, then return to their homes where brawling and destruction of property invariably ensue. (Morris and Ogan, 1972, 116)

Few law enforcement agents serve Nasioi villages. The natives had apparently lost their respect for traditional forms of justice (based largely on fear of sorcery), and native dislike of European justice kept them away from the Australians.

Morris and Ogan concluded that

Development does not begin overnight, as with the discovery of a copper deposit, but may have a long history which shapes present conditions in a way incomprehensible to those unaware of that history. Development is not adequately described by the presentation of gross statistics totaling millions of dollars, but must be analyzed according to particular effects of those dollars at different social levels. Finally, . . . development in economic terms may involve social decline in various forms. It is the tragedy of the Nasioi that the economic benefits are not distributed in the same manner as the social costs. (Morris and Ogan, 1972, 118)

NOTES

1. The similarity to urban renewal or today's "gentrification process" is strikingly similar. Where were these poor evicted families to go? TVA advised "all public organizations that could and would help" (Davidson, 1948, 257), most often the assistant county agent of the affected area. Uprooted people more often that not resettled in areas near their former residences, even if their new land was not as fertile as their old farms.
2. These facilities include (1) a plant for gaseous diffusion for separation of uranium-235 from the more common U-238, (2) the Oak Ridge National Laboratories, working on reactor technology, chemical technology, and basic research in biology, chemistry, physics, and metallurgy, (3) the Oak Ridge Institute of Nuclear Studies, and (4) the Agricultural Research Laboratory, maintained by the University of Tennessee and by the federal Nuclear Regulatory Commission.
3. The town is named after Paraguay's President Alfredo Stroessner.

REFERENCES

Bareau, Peter, 1978, "Boom Town Depopulates the Jungle," *Euromoney,* July, pp. 154-155.

Burman, Jose, and Levin, Stephen, 1974, *The Saldanha Bay Story,* Human & Rousseau, Cape Town, South Africa.

Business Week, 1980, "The Energy Powerhouse Behind Australia's New Boom," June 2, pp. 40-46.

Carter, Jeff, 1971, *The New Frontier,* Angus & Robertson, Sydney, Australia.

Davidson, Donald, 1948, *The Tennessee* Vol. 2, *The New River,* Rinehart & Co., Inc., New York.

Govan, Gilbert E., and Livingood, James W., 1963, *The Chattanooga Country,* University of North Carolina Press, Chapel Hill, North Carolina.

Kamm, Henry, 1980a, "Gold-Rush Era is Revived in the Outback of Australia," *New York Times,* October 15, p. 2.

Kamm, Henry, 1980b, "At 'Top End' of Australia, a Raucous Frontier Town," *New York Times,* October 18, p. 10.

McDowell, Edwin, 1977, "Conquering the Amazon Jungle," *Wall Street Journal,* April 5, p. 20.

Morris, J., and Ogan, E., 1972, "A View From Bougainville," *Waigani Seminar,* The Australian National University, Canberra, Australia, 106-118.

Rushman, Gordon, 1976, "Towards New Cities in Australia," *Town Planning Review* **47**(1):4-25.

Schumacher, Edward, 1982, "Paraguay Town's Fortunes Ebb as Dam Rises," *New York Times,* November 14, p. 8.

Wilson, R. K., 1980, *Australia's Resources and Their Development,* University of Sydney, Department of Adult Education, Sydney, Australia.

PART III

THE NEW
ENERGY RUSH

14

Scotland and North Sea Oil

THE SCOTTISH OFFSHORE OIL INDUSTRY

Scotland's offshore oil industry hit full stride in the mid-1970s, and field production is expected to reach its peak by 1985 and end around the year 2000. Since the actual oil exploration and drilling occurs miles off Scotland's North Sea coast, residents are free of the fear of massive oil spills from the rigs themselves though not of the smaller ones that could come from the tankers. The structure of Scotland's oil industry, however, imposes its own burdens on these people.

I (Malamud, 1981, 18-22) would describe the basic elements of the Scottish offshore oil industry as: platform construction; on-shore processing, storage, and transportation; and auxiliary services (e.g., warehousing, ports, and administrative headquarters). Of these activities, it is the construction of concrete and steel platforms hundreds of feet tall that affects the neighboring towns most acutely.

Platform Construction

The major burden of the oil industry falls on towns chosen to be assembling yards for the huge exploration rigs and even more massive drilling platforms. Most offshore drilling worldwide occurs in relatively shallow water where there is fairly placid weather, such as on the Gulf of Mexico. The conventional steel platform is perfect for these conditions. Building sites for these structures require large, flat areas of land surrounding fairly shallow water. Dozens of sites on Scotland's east coast are suitable for steel platform construction (see Fig. 14.1).

The stormy North Sea, with waters up to 750 feet deep, required radical innovations in drilling platform design when exploration and production began in the 1970s. The result was the concrete platform, where construction sites need less land than those for steel structures, but must surround deep water protected from storms. The few suitable sites in northern Scotland are on the Atlantic coast, away

Figure 14.1
Major Scottish oil industry development sites (Malamud, 1981).

from the drilling sites to which the platforms must be towed. Northern Scotland's Atlantic coast is far more picturesque and isolated than its North Sea coast, a geographical accident that has caused several bitter controversies sweeping Scotland and its oil industry.

Onshore Processing, Storage, and Transportation

Oil and natural gas flow through underwater pipes to landfalls on Scotland's east coast after drilling. For instance, oil from the Forties offshore field flows to Cruden Bay, and gas from the Frigg field comes ashore at St. Fergus. Brent, Cormorant, and Ninian field oil flow into the Shetland Islands, north of the mainland. Although it is ecologically desirable to have as few landfalls as possible, the enormous expense of laying underwater pipe requires that the pipe from each field come ashore as close to that field as is feasible.

The gas coming ashore requires coastline processing plants to remove seawater and liquid impurities, but oil can flow directly to the refinery without pumping. Scotland's only refinery, which is at Grangemouth, is far too small to process all the North Sea oil. With no new refineries under construction as of 1980, Scotland must export most of its crude, requiring massive storage depots and tanker terminals. However, the British government's desire to refine two-thirds of the North Sea oil in Scotland makes such sites as Nigg Bay, Campbeltown, and Sullom Voe likely refinery locations.[1] The increasing size of oceangoing tankers forces construction of a few massive terminals. Because northern Scotland lies almost in the Arctic Ocean, these tankers need naturally sheltered harbors for year-round operation. All this makes siting terminals and their neighboring storage depots and tank fields as difficult as finding good locations for concrete platform construction yards.

Auxiliary Facilities

Oil exploration, drilling, piping, refining, storage, and tanker shipping require huge support industries. Ports must serve vessels supplying the offshore rigs. Airports must receive workers arriving from distant cities and be able to ferry them to the rigs—almost always by helicopter. Warehouses, shops, engineering, and administrative offices are also necessary. All forms of ground transportation to these coastal bases are needed, not just for people but for supplies going to the rigs and shore bases. This doesn't even include infrastructure and services that are necessary for workers and their families who live onshore or offshore.

OIL'S IMPACT ON THE SCOTTISH LABOR FORCE

Most northern Scots lack the engineering and craft-labor expertise required of the drilling rigs and in the supply base towns and platform-building yards. The oil industry utilizes hundreds of skilled workers from southern Scotland's industrial belt, which has been crippled by high unemployment. Workers there know that oil-related jobs will be lacking in that zone, and flock north. This benefits the oil industry in that it can employ already skilled southern Scots at the high British wage scale, which is cheaper than training unskilled northern Scots and having to pay them the same wages.

The Scottish oil industry also employs hundreds of outsiders, particulary salaried employees, in order to have the best skilled labor available but also to avoid the often unruly British unions.[2] Scottish drillers on the rigs very often take their orders from foreign supervisors. Scots do not even have the consolation of knowing that allowing a foreign-dominated industry to operate in their land will help their overall employment.[3] Moreover, the single largest group of employers are the platform building yards, where one large order can mean the difference between prosperity and depression for months.

THE SCOTTISH BOOMTOWN EXPERIENCE

Elsewhere I have discussed the problems affecting dozens of Scottish towns on both coasts in their adjustment to the sector of the oil industry assigned to them (Malamud, 1981, 26-53). Drumbuie, a hamlet with only 24 residents, became the center of Scotland's most bitter siting dispute, resolved in 1974 when the Secretary of State for Scotland rejected the construction plan. Many other construction yards were built on both coasts, however. It was clear that these small communities tempted fate by basing their whole economies on platform construction. By 1981, for example, Scotland's three major platform building yards at Nigg, Ardersier, and Loch Kishorn all had received many orders, kept their work force fairly stable, and the Loch Kishorn yard was expected to be the western Highlands' major employer. None of these yards, however, had received a single order from 1975 to 1977 (Scottish Economic Bulletin, Summer 1977, 6, and Fall, 1977, 50). The Portavadie yard, moreover, had yet to receive an order by early 1976, and the Ardyne Point yard had unused capacity then.

Neither oil and gas extraction nor gas purification onshore has created boomtown problems. Most of the oil and gas must go to tanker terminals and their storage depots for eventual export, since Scotland's only refinery, at Grangemouth, can process only a fraction of the North Sea crude. Intense opposition to new refineries scuttled three planned projects on the Clyde. Others were planned for Nigg on the Cromarty Firth, at Sullom Voe in the Shetland Islands, and at Flotta in the Orkney Islands.

The proposed Nigg refinery and terminal were expected to ease the burden that years of steel platform construction would have imposed on the nearby boomtowns. This explains the enthusiasm with which the area residents welcomed news of the planned refinery in 1975; they were anxious to retain the skilled-labor jobs that would otherwise have vanished when the platform work slackened off. The Secretary of State for Scotland approved the refinery proposal, adding stiff provisions requiring the oil companies to protect Nigg's well-being.

Cromarty Petroleum, owned by the American industrialist Daniel K. Ludwig, expected to create 900 permanent new jobs in the area, and assured the residents that heavy demand for the gasoline it intended to produce at Nigg assured the workers of continuous employment. By 1981 the British government appeared to have given its final approval for Nigg as one of three locations for its new refinery, although ground has yet to be broken for it.

Although construction of the Flotta terminal was going smoothly as of 1979, housing construction, pier, and shipping improvements were moving more slowly. The Orkneys are the site of the huge Royal Navy base at Scapa Flow. Its closure in 1957 had accustomed the residents to large industries coming and going. In 1972 the Orkney County Council began

to make a list of sites thought to be attractive to the oil industry, and of areas to be preserved. The Council passed a law enabling it to buy land, exercise port jurisdiction over some of its coastline, and enter into equity of the firms wanting to become involved in oil development. The Council purchased the Flotta terminal site from the industry and leased it back, requiring the companies to get its approval at all operating stages. The Flotta terminal was in full operation by 1981, and about to receive oil from Texaco's Tartan field (*Business Scotland,* 1981).

The Shetland Islands oil terminal at Sullom Voe offers a classic example of modern industry's first intrusion on an isolated rural community. Malamud describes the difficulties this remote region faced in adjusting to construction of a huge tanker terminal. (1981, 34-43).

The islanders were indifferent to 1969-1970 oil discoveries elsewhere in the North Sea and unaware of oil's future impact on their lifestyle. The Shetland County Council had never prepared a development plan and was unprepared for the tanker terminal, rig-servicing base, and gas-liquefaction plant that the industry announced it wanted to erect there. The Council's three development officers had to quickly draw up a plan, without much guidance from the industry, whose experts differed among themselves as to the Shetlands' role.

On October 17, 1972, the County Council approved an interim development plan, which

sought for the first time to provide a framework for planning control, to guide proposals for development throughout the islands and to identify priority areas for detailed work. . . . In each district it identified focal points for housing, services and industry. (Nicolson, 1975, 72)

The Council wanted to build up present industries and limit oil bases to as few new places as possible: Lerwick, Sullom Voe, Swarbacks Minn, and Baltasound, all of which were already developed to some extent. The Council knew that Sullom Voe, with deep water surrounded by ample flat land, was the likeliest site for the new tanker terminal, and wanted this to be the islands' only major oil development site. The Council also knew that the oil companies needed Sullom Voe more than the islanders needed the oil, and that they would not try to dominate the islanders.

After extensive negotiations between the Council and the oil companies, Britain's Parliament passed the 1974 Shetland County Council Act, giving the Council much that it had requested. The most important long-term aspect of the Act was its granting the Council's right to set up a reserve fund from oil income. This enables the local economy to prosper during the oil boom, and to avoid decline afterward. Follwing the Act's passage, the Council set up the Shetland Finance Company to borrow funds to build the Sullom Voe complex.

The Council was wise to insist on active participation in oil industry development activities. Even more than Drumbuie, the Shetland Islands had absolutely no infrastructure upon which to base industrial development. A terrible housing shortage and accompanying real estate inflation soon engulfed long-time residents and newcomers alike. The boom led to higher crime rates as natives found themselves in the midst of hordes of foreign workers. Shetland roads, not even accustomed to automobile traffic, now had to withstand the weight of huge trucks. The activities of the farming, fishing, fish processing, and textile industries may have declined as many of their workers defected to the oil companies.

The Shetlands offer vivid illustration of an oil boom's effect on the area's local economy. Oil pollution of the sea bottom, the unwillingness of tourists to visit formerly scenic areas, and the inevitable loss of labor by traditional industries have all affected the islands' economy. By the end of 1975, the islands had only 215 unemployed workers (Lewis and McNicoll, 1978, 122), but many non-oil jobs were going begging.

The islands' major future problem is that oil-spawned technology is not likely to be transferred to the more traditional industries, because of the "restricted nature of communication" between those in and out of the oil industry, and of the gap between the oil and non-oil industries themselves. These make it unlikely that the islands will be able to create any industries not tied to oil—a necessity for growth in the post-oil era.

Among several tiny communities near Sullom Voe that must bear the full brunt of the oil boom, one primary example is Graven (population under 30 residents), which was to be the center of a major industrial complex attached to the Sullom Voe terminal. Very small amounts of good farmland are nearby, but the complex must have plants for removing gas and seawater form the incoming crude oil. One proposed solution to the lack of flat land is to store much of the oil underground. The oil companies selected nine terminal sites: one for liquefied natural gas ships, one for small tankers, two for large tankers, and five for medium-sized vessels. Some oil will definitely be stored near Graven, but the townspeople run only a slight risk of having a nearby refinery, gas liquefaction plant, or petrochemical complex because of the companies' need to have these plants close to their markets. The Graven area will instead contain a power generating station, several small light-engineering firms, and the nearby port.

Towns such as Graven had to absorb at least 1,000 new permanent residents working at Sullom Voe, plus the same number of temporary construction workers. These towns also had to build schools, stores, houses, recreational centers, and supply the social and welfare services to almost 4,000 new residents. The islands' entire 1974 population was only 18,000, with just 2,000 in the Sullom Voe area. Malamud described the strains put on the socio-economic structures of these tiny towns, especially Brae, Mossbank, Voe, and Toft (Malamud, 1981, 41-43). None of the four villages had sufficient paved roads, drainage, telephones, electricity, water supply, and street lighting, all of which the oil boom will make essential.

Considering all this, the County Council came up with the April 1974 decision creating the Sullom Voe District Plan, which included water and gas separation plants, a liquefied natural gas plant, and a liquefied petroleum gas plant. Not wanting to create a new town for new residents, the council agreed to create "what could be at least a new village" (Malamud, 1981, 42) at Firth, near Toft. Firth was to have 350 new houses, Mossbank 250, Brae 275, and Voe 125. Since the oil was expected to begin flowing ashore by 1976, housing and other infrastructure for the first newcomers had to be ready by early 1975. Expanding the existing towns could be completed by 1976, but creating Firth probably had to wait until 1976 or 1977. This new town was to have a worker construction camp with housing and all services except health care for 600 to 1,200 workers.

The Shetland planners knew that they had to do more than upgrade the quantity of its infrastructure and service level. Quality improvements were also necessary. The local doctors had to become thoroughly familiar with occupational safety and health problems long familiar to their colleagues in industrial areas, and, in most of these areas, with diving-related health problems as well. The islands also needed health care professionals having specialties in a greater variety of areas.

By 1981 "the impact of oil development [was] widely felt nine years after oil reserves were found." Thousands of English, Scottish, and Irish workers had built a huge complex of pipelines and storage tanks. The traditional industries, especially knitwear, declined as sharply as they had been forecast to do years before. Despite these effects and the increase in pollution, "to this day, Shetlanders remain the model for other isolated peoples trying to resist the onslaught and blandishments of oil exploration" (Lee, 1980, 53), and the local economy is more robust than anyone imagined several years before that it would be. The Lerwick waterfront now has bustling workshops and docks.

The Sullom Voe oil terminal opened in May 1981, and was supposed to be in full operation by mid-1982. The terminal now receives 1.4 million barrels of crude every day, and handles as many as 20 oil tankers a week.

The trust fund is now so large that it supplies old-age pensioners with gifts beyond their normal payments from other sources. The fund money is also upgrading the fishing industry. The fund is expected to reach $100 million by the year 2000 (Rattner, 1982, A-2).

As of 1982, the council still kept ownership of the land beneath the oil facilities. The islands' population has hit 23,000, up from 18,000 in 1974. "The archipelago . . . went from having the highest proportion of residents in Britain over 50 to having the highest percentage below 30" (Rattner, 1982, A-2). Crime, alcoholism, and traffic accidents have predictably risen.

The problems confronting the east coast cities of Aberdeen and Peterhead as they became oil company service bases, combining industrial services (e.g., docks, vessel repair, warehouses) with administrative and engineering office building centers have been catalogued elsewhere (Malamud, 1981, 43-49). Before the oil boom began, Aberdeen was northern Scotland's largest city and transportation center, and it naturally became that area's oil capital when the boom began. As in the smaller boomtowns, Aberdeen had a hard time satisfying the demand the oil boom placed on housing, warehouse space, docks, and land near the docks needed for storage.

Today, most Aberdonians will probably claim that oil development has brought both benefits (mainly jobs) and problems, (mainly a housing shortage) to their city. Aberdeen faces the same problems of integrating its alien population that confront the smaller boomtowns (Malamud, 1981, 45-46). Also, Aberdeen and the other northern Scottish cities have primitive sewage treatment, so pollution will certainly worsen. The lack of laws requiring smokestacks to have smoke control devices and forcing power plants to have cooling towers further adds to the pollution.

By 1981 Aberdeen was "firmly established as the oil headquarters of Europe and the world's second most important oil city after Houston" (Moreton, v). [4] Offshore activity is anticipated to pick up during 1983, and almost 40 new oil or gas fields are expected to begin producing by 1991. A total of about 55 fields will be operating by 1991, compared to the 15 now producing. Of course, all these predictions will be pushed back unless the worst European economic depression in fifty years does not abate soon.

Even more than Aberdeen, Peterhead is considered a classic boomtown. The Peterhead area is involved in offshore servicing and is a major landfall for offshore piping. It has run into problems accepting petrochemical plants based on offshore gas coming ashore at nearby Cruden Bay. Residents object to the noise, the danger of gas leaks, and the gas odors. The local government is having trouble providing roads, drainage, and housing.

The oil boom helped revitalize the decrepit port. Peterhead is now a major warehouse and workshop base, serving rigs and sending supplies to pipelaying barges. Peterhead is also an office center, second in the area only to Aberdeen, guaranteeing a demand for white-collar jobs virtually unknown in Peterhead's history. The cost of living is relatively low, but the housing situation is as bad as anywhere else in Scotland. City leaders had been too conservative in anticipating Peterhead's housing needs, and ended up paying far more for land than they had to. The authorities have had problems finding areas within the city suitable for building. Peterhead's fishing industry started to decline around 1978, as did Aberdeen's, the victim of rising costs and increasing levels of fish imports. Many fishermen have been forced to take oil-related jobs.

The overall effect of the boom on Peterhead's economy has been good, but natives and newcomers have paid a price. There is little mixing between these two groups. Neither the young nor the old have enough recreational opportunities. Juvenile delinquency and most of the other boomtown syndrome problems have become major social concerns.

By 1980 Peterhead looked forward to an ever-expanding role in Scotland's oil boom. Two major firms—British Gas and Mobil—were given final approval in June 1980 to build the nearby St. Fergus terminal and a billion-dollar pipeline from the offshore fields, both of which will probably be completed by 1985. However, the area's remoteness from its markets probably rules out the construction of a petrochemical plant, and this will hamper the gas industry's contribution to Peterhead's growth.

While the oil boom has generally helped Peterhead, the city must deal with the future. As Scotland's classic boomtown, Peterhead will suffer after the oil boom ends, especially because it has failed to attract a diverse industrial base.

Some smaller Scottish cities have also become service bases, benefiting as Peterhead did from Aberdeen's inability to handle the oil industry's full demand for this type of service. Montrose and Dundee are two such cities. Dundee will probably emerge as an engineering center since it can't compete with Aberdeen as an exploration and development center. Dundee's southern location puts it much further from the oil fields than Aberdeen or Peterhead, and the city lacks a good airport. This didn't prevent Dundee from becoming Conoco's marine headquarters by 1979. Montrose has also grown slowly.

All these supply-base towns profited from the oil companies' tendency to build their own marine and land bases rather than share them. As the bases proliferate, they spread to more towns up and down the coast.

FINAL COMMENTS

The boomtown syndrome afflicts both large port cities and tiny, isolated rural hamlets. None of Scotland's boomtowns suffers form severe environmental damage, making compensation problems uncommon. Scotland also has a highly centralized government planning network, fostered by its close political ties to London, that would not be able to exist in a loosely knit federation such as the United States.

Americans, however, should examine the local planning agencies that the previous section revealed; a County Council, inadequately prepared as it may have been, learned to deal with each development plan. The most important person in Scotland's oil boom, the Secretary of State for Scotland, holds a position with no American equivalent. The Secretary's status as final arbiter kept the Scottish court system free of lengthy, bitter challenges to the various development plans while assuring outside groups their right to be heard.

The ties with London also pose problems for Scottish

planners. The Conservative government of Prime Minister Margaret Thatcher seems unaware of the effect its tight-money policies will have on the ability of local managers to build the infrastructure to meet this growth.

The future of Scotland's boomtowns may well rest more in Edinburgh than in London, however, after Scotland achieves more self-rule under so-called "devolution." The Scottish assembly will provide environmental protection and social services, while London will retain broad authority over North Sea oil. Local Scottish officials, however, will still be responsible for new infrastructure. This three-way split of authority over Scotland's oil industry will require extraordinary levels of cooperation and coordination of planning.

No amount of planning would have been able to reduce the economic and psychological traumas that Scottish boomtowns suffered. Future research should determine the manner in which these towns obtained funds to adjust to the oil boom, the permanent changes in their political structures, the postconstruction fate of boomtowns unsuited for refining or other operation-phase activities, and the extent to which natives and newcomers avoided value conflicts and mutual alienation. The social elements of Scotland's boomtown syndrome deserve intense future scrutiny.

NOTES

1. Even though most of the large North Sea fields are in Norwegian waters, sea-bed obstacles prevent the laying of pipe from Norway's fields to the Norwegian coast. This places an even heavier burden on Scotland to build storage depots and shipping terminals.
2. Nearly all the full-time offshore drillers are American, Norwegian, and Spanish. Dutch, German, and Norwegian companies build nearly all the rigs. Once they are in place, American firms, with years of experience in the Gulf of Mexico,

lay most of the pipe, which is made of Japanese steel, and they supervise most of the drilling.
3. In 1976 the oil industry employed only 14,000 workers, many of them foreign, in a part of Britain having 134,000 unemployed workers (Jones and Godwin, 1976, 20).
4. In 1980 about 3,000 new jobs were created in Aberdeen, versus some 1,000 in 1979.

REFERENCES

Baldwin, P. L., and Baldwin, M. F., 1975, *Onshore Planning for Offshore Oil,* The Conservation Foundation, Washington, D. C.

British Business, 1981, May 8-14, vol. 5 (2).

Business Scotland, 1979, "Long-term Kishorn," December, **23**(12):15.

Business Scotland, 1981, "Texaco Tartan Oil Comes on Flow," February, **25**(2):7.

Jones, Mervyn, and Godwin, Fay, 1976, *The Oil Rush,* Quartet Books, London, England.

Jordan, Philip, 1979, "Oil and the Men," *The Guardian,* September 19.

Lee, John, 1980, "Shetlanders Keep Their Cool in an Oil Boom," *U.S. News and World Report,* May 5, pp. 50-53.

Lewis, T. M., and McNicoll, I. H., 1978, *North Sea Oil and Scotland's Economic Prospects,* Croom Helm, London, England.

Malamud, Gary, 1981, "A Comprehensive Solution to the Boomtown Syndrome," master's thesis, New York University.

McDonald, Murdoch, 1980, "Optimism in the Highlands," *Business Scotland* **24**(10):13-14.

Moreton, Anthony, 1980, "Basking in New Prosperity," *Financial Times Survey,* December 10, p. v.

Moreton, Anthony, 1980, "Europe's Oil City Likely to Expand," *Financial Times Survey,* December 10, p. v.

Nicolson, J. R., 1975, *Shetland and Oil,* W. Luscombe Publisher, Ltd., London, England.

Rattner, Steven, 1982, "Oil Boom Brings Cash and Crime to Shetland Islands," *New York Times,* January 4, p. A-2.

Scottish Economic Bulletin, Summer 1977, **12**:6.

Scottish Economic Bulletin, Fall 1977, **13**:50.

Turnock, David, 1979, *The New Scotland,* David and Charles Publishers, Ltd., Newton Abbot, Great Britain.

van der Vat, Dan, 1978, "Aspects of Oil, 3: Effect on Scotland's Infrastructure," *Times,* October 5.

15

American and Canadian Energy Boomtowns

Scotland may be in its first energy boom, but many areas of the United States and Canada have seen it happen before. Previous chapters discuss the old gold-rush and silver mining ghost towns that litter the Western landscape. Today, some Colorado towns sit atop radioactive tailings from the uranium mines that spawned these communities.

OPEC, of course, is responsible for these areas' recent revival. The new synthetic fuels and shale oil industries (if they ever pick up) will put enormous pressure on the western Rocky Mountains' water supply, while open-pit mining on an unprecedented scale will set environmentalists, ranchers, and farmers against energy developers and those residents who will profit from the boom. Unlike Scotland, western North America lacks the centralized planning necessary to impose decisions and deadlines without lengthy court fights.

In Scotland, land was never the central issue; offshore oil, not coal, is the principal source of the energy boom. All projects planned for the western United States and Canada involve direct environmental degradation, from air pollution to acid runoff into streams, to the scarring of vast tracts of land. Compensation assumes critical importance there.

ROCKY MOUNTAIN BOOMTOWNS

The federal government owns 80 percent of the resources of the Rocky Mountains and 50 percent of their land; it is also the largest employer in the area and controls the use of most of its resources, especially water. While the region's residents resent Federal control, the $20 billion in federal aid (as of December 1980), in land and forest management and in aid to farmers, exceeded the $14 billion in federal taxes those residents paid.

The oil-and gas-rich Overthrust Belt extends from Montana to Arizona along the western slopes of the Rockies. Montana and Wyoming are the richest states in coal to be strip mined, while northwest Colorado, southwest Wyoming, and northeast Utah have kerogenladen marl limestone (shale oil). Unlike drilling for North Sea oil, the extraction of these resources will involve considerable disruption of land. Almost the entire American energy boom of the next 20 years will occur in this pristine region (see Fig. 15.1).

Colorado's West Slope region has huge reserves of coal and shale oil, so most of the state's boomtowns are in this isolated area, west of Colorado's major cities and tourist resorts. If Exxon were ever to build its once-planned 150 shale oil plants in the West Slope, Rio Blanco and Garfield Counties could experience population increases from 755,000 to 1.5 million residents (Kelly, 1980, 37).

Craig (Moffat County) and Carbondale (Garfield County) are two such boom communities (see Malamud, 1981, 60-62 for a detailed account). To deal with its housing problem, Carbondale made up a Comprehensive Plan, which zoned 140 acres for largely detached-housing development, 280 acres for medium-density housing, and 95 acres for high-density dwellings. These zones were to accommodate 500 units (for 2,000 people) in low-density areas and 1,150 units (for 3,000 residents) in the high-density areas. The town, however, found it difficult to persuade the housing industry to build and borrow in an area of high costs and uncertain demand, and to assist local banks in obtaining money to lend.

Carbondale also intended to expand and improve its water supply and sewage systems, but had difficulty obtaining the funds for these capital projects because the tax revenue to cover their costs wasn't going to arrive until years later.[1] Colorado had no law requiring energy firms to provide funds, so Carbondale urged the firms operating there to do so. Even if it received the funds, the townspeople knew that more sources of money were necessary, especially to deal with the even larger expansion due in the late 1970s and early 1980s.

In Craig, the pressures and frustrations of dealing with the boomtown syndrome led to resignations of the city engineer, water superintendent, city clerk, police chief, and mayor. As town revenues lagged behind population growth and the need for capital

spending, the quality of life declined. All the energy projects causing Craig's boom lay outside the community's jurisdiction and paid no property tax to Craig itself.

Some other Colorado boomtowns are Rangely and Meeker (near oil shale areas), Paonia and Somerset (near deep coal mines), and Ridgely. In all of them, as always, housing posed the worst problem. Occidental Petroleum, however, agreed in 1979 to pay Meeker two years' advanced rent on an apartment building to house its workers. Ridgely's 1976 population was 1,900, but more than 9,000 were expected by the late 1970s. Water, sewage, and school services were all inadequate. Meeker's population had doubled between 1970 and 1977, and the energy firms had lured away many old-time workers from other industries. Surrounding Rio Blanco County wanted development confined to areas within three miles of Rangely and Meeker. Paonia is in Delta County, where most residents working in Gunnison County's coal mines live. While Colorado law allowed tax revenue sharing between two such counties, nothing requires it. Paonia's town services, as in most boomtowns, were operating nearly at 100 percent capacity.

In the future, many other Colorado towns will grow quickly if energy development on a massive scale occurs there. None of them can afford preboom infrastructure construction by themselves. Colorado's boomtown problem is so widespread that the state developed a list of impacted communities (Malamud, 1981, 63-65).

After a long economic depression and substantial population losses, Wyoming's personal income soared by 25 percent from 1974 to 1976 (Slocum, 1977, 1). The state is a center for coal, uranium, and soda ash mining, which helped Wyoming achieve the country's second lowest unemployment rate in September 1977.

Many Westerners familiar with boomtowns call this phenomenon the "Gillette syndrome." Gillette and Rock Springs, another classic energy boomtown, lie within the sections of Wyoming expected to be most heavily affected in the energy boom of the 1980s. (See Malamud, 1981, 65-67, for a detailed description.)

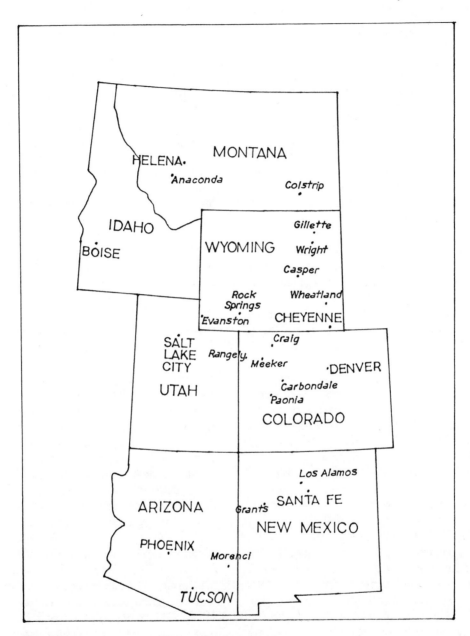

Figure 15.1
The new energy-boomtowns of the Rocky Mountains.

Wheatland, Wyoming, a town near a new coal-fired power plant, had about 2,500 residents in 1976, 5,000 in 1977, and an estimated 9,000 in 1980. It borrowed $3 million for sewage treatment, electricity, and other vital services. The utilities operating the plant run an "Impact Alleviation" office, and are providing a park for about 500 trailers, are investing $100,000 annually in a human services team, and are involved in other planning efforts to deal with family conflicts, drug and alcohol problems, child abuse, and other social problems. But one of Wheatland's problems was that many ranchers were not willing to sell or lease their land, even though the cattle business was slumping in 1977.

Evanston is another Wyoming oil boomtown. Workers by the hundreds live in trailers and tents. Amoco and Chevron were building two gas processing plants nearby in late 1980. Evanston's population was 4,460 in 1975 and was expected to be 15,000 by 1985, according to a 1980 estimate (Kelly, 1980, 38). Motels and stores were booming, but raw sewage was flushing into a nearby river. The town's crime rate doubled in one year, thanks to barroom brawls, burglaries, and family violence. School enrollment went up 20 percent in one year. Amoco and Chevron contributed $1 million to the schools, but the town used the money up long ago for buses and classrooms. The town soon had traffic jams along torn-up roads. Even a vacated chicken coop became somebody's home. As in every boomtown, housing is probably the town's most urgent need, with hundreds of residents on the waiting list for trailers.

One large Wyoming city affected by the energy boom is Casper, whose 1972 population of 39,000 has soared to 51,000 (*New York Times*, 1982). A stagnant 1 percent annual growth rate in the 1960s has become 6 percent since 1974. Observers expect surrounding Natrona County's population to double by 2,000. The city has become wary of people arriving whom it does not expect to stay long. Even so, the air is crystal clear and there is room for more people. Although the job picture for women has improved, "life continues to be dominated by a traditional Western concern for male prerogatives." Signs of downtown decline have begun to appear as suburbs expand. Casper has the normal boomtown problem of inadequate infrastructure. "Calls to the sheriff's office have risen more than twice as fast as the population since 1974" (*New York Times*, 1982). Overall city spending has gone up 3½ times in that period, and the school budget rose almost 60 percent in 2 years. Portable classrooms are in use, but a student increase is still to come from young couples recently settled in Casper. Since 1978 average rental housing costs have doubled and the vacancy rate is down to 1 percent, not much different from that in apartment-starved New York City.

Coal development could raise Montana's population from 700,000 to one million, but the employment situation of Montanans will not improve much because the capital-intensity of high-technology synfuels and mining operations will require out-of-state engineers and skilled workers. This was the same irony that northern Scotland faced. While most Montanans live in the western part of the state, the coal is on the eastern side. The urgent task for Montanans, if there is ever an overriding need for their coal, is to renegotiate the coal-related land leases for more money. The state should determine the desirability of encouraging large-scale coal mining. Much of eastern Montana's coal lies underneath Indian-owned land. The state should determine the best manner in which to reimburse the Indians for land leased for mining, but persuading the Crow to give up their land will be very difficult. One of their chiefs states that the Indians, in turn, should enact land use, zoning, and tax laws.

New Mexico's best-known boomtown is Grants, center of a uranium mining region. The population increase from 9,000 in 1975 to 14,000 in 1979 accompanied a doubling of the crime rate from 1970 to 1979. Then the uranium industry collapsed in 1980. "Dozens of companies and thousands of jobs have evaporated," with Grants especially hard hit (*Changing Times*, 1982, 36-38). In a year, Grants' school population declined by 500 students from the 1980 level, a sure sign that many suddenly jobless miners had pulled out (Schmidt, 1981, 1). Grants today remains depressed, a victim of the declining demand for uranium, seen in the decline of its price from $40 to $23 a pound in a year.

One-third of the uranium workers in the New Mexico-Wyoming-Colorado area were out of work by 1982. Not even a rapid buildup of American nuclear power plant construction will help quickly, since uranium supply now far exceeds the demand. Facing these bleak facts, Grants' leaders are "scrambling in a belated effort to attract new industry and employers and they hope to break the painful cycle of boom and bust that has marked the history of so many Western towns that have become too dependent on a single mineral resource" (Schmidt, 1981, A-16). Despite these efforts, "the town is reeling" for the third time in 30 years from reduced uranium demand. Ten years ago Grants had many expanding businesses, but Grants today contains many empty stores, and apartments and houses for sale.

The area around Grants is reeling, too. Twenty-five New Mexico mines have recently closed, and almost half the state's peak of 7,000 uranium workers are jobless. Poor planning is to blame for part of this desperate situation: "Both the Federal Government and the uranium industry anticipated a much higher demand in the latter part of the 1970s than proved to be the case" (Schmidt, 1981, A-16).

The energy rush has also returned to areas not far from the Rockies, such as southwestern Oklahoma. Towns such as Elk City and Hammon in the state's oil and gas belt have become typical boomtowns in the 1980s with all their value conflicts and strained infrastructures. Hardscrabble or marginal landowners and farmers have become wealthy overnight, but most unskilled workers face higher joblessness. (Padilla, 1982, 31).

Throughout the Rockies, state governments, landowners, and environmentalists oppose federal control of the area's energy development. In 1976 private industry planned to spend $60 billion in 15 years on coal mines, power plants, synthetic fuel plants, coal slurry pipelines, and power transmission lines. Residents, afraid of development they know they cannot

stop, want to control its pace. The level of residential distrust of the boom depends on the benefits they will derive. Arizona and New Mexico, with their large cities and depressed, undiversified economies welcome the boom more than Wyoming and Montana. Large Western cities such as Denver, Salt Lake City, Billings, and Casper will benefit, much as Aberdeen has, as centers for the energy firms' headquarters, but rural areas will suffer as they did in Scotland. Nature unkindly placed all these precious resources far away from areas destined to become population centers; without more careful planning, boomtown growth is inevitable when large numbers of people invade remote, energy-rich rural areas.

HOUSTON—AMERICA'S MOST SPECTACULAR OIL BOOMTOWN

Probably no other major city has come to symbolize oil-induced breakneck growth as Houston has. It is today the unquestioned leader of the Sunbelt boom, despite a recent slowdown in growth.

Houston has gone through three distinct periods of growth. From its founding in 1836 until 1875, it was a frontier town. Houston was "conceived for land speculation, its site chosen in part through logic and in part through chance, with the unusual advantage of being a political focal point . . . " (McComb, 1969, 18). But the bad weather, mud, sickness, discomfort, and perhaps the desire for fresh land speculation ended Houston's brief role as capital of Texas. The frontier town thrived as a trading center, and relied heavily on its connection to Galveston and the open sea via Buffalo Bayou, one of the area's few deep rivers. Local farm products went to Houston, then to Galveston for shipment. Even the trading activity stopped in May and did not pick up again until Houston's torrid summer ended in September. Roads were so bad year-round that floods and mud obstructed wagon travel into Houston whenever dust did not.

The railroad was the obvious answer to Houston's problems. When the Civil War began, Houston was developing into southern Texas' major rail junction. By 1873 Houston was tied to the now nationwide rail network. The Bayou, however, was even then usable only by small, shallow-draft boats. Houstonians then began earnestly considering a deep-water channel big enough for oceangoing ships, much as Los Angeles' leaders would shortly build a port from scratch. A 6-foot-deep, 100-foot-wide channel opened up on the dredged bayou in 1876. By now, Houston was also hooked up to Western Union's nationwide telegraph system. Around this time, Houston's first banks opened. The setting up of the Houston Board of Trade and the Cotton Exchange completed Houston's transformation into a "commercial emporium."

In it early days, Houston could rival the worst of frontier communities in flagrant drunkenness, gambling, prostitution, thievery and violent death. . . . As time went by, the city government, police and society managed to suppress extreme lawlessness, but crime and vice continued in Houston, a part of life as in other communities. (McComb, 1969, 65)

Police protection remained inadequate until after the Civil War, as did sanitation and medical care. The high humidity, poor drainage, and the abundance of insects—especially mosquitoes—all led to many epidemics from 1839 to 1867, mostly of yellow fever. Strict quarantining reduced the problem substantially. By 1875 Houston had become more sophisticated.

Houston then grew rapidly during an era of transition, spanning the years 1875 to 1930. Business now became less trade-oriented, but trade in cotton, oil, and lumber still were most important. The channel was widened several times so that Houston was already America's eighth largest port—years before anyone knew about oil in Texas. The channel and the railroads were fully developed by 1930, but the road system was not.

As late as 1882, however, "Houston amounted to 'a huddle of houses arranged on unoccupied lines of black mud' " (McComb, 1969, 100). Not until the automobile age did Houstonians consider it important enough to pave their streets. When the auto arrived, Houston adopted it as fervently—and drove out an

extensive interurban trolley system just as quickly—as Los Angeles did.

When drillers struck oil at Spindletop in 1901, Houston found itself in the middle of a rapidly expanding oil production region. When the Humble field opened up near Houston, the city became the center of a pipeline network. From 1905 to 1930, fields throughout southeast Texas (see Fig. 4.2 in Chapter 4) began producing. The Houston area, safe from Gulf of Mexico storms, proved the perfect place to set up refineries, eight of which lined the ship channel by 1930. The oil industry in turn brought more than 50 businesses to the channel. Banking activity, of course, rose to finance this development. Houston was the twenty-sixth largest American city in 1930, with more than 290,000 residents (McComb, 1969, 122), but its most expansive growth lay ahead.

Throughout this transition period, Houston suffered from inadequate water supply and other city services. Not until 1887 did Houston find pure water in artesian wells to replace polluted Bayou water. The Bayou has been filthy ever since, and the city does little to clean it. The city had to buy a privately-owned water works before Houston was assured of large amounts of sufficiently pure drinking water.

Almost from the beginning, Houston suffered from a lack of planning in the city government. In 1892 it was still "an overgrown, dirty village, seemingly blundering along without any policy or defined government of management . . . the most dirty, slovenly, go-as-you-please, vagabond appearing city of which I have knowledge" (McComb, 1969, 137), to one resident. Although the city bought several acres for a park in 1899, it is today all but inaccessible since it is cut off from potential users by freeways, the bayou, and downtown skyscrapers, and has limited parking space. By 1900 residents were becoming aware of the city's poor appearance. In 1911 the electric utility began putting its lines underground, following the examples of the telephone and firefighting services. But the lack of funds and the opposition of developers continued to stifle effective zoning and planning.

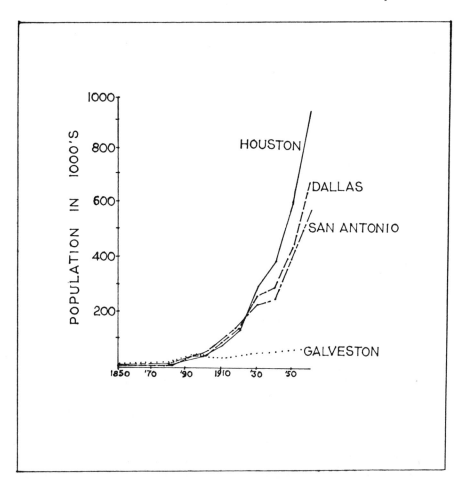

Figure 15.2
How Houston has outpaced fast-growing Texas rivals (McComb, 1969).

Houston's most rapid growth has occurred since 1930, with the population having reached one million in 1960; Figure 15.2 shows that Dallas and San Antonio, try as they might, have failed to keep up.

The diversity of local industry and the ability of Houston's leaders to bring in federal grants helped the city weather the Depression reasonably well. World War II brought major improvements to Houston's port, making it second only to New York by 1948. By now, Houston was also a key air traffic center. Its roads, however, continued to lag. Houston began upgrading its street system, traffic signals, and freeways to encourage passenger car traffic. Houston in the 1960s had become as sprawling a city as Los Angeles, but "the fact that there exists a practical limit to the number of automobiles that can travel to a central point at the same moment, and that a vehicle of public transportation, such as a bus, can move more people and occupy less room, has never been recognized in city policy" (McComb, 1969, 179). The rising number of cars has forced buses to slow down, making them even less attractive to residents.

Houston became a petrochemical industry center and headquarters for much of the natural gas industry in the 1940s, during which its population grew 54 percent. Houston in 1948 was America's fastest growing city. The war, which gave a boost to industry along the ship channel and elsewhere in the city, had much to do with this. This growth was almost totally unplanned. A French journalist reported in 1962 that "there is no plan. I am horrified. Everyone is doing just as he pleases, building here and building there. . . . Houston is spreading like a spilled bucket of water. If something isn't done about it quickly, it will be horrible, horrible" (McComb, 1969, 299).

There is a reason for Houstonians' seemingly uncaring attitude about the nature of their town:

Through Houston's modern civic and social history seeps a pervasive conservatism, reflected to varying degrees in politics, public schools, and reactions to urban problems. It is the conservatism of a nineteenth-century robber baron—exploitative, laissez-faire, and at times generous in philanthropy. Its roots lie in the Southern heritage of the town, the expansive, opportunistic nature of the area, and the strong business orientation of the economy. It gives to the people a certain bold, reckless, stubborn, independent, and sometimes lawless attitude, which means that the conservatism both helps and hinders the development of the city. (McComb, 1969, 206)

Houston's infrastructural development has only been hindered. It has been unable to deal with the severe flooding and land sinking that comes with its location on the bayou. The city has found new sources of fresh water, but it never cleaned up the polluted bayous. Despite cleanup efforts, the city's sewage treatment system has not operated effectively. Buffalo Bayou water contained not only sewage but bacteria and viruses.

The city's police department was as understaffed and undertrained from the 1940s through the 1960s as its pollution control staff, and it has recently been embroiled in many brutality lawsuits. Houston's police force may be as embattled in 1983 as it has ever been. Even the new police chief, Lee P. Brown, called the department "understaffed, ill-equipped, . . . plagued by attrition and morale problems, regarded . . . as

'discourteous and disrespectful,' slow to respond to calls and prone to racial slurs" (King, 1983, A-8). He also described a poor management structure that rendered the police incapable of fighting a spectacular increase in street crime since 1970. There also are just too few officers: 1.9 to every 1,000 residents versus 5.8 in Washington, D. C., and 3.3 in cash-starved New York (excluding the large transit police force there).

Planning is still almost nonexistent, but McComb claimed that Houston need not have sacrificed urban planning to achieve its phenomenal growth. "Fourteen other places in the United States, all zoned, enjoyed a much faster rate of expansion between 1920 and 1960" (McComb, 1969, 220). Although some developers and industrial groups have practiced zoning (e.g., in locating heavy industry on the Ship Channel and away from downtown), the city government has shown little interest in parks, housing projects, and slum clearance beyond the Civic Center areas.

Houston is not just a case of conservative office-holders indifferent to public wishes. The public itself wants it that way. A city unwilling to support a large public hospital system found it easy to spend money on the fine arts and for lavish, entertaining spectacles, such as the gaudy Astrodome.

The 1980 census showed Houston to have 1.6 million residents.[2] Yet Houston still has no conventional zoning laws, and it still has to grapple with perhaps the nation's worst urban traffic problems.

Morning and evening rush hour in Houston, particularly when summer temperatures reach 110 degrees and higher, is considered the worst in the country. . . . A number of factors contribute to the traffic problems, not least of which is growth that overwhelms services of all kinds and exceeds the city's ability to build roads fast enough. Moreover Houston, like Los Angeles, is growing out, not up, further increasing the load on roads.

These problems have been rendered nearly insoluble . . . by a failure to control development that often made it impossible to extend or widen streets. (King, 1982, A-12)

Recent developments may yet prove McComb wrong. Houston recently elected a (relatively) reform-minded mayor, Kathryn Whitmire. Part of her campaign dealt with Houston's chaotic infrastructure and inattention to planning. In 1982 the city council passed ordinances to stop developers from "hemming in highways with skyscrapers and cutting off streets with shopping centers . . . a dramatic shift from the past attitude that a landowner could do as he pleased with his property" (King, 1982, A-12). New rules require city blocks to be less than 1,400 feet long, to avoid the cutting off of through traffic. All development must now get Planning Commission approval. The laws also extend Houston's jurisdiction over development to five miles outside its borders.

A Boston planner first mentioned a zoning plan in 1913. This, plus other proposed ordinances in 1929, 1938, 1948, and 1962 were all defeated by the conservatism of residents plus developer opposition. It will be up to Mayor Whitmire to try to keep alive Houston's fledgling awareness of urban planning. She may have an unexpected ally: the slowdown of the rapid growth that has helped Houstonians equate chaos with prosperity. After 30 years of "furious" growth, Houston's economy has begun to slow down, victim of the worldwide oil glut and recession. Hard times will expose Houston's (and Texas's) lack of a comprehensive public assistance program and may reduce the willingness of outsiders to continue to flood into the city.

THE CANADIAN ENERGY BOOMTOWN EXPERIENCE

Canada is undergoing an energy and resources boom as massive as America's. Canada, too, has seen it all before, in towns such as Whitehorse, Yukon Territory (gold mining), Sudbury, Ontario (nickel), and Asbestos, Quebec. Robinson (1979, 55) provided an estimate of 190 resource towns in Canada today, with a total of about 700,000 residents.

Studying the development of resource towns, Stelter and Artibise (1978, 7-16) looked at the changing philosophy underlying Canadian boomtown con-

struction, and remarked that these towns "continue to be a product of past decisions." Canadian boomtowns are not much different from those elsewhere. Each revolves around an industrial project going back to early mining days. Town development usually went uncontrolled, and town welfare considerations always received low priority relative to those of production. The towns' fate always depended on the availability of markets for the commodity they produced.

Canadian boomtowns had weak and small middle classes, confined to some professionals and merchants; the distance from major markets, high development costs, and the resource industry's high wages hampered new industrial formation. Most boomtowns looked ramshackle and poorly built. Some boomtowns drew populations from neighboring cities (with native labor forces and outside management), while others had wholly alien populations. Service and supply towns originated from a group of decisions by more than one firm, while company towns depended on one industry. Some service-supply towns were originally boomtowns. Resource towns built before 1920 were privately planned and unregulated. Urban reformers inspired the design of towns built between 1920 and 1940. Proven practices in Britain and the United States and the expectation of provincial government involvement and even coplanning by the governments and industry contributed to towns designed after 1945. Robinson (1979, 56-58) cited 48 resource towns built from 1945 to 1958, and 19 from 1958 to 1971. The provincial government developed Elliot Lake, Ontario, to serve the workers of several mining firms. However, too many of these northern mining towns resemble the suburbs of Toronto or Montreal. The center of a well-designed mining town must be under one roof for easy communications during the long, dreary winters. Multifamily housing is essential for the same reason.

Working against careful design of resource towns is their limited expected lifetime. Even for those lasting a long time, the boom-bust cycle plagues planners. Sudbury is a classic boom-bust town. "Without a more comprehensive approach to planning in the area of resource management, resource towns will continue to be the most unstable and precarious of Canadian communities" (Stelter and Artibise, 1978, 15).

Robinson (1979, 61-64) showed ways in which planners can help lengthen the life of these communities before they even exist. "Practice has been to locate the town site next to the plant site," leading to creation of numerous but tiny hamlets much too small to develop the public infrastructure necessary to keep new residents reasonably content. A better idea, that was used in designing Elliot Lake, is a central town near several resource development sites. (Fort McMurray, Alberta, in the heart of the tar-sands belt, was designed this way.) Often it may be still better to expand an already existing town, as occurred in Lanigan, Saskatchewan, and Drayton Valley, Alberta (Robinson, 1979, 62). Robinson made clear, however, that "the type of new resource town to be built and, in turn, its most appropriate location, should be determined only in conjunction with a regional plan of settlement" (p. 63), determined at the provincial level. He also discussed the new towns' financing problems, described in Chapter 1 of this book.

Concern about rapid energy development is not limited to the Canadian north or west. Leaders of Newfoundland province are afraid that exploitation of the massive Hibernia offshore oilfield will create social problems and affect the province's lucrative fishing industry. These officials want to see drilling occur slowly. Newfoundland's energy laws are tougher than Canada's federal laws, and Newfoundland insists that it, not Ottawa, owns the oil and will determine the pace of its exploitation. Ottawa disagrees as to whether NewFoundland or Canada owns the oil while it lies underwater, but both levels of government agree that the province owns the oil once it comes ashore. Since the oil can be drilled only as rapidly as it is processed or stored onshore, the province will have the last word about the severity of boomtown development in its communities. Scotland does not have such an enviable position versus the British government.

Pending a return to relative prosperity, the tar sands

areas of northeastern Alberta province will boom just as explosively as the Colorado and Wyoming Rockies (see Fig. 15.3). In the heart of the tar sands belt is Fort McMurray, the region's largest permanent settlement. During most of the century, its population stayed at several hundred. Since 1965 the town has grown rapidly, much faster in fact than Yellowknife or Whitehorse, two far northern Canadian capitals, and Grande Prairie, a service center in western Alberta (see Figs. 15.3 and 15.4). Fort McMurray's population is much more heterogeneous than that of a stereotyped boomtown, and is not dominated by young, male, single adults and transients.

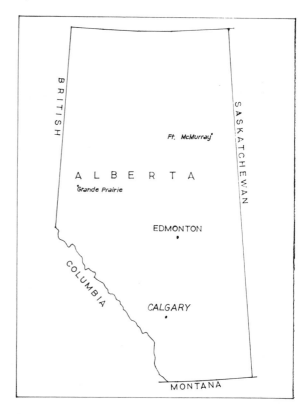

Figure 15.3
Alberta's booming communities (Fitzgerald, 1978).

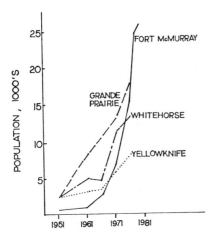

Figure 15.4
Rapid growth in the Canadian Rockies (Fitzgerald, 1978).

For decades, the population swelled and receded with each of the "boom" periods of oil sand development. Suddenly, in the early 1960s, the fluctuation stopped and the growth curve has gone up steadily ever since. In November of 1962, it became clear that the coming influx of population could not be handled by the town under the provision of the Town and Village Act of Alberta. A 1956 "New Towns Act" came to the rescue, providing the means to finance the sudden growth of demands on municipal services. As a New Town, which Fort McMurray became in 1964, the Board of Administrators of the town could borrow from the province for sewers, streets, water supply and related service funding. (Fitzgerald, 1978, 198)

Only one company is involved with mining there. Alberta's New Town policy enabled Great Canadian Oil Sands to place one of its officials on the town's board of administration, helping company and community work together on housing construction by the firm and extension of services by the town. A national credit agency helped the company work out mortgages for its employee-residents.

Those waiting for homes were billeted in the town's ever-growing trailer court developments. . . . As housing was made available to those already waiting, others moved into the trailers, and the temporary community continued to expand. Trailer courts are still very much in evidence in Fort McMurray, a sign of constant expansion. (Fitzgerald, 1978, 199)

By the end of 1964, the town had 1,804 people, a figure that grew to 6,847 by 1971 and shot up to 16,000 in 1975. The town was forecast to have 30,000 residents by 1980, but the recession, at least as bad in Canada as in the United States, may have delayed that milestone. A new project was to be responsible for much of this growth.

While most technical and management people were imported, the native populations were doing much of the work, and their unemployment rate plummeted.

New schools have been built and are being planned, hospital facilities are being increased, social organizations are being created . . . [and now the town has dealings with two nearby colleges. A new highway now reaches Edmonton. While Fort McMurray] is certainly in for more and more expansion, [it] occupies a peninsula . . . [suggesting] that the town is limited in the amount of growth it can accommodate. . . . The dilemma facing planners who take up the challenge to provide more room for more people is one directly related to . . . the oil sands. So much of the Athabasca valley area is underlain by rich oil sands . . . that it would be folly to block future resource development by construction of new towns. There will have to be very serious study to determine which sections of the highly valuable real estate can be given over to land development. (Fitzgerald, 1978)

Few boomtown investigations have been as thorough as an Alberta study of Fort McMurray society. Based on a June 1979 structured interview survey of 430 adult residents, the "Study of Human Adjustment in Fort McMurray" concluded that

Fort McMurray in 1979 only partially resembles the stereotype of fast growing resource towns. It does not appear to be a "high rolling," problem-ridden, grossly under-serviced community. . . . In some ways, however, the popular conception of Fort McMurray is correct. The community has experienced rapid population growth, multiplying its population over 20 times in the last two decades. . . . High population turnover continues even though the community has again stabilized following completion of Syncrude [Canada, Ltd.'s] construction. The population has a high proportion of those with relatively unstable employment histories and the population shows high geographic mobility moving to Fort McMurray. . . .

Residents are relatively dissatisfied with the quality of their neighborhoods and with external design characteristics of their housing. . . . Street and road maintenance and animal control were judged to be of poor quality. . . . Service quality may not always be high but, again, there appear to have been improvements, particularly in the provision of health services, recreation facilities, and retail shopping. . . . Fort McMurray residents generally know few of their neighbours. Family breakdown and marital infidelity are perceived to be common. . . .

These generalizations are not intended to prove that Fort McMurray is a community without problems or that rapid growth and high mobility do not have social and personal costs. The adjustment to rapid change that has occurred did not "just happen" without a great deal of effort on the part of community residents and leaders. (Alberta Oil Sands Environmental Research Program, 1980, xxv-xxvi)

In their own examination of Fort McMurray and its surroundings, Parkinson and Detomasi (1980, 92-102) cited similar statistics to those in the Alberta study, but nevertheless stated that

Fort McMurray is, ultimately, a success story. In spite of population increases of 30 percent per year, when all predictions were to the contrary, municipal services did not break down. . . . Public facilities were constructed and new services were delivered. Houses were produced. . . . Municipal revenues were strained but the money for essential programs did arrive at the eleventh hour. The planning in Fort McMurray was far from perfect. It was hampered by insufficient information, by inadequate appreciation of the magnitude of the problem, by "thinking too small," and by pressures to make and implement decisions quickly. The main point is that with effort and improvisation, the planners, decision-makers, and citizens of Fort McMurray did it; they planned for and accommodated growth on a massive scale and the results were much better than one would have expected. (Parkinson and Detomasi, 1980, 95-96)

The authors mentioned the third major Alberta energy project in the region, Alsands, involving a new town about 60 miles north of Fort McMurray, and still another proposed project to be built "in the Cold Lake area 270 km. southeast of Fort McMurray." They dealt extensively with the town's evolving skill in planning for explosive growth, making clear that although

there is an excitement about planning there, . . . The town looks neglected, uncared for, lacking in civic pride. It has dirty unswept streets, broken sidewalks in need of repair, last month's garbage and weeds in the boulevards; it lacks landscaping, flowers, grass, and trees. But these are trivial matters which can be dealt with once the town has mastered the more serious physical and social problems

posed by its growth and finds some discretion in its expenditures. The point is that major or irreversible environmental insult appears to have been avoided. (Parkinson and Detomasi, 1980, 99)

Among the conclusions Parkinson and Detomasi reached about resource town planning in Alberta are that

1. It is necessary to plan for the needs of workers who come to build the town, as distinct from those who come to build the plant;
2. There is a need for a coordinated planning effort among the provincial housing authority, local government, and the industrial employer in order to assure the timely delivery of housing, infrastructure, and public facilities;
3. It is necessary to recognize the fact that housing so delivered will be beyond the means of typical industrial and goods and service sector employees and that subsidy from both industrial employers and the public sector will be required;
4. It is necessary for government to recognize that resource-based boomtowns like Fort McMurray are different in kind, not just in degree, and cannot be subjected to all of the existing legislative constraints, decision criteria, and approval processes which govern the growth of other towns in the province;
5. Capital grants for massive front-end public expenditures should not be the result of an annual request; schools, social and recreation facilities should be approved and built in advance of need rather than after need has been dramatically demonstrated;
6. Finally, and perhaps most importantly, Fort McMurray demonstrates that planning can be concerned with social and environmental objectives rather than economic efficiency and cost minimization even in a remote, exploding town. . . . In future developments, the net costs of pursuing social and environmental objectives rather than simple efficiency are likely

to be much lower than in Fort McMurray; it remains to be seen whether the choice will be made. (Parkinson and Detomasi, 1980, 100-101)

Once again, the concept of coordinated and careful planning among all levels of government and industry appears to be the only sure solution to the boomtown syndrome. The role of industry became painfully clear in May 1982, when the Alsands project was virtually scuttled (see Chapter 26).

Attention has also been given to new resource towns going up in British Columbia. Until the 1950s, perhaps the majority of these towns had "high labor turnover, community instability, male dominance and isolation" (Bradbury, 1980, 19). Planners were anxious then to upgrade the social structure of future resource towns, while industry and government wanted new town design revised to attract workers' families. More and more often, companies were reluctant to run town housing or stores, citing either the expense or administrative difficulties for their officials.

British Columbia passed the 1965 Instant Towns Act, which Bradbury thinks failed in the short term because it did not consider the dominance by one firm in these towns that could one day withdraw its job-giving business from the area. An act that encouraged the townspeople to own their homes and run their town also ensured that they would bear the brunt of an industry withdrawal.

Bradbury evaluates the province's current resource town planning policy and discusses some of the problems of living in these communities. The provincial government evolved an "instant town" concept that was to be different from the company town idea previously used by company and government planners. But regardless of the designation, these small towns suffered the boomtown syndrome. Bradbury's conclusion is that

The instant towns of British Columbia are still resource towns dependent on one resource and one company. As such they are dependent on the prices and the demands of a world market and economy. . . . Day-to-day work and living conditions of the workforce are dependent upon decisions made by corporate executives not only at the local level, but at the level of national and international centers of control. . . .

In the new instant towns, the insecurity and the isolation of company towns may remain, but now there are suburban type townsites, more recreational facilities, local government, and a new type of workforce. . . .

The emphasis on attracting families and promoting home-ownership meant that many families become locked into such communities by mortgages, high taxes, and high costs of living. The instant town legislation succeeded in transferring the costs of running a township from the company to the workers. The people, in return for the chance to govern themselves and own their homes whether they wanted to or not, pay the price of creating a new and livable townsite. . . . Whether the instant towns will in the future progress towards . . . "the stage of maturity" will depend upon the viability of the economic base and the economic fortunes of the companies on the world market as had been the case before instant towns were created. (Bradbury, 1980, 33-34)

Canada's boomtown experience is not limited to tiny communities. Larger cities have followed the examples of Houston and Denver. The most outstanding example is Calgary, Alberta's largest city, whose population doubled from 1960 to 1974, reaching 500,000 (Borders, 1974, 2). Dais (1979, 258-270) describes the ways in which zoning and development control have tried by different methods to deal with this rapid growth.

By 1979 thousands more were arriving every month. "Under such pressure, real estate values have soared, with those of some modest bungalows rising $2,000 a month" (Malcolm, 1979, 14). Banks, insurance, and computer firms are presently joining the oil companies in Calgary. As they do, real estate prices continue to skyrocket, creating a financial windfall for suburban farmers subdividing their property, but a nightmarish espense for the 2,500 monthly arrivals in 1982. This created a severe housing shortage in Calgary.

Many of Calgary's newcomers are young, unskilled, and poor easterners, who often turn to crime (Giniger, 1982, 7). Value conflicts definitely exist in Calgary, long a center of western Canadian resentment toward eastern cities such as Toronto and Ottawa. The city continues to grow so rapidly that its chief of long-term planning predicts that Calgary could have a million inhabitants by the year 2000 (Freeman, 1980, 37).

Edmonton, Alberta's capital, is also booming, though not as rapidly as Calgary. Its planners know they have to convince new companies to set up their headquarters there to keep the boom going, since the oil companies have their headquarters in Calgary. Nevertheless, Edmonton's population increases by 11,000 to 12,000 people each year, and had grown to 462,000 by 1975 (Trumbull, 1976, 53).

By 1982 Alberta reportedly had Canada's highest suicide rate. Its population was more than two million, up about 30 percent since 1971 (Freeman, 1980, 37). British Columbia's population grew 21 percent from 1971 to 1980.

Areas even further north also boomed in the late 1970s, only to fall on hard times by 1982. The 1898 Klondike gold rush left about ten ghost towns and 5,000 settlers in its wake within two years. A gas pipeline was to have been built between Alaska and the lower 48 states, passing through Canada, so that for a time in the early 1980s, "real estate values [were] soaring. . . . The average price of a house in Whitehorse climbed by about $1,000 a month during the second half of 1977, and at the end of March [1978] reached $56,240, up from $44,562 a year earlier" (Katzenstein, 1978, 46). Plans were that

> Whitehorse, which has a population of just 12,000 people, will be a supply center for the pipeline. Whitehorse residents . . . are horrified at the prospect of being surrounded by construction vehicles. And with the cost of living in the north the highest in Canada, it is feared that the pipeline will only increase inflation. . . . (Katzenstein, 1978, 46)

Fears were also prevalent that crime, alcohol abuse, and other problems would worsen, as they did in Alaska when the oil pipeline went up there several years ago.

To prevent this, the Canadian Parliament "set up a monitoring agency to oversee all aspects of the project.

This is in contrast to the Alaska oil pipeline, where the administrative authority was divided among several United States state and federal agencies (Katzenstein, 1978, 46). Local industry nevertheless feared that it would lose skilled workers to the pipeline. Yukon residents wanted the Canadian government to create a fund to assure the territory of getting some of the pipeline income to handle the Yukon's own social and economic needs.

All this may have become moot by 1982. The global energy glut has forced an indefinite delay in the pipeline. To make matters worse, "for the first time since the Gold Rush, there [was] not a working mine in the Yukon; after more than eight decades of continuous operation, the colorful White Pass and Yukon Railway from [Whitehorse] to the Alaskan coast is closed; the economy is sinking and people are fleeing" (Martin, 1983, D-1).

Even before the 1970s boom turned into the 1980s bust, the Yukon contained a relic of previous booms —Dawson, a town that sprang up overnight during the Klondike rush. By 1980 it had legally become Canada's smallest city, with 700 residents (Malcolm, 1980, 5). With gold then at astronomical values, prospectors began returning. Contemporary Dawson is a combination of "some new buildings built to look old, some old buildings restored to look old, and some old buildings just looking old" (Malcolm, 1980, 5). The streets downtown are unpaved dirt paths full of potholes. The atmosphere is raw frontier even today, with its laws seldom being obeyed. The post-1981 decline in gold prices probably guarantees Dawson its current status for some time to come.

NOTES

1. Five to eight years is a common time lag.
2. Houston is now America's fifth largest city, and one of only two of the country's five largest cities to have gained population since 1970—Los Angeles is the other. Houston is a rarity in America, a booming metropolis.

REFERENCES

Alberta Oil Sands Environmental Research Program, December 1980, *A Study of Human Adjustment in Fort McMurray,* Alberta Environment, Edmonton, Alberta, Canada.

Borders, William, 1974, "Thriving Calgary, Grown Wealthy on Oil, Adds Glamour to Western Canada," *New York Times,* October 6, p. 2.

Bradbury, John H., 1980, "Instant Resource Towns Policy in British Columbia: 1965-1972" *Plan Canada* **20**(1):19-38.

Changing Times, 1982, "Behind the Boom in the Rockies," **36**(3):36-38.

Dais, Eugene, E., 1979, "Development Control in Calgary: The Case of the Fortuitous Hybrid," in William T. Perks and Ira M. Robinson eds., *Urban and Regional Planning in a Federal State.* Dowden, Hutchinson & Ross, Stroudsburg, Pa.

Finsterbusch, Kurt, 1980, *Understanding Social Impacts,* Sage Publications, Beverly Hills, Calif.

Fitzgerald, J. Joseph, 1978, *Black Gold With Grit— The Alberta Oil Sands,* Gray's Publishing, Ltd., Sidney, B. C., Canada.

Freeman, Alan, 1980, "Western Provinces' Fast Growth Presages Big Changes in Canada," *Wall Street Journal,* December 2, p. 37.

Giniger, Henry, 1982, "Gaps in Prosperity Troubling Canada," *New York Times,* January 10, p. 7.

Katzenstein, Dorothea, 1978, "Canada's Yukon is Worrying That Gas Pipeline Might Affect Its Economy and Pioneer Life Style," *Wall Street Journal,* June 20, p. 46.

Kelly, J., 1980, "Rocky Mountain High," *Time,* December 15, pp. 28-41.

King, Wayne, 1982, "Houston's Council Tries to Control City Growth," *New York Times,* June 23, p. A-12.

King, Wayne, 1983, "New Police Chief Battles Crime Boom in Houston," *New York Times,* January 14, p. A-8.

Malamud, Gary, 1981, "A Comprehensive Solution to the Boomtown Syndrome," master's thesis, New York University.

Malcolm, Andrew H., 1979, "Calgary Thrives on Oil to Become the Houston of Canada," *New York Times,* April 9, p. 14.

Malcolm, Andrew H., 1980, "Dawson: A Pothole at the End of a Rainbow," *New York Times,* September 20, p. 5.

Malcolm, Andrew H., 1982, "Calgary Corrals the Bankers," *New York Times,* January 11, p. D-1ff.

Martin, Douglas, 1983, "Distress Signs in the Yukon," *New York Times,* January 7, p. D-1ff.

McComb, David G., 1969, *Houston— The Bayou City.* University of Texas Press, Austin, Texas.

Monaco, L. A., 1977, *State Responses to the Adverse Impacts of Energy Development in Colorado,* Massachusetts Institute of Technology, Cambridge, Mass.

New York Times, 1982, "Casper: Wyoming's First Metropolis," March 9, p. A-14.

Padilla, Maria T., 1982, "Oklahoma's Oil and Gas Boom Brings Cash, People, Problems," *Wall Street Journal,* March 16, p. 31.

Parkinson, Anna, and Detomasi, D. D., 1980, "Planning Resource Towns for the Alberta Tar Sands," *Plan Canada* **20**(2):(2-102).

Robinson, Ira M., 1979, "Planning, Building, and Managing New Towns on the Resource Frontier," in William T. Perks and Ira M. Robinson, eds., *Urban and Regional Planning in a Federal State,* Dowden, Hutchinson & Ross, Stroudsburg, Pa.

Schmidt, William E., 1981, "Glut of Uranium Hurts Miners, *New York Times* December 22, p. 1ff.

Slocum, Kenneth G., 1977, "Wyoming Boom Spurs a Range of Problems and Confrontations," *Wall Street Journal,* September 28, p. 1ff.

Stelter, Gilbert A., and Artibise, A. F. J., 1978, "Canadian Resource Towns in Historical Perspective," *Plan Canada* **18**(1):7-16.

Stevens, William K., 1981, "Houston, Fastest-Growing Big City, Showing Signs of Having Hit Prime," *New York Times,* December 16, p. A-20.

Susskind, D., and O'Hare, M., 1977, *Predicting the Local Impacts of Energy Development,* Massachusetts Institute of Technology, Cambridge, Mass.

Trumbull, Robert, 1976, "Financiers Flock to Invest in Booming Capital of Alberta," *New York Times,* November 23, p. 53.

16

The Latin American Energy Rush

As the only two Latin American nations endowed with vast oil reserves, Venezuela and Mexico offered their citizens extravagant promises of new wealth that would greatly reduce the yawning gap between rich and poor that has chronically plagued most Latin nations. Yet neither country has come close to realizing that dream. Mexico, in particular, suffered from grievous errors of judgment by the recently retired President Jose Lopez Portillo, and is today attempting to edge away from the economic abyss.

Both countries, as did Scotland half a decade before, turned into huge boomtowns. Planning in these countries was, if anything, more chaotic than that in Scotland. Having suffered years of minor-nation status, Venezuela and Mexico, like Iran, Indonesia, Nigeria, and nearly all the newly wealthy countries, embarked upon huge industrialization programs that benefited only the wealthy class and required enormous amounts of borrowing abroad. The 1982 oil glut caught some of these countries, especially Mexico, with huge debts payable at towering interest rates and with falling oil revenue. The oil boom also sent prices soaring, certainly in Mexico. Vast sections of the countryside were abandoned by peasants seeking their small share of the oil wealth in the big cities, Caracas and Mexico City, neither of which was capable of handling the huge influx. The Venezuelan and Mexican booms brought uncontrolled growth to their capitals and to other cities equally incapable of dealing with torrents of newcomers.

VENEZUELA

The founding member of OPEC, Venezuela took off on an economic binge when oil prices skyrocketed in 1974. Rather than enrich the poverty-stricken masses, however, the oil boom merely enriched the well-connected few, mainly in Caracas. Howe (1974a, 21), accurately indicated this contradictory effect: Caracas is now "a city of handsome skyscrapers, elegant mansions and luxury boutiques and restaurants [but also] a city of brutal poverty, with grim, unsafe and unsanitary slums, ill-equipped and overcrowded schools and hospitals, and legions of unemployed." De Onis (1977*a,* 7) called Caracas "a heat trap of compact concrete structures and endless asphalt." One-third of the city's labor force is either out of work or underemployed, and anywhere from 800,000 to 1 million of Caracas's 2.5 million residents live in slums (Howe, 1974*a,* 21; de Onis, 1977*a,* 7).

Diego Arria, the new governor of the Federal District including the capital city, wanted to impose some controversial measures, such as "a ban on private beaches, protection for green zones. . . . to the point of threatening influential landholders . . . and the banishing of 15,000 street vendors" who had added to downtown congestion, "delinquency, drugs and filth" (Howe, 1974*a,* 21). But critics have accused Arria of merely scratching the surface, and are especially skeptical of his idea of relocating 300,000 slum dwellers to areas outside Caracas and giving them work.[1]

Arria faces huge challenges almost everywhere in Caracas he looks. "Public transportation, garbage collection and other government services remain disorganized despite the city's affluence" (Mann, 1980, IV-5), a critical problem that years of extravagant spending have not relieved. Caracas suffers from

month-long water shortages, trash-littered thoroughfares and public beaches, gaping holes in streets and sidewalks that go unrepaired for years, dirty, overcrowded and rundown public schools and hospitals, sporadic police protection . . . erratic phone service, poor public transportation and a host of other [problems]. (de Onis, 1980, 3)

All of these, except the phone problem, are depressingly familiar to urban Americans, yet their cities at least have the excuse of empty treasuries. How could these be afflicting the capital of a country awash in oil revenues?

Caracas's problem is in part the result of split jurisdiction: half the city is run by the Federal District government, and half by the local city council. President Luis Herrera Campins has broken most of his 1979 campaign promises to raise the level of public services (e.g., putting in a new water supply system and thousands of litter baskets, and increasing police coverage). An American executive was quoted as having said that after his arrival in 1975, when "the city looked like a dream" (de Onis, 1980, 3), deterioration began setting in.

One journalist familiar with Caracas claimed to have seen much improvement in the last two years (Mann, 1982, X-10). The city has upgraded its outmoded airport, and the problems of "overcrowded hotels, poor public services . . . have been reduced substantially." These benefit primarily the tourists in Caracas. Even Mann admitted that the city "still suffers from nightmarish traffic jams, poor telephone service and high prices," but "the Government has improved many public services, cleaned up the streets and made life considerably easier for visitors and residents alike. It is also building a subway that is scheduled to begin operating in 1983." Nevertheless, "Caracas has been delivered to the automobile, and even some residential sections lack sidewalks." Among the sources of these problems appear to be a lack among the top federal and city officials of planning knowledge, and inefficiency bordering on corruption.

Venezuela's oil boom has spread all over the countryside, and not just to the oil fields, centered in Lake Maracaibo to the west of Caracas. Venezuela is following the example of countless other newly wealthy Third World countries of trying to use its oil revenue to build basic industries (e.g., steel and nonferrous metals) from scratch. Yet there is a tragic flaw to this process. An oil boom in any country creates such a huge balance of payments surplus that the local currency is much stronger than that of the country's trading partners. This in turn prices the oil exporting country's nonoil exports out of world markets. The oil boom thus spawns industries that can serve only the local market, which in many cases is far too small for the size of the industry being built.

Venezuela's large population and relatively modern economy make it appear better suited for heavy industry than other oil exporters, notably Saudi Arabia. The oil boom has spawned several prominent Venezuelan boomtowns. One of these is Puerto Ordaz, in the center of a very rich deposit of high-grade iron ore. U.S. Steel decided to build Puerto Ordaz in 1952 as a residence not just for its own workers, choosing to fill only half the available home-site lots. Both Reynolds Metals and the Venezuelan government recently built plants nearby; their workers also live in Puerto Ordaz. This "gleaming new city of 160,000 inhabitants" (*Nation's Business*, 1973, 62) was designed by city planners from Harvard and the Massachusetts Institute of Technology. By 1973 it had a hospital, schools, an airport, churches, shopping malls, and an excellent street and highway system. Puerto Ordaz expects to reach its full capacity of 450,000 residents by 1998.

Ciudad Guyana, near the Orinoco River delta east of Caracas, was founded in 1962 and had an early population of 30,000. This had risen to 300,000 by 1977 and was still going up rapidly, thanks to inexpensive hydroelectric power nearby that spawned a regional steel industry. By 1977 probably the "world's largest construction job . . . underway" (de Onis, 1977*b*, 58) was occurring there: a $4 billion steel mill. Aluminum, cement, and other nonferrous metals plants were also going up nearby. Fifteen years after its birth, Ciudad Guyana had become a "modern city ringed by shantytowns . . . [in which] the growing pains are serious. There is a critical housing shortage. The cost of living is 25 percent higher than in Caracas . . . skilled workers cannot be found locally and must be imported" (de Onis, 1977*b*, 58). As occurred at Nigg, Scotland, a luxury liner (in this instance the Cristoforo Colombo) was to become a floating hotel for 1,100 foreign workers. Trailer camps and prefabricated houses were built for another 4,000.

Venezuela's determination to make steel one of the mainstays of its postoil economy gives both of these communities a bright future, but there is no guarantee that they, any more than Caracas, will ever solve the problems of the boomtown syndrome.

MEXICO

It is the best of times. In the oil-rich boom town of Villahermosa— once a primitive jungle settlement—Mexican "oil cowboys" and Texan mud drillers race their shiny Ford Broncos through the bustling city, and an Apple computer store stands between rickety tortilla stands. Some say Villahermosa's prosperity is a model for Mexico's future. The oil discoveries in southern Mexico are now thought to be linked in one vast field—a geological blessing that could catapult Mexico from its position as the world's fourth largest oil producer into competition with Saudi Arabia for No. 1.

It is the worst of times. Nearly half of Mexico's workers do not have full-time jobs, and those who have steady work find their inflation-ravaged paychecks buy less and less . . . 25 percent of all Mexicans go without meat and almost 50 percent cannot afford milk. "The poor are much poorer now than they were during the revolution of 1910," says a Mexican writer. . . . "Is this progress?" (Nissen, 1982, 51)

Perhaps no other newly inaugurated leader has ever faced a national crisis worse than that facing Mexico's President Miguel de la Madrid Hurtado. He confronts a nearly bankrupt treasury, skyrocketing prices, one of the world's highest birth rates, massive unemployment, and huge foreign debts.

It all seemed so much brighter five years ago, when oil found under the Bay of Campeche turned Mexico overnight into a world-class economic power. Yet its leadership, especially de la Madrid's predecessor, Jose Lopez Portillo, lacked the economic judgment necessary to guide Mexico's booming economy. Lopez Portillo made the same kind of extravagant promises as those made by Venezuela's President Herrera, and corruption far more blatant than anything in Venezuela combined with the lack of a serious political opposition to make matters even worse.

Lopez Portillo at first promised his people slow, stable growth after the great oil discoveries.

But the sharp rise in oil prices in 1980 brought in far larger revenues than Mexican planners had expected. The government launched an expansive and expensive industrialization program while politicians made giddy jokes about buying Texas back. "We were suddenly rich," says one former government economist. "We did what all the once poor, suddenly rich do—we overspent." (Nissen, 1982, 52)

Then oil prices began to fall in 1981. Mexico had to stop refinery expansion and many vitally needed public-works projects. Private industry began laying off thousands of workers.

Increasing numbers of rural Mexicans are flooding the country's urban centers. . . . The largest cities—Mexico City, Guadalajara, Monterrey—are now choked with millions of homeless and jobless "campesinos" [see Fig. 16.1]. Meanwhile, farms have been left shorthanded and the country's food production has slowed down. (Nissen, 1982, 52)

The government has failed either to stop the mass migration or to encourage industry to build factories in the depopulating countryside.

Nowhere is the lack of planning for an economic boom more painfully evident than in Mexico City, which suffers from a population explosion now the most spectacular in the world. Nissen (1982, 53) describes Mexico City's incredible problems, all stemming from the central fact that

it sprawls across 425 square miles and crawls with an estimated 17 million people—making it unofficially the world's most populous city. By the year 2000 its urban area is expected to have as many as 35 million inhabitants, surpassing Greater New York and Greater Tokyo to become the largest metropolitan area of the face of the earth.

Perhaps its most intractable problem is transportation. Gasoline, until 1982, was priced way below world levels, adding to public reluctance to use the already overcrowded and unsafe buses. The new subway system still covers only a small area. Most Mexicans, unaccustomed to apartment living, have to move further and further away from the downtown

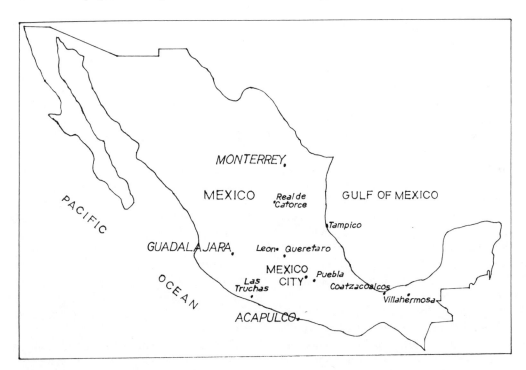

Figure 16.1
Mexico and its oil boomtowns.

area to find land on which to build houses (Riding, 1981, 2). Most of the area's factories are in the northwest section of the city, but most of its low-paid workers have to live in the east. All this adds to the appalling rush-hour traffic problem.

Mexico City hardly needed an oil boom to become a boomtown. In fact, the city's population grew even faster in the 40 years before 1970 than it did in the 5 years after 1970.[2] But it was after the 1975 oil boom that the city's growth reached crisis proportions. For the first time, Mexico City began attracting illiterate, unskilled peasants to whom it could not offer work. However, even its most hideous slums sometimes offer them electricity, sewage disposal, access to water supply, radio and television, all but unobtainable in many rural areas.

Kemper (1977, 84-91) examines growth patterns in the slums. They often progress from wooden shanties to concrete block homes; dirt paths are paved; connections to electrical, water supply, and waste disposal services become available; and schools and other community services appear. But at least a million Mexico City peasants probably live in the "ciudades perdidos," made of wood or tin. Most of them occupy their land quasi-legally or illegally. Many earn their living by scavenging through Mexico City's vast open garbage dumps. Kemper believes that newly arrived peasants avoid the "ciudades perdidos," populated largely by those who were city dwellers elsewhere. Peasants instead usually end up in "vecindades," multi-family houses with common toilets and water taps. About 20 percent of all Mexico City residents live in these quarters, which are far superior to the "ciudades perdidos." Since both types of housing are always filled to capacity, squatter settlements are the only refuge for thousands.

It apparently bodes the city government well to examine these settlement patterns. Perhaps urban planners can find ways to increase the attractiveness of the "vecindades" to prevent the city from sprawling even further beyond the reach of jobs and basic urban services. One has to wonder, though, about the wisdom of one radical idea, that of breaking the city

into "boroughs" as in New York City. New York may not be any better managed today than it was as a single political unit.

The Mexican boom has spread beyond the large cities. Coatzacoalcos, on the Bay of Campeche, became the center of a huge new petrochemical industry, and nearby Villahermosa also boomed in the early 1980s. However, the government planners have failed to expand infrastructure in these boomtowns. Their ports and the railroads to urban centers, neglected for decades, are huge bottlenecks today, hampering not only the nation but the citizens of these boomtowns.

The problem of exploding population is almost as acute throughout the country, which now numbers about 75 million citizens, up from 62 million in 1976. The imbalance between geography and population is now so bad that "some 85 percent of the people live in areas that have 15 percent of the national water supply. By 1982 a third of the population will be in Mexico City, Guadalajara, Monterrey, Puebla and Leon" (Riding, 1976, 2). To help forestall this

the Lopez Portillo government recently came up with a national urban development plan to spread growth to new areas by creating 13 integrated urban systems. Each was to center around a city (except for Mexico City, Monterrey, and Guadalajara), which will have new industries and services capable of absorbing an expanded population. (Riding, 1979, IV-7).

This plan was expected to cost more than $20 billion and last 20 years. Construction had already begun by the end of 1980 on "airports, roads, schools, housing, and hospitals to accommodate new settlers. And the government is offering big tax and energy incentives to attract industry" (Getschow, 1981, 33). The government wanted to limit Mexico City's population in the year 2000 to around 16 million. Its plans for Guadalajara and Monterrey were for each to have 3 to 5 million.

Coastal areas near the ports and energy supplies received special attention. One such area is Las Truchas, north of Acapulco on the Pacific coast, now a "sleepy farming and fishing community of 45,000" (Getschow, 1981, 33). The government is building manufacturing plants, a steel mill, and a large port. The area's population in 2000 is to be 1.5 million. "Modern hotels, shopping centers, public housing projects, and a red-light district already give the area a boomtown atmosphere" (Getschow, 1981, 33). Tampico, on the Gulf of Mexico near Coatzacoalcos and Villahermosa, is also booming.

Towns in the interior such as Leon and Queretero are also to get attention. Yet whatever the government attempts to do, Mexico City will continue to lure migrants, especially since it is still the capital and major market for goods and the nation's largest labor pool. Many industrialists, politicians, and members of the middle class do not want to leave their markets, power bases, and urban amenities.

Planning is often poor in the new urban centers.

In Las Truchas, for example, squatters occupy tin shanties at the town's edge as they wait for job openings. But about a fifth of the available public housing remains vacant; the brick homes are too small, too hot and perhaps too modern for peasants' tastes. . . . A Mexico City sociologist says peasants "prefer mud and log houses." Las Truchas officials worry about divorce, crime and other social problems that have risen with the city's growth. (Getschow, 1981, 33)

The fate of this plan in the new de la Madrid administration remains to be seen. So does the fate of efforts of planners from President de la Madrid on down to deal with this incredible national and urban boom.

Tragically for the Mexican leadership and people, the influx to the cities is not likely to abate during the oil glut gripping Mexico in 1983. Riding (1983, D-1ff) described the condition of once-booming Villahermosa early that year.

Shops and restaurants that opened in prosperity now cry out for customers, several half-finished buildings await completion and work on a new highway to nearby Coatzacoalcos has stopped. There even seem to be fewer people around. . . . "Many contractors have left, many migrant workers have returned to their home-towns, even peasants who found jobs in Pemex (the state oil monopoly) are going back to their plots". . . . The slowing of the pace has thus brought some relief to a long-sleepy farming region that never quite adjusted to the industrial revolution that exploded in its midst. . . .

[During the oil boom,] money—more than Tabasco (the Mexican state of which Villahermosa is captial) had ever dreamed of—soon strained the state's social fabric. "The attitude and mentality of the locals were not adapted to the new rhythm and new customs of those who came here. . . . The newcomers drove big cars, they went to bars, they filled restaurants, the red light district expanded. It was a tremendous shock for Tabasco."

The cattle-ranchers who had long dominated the state's economy found their farmhands leaving to work for Pemex. Shopkeepers and small-business operators were unable to pay the salaries necessary to dissuade secretaries and accountants from flocking to the oil company. With insufficient residential housing available, local homeowners saw an opportunity to raise rents to levels three times higher than the national average and more. This, in turn, pushed rents and house prices beyond the reach of local families. And for several years, inflation . . . was consistently 10 to 20 percentage points higher than elsewhere in Mexico.

The greatest impact, though, was felt in the rural areas where Pemex was actually drilling. Because the Government owns the subsoil Pemex could take over land that it required. But while compensation was paid, disagreements over the price frequently provoked angry incidents. . . . At that point, Pemex apparently recognized a potentially explosive problem and responded accordingly: it offered to share the cost of building and repairing local roads, started its own homebuilding program and agreed to pay a special tax to Tabasco equivalent to 6 percent of local oil production. It also set up a commission to deal with the complaints of local farmers.

With the additional funds, Villahermosa, whose population has tripled to 300,000 in less than a decade, was able to carry out urgently needed urban improvements to appease long-time residents and increase the compensation paid to peasants affected by Pemex operations. . . . (Riding, 1983, D-1ff)

Few on-the-spot accounts have offered a better example both of the boomtown syndrome and ways of fighting it than Riding's. However, his account came too early to explain in equal detail the oil glut's effects on Villahermosa's infrastructure or finances.

Mexico's energy boom has an ironic twist: It is bypassing many other towns that saw their boom die years ago. One of the many deserted Mexican towns is Real de Catorce, about 200 miles southwest of Monterrey (Riding, 1977, 4). In the nineteenth century, it was a boomtown of 40,000, the center of Mexico's silver rush. Now it is a ghost town, with only 600 residents, 1 policeman, 2 bars, and 5 shops. There are not enough people to support a clinic or a secondary school. The 1910 revolution destroyed Real de Catorce and many other communities. Any oil boom is almost certain to leave this and Mexico's other desolate communities even further behind.

NOTES

1. Each large Latin American city has wretched slums, usually on the hills outside the gleaming, modern downtown area; only their names distinguish one from the other. Caracas's are called "ranchos," Mexico City's are "ciudades perdidos" (lost cities), Rio de Janeiro's are "favelas". All suffer from appalling filth, high levels of disease and infant mortality, and lack of sanitation, education, and medical facilities, and are breeders of crime. They also suffer that perennial bane of boomtowns: a cloud of dust in the dry season and equally omnipresent mud in the rainy season.
2. From 1930 to 1970, Mexico City's population grew from 1.2 million to 8.5 million a 5% annual expansion rate. From 1970 to 1975, the figure grew to 10.5 million, a 4.3% annual rate (Kemper, 1977, 77).

REFERENCES

de Onis, Juan, 1977a, "The 'Monstrous Inequality' That is Plaguing Venezuela," *New York Times,* April 30, p. 7.

de Onis, Juan, 1977b, "A Tropical Ruhr Emerges in Venezuela," *New York Times,* June 7, p. 58.

de Onis, Juan, 1980, "Despite Its Wealth, Caracas Sits in Garbage and Smog," *New York Times,* March 17, p. 3.

Getschow, George, 1981, "Mexico Spends Billions to Foster Growth Outside Bursting Capital," *Wall Street Journal,* January 20(E), p. 33.

Howe, Marvine, 1974a, "Upgrading Effort is On in Caracas," *New York Times,* November 3, p. 21.

Howe, Marvine, 1974b, "Venezuela Views Oil Wealth as 'Last Chance' for Her Democracy," *New York Times,* October 25, p. 16.

Kemper, Robert V., 1977, *Migration and Adaptation,* Sage Publications, Beverly Hills, Calif.

Mann, Joseph, 1980, "Inflation Undercuts Venezuelan Oil Riches," *New York Times,* March 9, p. IV-5.

Mann, Joseph, 1982, "What's Doing in Caracas," *New York Times,* February 21, p. X-10.

Nations's Business, 1973, "Building a City in the Wilderness," **61** (8):62.

Nissen, Beth, 1982, "Hard Times for an Oil Giant," *Newsweek,* July 12, pp. 51-53.

Riding, Alan, 1976, "Mexico Facing Problems as Cities Sprawl," *New York Times,* July 1, p. 2.

Riding, Alan, 1977, "Dying Mexican Silver Town Still Foresees Shiny Future," *New York Times,* August 27, p. 4.

Riding, Alan, 1979, "Old, New Mexico City Has the Worst of Both Worlds," *New York Times,* February 11, p. IV-7.

Riding, Alan, 1980, "Mexico Struggles With Problems of Sudden Oil Affluence," *New York Times,* August 22, p. 6.

Riding, Alan, 1981, "Life in Mexican Capital: Adapting to the Impossible," *New York Times,* August 12, p. 2.

Riding, Alan, 1983, "Oil Impact on Mexican Town," *New York Times,* February 7, p. D-1ff.

17

Explosive Growth in the Persian Gulf

Since 1973 several nations along the rim of the Persian Gulf (shown in Fig. 17.1) have been caught up in unprecedented, almost giddy growth, forcing the world's most enormous transfer of wealth to countries that were just emerging from feudalism. The leader of these countries, of course, is Saudi Arabia, but other Gulf nations, including Kuwait, Bahrain, and the United Arab Emirates also are sharing in the energy boom. They are attempting an extraordinary jump from feudalism to the twenty-first century, but their orthodox, traditional societies are undergoing tremendous strain. Nowhere is this more obvious than in Saudi Arabia.

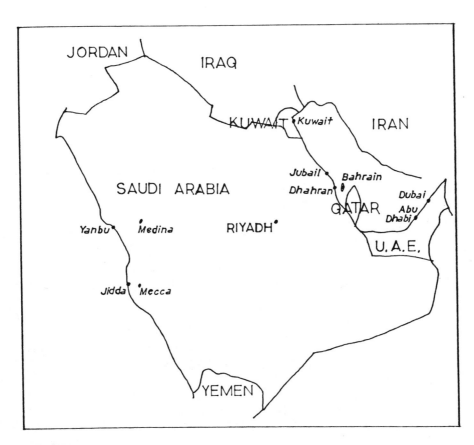

Figure 17.1
The booming Persian Gulf.

SAUDI ARABIA

Until well into this century, the world showed little interest in the wasteland of the great Arabian desert. A patchwork of rivaling sheikdoms until 1932, the largest area on the Arabian Peninsula was united by the extraordinary King Ibn Saud, who fortified his control of the land by placing his many offspring in key government and industry positions. Ibn Saud slowly strengthened his primitive economy by entering into deals with American and European oil companies to explore the great oilfields discovered in 1938.

Saudi Arabia remains religiously orthodox, its traditional role as the country containing Islam's two holiest cities, Mecca and Medina. Unitl 1973 this ultraorthodox society was able to remain intact even as oil revenues steadily increased. After the 1973 embargo and the quadrupling of oil prices, this was no longer possible. Saudi planners suddenly had to deal with unimaginable revenues that funneled into the treasury of an undeveloped country with a small population, and at the same time remember the dominance in Saudi Arabia of the principles of Islam. Probably nowhere else in the world is a country's five-year plan intended "to maintain the religious values . . . by applying, propagating and fostering God's Sharia [Islamic law]" (Kingdom of Saudi Arabia, Ministry of Planning, 1980a, 3).

The unified kingdom of Saudi Arabia started almost from scratch in 1932. The country had no federal budget until 1948, when oil revenues started coming in. The first local radio station began operating in 1949, the country's first university opened in 1949, the first municipal electric power system started up in Mecca in 1950, and the first newspaper was printed in 1952. Several oil installations were in place by 1950, as crude production quickly rose from 1 million barrels per year in 1938 to 600 million in 1946 and 200 million in 1950. Oil revenues also increased steadily, but skyrocketed after 1973: Saudi Arabia earned $57 million in 1950 and $25.7 billion in 1975 (Kingdom of Saudi Arabia, 1980a, 11). As has been seen in all boom environments, this led to reduced employment in agriculture, but increased labor forces in construction, trade, transportation, and government work.

Planning the growth of a country such as Saudi Arabia is not much different from planning that of any fairly large city elsewhere. Even the effort to be faithful to Islam has to include building an infrastructure almost from scratch. Saudi planners, however, have enough money at their disposal to be free of worry about front-end financing problems, since the development of Saudi energy was essentially completed years ago. Both the boomtown planning and the generation of enough money in a sufficiently short time to pay for it were under the government's control. Saudi Arabia has no parliament to defeat, reduce, or even debate the House of Saud's plans.

In no other boom economy do "revenues . . . exceed the physical spending capacity of the executive agencies" (Kingdom of Saudi Arabia, 1980a, 7) as spectacularly as they do in Saudi Arabia. Here too, however, "the supply of domestic resources, facilities and essential services can lag behind their demand." More than in most developing countries, the notoriously high level of government corruption means that "administrative and other inefficiencies can obstruct production schedules and cause damaging delays throughout the economy" (Kingdom of Saudi Arabia, 1980a, 7). Saudi Arabia, unlike most boom environments, suffers from a labor shortage and a capital surplus. Not until the Second Development Plan (1975-1980) did the country concentrate on infrastructure, required mostly to absorb the huge influx of foreign workers.

The First Development Plan was conceived in 1970, a year of balance of payments, deficits, and fiscal austerity (before the price explosion). The second plan began in 1975, when the nation was awash in oil money. Then, inflation and shortages in labor and infrastructure were the problem. The second plan concentrated on expanding the country's infrastructure, broadening government services, encouraging the influx of workers from the Saudi countryside and from Third World countries to the mushrooming Saudi cities. The fraction of the population living in cities grew from 36 percent in 1970 to 54 percent in 1980. Not surprisingly, the country's worst problems from 1975 to 1977 were a critical housing shortage, port congestion, labor shortages, rapidly rising labor and housing costs, and inadequate infrastructure. This plan tried to make the nonoil sector the main ingredient of economic expansion. During the length of the second plan, however, the government admitted that the oil sector's part of gross domestic product remained far higher than that of the nonoil sector.

By 1980 Saudi Arabia claimed to have in place "an adequate—if not yet fully sufficient infrastructural framework, to have reduced inflation, and to have increased per capita gross domestic product by more than 26 percent since 1975, during a half-decade of world recession (Kingdom of Saudi Arabia, 1980*a*, 14). Manpower shortages, however, became worse, and Saudi Arabia faced the common boomtown problem of encouraging other productive industries to locate in Saudi Arabia to provide for the day the oil runs out.

The Third Development Plan, to run from 1980 to 1985, intends to increase the use of foreign and skilled labor, then to improve their productivity by concentrating on capital-intensive efforts in manufacturing, farming, mining, and oil refining. It was also to "support Saudi society to deal with the problems of rapid economic and social change (Kingdom of Saudi Arabia, 1980*a*, 17). The big challenge, of course, is to do all this while adhering to the laws of Islam.

As in all boomtowns, the Saudi economy expanded at the expense of agriculture. The fraction of the Saudi labor force employed in farming went from 40 percent in 1974 to 24 percent in 1980 (Kingdom of Saudi Arabia, Ministry of Planning, 1980 *b*, 38). Since even the government admits that the money came in faster than it could productively be spent, some of the former agricultural workers reaped handsome profits in the burgeoning oil industry. They spent their new fortunes on high living, buying and speculating in real estate and other foreign assets.

The poor suffered from rapidly rising prices. From 1969 to 1976, the cost of food doubled and rents rose fivefold (Kingdom of Saudi Arabia, 1980*b*, 44). The Saudi government claims to have dampened retail price rises by imposing controls on rent and food prices, building new housing, and controlling producer prices by cutting state spending. Inflation is in part the result of scarcity of goods brought on by bottlenecks in the marketing network, so the government had to enlarge existing ports and upgrade the transportation and distribution systems. It also expanded its efforts to distribute land to poorer families and to allocate welfare and other transfer payments, granted wage and salary increases and strengthened subsidies on basic goods and services; all this was to protect the people's real income.

The Second Development Plan envisioned free health and social services, low-interest housing and personal loans, and subsidized prices for basic goods and services. The government also began requiring firms to give their workers medical care, insurance, and benefits for the disabled. It gave away more than 100,000 housing units during the Plan's duration, while providing interest-free loans to build 200,000 more; nomads "are given free land and wells if they will settle down and farm" (Martin, 1982*b*, III-1). The government could not, however, prevent the common boomtown phenomenon, where people with inadequate education, skills, or contact with the outside were left behind. When the Second Plan ended in 1980, infant mortality, malnutrition, and disease were all plaguing Saudi Arabia's poor, and they had insufficient health services to help them. The Third Plan intended to address these problems.

Under the Second Plan, the government built about 240 municipal water supply systems and 28 dams, upgraded the water supply systems of Riyadh and Jidda, built desalination and power generation plants, improved agricultural efficiency, and intensified gold, zinc, and silver mining efforts. The result of one of these efforts—the eightfold expansion of electric power generation—was that electricity consumption per capita rose more than 70 percent. Although nonoil manufacturing expanded, most growth was still "dominated by industries which supplied, and therefore depended on, the rapidly growing construction sector (Kingdom of Saudi Arabia, 1980*b*, 65).

In the late 1970s Saudi Arabia also upgraded its postal, transportation, telecommunications, and port networks. In 1980 the country had almost 400 post offices, a public intercity bus service, 130 docks for merchant ships (in 1975 it had 24), a paved road system expanded by well over 50 percent in five years, an enlarged railroad network, a new international airport at Jidda and another one being built at Riyadh, and an expanded air fleet. This formerly feudalistic nation also raised the number of its towns from 54 in 1970 to 106 ten years later.

The most crucial of its accomplishments was the construction of more than 40,000 housing units a year during the Second Plan, against 17,500 a year in the First Plan. The Saudi government intended from the start of the plan to encourage urban growth in areas able to support it through industrial expansion. Its major roadblocks were the difficulty of recruiting and training workers and of attracting construction firms to rural areas, combined with the failure of its planning and building codes that led to the frequent construction of buildings with poorly designed water and waste-disposal systems. By 1980 the government could nevertheless boast that more than half of its people lived in well-constructed buildings. The only problem was that, as in many other boomtowns, most of this construction was for the upper classes. High-rise projects quickly went up in Riyadh, Jidda, and other cities, but less middle and lowerclass housing went up. Saudi Arabia now has a housing surplus, but these units may be too expensive for the majority of Saudi families. To help some of them, the government made 150,000 loans for new home construction during the Second Plan. These new homeowners still need better water supply, waste disposal, roads, and utilities—a problem the Third Plan is supposed to remedy.

Whether or not the government helps uplift the Saudi poor, one large segment of the current population will almost certainly get no help—foreign labor-

ers and their families. Saudis have made certain that their economic and social policies exclude foreigners, especially unskilled workers. They "leave some Saudis fabulously wealthy, others moderately well-to-do and unskilled guest workers almost universally poor" (Rattner, 1981, III-8). Without property or income tax, wealthy Saudis get wealthier and the poor get poorer. But massive subsidies continue to assure lower-income Saudis of basic goods moderately enough priced for them to afford. The less prosperous in cities such as Riyadh, however, have to live in older and smaller apartments or in tents and shacks. Foreigners cannot own real estate, have modern apartments, or take government jobs, although they are eligible for food and telephone subsidies. This leaves real estate speculation—rampant in Saudi Arabia—to the Saudis. Other measures work against foreigners trying to acquire wealth, such as provisions that forbid them to own retail businesses and inhibit them from getting government contracts. These measures have helped many Saudis become wealthy merely by acting as front men for foreign interests. Poor foreign workers, however, lack these opportunities for wealth "on the sly." In fact, they are poorly paid, face deportation if they lose their jobs or misbehave, and must look for housing on their own.

The foreign workers face more intractable problems once they find housing. "Inflation, price-gouging, heat, substandard living accommodations and lack of entertainment" (Vicker, 1977*b*, 6) all work against them. Saudi Arabia has no cinemas and forbids alcohol consumption. With liquor available only on the black market, "in Riyadh, an illicit bottle of White Horse Scotch goes for $70" (Vicker, 1977*b*, 6). Even the Saudis have to go to Bahrain, Cairo, or Beirut to visit public bars and nightclubs. There is, of course, no officially sanctioned gambling. Kuwait, at least, allows horse racing, but no casino exists in Saudi Arabia or anywhere else in the Gulf states.

These restrictions impose severe hardships on a part of the Saudi population that is expanding rapidly. As of early 1981, 2.5 million of the 8 million residents of Saudi Arabia were either foreign workers (1.7 million) or their dependents (800,000). Even after the construction of a number of massive industrial projects, Saudi planners expect that more than half of the 135,000 residents expected in Yanbu and the 300,000 in Jubail (two of the largest projects) will probably be non-Saudis responsible for operating and maintaining the plants. Since few Saudis want menial jobs, most of the 2.5 million foreigners are from Egypt, Yemen, Sudan, Somalia, and other poor countries. Saudi Arabia also needs foreign workers because no more than 15 percent of Saudis are literate (Gupte, 1981*b*, A-10). The relatively few Western guest workers usually live in attractive cities such as Dhahran, and enjoy a lifestyle far superior to that of the African and Asian workers. One last Saudi law inhibits the material progress of these workers—few of them can ever become Saudi citizens, even if they are Moslem, since a royal decree is required.

The Saudi government could instantly reduce its need for foreign workers by tapping its female population. The orthodox state, however, is unwilling to employ women for any but "traditional female jobs, such as teaching and nursing" (Vicker, 1977*b*, 6).

The presence of millions of non-Saudis is not the only aspect of the country's boom that works against the government's ideal of a modern theocratic state. The explosive growth of the cities is also dimming this dream. As more Saudis become urbanized,

traditional hospitality and generosity are increasingly giving way to greed and fear, especially in the cities. Crime and corruption are growing. Ulcers, unheard of here ten years ago, are second only to car accident injuries as a major health problem. And psychiatrists, whom Saudis visit only on the sly, are doing a brisk business. In short, money has produced confused values, hypocrisy and anxiety. (House, 1981, 1)

Greed and a feeling of get rick quick before the fun ends have spread to many rich Saudis, who not only own huge amounts of foreign land and stocks but are also becoming more materialistic. "In only 20 years, the country has lost many of its traditions. With three-fourths of all Saudis under 30 years of age, many don't really know their own culture" (House, 1981, 1); they are getting accustomed to cars and movies

(available largely through video cassettes in a land with no movie houses). Urban residents have been showing less and less of the Bedouin hospitality to strangers that they had been famous for. While laws still control public behavior, modern Saudi men and women mingle at parties; smuggled X-rated movies can be seen on videotape recorders, and alcohol is consumed. These activities go on behind closed doors, and some royal family members also participate. In short, separate behavioral codes apply to public and private life.

Corruption has begun to flourish, with the always accompanying waste of government money, an example being in the building of apartment towers in Jidda and Dhahran that the poor cannot afford and the rich do not want. Yet as all this proceeds unabated, the Saudi government presents its nation to the world as the ideal Moslem state, a guide other Moslem societies should try to emulate.

Riyadh and Jidda

Such a booming country must inevitably have cities either undergoing wrenching growth or booming from scratch. Saudi Arabia contains examples of both types of community, and is a fascinating case study for the world's town planners.

In 1945 Riyadh was a mud-brick village, a forgotten town in a forgotten nation (Jidda was then the capital). As oil revenues steadily rose, it took on a more modern image as reinforced concrete slowly replaced the age-old brick design. Then the post-1973 nationwide boom focused special attention on Riyadh, now the capital city, which was totally unprepared. As Riyadh's population mushroomed to nearly 500,000 by 1976, and it became the destination of the world's businesspeople, hotel space quickly became inadequate and housing became scarce, especially for the lower classes. Contractors appeared unwilling to build housing for their imported employees as the regime wanted them to do. The city continued to grow at a giddy pace, its population nearing one million by

1980. Electric power demand has shot up by a fantastic 50 percent a year. The second Five Year Plan, by allocating $13 billion to urban street systems and sewers, $8 billion to housing, $3 billion for hospitals and clinics, and more money to schools, airports, and other urban infrastructure, was sure to encourage many more Saudis to come to Riyadh. The city has had to sprawl to the west, northwest, and northeast to accommodate its new residents, among whom will be foreign diplomats, as their embassies relocate from Jidda. A good deal of the infrastructural improvements are helping all Riyadh's citizens.

Residential construction is catching up with demand; in 1978, for the first time in a decade, housing costs actually declined. . . . Riyadh's traffic, often snarled, tangled and difficult, is improving, too. The city now sports a fleet of shiny new red and white . . . public buses, which will help alleviate traffic congestion. (Hayes, 1980, 28–33).

Though no longer the capital, Jidda has hardly been left behind. Arabia's chief Red Sea port long before the Saudi takeover, Jidda today has been called a "sweltering Red Sea boom town" (Pace, 1976a, 4). As new office buildings illustrate the booming private sector, the city's water supply is inadequate and many back streets remain dirt paths strewn with litter, evidence of the public sector's failure to keep abreast of oil revenue. The city suffers "power failures, deficient bus service and shortages of building materials." There is also " 'no one universal plan for electricity, sewage, water and telephone operations in the city'," say Saudi journalists. Though falling behind Riyadh in the space of growth, Jidda's population nevertheless exceeded half a million by 1976. At this time, the city had one hotel, terrible phone service, two decent restaurants, and an airport called "a virtual shed" (Rattner, 1980, 2). The government had ordered a two-year project to beautify the city by upgrading water supply and sewage disposal, putting up prefabricated housing, and enacting other measures to enhance the city's visual harmony. Whether or not this actually upgrades infrastructure to meet the demand is yet to be seen.

Another visiting journalist described Jidda in 1979 as a city with a long way to go to outgrow its boomtown atmosphere—

a jarring contradiction to the Saudis' stated goal of preserving Islam and maintaining their ancient society. . . . Outsiders forced to deal with the chaotic, frustrating and often mindless day-to-day occurrences of living in Jidda, a city that simply does not work, cannot help but wonder if the massive buildup is really progress at all. (Ferris, 1979, 26)

Among Jidda's problems, incredible in a society with the funds to do almost anything it wants to upgrade its cities, are blackouts, water shortages, communications breakdowns, extremely high levels of noise, and a primitive sewage system.

Jidda has expanded its services to tourists and businessmen in the last five years. The city now has 6 modern hotels, many diverse restaurants, 2 modern air terminals, fine telephone service, and 24 apartment houses for lower-income residents. Saudis coming to Jidda to make their fortunes may not care that much about these improvements' effect on the city's long-term effort to outgrow its boomtown appearance. Certainly, the foreigners, making up more than half of the city's nearly one million 1979 residents are not going to care, either.

Jubail and Yanbu

Perhaps an even clearer illustration of Saudi Arabia's breakneck growth is offered by two massive projects, Jubail on the Red Sea, and Yanbu on the Persian Gulf. The Saudi government wants the country to have a diverse industrial base, so in 1975 it ordered the construction of massive industrial complexes at opposite ends of the kingdom. To man these complexes, each is to have a nearby city built from scratch.

Saudi Arabia's Royal Commission for Jubail and Yanbu is solely responsible for the two projects. The royal decree creating the commission stated, among other provisions, that the Board of Directors should be the sole controlling authority responsible for implementing the basic infrastructure plans for the two cities, that the commission should have its own budget, and that the state should allocate funds to the commission via a special account not bound by current fiscal expenditure procedures. (Barker, 1981, 13-14)

Crown Prince Fahd (now Saudi Arabia's King) was named the commission's chairman. In practice, the commission has been as independent as it was supposed to be on paper. This also means, however, that the central government may be unaware of any subsequent cost overruns. The American builders, of course, have much to say about "planning and program management," but the Royal Commission has ultimate responsibility for setting policy.

The two projects began life in a different manner. The idea for Jubail was set out before design of any heavy industry began, whereas the major industry at Yanbu was being designed when the master plan for Yanbu was begun. In neither project did preliminary planning tackle most city-building problems. Various steps in preparation of the planning document disagreed with each other and with the basic Saudi intentions for them such as plans for the rate of population growth and mix. But

the Royal Commission chiefs . . . have tended to be dismissive of criticism initially, showing a willingness to consider the doubts only when the cities . . . have advanced to such a stage that concerns aired by [Westerners] can no longer be construed as attempts to dissuade the Saudis from the whole effort to industrialize. (Barker, 1981, 16)

Plans for infrastructure provision had to consider the need in both cities for water desalination plants that would also generate electricity. Seawater canals would both supply the desalting plants and send cooling water to the industrial complexes. "Permanent housing schemes are further down the list of priorities; the first residential design contracts for Yanbu were only signed in 1981 . . . and the urban design and health care studies are not expected to be finalized until next year" (Barker, 1981, 17). Both cities

must have airports and ports to connect them to the rest of Saudi Arabia and to provide the outlet for the mainly export-oriented industrial plants.

Jubail is the larger of the two projects, since it is being built in the heart of the great oilfields. Taylor offered an idea of the stupendous size of these projects, especially Jubail:

Some 324 miles northeast of . . . Riyadh, on desolate salt flats washed by the Persian Gulf and baked in 100-plus temperatures for much of the year, a whole new ultramodern city is emerging. When completed in 15 years, this megastructure will cover an area as large as Greater London and contain a population as numerous as that of Minneapolis. (Taylor, 1982, 57)

Each of these projects is being planned largely under the supervision of a single American engineering firm, Jubail by Bechtel and Yanbu by the Parsons organization. At Jubail, Bechtel suggested the petrochemical complex largely to "process and use" the $1 billion worth of natural gas that the nearby refineries were wasting every year.

Taylor made clear that the problems of building Jubail won't be the toughest facing Bechtel and the Saudi government.

Over the long haul, . . . getting Jubail to work and function as a thriving industrial metropolis could turn out to be every bit as challenging as building the city. For one thing, Jubail's planned industries will be cranking out a prodigious supply of basic industrial products that many experts argue the world has too much of already. [Moreover], it is not all that certain that the tradition-minded Saudis will want to move to Jubail in the first place. By and large, educated Saudis display a desire to remain in wealthy metropolises like Jidda, Riyadh and Dhahran, where easy money is to be found and white-collar jobs are plentiful. Yet to equip less-educated and poorer Saudis for the employment challenges of Jubail will take many years of social development that is now only in its earliest stages. (Taylor, 1982, 60)

Perhaps the government's most difficult task will be to convince its people, unaccustomed to job-induced mobility, to move to such a remote area.

Nevertheless, compared to other planned towns, Jubail is an outstanding example of unified, coordinated planning. Bechtel's philosophy was to put in all the infrastructure first, then build the industrial complex. To this end, the company supervised the construction of 300 miles of highways, two ports, 6,000 megawatts of power generation, an industrial port, and the desalination plant before anything else went up.

Yet even the planners of Jubail are unable to avoid the uncertainty of the energy industry and the reluctance of people to change their ways, even when it would benefit them financially to do so. They also cannot avoid the harsh weather conditions that plague energy projects from Alaska's North Slope to the Australian outback. Humidity at Jubail is almost always 100 percent and temperatures soar above 100 degrees nearly every day.

Yanbu, on the Red Sea, is a less spectacular sister project of Jubail. The Saudi government treats its great distance from the oilfields as its major advantage, since it makes Yanbu less vulnerable to an Iranian attack than the country's Persian Gulf oilfields and industries, and puts Yanbu closer to Western markets. Though smaller than Jubail, Yanbu nevertheless is an impressive effort for Parsons. By 1980 it had housing for 1,800 workers, a 60-bed hospital, and three schools. The government intends Yanbu's city to have 150,000 residents by the year 2000, less than half Jubail's intended population. It will also contain one of the world's major refining and industrial complexes, although Yanbu will not have any steel or aluminum plants. Two huge pipelines will connect Yanbu to the Gulf oilfields. Unlike Jubail, the Yanbu project could not rely on existing port, electric power, or desalination facilities. Despite the government's official justification for the project, Yanbu is "viewed by some as a political sop to the economically weaker western province" (Martin, 1982*a*, III-4) that had been the turf of the House of Saud's chief tribal enemy before 1932.

As the management services contractor for the Yanbu project, Parsons will help the Saudis with design and construction in 13 distinct areas, such as transportation-communications, water, sewage, electric power, port, airport, housing-community build-

ings, and others. The town of Yanbu, north of the industrial zone, will have "schools, mosques, hospitals . . . , shipping areas [and] a university" (*Wall Street Journal,* 1978, 4). Once the two cities are built, it should be evident to town planners which of the two companies has done a better job in a function for which neither was well known before.

Other Saudi Boomtowns

Though by far the most spectacular, Jubail and Yanbu are far from being the only new Saudi cities. The government is building three military cities: Khamis Mushayt near Yemen, Tabuk near Jordan, and the largest, King Khalid Military City, 220 miles north of Riyadh. When complete, the latter will be home for 70,000 Saudi military personnel from three army brigades and their families. King Khalid Military City, its site chosen for strategic reasons but making it extremely remote, will have

military structures, houses, and apartments, mosques, schools, entertainment facilities, a 300-bed hospital, and a telephone communications system. Wells 4,500 feet deep will supply the city's water. It will have an airfield. . . . And from power plant to corner barber shop, King Khalid Military City will consist primarily of low-rise structures built of precast concrete produced in plants at the site. (*Engineering News Record,* 1978, 24-26)

The Saudis are also building Kharj, an armaments manufacturing center south of Riyadh, which is to have 100,000 residents.

The oil boom is affecting many other Saudi towns. In the northeast, fishing towns such as Oqair, Darain, Bira, and Zahama are to be modernized. Another town, Jizan, is a "concrete block and mudbrick city in the southwest corner of Saudi Arabia, far from the boom belt" (Vicker, 1977*a*, 1). A traveler's report of a few years ago described Jizan as a "sleepy, disease-infected, rundown border town which ranks high on the list of places in this world one should avoid." Now, Jizan and the surrounding province also named Jizan, is headed by a member of the Saudi royal family. The area will take in about $300 million of the $142 billion in the country's Second Development Plan, a result of which is

This town of 40,000 or so people looks like a construction camp these days. Bags of cement are piled high on the jetty that thrusts into the Red Sea. Piles of sand and gravel block some of the streets. A score or so of ships wait in the harbor to unload more building materials.

For every man seeking work there are three jobs. . . . A new airport is under construction. A French company is building a three-berth port. Five hospitals in the province are in various stages of construction. (Vicker, 1977a, 1).

Prince Mohammed, the regional ruler, must coordinate the activities of each national ministry's office in Jizan province. His efforts are helped by the strict religious ways of Saudis, which ensure a low crime rate and little alcoholism or gambling. Wealth, however, has brought car ownership, and the old Islamic idea of fatalism—"Inshallah"(Allah wills it)—has made drivers feel unresponsible for their own actions, leading to numerous car accidents.

In small ways such as in Jizan, and in such gigantic ways as in Jubail and Riyadh, Saudi Arabia is dealing with new oil wealth to recreate the nation and its cities and towns. Only time will tell whether or not it has done so without creating a permanent boomtown syndrome afflicting its people and making them diverge forever from the government's treasured Islamic behavioral code.

GROWTH ELSEWHERE IN THE PERSIAN GULF

The oil whirlwind has swept through many of Saudi Arabia's Persian Gulf neighbors. Kuwait's oil resources were explored and exploited by Western companies at the same time as those of Saudi Arabia to the south. Kuwait, once an obscure sheikdom, today enjoys one of the world's highest standards of living. As does its rich neighbor Saudi Arabia, Kuwait offers "free medical care, education, heavily subsidized food,

free land and interest-free loans to build houses . . . , no income tax, property tax, sales tax or any other sort of tax" (Martin, 1982c, IV-1).

Kuwait needs foreign workers to keep its economy running as badly as does Saudi Arabia. Sixty percent of its 1.3 million residents are foreigners. While most of them are laborers from countries such as Yemen, others, especially those from India, are professionals. Regardless of their status, they have as slim a chance of becoming Kuwaiti citizens, and thus assuring themselves a permanent place in Kuwait's economy, as those foreign workers in Saudi Arabia.

The United Arab Emirates, among whose best known cities are Dubai and Abu Dhabi, are a prominent member of OPEC, perhaps beyond their actual importance to the cartel. Though not an oil exporting nation itself, the small island of Bahrain, just off the Saudi Gulf coast, has boomed nevertheless. Bahrain was long a center of pearl production and palm tree cultivation. The first oil concession was granted to the Bahrain Petroleum Co. in 1928, five years before it found oil. The petroleum boom and increased Japanese competition destroyed the Bahraini pearl industry.

With the discovery of oil in Kuwait and Saudi Arabia (1938), Qatar (1939), Abu Dhabi (1958), Dubai (1966) and Oman (1967), Bahrainis began emigrating. Unable to match its neighbors in oil production, the Bahraini government tried to set up the Bahrain Fishing Company, a venture owned jointly by local and foreign interests, to process and export shrimp. It also built an aluminum smelter in 1972 and a shipyard in 1977. These efforts succeeded in giving almost every adult male a job by the mid-1970s. This industrial base made Bahrain the Persian Gulf's communication, banking, investment, and education center. The area once reserved for palm tree cultivation soon sprouted housing projects. By 1971 Bahrain's urban areas held about 170,000 residents, 78 percent of the population—up from 50 percent in 1941. As Bahrain's housing stock went up, so too did housing prices, and the price of an average plot of land went up 50 times from 1946 to 1975 in the city of Manama.

"The economic order created by the oil industry transformed tenants into salaried labor, cultivators into wage earners, and the renters of land into entrepreneurs" (Khuri, 1980, 138). Farming employed a mere 6.7 percent of the work force in 1959, and only 2.9 percent in 1971. Few native Bahrainis make up this tiny agricultural labor force, and even fewer work today in such traditional industries as boatmaking, textiles, pottery, and basket and mat making. The new economic order also forced Bahrainis to upgrade education and literacy standards.

Though distinct from its neighbors in some ways, Bahrain shares their tendency toward a huge foreign labor force. About 75,000 non-Bahrainis, especially Indians and Pakistans, make up 46 percent of the construction work force, 41 percent of the community and social service sector, 37 percent of trade activities, and anywhere from a fourth to a third of the labor force in agriculture, fishing, and transportation (Khuri, 1980, 139). Bahrain must decide if it wants these industries if they remain dominated by foreigners who will always place demands on its infrastructure.

The long British rule, which didn't end until 1971, left Bahrain's infrastructure superior in many ways to that of its neighbors. Even Saudis come to Bahrain to use its excellent public school system, about 800 doctors and nurses, 50,000 automobiles, and 35,000 television sets.

Bahrain's social customs, such as the status of women, the level of censorship, and the tolerance of alcohol, are much more liberal than those of Saudi Arabia. The Gulf's first oil producer, Bahrain never became an oil giant. In fact, production of Bahraini crude started declining in 1970, and most of the crude processed at Bahrain's 255,000 barrels-a-day refinery comes from Saudi Arabia (Abercrombie, 1979, 305). Bahrain does have ample gas supplies, which run electric generators at its aluminum smelter, provide electric power, and run its water desalination plant. Its Ministry of Development and Industry set Bahrain up to replace Beirut as the Middle East's banking center. By 1979 about 150 banks had branches operating in an "offshore" tax-free environment. More efficiently perhaps than Saudi Arabia, Bahrain has set up an economy designed to survive in a post-oil age.

REFERENCES

Abercrombie, Thomas, 1979, "Bahrain: Hub of the Persian Gulf," *National Geographic* **156**(3):300-329.

Barker, Paul, 1981, "Saudi Arabia's Twin Cities," *Multinational Business* **1**:13-23.

Engineering News Record, 1978, "Saudis Cast $7-Billion City on Empty Desert Site," July 13, pp. 24-26.

Ferris, Thomas, 1979, "Riding the Saudi Boom," *New York Times,* March 25, p. VI-23ff.

Gupte, Pranay B., 1981*a*, "Swept By Change, Saudis Fear Loss of Old Values," *New York Times,* March 23, p. 1ff.

Gupte, Pranay B., 1981*b*, "On Saudi Arabia's Path to Prosperity: Long Trail of Abandoned Automobiles," *New York Times,* March 26, p. 1.

Hayes, Stephen D., 1980, "Riyadh on the Move," *Aramco World* **31**(4):28-33.

House, Karen E., 1981, "Modern Arabia," *Wall Street Journal,* June 2, p. 1.

Ibrahim, Youssef, 1979, "A Metropolis Rises in the Desert," *New York Times,* October 17, p. D-1.

Kingdom of Saudi Arabia, Ministry of Planning, 1980*a*, "Development and Development Planning in Saudi Arabia."

Kingdom of Saudi Arabia, Ministry of Planning, 1980*b*, "Progress During the Second Plan."

Khuri, Fuad, I., 1980, *Tribe and State in Bahrain,* University of Chicago Press, Chicago.

Martin, Douglas, 1982*a*, "The Saudis Build a Pittsburgh," *New York Times,* January 31, p. III-4.

Martin, Douglas, 1982*b*, "Saudi Arabia's New Capitalism," *New York Times,* February 21, p. III-1.

Martin, Douglas, 1982*c*, "Prosperous Kuwait Faces Retrenching," *New York Times,* February 22, p. IV-1.

Martin, Douglas, 1982*d*, "The Very Mixed Blessings of Pure Liquid Gold," *New York Times,* May 23, p. IV-3.

New York Times, 1981, "Indians Play Key Role in Kuwait," April 15, p. 4.

Pace, Eric, 1975, "Saudis Seek Balance in Riyadh Between Minarets and High Rises," *New York Times,* April 19, p. 2

Pace, Eric, 1976*a*, "Saudis Having Second Thoughts About Their Oil Boom Growth," *New York Times,* April 22, p. 4.

Pace, Eric, 1976*b*, "Industry Changes Saudi Landscape," *New York Times,* April 25, p. 16.

Pace, Eric, 1976*c*, "Remote Capital of Saudi Arabia Now Busy Cosmopolitan Center," *New York Times,* November 13, p. 2.

Rattner, Steven, 1980, "Jidda, Once Sleepy, Booms, But Riyadh is Taking the Lead," *New York Times,* December 26, p. 20.

Rattner, Steven, 1981, "How Saudi Arabia Mixes Welfare and Free Enterprise, " *New York Times,* March 1, p. III-8.

Taylor, Alexander L., III, 1982, "The Jubail Superproject," *Time,* July 12, pp. 57-60.

Vicker, Ray, 1977*a,* "Old Ways are Heeded in Remote Saudi Town Remade by Oil Money," *Wall Street Journal,* July 28, p. 1.

Vicker, Ray, 1977*b,* "Jobs Go Begging in Oil-Rich Mideast Lands," *Wall Street Journal,* August 22, p. 6.

Wall Street Journal, 1978, "Parsons Awarded Job for Complex in Saudi Arabia," May 3, p. 4.

18

Other Energy Boomtowns

Countries beyond the Persian Gulf have been quick to take advantage of the revolution in oil pricing. Some, such as Nigeria, have found vast oil resources of their own, while others, especially South Africa and Australia, have discovered they have so much coal they can become energy self-sufficient with great effort and a little ingenuity. All these countries are experiencing either the explosive growth of existing cities or the need to create new ones to be able to exploit their precious energy resources to the fullest.

LAGOS, NIGERIA

The only city in black Africa to suffer the oil-induced boomtown syndrome is Lagos, capital of Nigeria. Lagos was already the major city of black Africa's most populous and influential nation before Nigeria's membership in OPEC turned it overnight into a world oil power. However, the chronic corruption throughout the Nigerian government made it just as incapable of dealing rationally with Lagos's boom as the Mexican or Venezuelan leadership dealt with their cities' growth.

Modern urbanization began in the 1900s, as the railroad, the port, and many public buildings either were built or were enlarged. But Lagos did not begin to boom until after World War II; from 1950 to 1963, Lagos's population went up a remarkable 8.5 percent a year. Growth was so rapid in a city geographically unable to expand to accommodate it that the city of Lagos had a 1963 population density equal to that of Manhattan (about 25,000 people per square mile). Today's Lagos is centered on an island of two square miles on which 250,000 people live.

Lagos was thus Nigeria's unquestioned population center long before 1973. The lure of oil money proved as irresistible to the Nigerian peasant as it did to the Mexican peasant. Schools, piped water, health centers, and other urban wonders lured so many country people to Lagos by 1974 that the capital city had 700,000 residents, with another 1.3 million living in the surrounding region (Johnson, 1974, 12). This hectic population expansion created monstrous traffic jams and terrible housing shortages, overwhelmed health facilities, water supply, and electricity systems, and caused chronically high unemployment among the unskilled. Johnson remarked that without the oil boom, Lagos would probably have been able to deal with growth in a similar manner as its coastal neighbors, Dakar (Senegal) and Abidjan (Ivory Coast), in which expansion came with urban planning and without the loss of esthetics.

Lagos did not learn from its neighbors. "The city is suffering growing pains. Over-rapid expansion has wreaked havoc with roads, lights, water and telephones," (Darnton, 1976, 2) as the population doubled since 1966 to 1.5 million. With the urban lure of a Mexico City and the proximity to the oilfields of an Aberdeen, poor Nigerians and foreign businesspeople flock to Lagos. The latter have driven rents up several hundred percent, a situation unbearable to the former group. The poor, of course, have to deal permanently with atrocious traffic, since they are as unlikely as Mexico City's urban poor to return soon to the countryside.

Corruption has hindered efforts by the government to build new highways, a sewage plant, and other vital infrastructure improvements, as well as to reduce air pollution and cut traffic levels by imposing strict odd-even driving rules. Drivers with even-numbered plates were not to operate their vehicles on odd-numbered days, and vice-versa, but police venality no doubt reduced the effectiveness of this rule. The boomtown problem most visible to both Nigerians and foreigners is the inability to provide adequate electric power. Perhaps no city in the world is as vulnerable to blackouts as Lagos. "Nobody with any money gets by in Lagos without a generator" (Cowell, 1982, 2). Not even a tripling of the country's power generating capability in eight years has kept pace with demand. Utility officials cannot coordinate supply to industrial and residential areas that have risen without any planning.

Lagos in 1982 is a city "bursting at the seams. The traffic jams, or 'go-slows' in local parlance, are among the world's most stubborn, the prices are the world's highest, and with the congestion and heat, it probably ranks among the world's most irascible cities" (Cowell, 1982, 2). Lagos is a superb illustration of the fact that a boomtown's size has nothing to do with the inability of local officials to deal with the boom or with the severity of the boomtown syndrome among its inhabitants. Inflation, corruption, and black markets are facts of life. A typical house rents for $75,000 a year, with three to five years rent payable in advance. "For Nigerians, as well as the many foreigners who are here to cash in on the oil money, the city is an irritating, dangerous, chaotic place" (Cowell, 1982, 2). Even the government considers it a place of permanently snarled traffic, woefully inadequate sanitation, and a high crime rate. Quinn (1981, 19) claimed that he has seen more crime and less polite people elsewhere in western Africa, but admitted that "Lagos isn't the most pleasant city in West Africa . . . the traffic is horrendous in Lagos. What can you expect from a city of three million people with hardly any working traffic lights?" So frustrated is the Nigerian government that it is using billions of petrodollars to build a new inland capital at Abuja, just as the Brazilians did a generation ago. But the world oil glut, which has hit Nigeria harder than perhaps any other OPEC member, may quickly render Abuja a ghost town.

The entire Nigerian society has fallen victim to the oil boom and its aftereffects. Economics professor Peter Kilby (1981, 26) described this national boomtown syndrome that has been repeated in oil-exporting countries from Iran to Indonesia, Mexico, and Venezuela. Behaving as other countries unable to deal with the oil glut, Nigeria's solution to economic hard times was the January 1983 expulsion of thousands of Ghanaians and other Western Africans.

THE NEW ENERGY BOOMTOWNS OF SOUTH AFRICA

South Africa is today one of the few countries that has successfully weathered the world oil shortage despite its lack of oil. The nation has instead turned to its huge coal reserves, both to supply power generation plants and to find an innovative answer to its transportation fuel needs.

Coal also serves as a major export commodity. The government decided that the country needed a port near Durban on the Indian Ocean to relieve chronic congestion there. The town of Richards Bay began to develop in 1965 as a harbor to ship Transvaal coal (see Fig. 4.1). Previously a village of 180 residents, Richards Bay had by 1980 grown into a small city of 10,000 with several well-defined suburbs. Various government agencies provide generous financial assistance to industries taking advantage of the port and the ready access to coal. Resulting from this assistance, some of those firms have built an aluminum smelter, a coal exporting port, a plant processing sand into minerals, and a phosphoric acid plant in the zone of Richards Bay clearly delineated for such industries.

A variety of dwellings, a local clinic, and ambulance transportation to nearby hospitals were part of the overall plan. Richards Bay has an airport, hotels, two elementary schools, one high school, stores, clubs, a beach, and other recreational facilities. Richards Bay gets its water from two nearby lakes.

Richards Bay is largely a company town. The Richards Bay Coal Terminal Company, the area's major employer, either bought or built homes for its employees. The company, however, was not the town's sole planner. The harbor and railroad to the coal veins were designed and built by the South African Railways and Harbors Administration. The Department of Planning and the Environment, builders of the town and its infrastructure, oversee the activities of the Richards Bay Town Board, which in turn supervises daily activities there. The Planning and Environment Department planned and built extensive parkland throughout the Richards Bay area. The government expects Richards Bay to have 100,000 whites by the year 2000; a separate city for blacks is being developed nearby.

The Witwatersrand itself is the site of two new

energy cities. Bereft of oil but blessed with coal, South Africa decided after World War II that it had to develop a way to turn some of its coal into the liquid fuels required to run its transportation system. The culmination of these efforts was the country's first large-scale coal liquefaction plant, based on the Sasol process, built between 1952-1955 about 50 miles from Johannesburg. From coal mined at the nearby Sigma colliery, the plant also produces petrochemicals, liquefied petroleum gas, and industrial gases. To house the Sasol One plant's workers and their families, the city of Sasolburg was built nearby, starting in 1954. By the late 1970s, Salsolburg had 27,000 residents living in 5,500 houses and about 800 apartments. To encourage employees to live there, the government made housing loans available (to married men only). Each residential area has shops, and Sasolburg has several nursery, elementary, and high schools, a theater, library, cinemas, a variety of houses of worship, and recreational facilities. Its boosters claim that it is a city built "with modern town planning techniques and up-to-date architectural design," with curved streets and extensive parks (Sasol Ltd., 1980, 9).

Sasolburg has gone beyond its initial role of supporting the Salsol One plant to become a major chemical industry center. Plants in the region produce explosives, chemicals, plastics, synthetic fibers, fertilizers, synthetic rubber, fungicides, and other agricultural chemicals.

To expand its synthetic fuels effort, South Africa built the Sasol Two and Three plants near Sasol One. These two plants use coal from a different source — from the Bosjesspruit mine — it was decided to house their miners and the Sasol Two and Three workers not in Sasolburg but in another new city, Secunda. The government decided against expanding the nearby towns of Trichardt and Evander, doubting their infrastructures' abilities to deal with a vastly expanding population. Construction of Secunda began in March 1976, and it was proclaimed a town on June 22, 1977. A Sasol subsidiary built the town, working with the Transvaal government and several federal agencies. By 1981 Secunda had about 28,000 white residents and 5,500 permanent and temporary dwellings (Secunda Health Committee, 1980, 2).

The town developer's status as subsidiary for the main industrial firm means that Sasol can provide money for Secunda's development and that town officials can plan growth with much better knowledge of future industrial activity than most boomtown officials enjoy. Secunda's leaders also have had much fewer front-end financing and funding difficulties than those confronting other boomtowns.

It is evident that the township developer made a major financial contribution to the establishment of the necessary infrastructure for essential services. Without this contribution it would not have been possible to install essential services and levy reasonable tariffs. Notwithstanding this contribution the local authority had to find capital to the extent of (ten million rands) on the open market. (Secunda Health Committee, 1980, 5)

Secunda claims to have all the urban amenities of Sasolburg and Richards Bay. South Africa is confident that the size of its coal reserves will keep all three towns and their related industries going for decades to come.

All this new activity has affected Johannesburg, the grandest boomtown of them all. By 1969 Johannesburg had 1.2 million people and a booming financial district. It also had a skyline, traffic jams, and an overloaded water supply and transportation system. Predictions of a future Johannesburg-Pretoria "megalopolis" were already common (*International Mangement*, 1969, 57-60).

Only in South Africa can a city owe its existence to racism. Atlantis lies on the Atlantic coast, some 30 miles north of Cape Town. It is the culmination of a government effort to "relieve a severe housing shortage in the 'colored' (mixed-race) areas of Cape Town and to promote industrial 'deconcentration' " (Lelyveld, 1982, 2). (This is especially ironic, in view of the housing *surplus* in Cape Town's white areas.) The government planned for a city of 500,000 "coloreds" by 2000, partly to concentrate new industrial growth in Cape Province in Atlantis's industrial zone. About 30,000 "coloreds" lived in Atlantis by early 1982, and the 500,000 figure is not expected to be reached until the year 2020. The industrial park, however, is filling up quickly; 54 firms are operating there, although "coloreds" are unwilling either to move to Atlantis from Cape Town or to commute there. The town itself may be one reason: "For all the promises in the glossy brochures, there is nothing futuristic about the Atlantis that has come into being. What the visitor finds is a fairly typical South African township for nonwhites with drab mass-produced housing unimaginatively arrayed" (Lelyveld, 1982, 2). There are no restaurants, movie theaters, bus service, hospitals, or schools. Not surprisingly, there is a lack of civic pride, since the elected management committee has little power. One can only assume that the same amount of planning went into the black areas around Richards Bay, Sasolburg, and Secunda.

THE NEW AUSTRALIAN ENERGY BOOMTOWNS

Australia is in the midst of a similar energy boom. Coal and crude oil were two of Australia's most produced resources in 1976. Most of Australia's anthracite coalfields are in eastern Queensland and New South Wales (see Fig. 4.3). Most oilfields are along the coast of Western Australia. "Investment in the (coal) mines, service towns, and rail and port facilities could total between $2,000 and $3,000 million, if they were all to be developed in the next decade" (Wilson, 1980, 184). Of course, these plans depend largely on the growth of Japan's steel industry and other markets in the Middle East, Asia, and Latin America.

Australia's offshore fields have yielded significant amounts of natural gas but little oil. Most gas fields lie in the "northern cyclone belt" (Wilson, 1980, 192). In recent years, Australia has discovered the free world's third largest uranium reserves. Most of Australia's uranium lies in northern Queensland and along the coast of Northern Territory. Since Australia in 1980 neither had a commercial nuclear power plant operating nor planned to build one by 1990, much of the mined uranium is to be exported. The mining and export of uranium is a highly controversial topic in Australian politics, not only because of the uranium glut that has hit other producing areas (e.g., the American Southwest) but because of a uniquely Australian concern. The country's Aborigines, with increasing political power in recent years, must decide if the royalties they derive from the mining on their land will make up for the social turmoil created by mining.

Along with Kalgoorlie and the other boomtowns mentioned in Chapter 13, Australia has many boomtowns devoted to energy, among them the Bowen Basin coal towns in east-central Queensland and gas field centers in the Cooper Basin.

REFERENCES

Baker, Pauline H., 1974, *Urbanization and Political Change—The Politics of Lagos 1917-1967*, University of California Press, Berkeley, Calif.

Cowell, Alan, 1982, "Nigerian Capital: A Torrid, Irascible, Booming City," *New York Times,* May 7, p. 2.

Darnton, John, 1976, "Winds Gone, Rains Due, an Unsettled Mood Hangs Over Lagos," *New York Times,* April 17, p. 2.

International Management, 1969, "Johannesburg Booms Again," **24**(5):57-60.

Johnson, Thomas A., 1974, "Nigerians, Rejecting Rural Lives, Flock to Capital, " *New York Times,* March 14, p. 12.

Kilby, Peter, 1981, "What Oil Wealth Did to Nigeria," *Wall Street Journal,* November 25, p. 26.

Lelyveld, Joseph, 1982, "South African Racial Policy Begets City for 'Colored'," *New York Times,* April 2, p. 2.

Quinn, Bowden, 1981, "A Bad Rap for Lagos," *New York Times,* August 25, p. 19.

Richards Bay Town Board, Promotional material, Group Printing and Packaging Mobeni, Durban, South Africa.

Sasolburg Municipality, 1982, Promotional literature, Salsoburg, South Africa.

Sasol Ltd., Public Relations Division, c. 1980, "Sasol One" and "Liquid Fuels from Coal: Meeting the Challenge," The Penrose Press, Johannesburg, South Africa.

Secunda Health Committee, c. 1980, Promotional literature, Secunda, South Africa.

Wilson, R. K., 1980, *Australia's Resources and Their Development,* Department of Education, University of Sydney, Sydney, Australia.

PART IV

COMPONENTS OF THE BOOMTOWN ALLEVIATION PROCESS

19

Current Compensation and Siting Practices

Governments and industry have paid little attention to the effect of a project location on the loss felt by the area residents. When economics forces the choice of an especially bitterly opposed site, the ability to direct limited compensation money to the most severely affected residents can mean the difference between a smoothly run project and one endlessly delayed by lawsuits and demonstrations. Many current assistance programs, especially at the federal level, rarely meet the expectations of impacted residents. Researchers have come up with several suggestions for more effective ways of choosing sites for energy projects and compensating only those residents of the affected region who are truly deserving of aid.

CURRENT FEDERAL COMPENSATION PROGRAMS

Brody (1977) examined some of the federal programs now offering assistance to communities and individuals affected by external shocks. The federal government has numerous reasons for offering aid: charity; compensation for losses caused by responsible agents, usually acts of nature; inducement to buy local cooperation and to encourage local planning; agreement to share the risk of anticipated destructive events with local residents and governments and with private industry; and correction of capital market failures created either by towns having to spend funds on infrastructure improvement years before the tax dollars come in, or by a jurisdictional mismatch, in which the facility is outside the boomtown's jurisdiction.

The types of federal assistance available are direct payments and grants; technical assistance in predicting population growth, future facility needs, or in obtaining financial aid; federal loans to state and local governments to deal with the front-end financing problems (which are useless when state constitutions limit the extent of local borrowing); and subsidizing the payments of insurance by private firms.

The type of federal aid should relate to its intended purpose. Direct payments and grants can be charitable, compensatory, or inducive. Loans are primarily to correct front-end financing problems. Insurance subsidies are a form of risk-sharing. The federal government, ideally, bases the type of aid it will give on its impression of the affected town's needs.

The federal government can direct funding in a number of ways. Those responsible can earmark the funds for a certain purpose, provide them for a recommended use, or offer them on an unrestricted basis. Funds can be disbursed directly to state or local governments or to individuals, or they can be channeled through authorized federal agencies. At the same time, the state authorizes the governor, the state legislature, or a state agency to control the federal funds. Whether individuals or government should be the ultimate beneficiary depends on the purpose of the aid. If it is to compensate for losses caused by responsible agents, the affected individuals themselves should get the money. If "buying" local cooperation for the project is the funds' purpose, then the local government should receive it.

Brody (1977) examines the Trident Community Impact Assistance Program, the Economic Adjustment Program for Defense Impacted Communities, Relocation Assistance Act efforts, and Disaster Relief. I have condensed Brody's descriptions elsewhere (Malamud, 1981, 78-81).

The federal programs intended mainly for energy-impacted areas deal either with grants and loans to boomtowns for planning, capital construction, and other activities, or reimbursement of state and local governments for loss of tax or royalty revenues from energy development on federal lands.[1] Neither of these involves aid to individuals.

One grant-loan program is the Coastal Energy Impact Program, set up in 1976 (Malamud, 1981, 81). One of Washington's reimbursement programs arises from the Federal Coal Leasing Act (81-82). One reimbursement program involves payments in lieu of taxes—aid given in annual payments to local governments to be used as they wish. These governments administer areas in which federal lands are located.[2]

Effective aid programs must consider variations in local conditions and needs, and should give local governments most of the responsibility of disbursing federal funds as they see fit. By that definition, many federal aid efforts have been ineffective: poorly timed, inadequately staffed, and entangled in red tape. Gulf Coast residents criticized federal relief efforts after the devastating 1969 Hurricane Camille as slow, unco-ordinated, and politically motivated,[3] and Wilkes-Barre, Pennsylvania residents expressed similar feelings after severe 1972 flooding. Victims of January 1982 mudslides in central California also complained about red tape and the 8-16 percent interest rates applicable to loans from the Federal Emergency Management Agency (they had been 1 to 3 percent until 1981). Congress also limited FEMA's lending to those who could prove their ability to repay. FEMA blames the problem on public misconception about its mandated role, which is merely to help other government and private agencies rebuild damaged economies rather than to do the job alone, and insists that the high interest rates are Congress's responsibility.

National politics also affect the level of federal aid to Western boomtowns. By the end of 1980, the federal government was spending about $50 million a year to help towns disrupted by coal and uranium mining build new sewers, water lines, schools, and hospitals. When Western states and towns complain that this is not enough money, they blame the Administration, which in turn blames the Congress, dominated by Eastern interests. Much of the current $50 million is the responsibility of the Department of Energy's Office of Shale Resources Applications. Reagan Administration efforts to dismantle the Energy Department can only hurt this funding effort.

A final problem with federal boomtown aid is that federal laws, designed mainly for sudden disasters, "leave the government ill-prepared for disasters that last weeks or months" (Rosenbaum, 1977, IV-1), such as drought, severe winters, and disruptive long-term energy development. Despite Reagan Administration efforts, however, federal aid will continue to be a crucial part of any boomtown relief plan, but not necessarily the most important part; its inherent bureaucracy will never make it popular with Westerners unless they have no other source of funds.

CURRENT STATE COMPENSATION PLANS

Westerners may be no more receptive to state impact assistance than to federal aid; for example, western Coloradans often consider Denver as far away as Washington. Sheer geography, however, should give state officials insight into local problems that Washington cannot match. Despite the similarity of their future as energy development areas, the states have widely varying aid programs.

Colorado

As of 1977, Colorado has a Socio-Economic Impact Coordinator, whose staff deals with secondary energy development impacts. The coordinator's assistant serves as a contact for towns such as Craig and Somerset, and represents state interests by attending town gatherings. The coordinator's office

1. develops local impact assistance teams containing industry, state, and local government officials, and federal representatives
2. worked on a 1977 census in six energy-impacted counties to improve federal grant allocations
3. ranks Colorado towns according to the expected severity of the impact, updating the list periodically.
4. prepares fact sheets on all impacted towns, including the development of population, financial data, sewer and water supply needs, police, fire, recreation, housing, and educational statistics
5. assists towns with grants from the state's Oil

Shale Trust Fund and coordinates that fund's activities with other funds
6. monitors statewide energy activities
7. is studying boomtown financing

The state has professionals available to provide expertise on impact response methods to communities.

Colorado did appear, at least in 1977 and 1978, to lead most other Western states in impact aid planning, but Colorado's effort is still developing in sophistication, and local residents are far from satisfied with it (Monaco, 1977).

North Dakota

This state's Coal Impact Office makes grants covering the extraordinary expenses its boomtowns incur by hosting coal development projects. The state, however, refuses to finance projects normally funded by private sources or by homeowners. The office keeps firm control over the uses to which the towns can put the aid money. Unlike Colorado, however, North Dakota had in 1977 not yet developed an accurate, reliable information system with data on the size of impact problems.

Texas

In 1977 this state was only starting to become aware of the local effects of energy development. The government's criteria for permitting drilling had nothing to do with socioeconomic impacts, but state agencies did consider the environmental impact of surface mining.

Wyoming

Wyoming's Community Development Authority can issue up to $100 million in tax-free bonds to finance infrastructure and housing, but its bonding authority was legally uncertain in 1977. The Farm Loan Board distributed severance tax revenues to coal-impacted areas, with the money having to go to road, water supply, or sewage projects.

HOW INDUSTRY CAN HELP AFFECTED TOWNS

The "let the private sector do it" philosophy so popular in the U.S. in 1983 assumes that industry will be more able to help boomtowns than any level of government.[4] Industry, however, has been slow to recognize its obligation to help these communities.

One of the boomtown's basic problems is that the "risks, uncertainties and a lack of foresight cause the mismatch between supply and demand for housing" (West, 1977, 1) and other services. Energy firms must be more willing to reveal their plans to housing developers and infrastructure builders, since these town features are essential to maintaining a high enough quality of life to keep worker productivity high.

Energy companies can merely pay their taxes or they can become more active in easing the problems created locally by their activities. The companies can take this second step by giving financial aid, offering know-how, helping plan, build, and operate public facilities, and coordinating impact monitoring. A description of the variety of ways in which industry can carry out each of these steps is given in Malamud (1981, 87-88).

Industry will be more likely to help if

1. assistance is necessary to mange energy-stimulated growth
2. a firm's failure to assist will cause extremely bad impacts[5]
3. assistance will increase productivity and reduce labor turnover during construction and operation
4. construction delays cause soaring costs that outweigh the saving to the firm if it fails to offer assistance

5. the firm considers a project a key element in its strategic planning
6. local opposition is limited[6]
7. the town shows willingness to share the responsibility for local development[7]
8. assistance is likely to help the project succeed on schedule
9. the project has a long life expectancy
10. local services and infrastructure are not seriously lacking before construction begins
11. the firm does not expect the local government to discriminate against it (West, 1977)

It is therefore up to both industry and local governments and residents to encourage timely industrial assistance to the affected communities near an energy project. Local leaders and residents have a variety of ways by which they can influence corporate policy toward them (Malamud, 1981, 89).

CURRENT SITING MECHANISMS IN THE UNITED STATES

Current energy project siting procedures deal heavily with environmental damage. This section will examine the effects of these procedures on residents near energy sites and in boomtowns.

The 1969 National Environmental Policy Act (NEPA) forced all federal agencies to consider environmental effects, including preparation of an Environmental Impact Statement (EIS), when a major federal action was to be taken. The EIS is now a standard requirement of all energy firms when they apply for federal permits to build any project and is a clear part of the U.S. energy project siting process. Residents to be affected can express their opinions well before construction begins, since the federal agency responsible for issuing the permit must get the public involved in its decision making. But unless a project is unusually large, only a limited number of citizens participate.

Citizens have often joined public policy disputes in the U.S. whenever they feared losing scenic or recreational areas.

On the whole, citizens become involved . . . most effectively when they deal with small-scale, specific issues, especially at the lower levels of government. As more people become involved and as more special interests are represented, the problems become more complex . . . and the familiarity of members with specific issues diminishes. (Organization for Economic Cooperation and Development, 1980, 31)

and general public interest in the whole dispute probably does, too. NEPA's effect on public involvement in siting procedures is best illustrated by examining several energy policy disputes.

The controversies surrounding the Bodega Head nuclear plant in California and the Kaiparowits fossil fuel plant in Utah offer dramatic evidence of the difference NEPA and the EIS has made in siting procedures (Malamud, 1981, 90-95). The Bodega Head siting dispute in the early 1960s involved the local utility, local officials, business people, and news media, but not public opinion, which had been all but ignored. Yet the plant was to be built in a heavily populated area. The Kaiparowits plant, on the other hand, was to go up in the remote vastness of southeastern Utah. Yet the area's very remoteness brought environmentalists into the dispute. The events leading up to the decision not to build the plant showed the extent to which NEPA and the EIS requirement enabled local residents to join the environmental groups to demand a substantive review of the lengthy licensing procedure.

The Midland nuclear plant controversy in Michigan (OECD, 1980, 58-75) differed from Bodega Head and Kaiparowits because Dow Chemical, Midland's only major employer, stated that it firmly supported the plant. This, of course, induced most Midland residents to favor the plant, too. Only environmental groups opposed it. Unlike Kaiparowits, where most of the residents favoring the plant (electricity users) lived far away, the Midland plant would have directly affected all the Midland citizens. This suggests that local residents should have the major voice in expressing their feelings about a project. When their lack of organizing ability prevents a majority of opposing residents from forming a united opinion, environmentalists provide a useful organizing role. When (1) the

majority of residents favor a project (unlike Kaiparowits) and (2) the town's major employer has not forced the residents into supporting the project by threatening to close its manufacturing plants down if the energy project is not built, then the environmentalists should not create national or statewide publicity unfavorable to the project and to the residents supporting it.

Residents to be affected by energy projects can now express their concern about the degradation of their area and communities resulting from energy development, including the boomtown syndrome, and can do so well in advance of any agency attempt to grant a permit. Without NEPA and the EIS, this would never have occurred. These siting disputes also show the need for all the participants in these disputes to be willing to work toward a resolution of the conflict. The Midland case was particularly bitter, with no resolution having been reached by 1981, partly because the dispute had become more legal than scientific or ecological.

SITE SELECTION ABROAD

France

To an extent unknown in the United States, France's central government, through its nationalized electric utility, Electricité de France (EDF), is responsible for "the determination and preliminary selection of sites . . . in conjunction with the regional and department authorities" and central government agencies from the health, industry, and equipment ministries. They then consult the elected officials and other authorities in those areas containing the most likely sites to continue assessing technical and economic feasibility, safety, and environmental impact. In France, however, no local or regional government body has "any legal right to restrict the government's freedom of action regarding site selection" (OECD, 1980, 84).

The public does not become actively involved in French siting procedures until a six- to eight-week public inquiry is convened—after all the intergovernmental discussions. The inquiry results become part of the information available to the central govern ment's minister responsible for electric power, who then submits to the national Council of State a draft decree stating whether the project is in the public interest. The siting procedure, which neither the public nor the courts can delay to any great extent, ends when the decree is signed.

West Germany

The West German legal system contains administrative courts that handle citizens' complaints against acts of any governmental authority. Neighbors of an energy-generating project can sue the developer if they think their rights have been violated.

Several of the West German regional governments have made special attempts to solve energy facility siting problems because of rising local opposition to federal and regional siting decisions. The Federal government alone, however, has the power to select potential energy facility sites, among which the provinces can make their own choices. Only industrial and special sites are eligible for selection. Major energy plants can go up in developed areas only if they replace similar plants. Since local land-use plans provide the public its only chance for early participation in the licensing process, a license proposal for a site not identified as suitable in a local plan will involve the public only at the very late stages.

Great Britain

Since environmental impact statements are not required in the U.K., the ecological effects of many North Sea Oil-related projects have not been analyzed. Most central government officials put their faith in the current planning system which, while often addressing visual impacts, fails to deal with offshore effects on ecology and with marine impacts in harbors.[8] As a result, the "long-term ecological and social effects of oil-related North Sea operations in Scot-

land have not been attended systematically within the Scottish planning system." Few Scottish planners know these long-term effects.

With environmental impact assessment, Peterhead would have dealt better with its harbor expansion, and Nigg would have adjusted to the presence of 3,000 platform-building workers. The assessments made in Scotland have generally been long on project description, short on impact analysis and the listing of alternatives, and downright scanty on environmental information. Of all the impacted regions, Shetland, apparently alone, had consultants prepare detailed environmental impact statements before and after Sullom Voe's selection as the main development area. The Shetland County Council made sure that these studies were to be the basis of a development plan that only then would decide the scope and speed of development, and not be a justification of development plans already made. These studies managed to predict the scope of construction far better than the British government did itself. Most American impact statements, by comparison, assume that the project is necessary rather than first considering its need.

Scotland, however, lags behind the United States in several key impact assessment aspects. While the United States has never settled on any one environmental or social impact assessment method, Scotland in 1975 had not even developed alternative methodologies; each Scottish town had to do so for each project, generally by calling in outside consultants. Aberdeen University has been preparing a manual for local use in assessment decisions.

Australia

In 1974 Australia passed its own Environmental Protection Act, apparently very similar to the United States's NEPA. It requires environmental impact statements and, in some cases, public inquiries for projects. Since Canberra controls the export of minerals, and the small domestic market assures the export of most extracted Australian minerals, the federal government has the power to require an EIS.

The Australian states control the process of issuing production leases and the extent of the required restoration; they can also ask for environmental studies and hold inquiries. This can cause delay, much of it political. The 1974 law requires mining companies to refer new proposals to the Minister of the Environment, who decides on the need for an EIS.

The Minister's decisions are not usually subject to public discussion. If the public believes that the Minister is considering a proposal, the Act allows the public to ask the Minister for comments, and requires the Minister to respond promptly.

The mining company, not the Ministry of the Environment, prepares the EIS. If the Ministry decides to call for a public inquiry as part of EIS preparation, the Minister must give the public six weeks advance notice, and give interested persons the same amount of time to send in written opinions. After the inquiry, the final impact statement is issued publicly. Since the Minister of the Environment's opinion can be overturned by the Cabinet, this whole decision making process can become highly politicized. Bambrick urged that "specific policies . . . should ensure that state and federal environmental investigation are complementary rather than competitive . . ." (1979, 119).

The federal Department of the Environment claimed in 1975 that the states agreed to coordinate environmental regulation efforts to make sure that only one EIS will be issued for a given project. More formal methods for state-federal cooperation have since been set up, but have not prevented frequent bickering between them. Certain states—New South Wales, Queensland, and Western Australia—have had glaring mining-conservation confrontations with Canberra; the state in these disputes was normally more proindustry than the federal government.

The passage of the 1974 Act was one illustration of the 1972-1975 Labor government's having been the first to take a stand on environmental matters. More recent liberal governments have been slow to return them to the states and to industry. From 1975 to 1978, 6,000 proposals were considered, of which 1,270 were judged to be of environmental importance. Yet only 19 environmental impact statements for mines had been issued as of 1979; in the other instances, the project was considered not to warrant an EIS, or the mining company agreed to include some environmental protection measures in its plans.

Australia is so vast and its mining areas so far from major cities that it does not have to worry about the effects of mining or energy exploitation on large numbers of residents. Only in areas populated by large numbers of native aborigines is the social impact of mining going to become a major aspect of the project's overall effect on the nearby region. Moreover, only in these areas will there be any problem of compensating the residents affected.

COMPENSATION POLICIES ABROAD

This section deals only with those government or industry payments to afflicted residents beyond those normal tax payments made by any industry to the country, region, or community in which it operates.

For every 2,000 workers at a French nuclear plant site, EDF estimates a population increase of 3,000 residents in the surrounding area. The French authorities know that

Arrangements have had to be made to ensure that such a large increase in population compared with the local population does not cause serious difficulties from the point of view of the conditions of life of the workers and their families. . . .

These arrangements now come within the framework of what has been called the "regime for major construction sites." This regime, which does not only apply to nuclear power plant sites, is designed to ensure that the conditions of life of workers on a large site resemble those of the local population as closely as possible. . . .

These arrangements are made in collaboration with the local communities concerned at no cost to the latter which cannot be covered by the new tax revenue brought by the plant, i.e. with no increase in local taxes; this is true even if, in addition to specific accompanying facilities such as housing and schools, it is found necessary to provide other facilities in advance to improve the future quality of life, such as sports fields, swimming pools, etc.

Local communities may be self-financing or may borrow with the help of the financial facilities given them, the financing being covered mainly by the large new tax revenue going to the local communities from taxation of the plant. (OECD, 1980, 119)

To avoid the front-end financing problem,

The French Government has agreed to make advances against the taxes which a plant will later have to pay. These advances may cover any annual repayment installments on loans which local authorities have had to arrange with the national financial organizations existing for that purpose. (OECD, 1980, 129)

The ENEL, Italy's version of EDF, makes special contributions to impacted Italian towns before plant construction begins. These payments equal about $2 per kilowatt, or $1.8 million for a 925-megawatt plant (OECD, 1980, 130).

In Switzerland, utilities offer several benefits to affected towns, such as contributions toward building a reservoir, repair of local roads, reduction of one plant's height by about 65 feet, and the supply of free electric power at the plant gates.

Japanese utilities pay a Fixed Assets Tax to the cental government equal to an amount between 1.4 and 2.1 percent of the construction cost. The impacted town receives one quarter of the total. It is not clear, however, whether or not the tax is paid or the town receives its share before plant construction. The utilities also have to obtain local fisherman's co-operation and pay indemnities to those thrown out of work because of the plant.

Australia rarely has to consider compensating affected citizens. Those most likely to suffer impacts are the aborigines living deep in the outback, far from the largely white cities of the coast. A very controversial subject in Australia is the amount of power the aborigines should be allowed in deciding the fate of resource projects and the compensation they are to receive upon approval of a project. Australian planners must remember that although aborigines are considered primitive by Western standards, they value their land, culture, and lifestyle, are increasingly sensitive to the prejudice of nonaborigines, and have ideas of time and work much different from those of whites.

The Northern Territory's Aboriginal Land Rights Act of 1977 allows mineral exploration and development on aboriginal land only if they agree to it. However, it also allows national considerations to outweigh aborigines' decisions against mining. In 1979 aborigines held 18 percent of the Territory's land, but they may claim another 23 percent (Bambrick, 1979, 73). The Act does not offer the aborigines any guidelines for their financial dealings with the mining and energy companies, who inevitably consider any resources they discover to be Australian, not an aboriginal asset. In 1977 one aborigine leader said, however, that "we want not only royalties, but a fair share of the profits" above an "accepted" level. The aborigines' Northern Land Council also wants aborigines to be able to use most of the infrastructure near the mining area, and to obtain the free use infrastructure actually in the mining zone once mining ends. Aborigines insist that whites be forbidden to live in the new mining towns unless they work there or are related to workers. They also demand that the Council be able to refuse entry to anyone for any reason, and that the mines hire as many aborigines as possible with working conditions and hours that they consider appropriate. Finally, the Council insists on strict environmental safeguards, monitoring, and reclamation. The Council can be agreeable to mining projects, indicated by its approval on November 3, 1978 of a uranium mine project.[9]

NOTES

1. In other words, the lower level of government would have received the tax or royalty had the land not been federally owned.
2. These reimbursement programs are absolutely critical to Alaska, whose land is 96.4% federally owned, to Nevada (86.6%), Utah (66.1%), Idaho (63.7%), Oregon (52.6%), Wyoming (47.8%), California (45.2%), Arizona (42.8%), and, to a lesser extent, Colorado, New Mexico, Montana, and Washington (Brody, 1977). Federal ownership of much of their land is one reason for the "sagebrush rebellion" now sweeping the western states.

3. Families with friends in relief agencies allegedly received better service than other families.

4. After all, the firms doing the developing should know better in many instances than the federal or even the state government about the scope and duration of their work.

5. These implications include giving the firm the notoriety of having caused environmental degradation.

6. If opposition is too high, the project will stop.

7. For example, if the town seeks federal and state aid on its own without waiting for industry to help, it is showing willingness to share the responsibility for development.

8. For example, Scottish law does not require sewage treatment plant installation.

9. All this bears substantial resemblance to the dealings Washington will increasingly be forced to have with Indian tribes living above rich Rocky Mountain energy resources.

REFERENCES

Bambrick, Susan, 1979, *Australian Minerals and Energy Policy*, Australian National University Press, Canberra, Australia.

Brody, Susan E., 1977, *Federal Aid to Energy-Impacted Communities*, Massachusetts Institute of Technology, Cambridge, Mass.

Malamud, Gary, 1981, "A Comprehensive Solution to the Boomtown Syndrome," master's thesis, New York University.

Organization for Economic Cooperation and Development, 1980, *Siting Procedures for Major Energy Facilities*, OECD, Paris.

Rosenbaum, D., 1977, "The U.S. Has a Heavy Investment in Disasters," *New York Times*, February 6, p. IV-1.

West, Stanley A., 1977 (Aug.), *Opportunities for Company-Community Cooperation in Mitigating Energy Facility Impacts*, Massachusetts Institute of Technology, Cambridge, Mass.

20

Theories of Siting and Compensation Improvement

Governments and energy companies can, and do, consider impacted residents in their siting and compensation schemes. Many questions relating to the boomtown residents themselves remain unanswered, however. Most current siting and compensation methods appear to assume that all the town's residents are equally deserving of consideration in the siting process before the plant is built, and of compensation after construction starts. The town itself, then, receives the aid, not the individual residents.

The following theories put forth primarily by Massachusetts Institute of Technology urban and energy policy researchers, suggest that a truly fair solution to the boomtown syndrome requires a more thorough look at the different degrees of loss and suffering imposed on various classes of residents. They suggest a siting scheme called auctioning and a variety of new compensation plans, both to overcome local opposition to energy development and to help determine the costs of the boomtown of development-related dislocation. These theories offer a way to reduce the local bitterness brought on when someone's property is seized to build something the owner opposes.

THE O'HARE-SANDERSON COMPENSATION MODEL

The extent of a resident's alienation or loss and the timing of the aid offering must be considered in any fair compensation system. For example, O'Hare and Sanderson (1977) consider boomtowns as dynamic rather than static, and avoid "identifying a community with the people who live in it at a particular time" (O'Hare and Sanderson, 1977, 102).

The basic purpose of any fair compensation program must be to determine those boomtown residents truly deserving of aid. The various sources and recipients of these funds have changing stakes in the outcome of the project and changing decision making power as the development process evolves. Compensation becomes most urgent when stakes are highest but decision making power is lowest. This situation will cause trouble unless the decision makers both wish to act in the impacted group's interest and know this group's needs. In site selection, the developer may not care about the town's original residents. Since town planners cannot identify immigrants before they arrive, town leaders will ignore the immigrants' needs.

The O'Hare-Sanderson theory examines the choices available to the groups of participants. Residents are clearly better off as more options are available to them and as fewer options are denied them. Their type of analysis is based on the Pareto criterion, which argues that "a state of affairs S_2 is preferable to S_1 in the view of an individual if it offers him more choices, but does not foreclose any that S_1 provided." If S_2 does not include all of S_1's options, then the criterion is as follows: "If a state of affairs S_4 offers an individual a choice which state S_3 forecloses, S_4 is preferable to S_3 in the individual's view if he did not choose any of the foreclosed options under S_3 and chooses one of the new options under S_4" (O'Hare and Sanderson, 1977, 121).

This analysis can help planners determine those boomtown residents deserving of compensation. If someone is no worse off after the boom than before it, that person needs no compensation. The first half of the Pareto criterion excludes immigrants from assistance, since none of their preboom options vanish. Therefore, O'Hare and Sanderson claim that newcomers should not be considered when awarding compensation to victims of boomtown growth. Immigrants must know exactly what to expect before they consider moving to a boomtown—that the boom will not last forever, and they will probably have to move on.

Some of the boomtown's original residents will benefit from rapid growth, while others will suffer. Those most likely to deserve transfer payments are fixed-income people; workers in occupations with labor surpluses and falling wages; working women, who generally cannot join the construction boom and who must compete with incoming women for those jobs available to most females; farm workers who suffer from strip mining; businesses dependent on farming (e.g., processing and canning); and consumers of services brought into short supply (e.g. schoolchildren, the elderly, and overworked doctors).

Those deserving of compensation can only be found among the original residents. Therefore, merely giving money to the boomtown's government or to its general population is inefficient. To set up a proper compensation system, planners must consider boomtowns as disasters against which insurance can be written (i.e., town residents pay premiums and receive payments if the disaster occurs), and avoid giving boomtown compensation money to its government. Those who benefit, namely the developer and the ultimate energy consumers, should pay boomtown "premiums." Many sufferers from energy development do not live in the boomtown's jurisdiction. "It is rare that the constituents of any local government are the same group as the person affected in a boom" (O'Hare and Sanderson, 1977, 130). Government may also disburse its aid so slowly that immigrants ultimately benefit as new residents, especially if the money becomes part of capital investment projects that the immigrants, with their superior numbers, can control. Finally, government will not likely compensate old-time residents who leave. If those who legitimately receive money decide to give it back to the government as taxes, they can do so. Although O'Hare and Sanderson never fully consider the way in which an individual compensation plan will work, they remark that

It is preferable to construct a schedule of "boomtown disaster relief" under which individuals qualify for fixed payments insofar as they meet specific qualifications like "retired person," "non-landowner," or "agricultural supplies retailer". . . . The size of the compensation should also be included in the compensation schedule. . . . The compensation should *not* be made in view of the residents' subsequent good or bad experience during the boom itself. The compensation is for suffering . . . and any subsequent advantage a citizen gains from the development is appropriately considered his own. (O'Hare and Sanderson, 1977, 133)

These ideas appear to ignore certain political realities, such as the way in which the federal or state government is going to identify individuals deserving of aid unless people insist loudly enough on it (not a very likely event in many towns), or unless the local government identifies them for higher governmental levels (one wonders what local government will do this in return for nothing). Nevertheless, wise town planners will not confuse a town with its residents. Moreover, a local government in a developing boomtown will lose much of its aid if the planners adopt the O'Hare-Sanderson model. The town government must then rely on its taxing power, half of which disappears if the energy project is outside the town's jurisdiction.

Few ways exist in the real world for a local government to raise the enormous sums of money it will need with a small tax base on which to work. A town realistically cannot expect its original residents who receive aid to contribute much of it to the local treasury in this age of tax revolts. In most boomtowns the size of Drumbuie, Scotland, the boundary between the town and its individual residents becomes very thin.

In a separate study, undertaken with Susskind, O'Hare (1977) did acknowledge that the local government will deserve direct compensation under certain conditions, because: only the local government will provide money toward building roads and other necessary facilities; giving money to government is far simpler and more direct than giving to individuals; and aid to a town can help the town's government improve its decision making abilities.

Future boomtown research must determine the validity of the O'Hare-Sanderson theory by examining the limiting size of a town for which the boundary between town and citizens is important; the number of original Scottish boomtown residents who became out-migrants; how well the compensation system worked there; and the source of most of the aid—the oil companies, the Scottish or the British central government.

OTHER COMPENSATION IDEAS

Vander Muelen and Paananen (1977) were also concerned about the need for equitable compensation of boomtown residents as part of the overall economic efficiency of rapid energy resource development in the western U.S. They, as did O'Hare and Sanderson, examined the Pareto choice criterion, concluding that it will be satisfied if those who benefit from energy development compensate those who suffer, and if overall welfare increases. Vander Muelen and Paananen believed that the cost of arranging compensation payments—and, implicitly, government's unwillingness to undertake fair compensation—will go down if planners can reduce the number of groups bargaining for the aid.

The authors remarked that investors, workers, environmentalists, consumers, and original residents are affected when industry develops energy resources. The environmentalists' lack of an economic stake excluded them from consideration. "While the costs of rapid growth affect all original residents, benefits from gains in earnings are not as evenly distributed" since many residents are retired or work outside the energy industry. Therefore, "original residents as a group are not automatically compensated for costs imposed on them during impact" (Vander Muelen and Paananen, 1977, 318). The authors claim that providing funds to local governments fails to attack the problem of rapid growth, but merely accepts it and tries to deal with it. "The most pressing equity problem is the impact of rapid growth on the welfare of original residents. The related efficiency problem is the failure of present policy to force investors to take account of the costs their decisions impose on original residents" (Vander Muelen and Paananen, 1977, 319). Vander Muelen and Paananen suggest that investors be required to contract with the boomtown governments, including a time schedule and penalties for breaking the schedule, plans for housing, and plans for payments to the town.

These suggestions form part of an investment strategy, an idea discussed by many researchers and that is covered in Chapter 23. It requires far more certainty in government's and industry's strategic planning for resource development than either has shown so far. It also demands that local governments have a better grasp of growth management than all but a few have displayed. Nevertheless, the investment strategy is part of the overall boomtown solution.

Discussions of compensation are not limited to political science or economics journals. Legal scholars have developed an extensive literature of compensation law. Costonis (1975), for example, showed how fair compensation can serve as an intermediary between police and eminent domain powers[1]; Sax (1971) remarked that the idea that "public rights" may be vindicated without mandatory compensation should be more popular in legal circles than it has been; and Michelman (1967) argued that legislatures and government agencies have been avoiding their responsibilities in the compensation process.

An answer to these legal questions must be part of any boomtown solution. Their resolution will reduce the animosity of landowners and other affected residents to energy development. Future boomtown investigation must examine the progress made in the courts and legislatures of Western states toward creating some kind of equitable compensation system that neither ignores the grievances of landowners nor awards them such huge compensation payments that future energy development is unnecessarily hampered.

THE "AUCTION" CONCEPT OF SITING AND COMPENSATION

Michael O'Hare of the Massachusetts Institute of Technology developed, both working alone and with Susskind (1977), an alternative plan to the traditional payment scheme (Malamud, 1981, 115-117).

The "auctioning" concept is basically a competition among those local governments anxious to have the project in their jurisdictions. Each government will set up an environmental impact statement for its site, arrange direct payment from either government agencies or energy companies to those individuals most affected by the project, make a legal commitment to the project by setting up zoning changes or plans for infrastructure construction, and determine the correct compensation level.

Each town then makes a bid, determining the minimum level of per capita compensation and of total payments. The development agency receiving the bids will consider the compensation levels when determining the cost-benefit ratio for each town (i.e., determining which town will suffer and which will benefit most), finding the proper site and paying that town's demanded compensation. O'Hare and Susskind claimed that very rarely will the feasibility of only one site eliminate the auctioning possibility.

One problem planners will face is to avoid encouraging towns to overbid and ask for more compensation than they deserve. The agency should use the "Dutch auction" scheme of awarding the facility to the lowest bidder but paying compensation to the town equal to the payment demanded by the next lowest bidder. This will probably work in most cases, since competing towns rarely know the others' bid levels. O'Hare and Susskind know that even their scheme will award the same amount of compensation to each resident, and that some townspeople will get too much compensation and others too little. However, they claim that the compensation error with an auction process will never be worse than that without an auction (O'Hare and Susskind, 1977, 27).

O'Hare and Susskind discuss the process by which each town sets up a bid. The first step is a referendum, in which each resident states his own cost. Then the local government selects the bid, and the residents determine the means by which they can make up for compensation errors. The residents can even set up a temporary political unit if the entire town is not affected or if parts of a few towns are involved. If the development agency offers planning grants to likely bidders, each one can select a private firm, use the agency itself, or have its own planners predict the impact and the costs. If local residents, many of whom may be ignorant of the impact created by large energy facilities, are afraid to bid at all, the development agency can set a cost estimate for the town upon which the town can base its bid. The entire bidding process rests on the assumption that it can prevent people who claim that their suffering is not compensable in cash from vetoing the bid.

This theory offers promise because it does not pretend to ignore the hostility with which most local residents will greet a proposed energy project. It offers those residents with high per-capita stakes a chance to influence strongly, and perhaps to dominate, the referendum in which the town sets its terms. One problem not addressed by O'Hare and Susskind is that many small towns in the Rocky Mountains and other energy-impacted areas are much poorer than those in areas blessed by a steadier economy. The residents may, out of desperation for hard cash, and out of ignorance of the boomtown syndrome, insist on setting an unrealistically low bid; the cost will be far higher than anything the town's low bid can compensate. Nevertheless, development agencies cannot be expected to investigate the emotional condition of each resident of every possible project site. Another problem is that most local governments do not know the impact of a proposed energy project, unless they have already experienced it. If four of five possible project site towns find themselves in such a situation, they will all ask the development agency to do everything but set the actual bid. This takes decision-making power out of the hands of those at the local level, who should be making most of the decisions, since they will suffer the highest per capita cost.

Additional research must investigate the extent to which the auctioning concept has found use in actual project siting procedures, and the modifications that O'Hare and Susskind may have made in their theory since 1977, in response to these real-world developments. Nevertheless, auctioning promises to be one way in which townspeople can determine the compensation they are to receive for the inevitable inequities of the siting process. This concept also ties together the siting and compensation processes, something that most central governments often forget to do.

NOTE

1. Traditional law recognizes two types of seizure: seizure reasonably related to a valid public purpose, under the government's "police power," and seizure under the government's power of "eminent domain." Police-power seizure requires no compensation from the government, which an eminent domain seizure requires "just compensation," fixed by a jury according to rigid standards.

REFERENCES

Costonis, J., 1975, " 'Fair' Compensation and the Accommodation Power," *Columbia Law Review* **6:**1021-1082.

Malamud, Gary, 1981, "A Comprehensive Solution to the Boomtown Syndrome," master's thesis, New York University.

Michelman, F. I., 1967, "Property, Utility and Fairness," *Harvard Law Review* **80**(6):1165-1258.

O'Hare, M., 1977, "Not On My Block You Don't," *Public Policy* **25:**407.

O'Hare, M., and Sanderson, D., 1977, "Fair Compensation and the Boomtown Problem," *Urban Law Annual,* vol. 14, Washington University, St. Louis.

O'Hare M., and Susskind, L., 1977, *Managing the Social and Economic Impacts of Energy Development,* Massachusetts Institute of Technology, Cambridge, Mass.

Sax, J. L., 1971, "Taking, Private Property and Public Rights," *Yale Law Journal* **81**(2):149-186.

Vander Muelen, A., Jr., and Paananen, O. H., 1977, "Selected Welfare Implications of Rapid Energy-Related Development Impact," *Natural Resources Journal* **17**(2):301-323.

21

Predicting Population and Serving Social Needs

THE SOCIAL WORKER'S TASK

Even the most rational financial compensation method cannot remove the social, noneconomic, nonfinancial losses imposed on boomtown residents—alcoholism, crime, vandalism, mental depression, and all the other problems discussed in Chapter 1. While siting and financial compensation mechanisms have received intense study, Bates (1978) remarked that behavioral scientists are only now starting to understand the social effects of boom-bust cycles related to energy development. Social workers have conducted few clinical or epidemiological studies of the effects of rural exploitation on newcomers and old-time residents, mainly because social workers were never involved in energy development policy and because that profession's ignorance of the problem is severe. Bates explained the manner in which social workers in a developing boomtown have to get the best results from their involvement.

Bates stated that the social worker must encourage open conflict among residents and help them express feelings that they are not used to expressing, help diverse groups organize themselves, and show extreme patience. The worker must also follow the Middleman-Goldberg structural approach to serving these residents. This individual must

1. be accountable to the client, preferably by developing a service contract with the client
2. follow the demands of the client's task by looking beyond each client to see if others face the same task, and by working with the clients on others' behalf and with others on the clients' behalf
3. maximize the supports in the clients' environment by avoiding the taking of the central position in helping the clients
4. take a broker's role before assuming a mediator's role, and take a mediator's position before assuming that of an advocate
5. use extreme care in working with socially impacted communities.

HOW PLANNERS CAN EVALUATE SOCIAL IMPACTS

Numerous techniques exist for forming social impact assessment statements such as social indicators, model building, demographic analysis, matrix methodologies, computer methods, social forecasting, cross-impact analysis, impact monitoring, and many others. The topics investigated include housing, energy development, transportation, facilities siting, land use, coastal land management, rural development, and boomtowns themselves. Finsterbusch and Wolf claimed that social impact assessment focuses very little attention on individuals. While most of their book is highly abstract and not very useful to small-town leaders trying to plan social impact analysis, it does discuss the various social impact assessment methods available. One especially intriguing idea is that of Gene Willeke of Georgia Tech University (Finsterbusch and Wolf, 1977, 317-323), who suggests that planners identify the various "publics" and try to communicate with them.

Willeke believed that planners can accomplish this task by identifying subgroups in a large population according to location, interests, and social characteristics (e.g., age, sex, income, and education). Several methods are available for subgroup identification: self-identification (in which citizens contact agencies or attend meetings), third-party identification by a citizens' advisory committee, and staff identification by the planners themselves. Field interviews, geographic, demographic, historical, and comparative analyses are all useful methods of analyzing these subgroups.

While the boomtown syndrome's social elements may be the most severe, they are also the least evident to researchers. Experts have far to go before they can develop a system of social compensation as elaborate as the financial compensation schemes discussed earlier. Social impact analysis probably will not become enough of a science in the next few years to help most boomtown residents; these citizens will have to rely on financial compensation to ease all their burdens for some time to come.

PREDICTING POPULATION GROWTH AND SERVICE DEMANDS

The ability to predict the increase in population accompanying an energy boom will obviously be helpful to social and economic planners in the affected region. Sanderson and O'Hare studied and evaluated the abstract mathematical and computerized models available to planners trying to predict the rate of population growth in communities likely to become boomtowns. Without this knowledge, no one knows the amount of new infrastructure and housing to be required or the level of social and health services to be needed by workers and their families.

The problem with most of these models is that they

vary in their methodology, output, assumptions, and quality. . . . They either simulate community development over time or combine various submodels providing community 'snapshots' at selected points in time. . . . Underlying assumptions often conflict, reflecting their different sources. . . . Model quality, measured by special features, tests, exportability and usefulness to policy-makers, reveals careful and thorough work in some cases and hurried operations with insufficient in-depth analysis in others. (Sanderson and O'Hare, 1977)

Predictions of energy project impacts small enough to affect individuals are concerned with variables, values, equations, parameters, calibrating models, outside variables, accuracy, precision, and testing of assumptions by sensitivity analysis and experimentation.

Simulation models find year "n" results, which become the input for the year "$n + 1$" calculations using the same basic equation, and simulate change over time. Coefficient models use different equations for each year. Each submodel predicts one variable's value at one point in time. The equations themselves often have to be changed to remain useful.

Planners at any level of government have to understand the qualities of a good model before selecting one. A good model predicts variables that are relevant to the planner's needs. It also works in a useful time interval or series of time intervals (i.e., not in minutes or decades, but in weeks, months, and years), and in a jurisdiction matching the planner's own. Planners also have to beware of common modeling errors. The most frequent is that a model's faulty structure causes computation of incorrect values for the desired variables. Incorrect parameters may also cause values to be computed for the wrong variables.

Several types of projection methods are available to planners. Employment models assume that the local economy consists of export (often called basic, or primary) and local (or secondary, nonbasic, or derivative) sectors, and that the size of the local sector depends on the size of the export sector.

Population models assume that this variable depends on the expected growth in employment from the project. They use family size, employment patterns, unemployment, and migration as key variables, and predict population based on the population-per-worker and employees-per-household ratios. Most population models fail to consider multiple-worker families, newcomers' lifestyles, demographic changes in boomtowns, and the fraction of available jobs filled by long-time residents.

Service impact models project service demand by multiplying population estimates by per capita "adequacy" standards (e.g., police officers-per-person or hospital beds-per-thousand residents). These standards supposedly measure the need for services, but the planner has to define adequacy, a variable that for each town will depend on the price elasticity of demand,[1] regional variations, and social customs. Most of these models overlook current service usage, residential settlement patterns, and population age distributions. Current service usage affects the level of future service needs, settlement patterns help to determine future infrastructure needs, and age distributions influence the need for housing and education.

Public revenue and spending models deserve little confidence, since they are often based on faulty assumptions. Revenue levels depend on tax rates, assessment methods, and local tax bases; revenue levels change with an area's social and political atti-tudes, and cannot be exported from one area to the planner's. Several expenditure models make assumptions about inflation, changing productivity, and changing land and fuel costs. With the economy's being whipsawed by wildly fluctuating energy prices and by land speculation, there is very little reliable information available for making this kind of local projection.

Sanderson and O'Hare provided an exhaustive list of available models and an equally thorough summary of the models' inputs, outputs, and processes for obtaining results, but also warned planners intending to use them that

Those purchasing projection studies should be aware that many studies have been low-budget projects, done *very* quickly (in the interest of "timeliness"), lacking careful consideration and analysis of the problem at hand; few adequately reference their sources of information or report any testing of their models. Defects like these reduce a study's usefulness and hinder the development of better projection methods. Lack of testing is less serious when procedures are either explained or well-enough referenced to allow their replication elsewhere, but too many studies report numbers without explaining their derivation.

Besides these weaknesses, we found several omissions common. Most studies ignore the price elasticity of demand for services and omit procedure for defining "need." Does the cost of providing services affect the quantity of service desired? Experience tells us that if tax bills increase—especially relative to income—people decide they don't want so many public services after all. If there is a relationship between service costs and demand, does it change from place to place or from generation to generation? Most important, does everyone "need" the "average" service level? Do they "need" the level recommended by some professional group? How do we decide what people "need" in a particular rapidly growing community in the year 1990?

These questions are neither trivial nor easily solved; purchasers of projection studies expecting to buy models which address these questions and which overcome the weaknesses prevalent elsewhere, should carefully consider the constraints they place on consultants. (Sanderson and O'Hare, 1977)

NOTE

1. This is the extent to which a change in the price of a service will cause a change in the opposite direction in the demand for it.

REFERENCES

Bates, V. E., 1978, "The Impact of Energy Boom-Town Growth on Rural Areas," *Social Casework* **59**(2):73-82.

Finsterbusch, Kurt, and Wolf, C. P., eds., 1977, *Methodology of Social Impact Assessment*, Dowden, Hutchinson & Ross, Stroudsburg, Penn.

Sanderson, D., and O'Hare, M., 1977, *Predicting the Local Impacts of Energy Development*, Massachusetts Institute of Technology, Cambridge, Mass.

22

The Tax and Disbursement Systems' Effect on Boomtowns

Prospective boomtowns cannot solve their problems without receiving adequate financial aid at the right time; the front-end financing problem and the jurisdictional mismatch threaten nearly every boomtown's finances. This chapter illustrates the variety of ways in which national and state governments receive revenue from energy development and channel aid to local governments needing financial help to deal with it. Few of these were intended to help towns undergoing explosive population growth.

THE ROLE OF THE FEDERAL GOVERNMENT

The federal government collects royalties on its land leased to coal developers. Since the federal government owns more than half the land in several Rocky Mountain states, it will collect vast sums as the West is opened further to development. Washington now allots 50 percent of its royalty revenues to the states to spend almost any way they wish; the states receive the money as direct payments or low-interest loans. This clearly is not a system of rapid assistance to towns undergoing rapid population growth.

The federal government can offer grants and loans to boomtowns for infrastructure building and other purposes, and can reimburse state and local governments for loss of tax and royalty revenues from energy developed on federal lands. This does not, however, assure timely disbursement of aid to boomtowns when they most desperately need it.

THE ROLE OF THE STATES

Each state has the power to levy severance taxes on any energy development project within its borders. Despite their huge revenue potential, severance taxes took a long time to be accepted in most Western states.

Among available revenue sources for the states are state income and property taxes, energy-related excise taxes (e.g., severance taxes), bond issues, and various 179 types of federal aid. The states rely on taxation for most of their revenue, but energy excise taxes offer the most direct, efficient way to channel revenue from the source of boomtown growth to those most heavily affected by it.

The states parcel out aid through mechanisms such as project grants, unrestricted grants, block grants, and loans. The aid's purpose can be to correct capital market failures, offer compensation, or ensure orderly development. As occurs with federal aid, the type of state help must suit its purpose to be most effective. Loans therefore offer the best way to deal with capital market failures, and recycling excise tax revenues is the best compensation method.

Monaco (1977) analyzed Colorado's financial situation at the start of the synthetic fuels age. The state faced several obstacles to effective boomtown financial aid in 1977. The state constitution forbade the government to borrow on a boomtown's behalf, a problem facing many other states. While fiscal prudence is always desirable, "state indebtedness, if managed carefully, can be a useful tool for assisting boomtowns" (Monaco, 1977, 29). If the state knows the pace at which development will proceed, it can borrow in the financial markets or from the federal government and then lend these funds to the boomtowns, with the full knowledge that these communities will repay the loan with tax revenue over time. The Colorado legislature, often beset by political bickering when considering relatively minor matters, will have to amend the state constitution to enable the state's many boomtowns to borrow.

State law can also stymie boomtown growth management. For years, Colorado law forbade the state to levy a severance tax on any resource extraction industry. Then in 1976, Colorado "imposed a 4 percent severance tax on its coal, . . . and its production has increased 75 percent since then. Colorado's annual revenue from the tax is $1.2 million" (Utah State Department of Community and Economic Development, 1980, vol. VI, 6). By 1980, Colorado's passage of a coal severance tax left Utah and Arizona as the only Western states then without such a levy.

The high concentration of mobile homes in boomtowns is still another hindrance to boomtown management through tax collection. These dwellings are considered motor vehicles for tax purposes; their owners pay sales taxes, ownership and license fees, but no property tax, and the vehicles depreciate in value. "Mobile home owners pay only about one-fourth of the tax charged to owners of comparable conventional housing" (Monaco, 1977, 32).

Colorado's population distribution prevents the state's boomtowns from faring better in obtaining financial aid. Most residents live in Denver, Boulder, Colorado Springs, and other cities along the Rocky Mountains' eastern slopes, while Craig and Colorado's other boomtowns lie in the Overthrust Belt running along the western foothills. This causes relative apathy among most Colorado politicians toward the state's boomtowns and their special needs.

Wyoming's sparse population is more evenly distributed geographically than Colorado's, so Wyoming's legislation is more forceful toward industry. In 1975 Wyoming passed laws repealing tax exemptions for industry and permitting towns to raise their debt ceilings. Wyoming enacted a severance tax on coal mining in 1969. The tax rate, only 2 percent in 1978 (Susskind and O'Hare, 1977, 43), had reached 17 percent by 1981. In 1977 Wyoming also collected a 3 percent sales tax, from which one-third of the revenues reverted to the state's "political subdivisions." These sketchy figures suggest that Wyoming's tax system is more receptive to its boomtowns than that of Colorado, bereft until 1977 of a coal severance tax.

North Dakota enacted a severance tax in 1975. Forty percent of its revenues went to local taxing districts, 30 percent to the state's general fund, and the remainder to a special trust fund. Unlike some states, North Dakota has made sure that much of its general fund revenues flow directly to local school districts. As the schools' population rises, so does the aid.

Montana's severance tax of 30 percent is perhaps the nation's steepest levy directly imposed on energy development, and was the recent subject of heated political and legal activity. In July 1981, the U.S. Supreme Court upheld the constitutionality of Montana's tax, but left to Congress the nagging "question of what is an 'excessive' rate'" (*Business Week*, 1981, 94). Future work should look into the effect this high tax rate has had on energy companies' willingness to explore and extract Montana's resources.

In 1981 Utah still had neither a severance tax nor a provision allowing the state to distribute any of its tax revenue with local governments. County administrations cannot even share their revenues with their own communities. Only by doing so can communities within a given county share any kind of energy-generated revenues.

Searle (1977) offered a complete picture of Utah's tax system in the late 1970s. Business and personal state income tax revenues go to school districts. State sales tax revenues flow into the general fund. Communities can impose sales "option taxes" if they wish; the income generated from local sales taxes goes back to the political units in which the sales took place. Local property tax money goes to school districts and local governments. Property taxes collected in boomtowns do not usually meet the related need for additional revenues if, as so often occurs, these towns contain many mobile trailers. Energy firms, as in other states, can escape local property taxes in Utah by setting up operations outside the town limits. A privilege tax is imposed on all firms doing business on the 75 percent of Utah's land under federal ownership and thereby exempt from property taxes. This is the only tax among all those in Utah that can benefit boomtowns directly.

Even more helpful will be a coal severance tax and a sensible increase in the one percent tax on metals-extraction firms. Only with a severance tax will the ultimate consumer of energy provide capital for energy-impacted areas. Since Utah's constitution forbids state revenue sharing with its towns, the state will have to enact its severance tax as a local options levy if it is to help those towns needing the most financial help in delivering vital services.

Utah communities and school districts can incur debt up to 2 percent of taxable property value for county borrowing and 4 percent for town and district borrowing. Under special (i.e., boom) conditions, this figure becomes 8 percent, but this still does not offer a boomtown all the help it needs. Moreover, boomtown bonds rarely are of a high quality, since the uncertainty of energy development makes bond repayment equally uncertain. Utah's constitution forbids the state to guarantee local bonds, but allows the energy firms involved to do so. In 1975 the state allowed its towns to issue bond anticipation notes in the amount of anticipated increases in property values or expected debt retirement. Revenue and special improvement bonds provide limited help in boomtowns. The existence of municipal improvement and special service districts also allows towns more leeway in issuing bonds. Service districts, for example, can issue bonds up to 12 percent of taxable property value, far beyond the 8 percent allowed towns, counties, and school districts. Other recent Utah acts allow special districts to finance schools, water systems, and housing.

In Utah, the type of government in any given area determines, among other things, the amount of energy-generated revenue it receives. In 1972 the state legislature enabled Utah's government to ask each county's residents to select, in a referendum, the type of government they desired, out of 16 varieties. Eight of these will involve consolidation of the county's incorporated and unincorporated areas' tax bases. Local residents, however, are often afraid of losing their identity and autonomy, while county residents outside the towns do not want to share their new wealth with traditionally more prosperous towns. One flaw in the 1972 scheme is that the newly formed government will normally have a county's 2 percent debt limit, rather than the 4 to 12 percent available to a city.

Utah's Agenda for the eighties, an overall plan for the state's economic, social, and political development in the next ten years, declared that

The current debate over the best source of funds for boomtown assistance programs is still unresolved. The financial assistance could come from the company, state governments, the federal government, or some combination of the three. The latter seems to be the most reasonable with the federal government taking the lead in coordinating and putting together a front-end financial package for the impacted community. (Utah State Dept. Comm. Econ. Dev., 1980, vol. VI, 4)

Only by better intergovernmental planning than that so far shown by all governmental levels will this occur. The state, however, appears to have a larger responsibility than the agenda gives it, since only the state can enact special severance taxes, which will assure that the energy consumer and not the afflicted resident pays the ultimate cost for energy-encouraged boomtown growth, and the revenues generated can flow directly to the impacted towns rather than to a general state fund or to school districts, neither of which can be expected to provide the money needed for any type of infrastructure or service provision required at a given moment.

FOREIGN TAXATION OF ENERGY-RELATED PROJECTS

Chapter 19 examines European and Japanese compensation and siting policies dealing with nuclear power plants, and this chapter covers nuclear plant taxation in those countries. It also describes the changing attitude to the Australian government toward taxation of energy exploitation there.

Electricité de France (EDF), France's nationalized utility, has to pay "local taxes on each [power] plant equivalent to those payable on all other industrial establishments" (Organization for Economic Co-operation and Development, 1980, 122). These taxes consist of a land tax and a "taxe professionelle." There is a limit to the amount of tax money that a town in which a plant operates is able to receive; the rest of the revenue goes to a regional fund, which in turn distributes the money to towns adjacent to the plant site. Each town's share depends on the number of plant workers living there. The taxe professionelle, however, has not been widely accepted in practice.

Belgium's two nuclear plants were constructed and are operated by a consortium of Belgian utilities combined with France's EDF. Each plant is liable for taxes on the income it generates, communal taxes, and a variety of provincial levies. The income tax is proportional to the overall plant investment. The central government receives 30 percent, the province 10 to 20 percent, and the plant's town 20 to 50 percent of the tax revenue. The amount of provincial tax depends partially on the number of employees at the plant.

As in Belgium, Swiss nuclear plants are built and run by private firms, and each group of companies operating a plant is taxed on capital and income. Each Swiss canton (province) sets, by statute, the bases and rates of tax to cover all plants within its boundaries. If a plant occupies part of the land of two towns or cantons, a national law apportions the tax payments. While "the tax revenue of the commune in which the plant is situated is quite adequate to cover the costs which the commune may have to bear . . . the tax revenue of the other communes in the canton . . . is very small" (OECD, 1980, 125). This suggests a jurisdictional-mismatch capital market failure; however, "during the construction period . . . [the nearby towns] may benefit from the capital tax which increases in proportion to the growth of the share capital of the construction company" (OECD, 1980, 125). It still is not clear, however, whether this provision assures these towns of having the right amount of funds at the right time, as they must absorb many new construction workers and their families.

Japanese electric power plants pay a fixed assets tax, set by the plant site community at 1.4-2.1 percent of the construction cost. The town, however, receives one-fourth of the tax revenue. The national government collects the rest of it, but disburses much of it as "subsidy payments" to nearby towns. Here, too, one does not know, without more information, to what extent these nearby towns experience capital market failures.

A tax apparently unique to Japan is based on the nuclear fuel; the tax equals 5 percent fo the value of the fuel placed in the reactor during start-up of subsequent operation. Japanese plant operators also have to pay a business office tax of 1.5 percent of their income, a real property acquisition tax, a special landholding tax, and a tax for promoting nuclear power development, which in 1980 equaled 85 yen per thousand kilowatt-hours of electricity produced. It is paid to the central government, which then provides grants to local governments for infrastructure financing. These grants cover the period between the beginning of construction and the start of operation and can be viewed as a kind of advance payment.

Australia's energy tax policy changed twice in five years with the 1972 election of the Labor government headed by Gough Whitlam and his controversial firing by the country's Governor-General, Sir John Kerr,[1] in 1975, followed by Labor's defeat later that year. In 1978 the ruling Conservatives abandoned the idea of a resources tax on oil and uranium production, claiming these levies would discourage exploration and private investment. The Labor opposition called for an "excess profits tax," insisting that it was the only way to keep most mining earnings from going overseas. Australia has a long way to go before it reaches the level of sophistication evident in Japan's and Western Europe's taxation-disbursement systems.

Many countries have developed mechanisms for channeling tax revenue not only from energy plants but from more widespread sources to needy boomtowns. More research can determine the extent to which these boomtowns experience capital market failures of either the front-end-financing or the jurisdictional-mismatch variety. This type of financial aid, combined with special programs similar to U.S. disaster aid, can go far toward alleviating the severe financial problems central to the boomtown syndrome.

NOTE

1. Sir John Kerr was the top representative of the British Crown in Australia.

REFERENCES

Business Week, 1981, "A Drive to Cap Severance Taxes," July 27, p. 94.

Monaco, L. A., 1977, *State Responses to the Adverse Impacts of Energy Development in Colorado*, Massachusetts Institute of Technology, Cambridge, Mass.

Organization for Economic Cooperation and Development, 1980, *Siting Procedures for Major Energy Facilities*, OECD, Paris.

Searle, Reed, 1977, *Utah Statutes: Programs and Policies for Financing Public Services in Energy Development-Caused Rapid Growth Situations*, Utah State Department of Community and Economic Development, Salt Lake City, Utah.

Susskind, L., and O'Hare, M., 1977, *Managing the Social and Economic Impacts of Energy Development*, Massachusetts Institute of Technology, Cambridge, Mass.

Utah State Department of Community and Economic Development, 1980, *Agenda for the Eighties*—Introduction, vol. I, II, VI, (December 9), UDCED, Salt Lake City, Utah.

23

Approaches to Government and Industry Planning

It's Catch-22. The companies say, "We gave to the feds." The feds say, "We turned it over to the state." The state says, "Come back when you can show us your impact." We're always playing catch-up. (Maxwell, 1979, 1)

This complaint from the city manager of Meeker, Colorado, vividly illustrates the lack of coordinated planning among industry and all levels of government. Such a situation all but indicates the failure of all these groups to refine their own planning abilities adequately.

Planning is the heart of any boomtown syndrome solution. It is the source of any financial aid plan, any effort to predict population growth and service demands, any attempt to serve the boomtown residents' social needs, and any effort to combine the siting and compensation processes rationally. The United State's failure to do any of these effectively stems from its chronic inability to define those functions best performed by each level of government and by industry. The spread of energy development cuts across federal, state, and local planning and decision-making, as well as boundaries. These governments' inability to unify their planning efforts is one price the United States pays for its political decentralization.

The British system of planning evolved in a far more centralized manner than that in America, enabling London to determine the ultimate course of developments in outlying areas. If Washington suddenly seized such powers, the Western "sagebrush rebellion" would undoubtedly get far more intense. The British exported their language and customs to Australia, but not their administrative system. As in Canada, Australia's provinces have far greater power and autonomy even than the American states, let alone Scotland or Wales. Sweden's small, homogeneous population and long, stable history have also produced a highly centralized and coordinated planning network.

BRITISH PLANNING AND DECISION MAKING

Local Planning

Many county and local councils became embroiled in the Scottish oil industry disputes discussed in Chapter 14. They often reflected local concerns of unfair financial or physical burdens being placed on those with the least power over their fate. Strategic planning for oil development was a national concern, just as this type of planning in the private sector is top management's responsibility. Implementation of oil development plans, however, can only occur at the local level.

Local Scottish governments knew that only London had the power to stop a project. British law requires the secretary of state for Scotland to approve every "planning decision made by a local council . . . of major significance [requiring] the rezoning of land within the existing development plan for the area" (Hutcheson and Hogg, 1975, 113). The secretary must hold a public inquiry if either the developer or a large number of residents oppose the council's decision. The secretary's mere presence shows that unless a council runs into no opposition at all, ultimate decision making rests in far-off London.

Regional Planning

British law requires each region to set up a planning council. Among these councils' responsibilities are to attract oil-related industries to their areas and to help local companies become involved in oil development. In two regions predicted to be heavily affected by oil, the Shetlands and Orkneys, the regional councils tried to increase their control of development. Chapter 14 discussed the Shetlands's successful attempt to control construction and operation at Sullom Voe

that evolved into the 1974 Zetland County Council Act. Its main provision was to allow a local group, the Sullom Voe Association, to run the terminal. The Association's charter allows the oil companies, some of which are represented in the Association, to make all operating decisions, but requires the Shetland Islands Council (the other Association member) to make all other decisions.

London's decision to leave considerable control of oil-related development to the regional councils gives them far more decision making power than the local councils have. The extent to which the Secretary of State for Scotland can intervene in regional decision making is unclear. Since national eagerness to rapidly exploit Britain's North Sea oil is no secret to the regional councils, one cannot readily imagine these groups, insulated far more from the outraged local landowner or fisherman than are the local councils, to challenge national policy.

The task of British regional planners is far from easy. Raine and Baxter (1979) discussed several problems these officials have in predicting "future economic and financial circumstances." The major one is that

the uncertainties at the national level about resource availability make the task of forecasting financial resources at the local level extremely hazardous; . . . the scope for reducing these inherent uncertainties is extremely limited. . . . It is sensible for regional planning to attempt to provide information that helps in the assessment of regional and sub-regional needs and so influence the regional resource allocation process. (Raine and Baxter, 1979, 214)

The authors made the crucial point that in evaluating the level of demand for funding, British planners have at least

analyzed patterns of past expenditure within their territories as parts of their reports . . . and have then attempted to relate past investment levels to current and projected client-group populations in order to assess the priorities for future investment. However, governments are unable to guarantee funds by program or even in total beyond the life of their administration, which is shorter (Raine and Baxter, 1979, 210) than the period taken by Britain's Public Expenditure Survey Committee (PESC), which helps ministers determine the size and allocation of funds to different programs. The PESC normally uses a five-year planning horizon (which often is reduced by 50 percent). The first year is almost gone before the plan is published and the fourth and fifth are often provisional. Few regional equivalents of the PESC exist in Britain. Financial allocations to local governments are hostage not only to the uncertainty of central government aid but also to that of local officials determining their tax levels. The authors showed how in one case—forecasting financial resources for transport—even short-term forecasting became speculative.

National Decision Making

For decades, Britain exploited the rich Middle East oilfields through its involvement with Shell and British Petroleum. Once it found vast oil deposits at home, the government decided to extract that oil as rapidly as possible to rescue its chronically weak economy. Since the oil companies wanted the same thing, the government and the industry have worked almost as one unit.

This alliance has not prevented the secretary of state for Scotland from rejecting industry plans, as the Drumbuie incident makes clear. The secretary, however, is one of five British cabinet members whose responsibilities include overseeing various aspects of North Sea oil development,[1] so overall British policy rests with the prime minister, to whom all of these officials report.

Since 1970, however, Britain has had five prime ministers and four exchanges of power at the top between the Tory and Labor parties. These frequent changes not only of party but of philosophy render long-range planning close to impossible.

The 1947 Town and County Planning (Scotland) Acts gave the Secretary of State for Scotland broad powers to deal with transportation, housing, health, and many other matters. The Acts also allowed him to become involved in land-use planning, but not in offshore natural resource development itself. This provision effectively subordinated Scottish to British interests; even if the Secretary objects to a plan affecting Scotland, his fellow cabinet members can overrule him if they unite on the issue.

Two of the agencies reporting to the secretary are the Scottish Development Department (S.D.D.) and the Scottish Economic Planning Department (S.E.P.D.). The S.D.D. enforces the Town and County Planning Acts, enabling the secretary to use his socioeconomic planning powers to force local governments to set up plans describing those areas to be developed or preserved. The S.E.P.D. converts the national desire for rapid energy development to planning programs for all Scottish government agencies to be implemented by the Economic Planning Board for Scotland, which is usually pro-industry. In theory and in fact, these roles are guaranteed to produce competition between the two agencies.

The secretary's powers go beyond those envisioned in 1947. He has been forced to involve the Scottish government in helping local planners. His power to call public inquiries gives the public one of its few opportunities to voice its opinions outside the voting process. The public cannot force the secretary to decide either way, appeal his decision once it is issued, or take the matter to the courts. The lack of British public-interest law firms forces local activists to foot much of the bill for public inquiry proceedings, often discouraging local opposition to national or regional policy. Moreover, the secretary may have residents' best interests at heart, but the local citizens near a proposed development site are unlikely to stop a central government determined to develop its resources. "It seems clear that few American states or towns opposed to development would be so tolerant of such subordination and the possibility of an overriding decision" (Baldwin and Baldwin, 1975, 143).

THE U.S. APPROACH TO PLANNING

The United States has no equivalent of the British Town and County Planning Acts. The federal government never considered urban planning and local land-use management any of its business, the states' role always depended on the cities' representation in the legislatures, the large cities (with a few exceptions) developed almost randomly with urban sprawl being the inevitable result, and the small towns and villages neither expected to have to deal with rapid growth nor developed any planning system at all. U.S. growth and land management is therefore haphazard and undeveloped, with only a few states, cities, and towns showing any imagination in recent years.

Beginnings of a Federal Boomtown Strategy?

In 1977 the Carter administration began developing a coherent boomtown assistance policy. The White House Conference on Balanced National Growth and Economic Development stated that the United States considered boomtowns a part of the overall government problem at the state and local levels: "Their tax bases have not proven to be sufficiently responsible to provide the revenues needed to meet rising public service needs, or in some cases, even to maintain existing levels and quality" (White House Conference on Balanced National Growth and Economic Development, 1977, 15). The Conference also considered Washington's need to support failing local governments, discussed the difference between managing and reacting to change, and brought out the need for a national economic and growth planning and decision-making system.

As in Britain, however, national domestic policies are often politically motivated. As the Carter administration became more budget conscious after 1977, it may not have carried out the Conference's own recommendations. The Reagan emphasis on lower-level government responsibility (and lack of emphasis on the ways in which these governments can obtain the funds for carrying them out) suggests that whatever strategy Washington may have once had about helping boomtowns is doomed, at least for the next few years.

State Planning: Problems and Promises

The quality of state planning efforts in the United States varies as widely as siting and compensation efforts. For instance, the Utah Industrial Development Board's plans in the late 1970s for energy development "made no allowance for . . . adequate housing supply, water and sewer facilities, tax base, transportation, medical and social services, and recreational programs" (Gaufin, 1980, 7). Moreover, Utah's Office of Energy learned in 1977 that the state did not have the level of funds required to implement the rapid development of energy resources. Utah's state planning coordinator blamed the lack of consistent data and of coordinated planning and budgeting processes for Utah's inability to form a coherent development policy, a problem that lasted until Utah developed its Agenda for the Eighties.

Although Colorado is accustomed to a variety of boomtowns, it never had to attempt estimating the extraordinarily rapid, short-term population growth likely to occur in its 1980s boomtowns.[2] One of Colorado's planning problems, which all Rocky Mountain states will face, is that industry changes its labor force and equipment requirements every time it improves an energy-related process's technology. If the energy firm always changes its employment outlook, the state cannot accurately predict total population or service demand and long-term planning is impossible.

Most coherent state energy development plans had by 1981 included a severance tax. Consumers in the East, however, have resisted these taxes, mainly because users of the West's coal are "locked into long-term contracts that force them to pass on the tax to consumers for years to come" (*Business Week*, 1981, 26). The states often receive severance tax revenue from consumers long after displaced Western residents have somehow been compensated, the energy firms have recouped their investment, and the state treasury has become swollen with tax revenue.[3]

Any subsequent change in severance tax levels allowed by the courts will force state planners in energy-producing areas to revise all their economic forecasts just as thoroughly as do changes in energy technology.

Local Planning: Growth Management Theory

Growth management . . . does not mean centralized control of economic activity. . . . [It] does involve generating enough cooperation among the groups . . . involved to develop the economic, political, and social tools . . . to implement solutions to these questions. (Gilmore, 1976, 537)

Impacted cities and towns themselves, and even the smallest villages, can control their growth rate in several ways. Gilmore's 1976 boomtown model, referred to in Chapter 1, discussed four general tactics to follow:

1. balancing investment between the public and private sectors, either by obtaining capital to raise public sector spending, or by controlling plant siting to reduce private sector spending to a level that the public sector can serve,[4]
2. developing resource use and conservation by passing land, air, and water use laws
3. developing the labor force with training and equal opportunity programs
4. retaining the population by keeping an adequate quality of life

Gilmore himself admitted that Western social, political, and economic habits will prevent many of these steps from being followed adequately.

Finsterbusch (1980) also proposed a rather general list of growth management components:

1. better planning, with the sort of models and social impact assessment techniques discussed in Chapter 21
2. better zoning practices
3. better negotiation with industry
4. better ability to get federal and state aid
5. better tax planning
6. better ability to obtain passage of state laws favorable to the town
7. better provision of new services
8. encouraging new associated and independent industries to enter the town to keep it from busting, a critical step that Gilmore ignored.

Gilmore insisted that the federal government had the major active role to play in preventing boomtown growth; and that the towns and counties should merely accept change, cooperate among themselves, and adapt "the innovations of others." The major thrust of this book, however, is that towns, states, and industry, not the federal government, must play the most active, innovative roles in controlling boomtowns.

Walt Axelgard, the mayor of Price City, Utah, in 1978, believes that a town must not rely on its own citizens to finance growth through raising property taxes and incurring debt. Axelgard (1978) suggests rather vaguely that "good planning, annexation policies, impact fees, and building permits are only a few of the ways to assess the costs of growth where they belong."

Nelson (1980, 61-65) reviews the ways in which towns control their growth rate through legislation. Most of them first try to pass routine zoning laws, which "stabilize the cost of growth, limit a community's population, and designate a community's land use and development patterns." They also set up holding zones and overzone.[5]

Growth management "attempts to control the type,

direction, and timing of growth by constricting development" (Nelson, 1980, 67), by controlling the quantity, type, cost, location or direction, timing, and quality of development efforts. Density and land use controls dictate the quantity of these efforts. Building codes, zoning laws, and tax abatement rules to encourage desirable types of development control their type. Raising the indirect costs of development through taxes and assessments influence their cost. Master land use plans and the placing of utilities help control their location or direction. Setting up holding zones and deliberately failing to expand utilities and roads control their timing. Contract zoning and flexible recruitment efforts are two of the techniques of controlling their quality.

Growth controls are often temporary. Towns can pass moratoria on building and rezoning requests and variances, or environmental moratoria based on an emergency lack of utilities. They can enact interim controls, based on the need to regulate growth rather than to designate use. Ramapo, New York, passed timing and sequential controls limiting all development to areas already served by local infrastructure. Towns can limit growth to service areas, in which municipal services and facilities already exist. Land banking and developing easements give the community control of a given property by condemning it, and either obtaining title or not doing so. Other temporary controls include transfer of development rights, bonuses, incentive, and conditional zoning.

Communities can also enact permanent controls. These regulate the use of flood plains, wetlands, and environmentally sensitive areas, or set up building and population ceilings. Developers can go to court only to challenge what they consider abusive growth management policies. Courts often consider these as a taking deserving of compensation. The town, however, can resort to bureaucratic delay if it loses in court. The courts generally "have held . . . that a community's zoning ordinances are presumed to be a valid application of its police powers" (Nelson, 1980, 65), and that the burden of proof is on the developer.

This shows the relevance to boomtown growth of Chapter 20's discussion of compensation law.

Any successful growth management strategy must contain provisions controlling land speculation. Lindeman (1976, 142-152) shows the ways in which this can upset the best-laid plans and free market ideals. He claims that the speculator's "'function' . . . is to hold . . . undeveloped land from the time the original user is forced to sell out until a 'final user'—i.e., a developer—is willing to buy it from him" (Lindeman, 1976, 143). The trouble is that speculation makes less land available to development and drives prices too high for developers.

Lindeman distinguished between those who buy land for productive reasons and those who speculate in it. To speculate in land, one must expect someone else to buy the land at a high enough price to justify one's own purchase. Most often, this subsequent buyer is another speculator, for a final user will buy only when the land is ready for development, not when the speculator wants to sell. This timing was the core of all the land booms in Miami and Los Angeles.

The average speculator seeks leverage, trying to borrow most of the money for the land purchase at interest rates that lag behind land price inflation. He must find a source of money that will enable him to make the lowest down payment and periodic interest payments possible. Most institutional sources of funds are either forbidden by law to make this type of loan or unwilling to lend at such high risks of default. Only the seller of the land is likely to provide the financing the speculator needs.

Since 1976 the U.S. tax code has granted tax benefits to those gaining from sales of capital assets (Lindeman, 1976, 144). Lindeman offers examples to show why both sellers and buyers in a speculative market benefit from leverage and the tax code, and explains that too much speculation in a given tract of land will make it less attractive to future speculators. Owners further down the speculative chain find themselves stuck with properties encumbered with heavy obligations. Being unable to sell, they are thereby unable to acquire additional funds with which to engage in more speculations. . . . A few of them may have to sell at losses if they experience some urgent need to be rid of their land and its obligations. (Lindeman, 1976, 148)

In most speculative land booms, most debtors default, often all the way back to the first seller. Various legal and financial factors often make the land less attractive to final users. The price may be too high or the land encumbered with mortgages or legal hazards to ownership. Lindeman emphasized the aftereffects of a boom. Supply restrictions can make the price of nearby nonspeculative land soar. As land prices go, so do those of everything else in the boomtown.

One final piece of growth management theory involves the "investment strategy" concept covered in the environmental management and economics literature. It is a plan for providing capital to boomtowns in a timely, efficient manner. Cummings, Schulze, and Mehr (1978) studied the dilemma of an investment planner trying to set up an investment strategy for providing capital for streets, water, police, and other public services. If the planner expects the population to grow steadily for several years from an original P_0 at time t_0, he must decide whether or not to provide adequate infrastructure at t_0 for population levels expected in year t_1, t_2 or t_3. Planning for a boomtown's wildly erratic population change, shown in Figure 23.1 (a), is far more difficult. Any investment to provide per capita infrastructure for a population level exceeding P_1 will yield excess capacity for all the years beyond t_4. Since most infrastructure will still be in place far beyond t_4, the planner must decide if he should invest enough for an infrastructure suitable for P_3.

The issue here is that of weighing deteriorating municipal services associated with low per capita infrastructure levels during the boom against high capital costs for excess capacities in the post-boom period that result from the maintaining near-norm per capita infrastructure during the boom. (Cummings, Schulze, and Mehr, 1978, 254)

The planner must find the optimal investment strategy

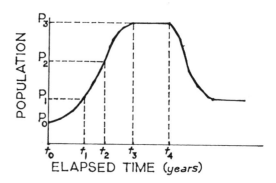

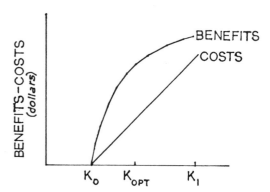

Figure 23.1
The investment strategy (Cummings et al., 1978).

to balance the capital costs from having too high a per capita infrastructure level against the social costs from too low a level. He must determine and measure the benefits of varying levels of infrastructure.

Cummings, Schulze, and Mehr developed the wage-infrastructure trade-off as the measuring device, in which wages should be higher in boomtowns than in stable towns to compensate immigrants for quality of life decline, including per capita infrastructure reduction—an idea counter to the Pareto criterion analysis suggesting that immigrants are not deserving of any compensation at all. They then studied 26 Rocky Mountain towns' 1970-1975 histories, and found that "individuals will 'trade off' a one percent increase per capita stocks of municipal infrastructure for an 0.035 percent decline in wages." (Cummings, Schulze, and Mehr, 1978, 252).

The researchers' mathematical analysis of the costs and benefits to the town for investing different sums in infrastructure produced the "*B* minus *C*" curve, of which Figure 23.1 (b) is an example. The field experience of Cummings, Schulze, and Mehr was that most boomtowns have a fully depreciated infrastructure before the boom, and assessed home valuation and (normally) low tax rates are just enough to provide maintenance and operations funds, but that nothing is available to finance new infrastructure. The towns, naturally, cannot easily increase their tax rates. Cummings, Schulze, and Mehr claim that their calculations can give planners some help in defining "the level of required front-end financing."

Cummings and Mehr (1977) provide a more detailed look at an optimal investment strategy problem. "Planning and executing [investment in infrastructure] is an important problem for boomtowns, and relatively little is understood about it" (225). Cummings and Mehr claim that the problems of investment planners are to estimate population size changes over time, to obtain adequate and timely funds, both matters discussed elsewhere in this book, and to determine the portion of the infrastructure demanded that should be supplied. The authors investigated only the third aspect of the planners' problem, shown in Figure 23.2.

In Figure 23.2, step 1 compares population estimates for any given year to the urban infrastructure standards desired (e.g., per capita infrastructure). Step 2 compares desired infrastructure with that already in place. Step 5 mentions goal violation costs, defined as the "social costs associated with the failure to maintain capital stocks at their desired, goal-determined levels as identified in path 1" (Cummings and Mehr, 1977, 229). The decision to invest has to consider the town's debt-incurring abilities (step 6). Either the town has a surplus, so that it can finance development internally, or it has a deficit. Since tax increases are politically undesirable, the town can borrow (step 6b), or obtain grants and other outside funds (step 10).

This model assumes that the town's citizens want to keep the sum of investment costs plus goal violation costs as low as possible. The town should invest only up to the point at which the last increment of investment cost equals the last increment of the present value of all future goal violation costs. Setting numbers for community goals and violation costs is very difficult, as is translating altered performance caused by changes in investment strategy into costs or benefits. Cummings and Mehr indicate that there is "no logically consistent, defensible way to associate costs and benefits with alternative levels of capital investments. . . . Prospects for successfully measuring goal violation costs associated with capital investment levels are not encouraging," (1977, 230) but Cummings and Mehr tried to measure infrastructure-related benefits anyway. Their model uses wage differentials versus quality of life, just as Cummings, Schulze, and Mehr do. Among their problems are that yearly estimates for capital stocks in boom and base communities are nonexistent, and that available wage and employment figures are for counties, not communities. Much more research on infrastructure benefit determination and quantification needs to be done.

AUSTRALIA'S FEDERAL AND STATE POLICIES RELEVANT TO BOOMTOWNS

With no tradition of strong central government, Australia has only recently begun groping for a well-planned, coordinated set of policies toward mining and urban growth, the two areas in which federal policy can influence the growth of boomtowns.

Mine Ownership and Taxation

The vast size of Australia and the widespread distribution of its resources have hindered the growth of comprehensive planning there. State governments traditionally let industry and the federal government in Canberra take the major roles in matters concerned

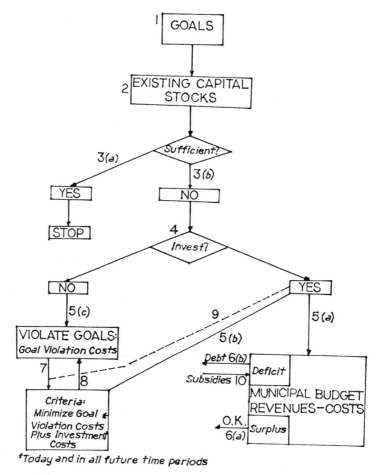

Figure 23.2
The optimal investment strategy (Cummings and Mehr, 1977).

with national welfare. The states tended to make agreements favoring multinational mining companies and their customers, many of whom are in Japan and east Asia.

Abrupt changes in government, referred to in Chapter 18, hampered national planning efforts in the midst of the new Australian resources boom. From 1975 to their recent defeat, the rule of the Conservatives brought an unprecedented federal interest in resource development. Since 1978 Canberra

has insisted on at least a 25 percent Australian equity in development projects, and expects that figure to rise to 50 percent (Wilson, 1980, 213).

However, the Conservatives had avoided a severance tax either on oil or uranium. On the state level, especially in Queensland and Western Australia, governments also were reluctant to drive away investors, and were willing to charge low royalties in return for insisting that industry build housing and other infrastructure. Both levels of government face the same issue, "the appropriate return to the community for the minerals [Australia] owns; how to achieve that without discouraging enterprise" (Wilson, 1980, 215). They also have to evaluate the effects of mining on their nation, among which are

1. the shifting of growth to the largest states in the east and west at the expense of the poorer central states
2. the increasing awareness of the need for national planning to consider issues likely to be avoided by local and state governments
3. additional pressure being brought upon rural industries and manufacturing
4. the federal government's insistence on equal ownership of mining ventures, by which Australian companies obtain foreign knowhow
5. national awareness of the trade-off between overall economic development and its effect on aboriginal society

Urban Growth and Development

Until 1972, the Australian government showed little interest in urban development, leaving it up to each state's planners. Almost 40 years ago, the south Australian Housing Trust built the new town of Elizabeth, 15 miles from Adelaide. By 1976 Elizabeth was "well on the way to reaching its planned population of 70,000" (Rushman, 1976, 20).

The failure of other state governments to play an active role in town planning has made land price inflation an old problem in Australian cities. One effort to fight it took place in Perth in the late 1960s, when a surcharge on the land tax was applied to unimproved land zoned for development. Local developers also agreed to produce home sites at an agreed rate and to sell 60 percent of the lots for about 4,000 Australian dollars less than the going rate. In return, Perth's government agreed to rezone the land and let the developers build and supply water and other services early in the construction phase. Supply

then increased quickly and prices leveled off. The city of Adelaide used this scheme several years later.

A growing consensus in Australia believes that developers should be forced to provide more services as a price for obtaining higher revenues through increased building efforts. By the late seventies, Australia had developed a number of measures to fight land speculation and price inflation. One of them is taxation of the "betterment"—the increase in the value of a plot of land from its undeveloped to its developed state, a measure made necessary by the lack of a capital gains tax (as of 1978). "For a tax on betterment to be successful, it has to result in a lower price for raw land rather than a higher price for building sites: it needs to be passed back rather than forward, otherwise it becomes a tax on development paid by the buyer" (Neutze, 1978, 205). Another idea is to impose withholding taxes on land zoned for urban development but not developed. The idea is to inhibit speculation in such land, but Neutze (1978, 209) explained that such a tax merely gives the local government more power, an unpopular step in Australia's strongly capitalistic society. Most of the other measures have failed to control land price inflation.

Resource development will not have much impact on urban growth, since natural resource towns tend to be very small. Unless Australia begins extensive projects to refine or process its minerals rather than merely export them, its resource towns will not see a major population increase. Perhaps this limited amount of refining and processing has created a lack of urgency that is hampering the development of coordinated planning. In Australia, the state and federal governments have been unwilling to set up regional councils strong enough to influence federal government decisions. Local councils have to band together to

press regional demands on state and Federal governments. Australia's small local councils seem too concerned that their identity could be lost in a regional body to recognize that they could play a much more significant role in such a body.... The best hope for effective urban and regional policy would seem to lie with a small but powerful coordinating body responsible to the premier or the Prime Minister, complemented by vigorous regional councils promoting the interests of their own regions. (Neutze, 1978, 236)

The lack of a federal new towns law also stifles new town planning, a problem that will become more evident if Australia decides to refine its minerals before they are exported. Each new town plan must originate from an agreement between Canberra and the affected state. The state then passes laws to freeze land prices, to allow it to buy land, and to set up the organization to develop the project.

One of the more prominent of Australia's eight new towns is Albury/Wodonga, in the state of Victoria. This small city had about 38,000 residents in 1971 and, at its 1961-1971 growth rate, will have 93,000 by 2000. The Victoria government passed laws to "establish land prices and to allow [the government] to use the federal funding to purchase at prices [prevailing] at the end of 1972 plus a margin to allow for inflation, rather than at current speculative prices" (Rushman, 1976, 17). Rushman neglected to mention whether similar laws were in force in New South Wales, in which two of the other famous new towns are located. In 1971, Bathurst/Orange, less than 100 miles northwest of Sydney, had 80,000 residents, and Holsworthy/Campbelltown, down the coast from Sydney, had 46,000. Their projected population in the year 2000 are 110,000 and 488,000 respectively. The eight new towns are scheduled to contain about 1.5 million residents then.

The federal government and those in the mining states will no doubt spread these ideas to resource exploitation regions, especially if economic growth enables Canberra to continue pumping money into the towns,[7] if rapid population growth in the large cities induces people "to move to a new city simply in order to get a roof over their heads" (Rushman, 1976, 23), and if industrial growth is rapid enough to induce companies to relocate.

Provision of Infrastructure

During the 1960s boom, resource firms provided most of the required infrastructure. This required direct foreign investment, since Australia's capital funds market could not supply the required investment locally. With the world economy in recession in 1982, driving demand for resources down, and with interest rates at all-time highs in the last three years, industry has begun to look for government assistance.

The achievements of Australian industry in the remote mining areas during the 1960s were remarkable. It built 24 new towns, each of which contained between 500 and 4,000 residents, 12 new ports, more than 20 airports, 1,000 miles of railroads, and spent 1.5 billion Australian dollars on schools, hospitals, shopping centers, and about 10,000 houses (Bambrick, 1979, 148). "In some areas, the cost of such infrastructure may exceed the cost of the mine."

The recession has changed all this, and industry and government disagree as to the extent of government involvement in the provision of infrastructure. If the government proves reluctant to help out, sharing of infrastructure among several industrial projects will surely lighten the financial burden.

Many state governments have recently announced their intention to raise money overseas for infrastructure and electric power supply, and Canberra approved all 12 state applications for this purpose. The federal government, however, refuses to share project risk with the states.

Political Changes in Federal Mining Policy

As in Great Britain and America, federal energy policy is highly politicized. The Conservative government of Malcolm Fraser gradually reversed the 1972-1975 Labor government's desire to get actively involved in mining. This desire was apparent in the 1973 Petroleum and Minerals Authority Act, which brought the federal government into exploration, mining, processing, transporting, buying, and selling natural resources; surveying reserves; and long-term planning. The Act had "the general power to do anything incidental to performance of its functions" (Bambrick, 1979, 171). The most sweeping provision allowed the national government to enter and occupy state- or privately-owned land if it had a warrant or the occupant's written approval. The highest Australian court declared the Act an illegal violation of states' rights.

In other ways, the Labor government encouraged rising nationalism, which bred resentment against multinational firms, especially the Japanese, operating in Australia. Federal policy was generally unfavorable to mining during the years 1972-1975, and favorable before 1972 and after 1975. By 1977 the official Conservative government policies were to restrain consumption, achieve higher energy self-sufficiency, encourage large mineral export projects, develop new oil and gas reserves, and upgrade research and development efforts. Australian policy has therefore shifted far to the right, as it has in Great Britain and the United States.

Metals Processing

Both the states and the federal government want to make Australia a major metals-processing nation, since it has by far the largest mineral deposits near the booming East Asian countries that offer a huge market for finished goods, especially steel. Whether or not processing is economically viable, state and local governments encourage metals processing because of the construction and operating jobs they offer. The state, moreover, can legally require processing near new mines when it issues the leases for them. The states can also set lower royalties on ore processed within its boundaries than outside them, offer to finance infrastructure or to take equity in processing efforts, offer tax incentives to industry, and give their own residents incentives to expand the Australian capital funds market.

The lack of a firm national hand in this matter, evident in the lack of a royalty imposed by Canberra on resource extraction, has therefore given the states great leeway in building any level of infrastructure for any project they want to promote. They would be even more eager to do this if mining companies were to stop duplicating each other's infrastructure building.

Decision-making Conflicts Between Canberra and the States

As in the United States, resource-poor Australian states will prefer purely federal to purely state control of mining, since the federal government can impose royalties to make sure that the general population receives some benefits. The United States has such a royalty, and it may be only a matter of time before Australia imposes royalties as well. Resource-rich states, such as Queensland and Western Australia, will of course oppose federal control.

The states have substantial control over mining within their borders, but not offshore. The states have challenged federal offshore-mining control several times in the High Court. One case involved the Petroleum and Minerals Authority Act, which the Court later declared illegal. Another disputed issue involves resources to be exported; the federal government wants to impose export taxes on them, while the states insist on the right to charge royalties that accrue only to the resources' state of origin. In Canada and Australia, state and federal mining policies often conflict when rival political parties are in control. When they do not conflict, they can overlap, as occurred in one Canadian province where, for a short time "combined federal and provincial mining tax exceeded 100 percent" (Bambrick, 1979, 188). Bambrick emphasized Australia's need for federal controls over exports and state controls over mining to be coordinated in a country that exports essentially all of its mineral resources.

The states have the major responsibility for environmental control, but Canberra has a role to play, too. Bambrick claimed that the Australian government affects and is affected by land-use considerations, and will probably be widely viewed as the ultimate source of any financial compensation payments. Australia, however, now has a complex system of taxation (both by federal and state governments), royalties (state), subsidies (both levels) and incentives that combine, however inefficiently, to form its mining policy.

Chapter 13 includes a discussion of some of Australia's new mining boomtowns. Many of them at one time received both state and federal help. Nevertheless,

Australia has had her ghost towns; not all the gold mining centers survived as [farming] towns like Ballarat and Bendigo. Some of [Australia's] present inland centers, like Broken Hill and Mount Isa, depend almost entirely on one industry, although they do service surrounding [rural] areas. . . . The concept of net social benefit is not necessarily clear in an economic system which has local, State and Federal priorities. (Bambrick, 1979, 198)

A Recent Attempt at National Economic Planning

In the late 1970s, Australia created the Bureau of Industry Economics, which has begun to examine the connection between Australia's mining industry and its other manufacturing industries and its service sector. The bureau wants to obtain data on mining's impact on the overall economy, and to forecast future trends in the mining industry and their effects on other industries and on employment. Bambrick felt that the widely differing attitudes in Parliament on mining's importance to the economy meant that "the present study, costly and complex as it is . . . could provide a background on which policy attitudes could be based. . . . With information at last available on the industry's relationships with the rest of the economy, policies to achieve specific objectives can be formulated" (Bambrick, 1979, 223).

PLANNING IN SWEDEN

Percivall (1979) described Sweden's land-use and urban planning apparatus. Its central government is organized into policy making ministries and policy executing agencies or boards that are independent of the ministries. The National Board of Physical Planning and Building is responsible for land-use planning.

Each of Sweden's 24 counties has its own administration to carry out the policies of the central government ministries at the county level. Some national agencies or boards (e.g., housing and education) have their own county-level offices that distribute central government funds. Each county's leaders elect a county council, which carries out the duties given them by the central government in Stockholm.

To make matters even more complex, the County Administration is Stockholm's major representative at the county level. "Its main task is to promote the coordination of national, municipal and county council administration in the county as well as representing county interests versus Government and Parliament." (Percivall, 1979, 13).

Stockholm has taken a greater role in lower-level planning in recent years. In 1949 it changed its eminent domain legislation to allow local governments to seize land required for urban development. A 1968 revision allows them the right to first refusal when land is sold in the open market. However, most land acquisition by towns has been by voluntary purchase. The 1947 Building and Planning Act allows two or more local governments to plan regionally, but they must have the prior approval of the County Administration and federal Cabinet.

ATTITUDES TOWARD PUBLIC PARTICIPATION

One key to resolving the boomtown syndrome is to make both oldtimers and newcomers feel involved in the boom events. But this idea of "public participation" has never been popular in Western democracies, although it is by no means a recent one.

Many of the utopian societies of North America had practiced forms of participation that manifestly influenced the physical arrangements as well as the process of building communities. However . . . , public participation remained a thwarted social concept. One reason for this is the rise of specialized professions, which combined with the ascendant economic influence of private entrepreneurial forces in public affairs to steadily remove and then exclude the ordinary citizen from meaningful involvement in decisions affecting the development of his community. (Perks, 1979, 294)

Among the authors researching different countries' levels of public involvement in land-use and urban planning are Fogg (Australia), Suetens (Belgium), Kimminich (West Germany), Bjerken and Percivall (Sweden), Elder, Lash, and Cooley (Canada), and Callies (United States) (see Bjerken, 1981; Callies, 1981; Fogg, 1981; Kimminich, 1981; Suetens, 1981). Except for the Canadians, they are generally skeptical about the value of public participation in town and regional planning beyond allowing the public to let off steam. Attitudes, however, vary from country to country. States within the U.S. are willing to recognize public interest groups more than those in Australia. Authorities in the field generally agree that the ultimate decision-making power in planning must rest with the legally mandated authority. In practice, this often leaves professional planners with that power.

Australia has no law assuring the public any right to be involved in government planning. Planners feel that only the better-educated part of the public ever participates anyway, that anarchy would otherwise result, and that public exposure to land-use planning brings in the speculators. Australians are mainly afraid that government by elected lawmakers will give way to government by plebiscite. Fogg, however, claims that Australia allows more participation than Great Britain does. While most Australian states have planning acts, they generally allow the public only to submit objections to laws already proposed. Fogg believes that only in local issues can public participation operate effectively.

In Belgium, at all planning levels, advisory commissions must be set up to assist in planning issues. At the local level, however, the king, not the towns, is charged with setting up a commission. Perhaps as a result, few towns had them. Commissions at all levels seem dominated by the representatives of government, industry, and labor. Any development plan from any level must have royal approval before becoming legal. As in Australia, once a plan is drawn up, its creators must announce it in the media and on notice boards (Suetens, 1981, 270). But all objections must be in writing, the people can only look at the plan during normal working hours, and the 90-day public review time is not enough to permit a serious reaction. Belgian planners, as do those in Australia, feel that only those in the public familiar with the issue and unintimidated by the planners' jargon will respond.

In West Germany, everyone favors public participation, but no one wants to enact or enforce related laws. Only in nuclear power plant planning does it become noticeable. The 1965 "federal law for the regulation of space [which] provides for the higher level guidelines for physical planning . . . does not contain a single provision giving citizens any right of participation" (Kimminich, 1981, 276). The 1960 "federal constitution act [which] contains the basic rules for town planning" requires making local plans available for viewing for a month, but gives the citizen no right to enforce his views. The 1971 "law for the promotion of urban construction" also does little for public participation. While many laws regulating the planning function require public hearings and a 30-day public display, none guarantee citizens the right to force their views on the planners.

In Sweden, demands for public participation rose in the 1960s. "It is also perhaps a characteristic of [countries with small populations] that a large 'silent majority' has no real chance of developing" (Percivall, 1979, 33). By the 1970s, the public was heavily involved in planning, as activities of civic interest, political, labor, and professional groups increased. Bjerken interpreted public involvement to mean tenants and other groups present in housing disputes. The 1947 Building Act, the 1959 Building Code, and rules issued by the National Board for Urban Planning are the three areas of Swedish planning and building laws. They fail to give the public any more influence over planning than do laws in the other countries just discussed. No laws now allow those affected by a building plan to vote on it, and laws by tenants and environmental groups rarely make much impact on building plans.

Although officially begun with the creation of the Community Planning Association of Canada in 1946, public participation developed very slowly there, as usual, against much bureaucratic resistance. Some officials believe that "participation can be an unwarranted surrogate for government" (Perks, 1979, 295-296). Even the public has had trouble accepting their need to be involved in Canadian planning.

Public participation has seldom been inspired by popular unrest or uprising. It is led and fed by social change agents, only occasionally by political leaders, and most commonly when public authority intervenes through technological or economic programs. It is more than a coincidence that the first planning-participation endeavors of formal significance in Canada were funded by the federal government and located in Quebec. [They] started up in 1961 and 1962. . . . Yet the advances made in these three regional projects . . . proved marginal and too frequently illusory. . . . By the 1970s, [the] enthusiasm [of the Canadian government] for animation or organization had waned, no doubt because the political returns had proven on balance to be counterproductive or fell short of unity on the benefit-cost ratio calculation. This diminution of government support was as true for Quebec as it was for the rest of Canada. (Perks, 1979, 296-297)

Elder (1979) discusses public participation through national- and provincial-level public hearings, Lash (1979) examines goal-setting at the regional level, and Cooley (1979) looked at local building design and management. Perks stated that

these case studies make apparent how inappropriate any general theory of participatory planning is, at least for Canadian conditions. Political level, substantive issues, and the numbers of interest [groups] involved determine how it may best operate and how rewarding it can possibly be. . . . Despite the articulate political skills, growing number of adherents, energies, and organizing capabilities among participation advocates, finding appropriate methods and criteria for performing a trade-off calculus other than by balloting remains one of the unresolved problems of planning participation. (Perks, 1979, 297)

In the United States, local governments seem to dislike increased public participation outside the traditional voting process. The federal housing, environmental, and coastal resource management laws requiring public involvement are on a higher level than that in which most citizens ever get involved. Callies claimed that public participation has been more "rigorously pursued" in housing matters than in any other area, despite the National Environmental

Policy Act and its Environmental Impact Statement requirements.

NOTES

1. The others are the Secretaries of State for the Environment, Employment, Energy, and Industry. The first of these will often resist an oil development project, the second somewhat less often, and the other two very rarely.
2. This is especially true if the early 1980s recession eases up by 1985.
3. This situation is analogous to the tolls motorists often have to pay to use bridges, tunnels, and highways on which construction had been paid off years ago. The tolls are one major source of maintenance and operating funds for the authorities running these facilities.
4. Gilmore (1976, 538) estimated that the "amount of new capital needed by local services is probably 5-20 percent of the new capital invested in the basic sector."
5. Holding zones are areas having unrealistic land use designations preventing development, but they raise due process and takings questions covered in Chapter 16. Overzoning classifies areas for uses for which no demand exists.
6. In 1973-1974, it spent 33 million Australian dollars, mostly in land acquisition.

REFERENCES

Axelgard, Walt, Memo dated July 20, 1978.
Baldwin, P. L., and Baldwin, M. F. 1975, *Onshore Planning for Offshore Oil*, The Conservation Foundation, Washington, D.C.
Bambrick, Susan, 1979, *Australian Minerals and Energy Policy*, Australian National University Press, Canberra, Australia.
Bjerken, M. T., 1981. "Public Participation in Sweden," *Town Planning Review* **52**(3):280-285.
Business Week, 1981, "Western Coal Sparks a Test of States Rights," February 16, p. 26.
Callies, David, 1981, "Public Participation in the U.S.," *Town Planning Review* **52**(3):286-296.
Cooley, Nancy J., 1979, "The Britannia Community Centre: A Lesson in Participatory Planning and Design," in William T. Perks and Ira M. Robinson, eds., *Urban and Regional Planning in a Federal State*, Dowden, Hutchinson & Ross, Stroudsburg, Pa.
Cummings, Ronald G., and Mehr, Arthur F., 1977, "Investments for Urban Infrastructure in Boomtowns," *Natural Resources Journal* **17**(2):223-240.

Cummings, Ronald G., Schulze, W. D., and Mehr, Arthur F., 1978, "Optimal Municipal Investment in Boomtowns," *Journal of Environmental Economics and Management* **5:**252-267.

Elder, P. S. 1979, "Public Hearings in Environmental Planning and Management," in William T. Perks and Ira M. Robinson, eds., *Urban and Regional Planning in a Federal State,* Dowden, Hutchinson & Ross, Stroudsburg, Pa.

Finsterbusch, Kurt, 1980, *Understanding Social Impacts,* Sage Publications, Beverly Hills, Calif.

Fogg, Alan, 1981, "Public Participation in Australia," *Town Planning Review* **52**(3):259-266.

Gaufin, Rhoda, 1980, "Toward a Growth Management Strategy for Utah" May 12, New York University.

Gilmore, J., 1976, "Boomtowns May Hinder Energy Resource Development," *Science* **191:**535-540.

Hutcheson, A. M., and Hogg, A., 1975, *Scotland and Oil,* 2nd ed., Oliver and Boyd, Edinburgh, Scotland.

Kimminich, Otto, 1981, "Public Participation in the Federal Republic of Germany," *Town Planning Review* **52**(3):274-279.

Lash, Harry, 1979, "Planning in a Human Way: The Public in the Process," in William T. Perks and Ira M. Robinson, eds., *Urban and Regional Planning in a Federal State,* Dowden, Hutchinson & Ross, Stroudsburg, Pa.

Lindeman, Bruce, 1976, "Anatomy of Land Speculation," *Journal of the American Institute of Planners* **42**(1):142-152.

Maxwell, Neil, 1979, "Mining Matters," *Wall Street Journal,* December 12, p. 1.

Nelson, D. R., 1980, "The Growing Problem," *Real Estate Review* **9**(4):61-65.

Neutze, Max, 1978, *Australian Urban Policy,* Allen & Unwin, Sydney, Australia.

Percivall, Martin, 1979, *Special Issue—Sweden,* International Federation for Housing and Planning, Stockholm, Sweden.

Perks, William T., 1979, Introduction to Part V ("Public Participation"). in William T. Perks and Ira M. Robinson, eds., *Urban and Regional Planning in a Federal State,* Dowden, Hutchinson & Ross, Stroudsburg, Pa.

Raine, J. W., and Baxter, R. S., 1979, "Forecasting Financial Resources in Regional Planning," *Town Planning Review* **50**(2):204-215.

Rushman, Gordon, 1976, "Towards New Cities in Australia," *Town Planning Review* **47**(1):4-25.

Suetens, L. P., 1981, "Public Participation in Belgium," *Town Planning Review* **52**(3):267-273.

White House Conference on Balanced National Growth and Economic Development, 1977, *Working Document, August 1* (revised as of September 9), Washington, D.C.

Wilson, R. K., 1980, *Australia's Resources and Their Development,* Department of Adult Education, University of Sydney, Sydney, Australia.

PART V

INNOVATIONS
IN BOOMTOWN
GROWTH
CONTROL

24

Innovations in National and State Planning

NATIONAL PLANNING EFFORTS

Earlier sections showed that the American central government has exercised far less control over low-level planning than has Great Britain's. Room for innovation still exists at this level. In 1978 Congress authorized the federal Energy Impact Assistance Program to channel funds to state, county, and local governments for planning and site acquisition and development, totaling 100 percent of cost for planning and 75 percent of cost for site acquisition and development. The Energy Department sends funds to these bodies through the Agriculture Department and the Farmers Home Administration. Although the state governors designate the impacted area from coal and uranium mining, processing, and transportation, Washington controls the approval and funding processes. The Department of Energy (D.O.E.), however, has ignored the impact of the synthetic fuels, oil shale, and tar sands efforts expected to carve up large chunks of western real estate. Although other federal programs help towns finance specific infrastructure projects, "these programs are already oversubscribed, targeted at different income and population groups, and often hampered by . . . funding curtailments" (Gernt, 1977). Gernt posed the question at the boomtown syndrome's heart: Is an adequate quality of life for workers the responsibility of industry or government?

The issue of boom towns growing out of the National energy priority for increased production thus demands a cooperative response from the Federal government, State and local governments, as well as industry. The Federal role should be one of short duration, only available during the planning and development stages before energy revenues begin to flow to the areas . . . and relatively unencumbered by Federal regulations. (Gernt, 1977)

This suggestion appears far different from Gilmore's emphasis on federal help, and more attuned to the national political temper of the 1980s.

An outstanding federal innovation in joint policy making that may deserve a long look is the 1965 Public Works and Economic Development Act, which set up Title V groups throughout the United States. These groups

insure an upward flow of ideas in the ultimate establishment of regional and national priorities, . . . provide a unique federal/state/local partnership that complements the traditional federal/state/local methods of operation, . . . encourage interstate planning, cooperation, and information sharing on common problems, . . . [and] allow the targeting of resources to specific regional needs which stimulate the economic development of that region. (Western Governor's Policy Office, 1978)

INNOVATIONS IN STATE PLANNING

Regional Planning Efforts

In the late 1970s, leaders of the Rocky Mountain states became aware of the extent to which that entire region was destined to become an enormous energy mine. They knew that only through regional planning were they ever going to prevent unrestrained growth in one state from spilling over to a neighboring state.

The White House Conference on Balanced National Growth and Economic Development requested, on October 13, 1977, that five multistate groups offer a regional outlook to the Conference. One of these groups was the Western Governors' Policy Office (WESTPO), comprising Alaska, Arizona, Colorado, Hawaii, Montana, Nebraska, New Mexico, the Dakotas, Utah, and Wyoming.

While the Conference's own future became more uncertain after 1977, WESTPO is active today. Its leaders, the governors of its 11-member states, meet often in Denver to plan strategy and to bargain with Washington to make sure their states will get boomtown impact assistance. WESTPO knows that changes in federal energy development plans will cause changes in state severance tax laws,[1] and that the states can then adjust their aid to their boomtowns as needed.

To help implement these plans, WESTPO's Western States Policy Office monitors federal energy activities.

WESTPO has long contended that "what we need are regional development institutions and programs controlled by elected officials . . . responsive to and capable of addressing the special problems and potentials of different regions of the nation" (WESTPO, 1978, 10), similar to the Appalachian Regional Commission and the Title V groups, three of which are in the WESTPO area. Future research must examine the Reagan Administration's commitment to such federally sponsored regional planning ideas, which WESTPO feels are the best approach to balanced national growth and economic development since most growth management and development problems are not confined by administrative and political boundaries, and since most growth management laws are at the state and local levels.

WESTPO has more specific objections to present federal boomtown assistance programs.

There is no single [federal] agency responsible for program and policy initiation relative to socioeconomic impact problems. . . . With the exception of the Coastal Energy Impact Program [discussed in Chapter 19], thre are no targeted programs relating impact aid to the nature and extent of actual impact situations. . . . While federal agencies administer numerous programs that relate to impact situations . . . almost no coordination exists among these agencies. (WESTPO, 1978)

Many of these agencies compete with each other to be the top agency. Among WESTPO's opinions are that the federal and state governments must create a way to include social factors in resource development plans; coordinating federal energy agencies' activities more efficiently requires their reorganization; and, most important, "all levels of government and the private sector must share the responsibilities of anticipating, assessing, and mitigating impacts of energy development" (WESTPO, 1978, 27).

Some of WESTPO's suggestions are that Washington should

1. grant and make low-interest loans to boom-towns, with the governor's approval, to cover costs that cannot be passed on to consumers
2. designate a single federal land agency as the main liaison with lower government levels to coordinate all federal assistance programs
3. consolidate, simplify, and streamline these programs
4. include state priorities into its funding plans
5. simplify its procedures to enable more impacted rural towns to apply for federal aid
6. strengthen the Economic Development Administration's Title IX program to include special funding aid to boomtowns
7. make sure that all federal decisions to develop a specific area for energy "trigger a simultaneous action to implement policies and programs that will mitigate negative social and economic impacts" (WESTPO, 1978, 39)
8. pass along as many of the costs of implementing these steps to consumers as are beyond local taxing abilities
9. allow the pertinent governor to veto a specific leasing plan of federal lands
10. have the White House coordinate operation of the various regional development commissions by setting up a federal Agency for Regional and Area Development

Planning Innovations of Individual States

Massachusetts

Although not a major energy producer, Massachusetts deserves attention because it has been in the forefront of efforts to include local residents in state planning, decision making, and policy making. By 1975 probusiness lobbying and the state's inability

to implement growth management policies had halted a trend in the early 1970s toward state land-use laws. The state did not try to educate the public before passing these laws, without which the state could not become more involved in land use planning. The state also failed to make the public understand land use as an issue not limited to realtors and environmentalists.

Massachusetts wanted to avoid overruling local land use controls so that it could encourage development of key facilities, or using top down growth management approaches. Its 1975 Growth Policy Development Act created Local Growth Policy Committees (LGPCs) to include public and government representatives. These groups are to provide information to local and state planning agencies and to the state legislature. The state requires the LGPCs to answer a questionnaire related to growth issues, and to hold public hearings on preparation of answers to it. The lack of county governments made the LGPCs' role in uniting neighboring towns' planning efforts especially vital.

Massachusetts's Office of State Planning reviewed the responses, and developed recommendations to the legislature so that it could carry out growth policies responsive to the needs of the state's regions and communities. Susskind and Elliott studied the LGPCs' efforts, interactions among their members, interactions between the LGPCs and their towns, and the impact of LGPC efforts on local growth policies and public education in growth management. They also looked at the extent to which educational level, location, population, degree of urbanization, interest in land-use planning before the LGPCs' existence, the traditional extent of citizen involvement in town affairs, and the degree of planning skill accounted for the LGPCs' impact on town policy, public attitudes, and the attitudes of individuals on the LGPCs themselves.

Susskind and Elliott are convinced that local residents can have a large impact on state land-use planning. Nevertheless, hostility to the state government, fear of financial reprisals if the town does not go along with the state, local leadership failures, and citizen apathy will be difficult to overcome — especially in money-starved states like Massachusetts that will be unable in the 1980s to conduct such elaborate efforts at citizen involvement without asking for federal aid and risking federal control.

Susskind and Perry (1977) studied the Office of State Planning's response to the LGPC reports, and generally approved it, claiming that OSP and the Governor have obviously learned a great deal from the growth policy process. Once the Legislature was to begin hearings on the report, the LGPCs and regional planners were to be able to respond to the OSP.

Yaffee (1977) examined one LGPC's work in far greater detail (Malamud, 1981, 159-160), trying to determine whether Harvard residents' attitudes validated the Act's assumptions that

> towns have some idea of their desired future and can reach a consensus,
> growth pressures force a town to act in some way to resolve unanswered questions,
> towns cannot deal well with these pressures,
> towns will want to enter planning arrangements with regional and state governments,
> and the LGPC will generally benefit the town.

Area residents validated the first assumption, went against the second, validated the third to some extent, rejected the fourth, and its LGPC members believed that their town had little to gain by cooperating with the 1975 Act.

Part VI herein will give some lessons drawn from these three studies regarding state attitudes toward town planning efforts. It appears clear, however, that Massachusetts has a long way to go before it can claim that the 1975 Act has begun to make its citizens more aware of, and willing to participate in, state growth management plans as they affected the towns and their residents. The state may have been mistaken in the manner in which it carried out the Act — it appears, after all, to be the very sort of top down plan it had intended to avoid, since the state decided on the form of the questionnaire it distributed to all the LGPCs, and refused to allow the committees to set the questionnaire up to suit their own needs.

Colorado

By 1977 Colorado's governor had set up an Energy Policy Council to advise him on state policy creation concerning energy-related matters. The Council contains members of the governor's staff, and the top officials of the Departments of Natural Resources, Local Affairs, Agriculture, and Health. The council intended to set up a state energy conservation plan and a state energy policy, the latter to be a basis for natural resource-related decision making. The state also has an Oil Shale Coordinator's Office concerned with oil shale impacted towns, but local residents belittled its efforts to make Denver aware of their problems. As of 1977, Colorado had allocated only the Oil Shale Lease Fund's money to aid boomtowns; all other state activities then involved only information gathering. Colorado, then, had begun innovating in planning by 1977, but it will still have to change its statutory and constitutional barriers to more effective boomtown aid before massive energy development resumes — once the early 1980s recession ends.

By 1980 Colorado had also set up a Joint Review Process, a system intended to coordinate the actions of all government agencies responsible for various aspects of reviewing any energy or mineral development project. One example of its operation concerned a proposed molybdenum mine that AMAX wanted to build at Mount Emmons. The Process was claimed to have sped up the government review and permit-granting processes considerably. An ingenious part of the process was a tour of neighboring boomtowns given for the local officials so that they could plan for rapid growth in their area. Another worthwhile feature was an agreement among AMAX and several government bodies to run a coordinated socio-economic study. Ironically enough, after all this effort, economic conditions forced AMAX to scuttle the entire project.

Vermont

Rohrlich (1976) discusses one especially unusual state law, again in nonenergy-producing New England. In 1973 Vermont enacted the nation's first land gains tax. It intentionally placed the heaviest tax burden on land speculators, and exempted landowners who either hold on to their land for more than six years or erect office buildings or their own dwellings on most of their land area.

Some landowners can raise their selling price to offset the high gains tax if they must sell within the six-year period, while others might hold their land back from sale if their cash-flow situation calls for such a decision. Rohrlich believed that the tax would discourage demand for land once prospective owners —especially speculators—became aware of the tax. This levy, therefore, could well depress both the supply and demand of land, and so may not itself affect the price of land; it could, however, restrict land deals to those between owners intending to hold the land for nonspeculative purposes.

Utah

By 1980 Utah had to devise a plan for dealing with a huge population influx, caused not ony by expected massive energy (coal, gas, oil, oil shale, and tar sands) projects, but also by the incoming defense and electronics industries. The state's Department of Community and Economic Development was asked to prepare both components of the state planning coordinator's Growth Management Strategy. One component, to be discussed later, is a Community Investment Strategy; the other is the Agenda for the Eighties, intended to allow Utah residents to voice their ideas about the preferred direction of the state's economic development, and to prepare policies for managing the state's growth that reflect the ideas expressed by a majority of the state's citizens.

I have summarized the Agenda's suggestions relevant to dealing with boomtown growth (Malamud, 1981, 162-164), some of which are passage of a minerals severance tax, an increase in the local income and sales tax and the state income and property tax, state and local revenue sharing, and local governments using a huge variety of growth management techniques (listed in Part VII). Subsequent research must determine the extent to which Utah has been able to carry out any of the rather broad plans discussed in the Agenda.

Utah's Community Investment Strategy is based on project priority lists on local and state levels, so that agencies at all government levels can coordinate their funding activities. Each agency must consider the impact of its decisions on other agencies' programs. Among state funds to be included are those of the Natural Resources Department, the Community and Economic Development Department, the U.S. Economic Development Administration, the Housing Department, and the Environmental Protection Agency (EPA). The Strategy is intended to give program implementers the funding guidance and decision making help they want, and to teach them how to determine their fund requests based on genuine need, not on the applicant's political skills in obtaining grant money. The Strategy should also help towns learn in advance if they can fund their projects, from which sources the money will come, and the time interval involved. All these measures will enable state and local planners and budget writers to coordinate their efforts far more than they had before, to work with data that is consistent at any given time, and to give priority funding to growth-influencing projects (Malamud, 1981, 164-165).

North Dakota

This state recently enacted a Joint Powers Act, which allows local governments to enter joint ventures to plan, finance, and operate public facilities (Peirce and Hagstrom, 1979). This should reduce the jurisdictional mismatch often responsible for capital market failures. Mercer County's use of this law to enhance its growth control efforts will be covered later.

Florida

Florida should be as familiar with boomtown growth as any state in the Rockies. Rapid population growth before 1970 and a severe 1971 drought induced the state legislature to pass the 1972 Environmental Land and Water Management Act, requiring the state to review the developers' plans when they cover more than one town; and the 1972 Land Conservation Act, enabling the state to buy threatened land if all other government efforts fail. It also passed the 1972 State Comprehensive Planning Act, creating a Division of State Planning to coordinate efforts to form "goals and policies for shaping land development within the state" (Fishkind and Peterson, 1979, 6) and the 1975 Local Government Comprehensive Planning Act, requiring each county and town to prepare a wide-ranging, economically viable plan to be approved by the state before July 1, 1979.

Fishkind and Peterson (1978-1979) reviewed a number of county and local growth control innovations recently undertaken in Florida. In central Florida, for instance, Clearwater, was America's first city to require a community impact statement for all projects that cost more than $500,000. In the north, Leon County (including the state capital, Tallahassee) is trying to tie its land-use plan to its long-range capital construction scheme.

Fishkind and Millman (1979, 13-18) developed "a model for assessing regional growth management strategies based on econometric methods." They claim it can accurately forecast industrial employment and personal income; cover changes in migration, population, and labor force size; forecast demand for electricity, sewage and water supply, changes in pollutant emissions and traffic patterns; cover revenues and expenditures; and develop equations predicting savings-and-loan deposits and housing starts.

NOTE

1. The pending lawsuit and Congressional action discussed earlier, and other similar actions to follow will also do so.

REFERENCES

Fishkind, Henry H., and Millman, Jerome, 1978-1979, "A Model for Assessing Regional Growth Management Strategies," *Business and Economic Dimensions* **14**(4):13-18.

Fishkind, Henry H., and Peterson, David, 1978-1979, "Growth Management in Florida," *Business and Economic Dimensions* **14**(4):4-12.

Gernt, Wallace, 1977, "Briefing Paper, Energy Impact Assistance," National League of Cities, Washington, D.C.

Malamud, Gary, 1981, "A Comprehensive Solution to the Boomtown Syndrome," master's thesis, New York University.

Monaco, L. A., 1977, *State Responses to the Adverse Impacts of Energy Development in Colorado*, Massachusetts Institute of Technology, Cambridge, Mass.

Peirce, Neal R., and Hagstrom, Jerry, 1979, "Mercer County's French Connection," *National Journal* **11**:266-269.

Rohrlich, George F., ed., 1976, *Environmental Management*, Ballinger Publishing, Cambridge, Mass.

Susskind, L., and Elliott, M., 1977, *A Survey of Local Growth Policy Committees and Their Impacts*, Massachusetts Institute of Technology, Cambridge, Mass.

Susskind, L., and Perry, C., 1977, *The Impact of Local Participation on the Formulation of State Growth Policy in Massachusetts*, Massachusetts Institute of Technology, Cambridge, Mass.

Utah State Department of Community and Economic Development, 1980, *Agenda for the Eighties*, December 9, UDCED, Salt Lake City.

Utah State Department of Community and Economic Development, 1980, *Program Outline—Community Investment Strategy*, May, UDCED, Salt Lake City.

Western Governors' Policy Office (WESTPO), 1978, *Balanced Growth and Economic Development—A Western White Paper*, vol. 1, January 29, WESTPO, Denver.

Yaffee, Steven L., 1977, *Municipal Involvement in the Formulation of State Growth Policy*, Massachusetts Institute of Technology, Cambridge, Mass.

25

Recent Growth Management Developments

Several American and Canadian cities and towns have developed a variety of ways to control the rate of their own growth. One must not assume, however, that energy boomtowns can adapt all these larger communities' growth management policies to their own needs. These policies are nevertheless worth examining here, for Hill (1974a, 2) stated that growth management efforts are proliferating throughout the United States, confronting lawyers, realtors, builders, planners, politicians, and would-be-homemakers with three basic questions: Where will America's new residents live in the 1980s and 1990s? Who decides which communities can adopt growth controls? Can communities shut their door entirely to newcomers?

EARLY GROWTH MANAGEMENT EFFORTS

Hill (1974a, 2) cited numerous attempts at growth management that began long before the present so-called "age of limited expectations" made it a rallying cry for towns all over the nation. In the 1960s, for example, Pennsylvania developers began suing communities that rejected their projects. By 1970, some Washington, D.C. suburbs were so overtaxing their waste treatment systems that they forced state and county leaders to impose moratoria on building permits and sewer hookups until these systems could catch up. Boca Raton, Florida passed a 40,000-residential unit ceiling. Palo Alto, California set aside ten square miles of undeveloped land by zoning it into ten-acre sections. Southampton, New York set a population limit of 127,000—more than twice its present level.

In 1973, San Jose, California imposed a two-year halt on any "new residential zoning that would reduce pupil-space in schools" (Hill, 1974a, 2). That same year, sewer connection freezes were operating in 40 Florida communities and 160 others in Ohio and Illinois. The next year, the federal Department of Housing and Urban Development found that 226 cities had passed some sort of freeze on such steps as building permits, subdivisions, water and sewer *209* connections. But few of these moves were made necessary by a lack of physical space; most were for economic reasons, such as the tax burden per capita would soar, even if new taxpayers came in. To reduce this threat, many towns want developers to pay more infrastructure costs by putting large surcharges on them.

Hill summed up the measures taken in these and other communities:

Beyond moratoriums, the repertoire of growth controls includes a variety of zoning practices—sequestration of open land, from which development is excluded; large-lot zoning, making home sites too expensive for anyone but the wealthy, and restrictions on commercial development and apartments or other multiple housing.

Another set of devices is special levies on large-scale developers —high permit fees, extra charges of schools and the other community services a new development entails; requirements that developers deed a sizable portion of their land to community facilities such as parks; imposts to pay for parks in other parts of a community, or simply fees—in the name of helping out with community overhead —that go into a city's general treasury.

Blending these measures in various combinations are "phased growth" plans, which in effect ration building permits and other development over a period of years. (1974a, 2)

These growth management efforts have stirred nationwide controversy—not merely their attempt to keep people out, but their alleged effectiveness in keeping lower-income residents away. They are often criticized for having helped add to the acute nationwide shortage of affordable housing for the lower and middle classes. Small wonder, then, that so many of these efforts end up in the courts.

RAMAPO AND PETALUMA: THE PIONEERS

Ramapo, New York and Petaluma, California, are the forerunners of local-level growth management in the United States. Among the researchers in the urban planning field to note these towns' feats were Fishkind and Peterson (1978-1979), who described growth management as

a process of (a) directing population growth and industrial develop- ment to areas which have resources available to support growth, (b) timing the growth process to synchronize with the ability of services, (c) avoiding the overburdening of fiscal, social or environmental infrastructure, and (d) minimizing negative spillover effects on adjacent areas. (Fishkind and Peterson, 1978-1979, 4)

Along with Hill (1974a) they referred to the story of Petaluma, which until 1956 was a farming town north of San Francisco. That year, a highway running along its eastern edge was widened to a freeway. This added to the growth of the entire Bay Area to create explosive growth in Petaluma, which mushroomed from 14,000 residents in 1960 to 25,000 in 1970, and 30,000 in 1971. Around 1969, the Petaluma public works department warned that the town's waste disposal system would reach its capacity after one more year of unrestrained growth, especially since nearly all the new growth was in single-family homes east of the freeway, where few houses existed before 1956. In June 1973 the residents voted four-to-one for a law passed the previous August limiting construction in the next five years to 500 dwelling units a year. A U.S. district court swiftly overruled that law, stating that Petaluma could not use its power of rejecting bonds at the polls as "a weapon to define or destroy fundamental constitutional rights" (Hill, 1974a, 2). That attitude shocked Petaluma's town planners, who felt that the courts could not force citizens to pay for the bond issues necessary to build and expand town services.

Petaluma dealt with only one segment of growth management. The first really sophisticated growth control effort took place in Ramapo, which made growth dependent for the first time on the ability to fund city infrastructure expansion. "By identifying the direction of future service expansions, particularly water and sewerage lines, Ramapo is able to limit and direct development where service capacity is available." The basis of the Ramapo technique is a "point-score system under which applicants for annually rationed building permits must show their projects will not unduly burden municipal services (Hill, 1974b, 20).

The Ramapo experiment has proven both legally sound and a model for other communities.

GROWTH MANAGEMENT AND THE COURTS

The fate of Petaluma's experiment, however, underscores the huge impact of court decisions on a town's freedom to control its own growth. As early as 1926, the U.S. Supreme Court upheld zoning as a legal exercise of a town's police power. Planners hoping to curb growth have since then been forced to "steer a course among legal guidelines and precedents as tortuously as a steel sphere bouncing off the obstacles in a pinball machine" (Hill, 1974*b*, 20). The basic problem for both planners and judges is to determine the extent to which zoning and town planning can go without violating people's right to be mobile.[1] The courts are today still trying to help towns decide the restrictions on growth they can reasonably and legally enact.

The courts have come down on other growth-limiting measures besides Petaluma's. In 1970, the Pennsylvania Supreme Court invalidated Concord Township's attempt to block a planned development because of the adverse effects of population growth. Two years later, a U.S. appeals court upheld the right of Sanbornton, New Hampshire, to zone half its area for 3- and 6-acre lots. Also in 1972, the U.S. Supreme Court refused to review a New York Court of Appeals ruling that upheld the Ramapo growth control plan.

In January 1973, the U.S. District Court in San Francisco ruled against Petaluma's plan. Three months later, the U.S. Supreme Court upheld the Long Island town of Belle Terre's ordinance limiting land use to one-family houses. This decision, of course, had the effect of barring poorer citizens from the town, and predictably brought intense criticism from civil-rights groups.[2] When towns have tried to comply with these groups, they have sometimes been overruled by state courts.

Some lawyers trying to untangle the knots left by past court cases say that

> growth management efforts solely to preserve the status quo and not motivated by proven socio-economic forces are legally shaky,
> growth management plans apparently aimed at lower-income people are legally shaky, temporary controls are on solid ground if their need can be shown,
> and a well-thought-out, long-range, phased-growth plan has at least an even chance of being sustained.

However, Hill questioned the legal system's ability to set clear guidelines on what may be basically a moral and economic issue, namely the extent of economic stratification within a town's society and the town's right to set that level for itself, often at the poor's expense—in short, "on what a representative American community should look like."

[Another] major legal problem is the fact that no two communities' problems, or proposed remedies for them, are ever identical, and rarely come before the same court. So, unlike other areas of law where precedents become guidelines, community-planning rulings often do not apply beyond the original cases. (1974*b*, 20)

The courts figure prominently in several of the following examples of imaginative growth management at the local level.

BOULDER, COLORADO

Perhaps America's most creative community in its growth management efforts is Boulder, Colorado. It enacted its first zoning ordinance back in 1928. Voter resistance, however, hindered subsequent growth control efforts based largely on water and sewer line location and extension. The courts also objected, claiming that the city was running its water and sewer systems as a public utility and therefore had to supply these services to new communities in the 58-square-mile Boulder area, even if it were against the city's wishes.

Meanwhile, Boulder's population soared eight percent a year between 1950 and 1977 (*New York Times,* 1977, 47), mainly because of the opening of an IBM office there, construction of a main highway to Denver, and the growth of the state university. By the late 1960s, Boulder residents, aware of the nation's new environmental awareness, began examining ways to control the haphazard, unaesthetic, rapid population growth. Residents approved a 1970 plan to "take all steps necessary to hold the rate of growth . . . to a level substantially below that experienced in the 1960s," and to "undertake a definitive analysis of the optimum population and growth rate for the Boulder Valley."

The next March, the City Council approved an interim growth policy, creating a citizens' commission to determine the ideal Valley population growth rate. Although the study, released in November 1973, suggested a three percent annual growth rate, the Council never enacted the study's permanent guidelines.

City Councilman Paul Danish, acting after the study's completion, was primarily responsible for Boulder's enacting an ordinance on November 2, 1976. This limited Boulder Valley growth to two percent a year by restricting the number of building permits to be granted each year to 450 houses. Its idea of developing a merit system to allocate permits came from earlier growth management efforts in Petaluma, California, and Ramapo, New York.

Developers considered this system too time-consuming and expensive. A Rocky Mountain Research Institute study concluded that the merit system and the rest of the Danish plan were not responsible for rising housing costs. "Competition for merit points has served as a real incentive to incorporate housing for moderate-income owners into project planning (Cooper, 1980, 16)." To broaden its growth management efforts beyond the Danish plan's limit, Boulder was to start a new growth study in 1981, considering the effects of the ordinance on housing supply,

demand, costs, and type. Planning director Frank Gray believes that the successor to the Danish Plan will be a growth control system capable of balancing job opportunities and commercial services with housing controls, while considering other concerns such as community energy and transportation needs. Critics, however, claim that Boulderites are simply trying to keep out less affluent Denver citizens, and the Chamber of Commerce agreed with a less radical comprehensive growth plan to join Boulder and its surrounding county into a growth control project to keep much of the population increase limited to smaller towns outside Boulder itself.

PHOENIX, ARIZONA

By the mid-1970s, the booming sunbelt city of Phoenix, Arizona, was suffering from severe urban sprawl, dirty air, traffic congestion, and overcrowded schools; these were similar to the problems afflicting San Jose, Albuquerque, and Denver (Gottschalk, 1974, 1). Unless Phoenix's sprawling suburbs have industries that can absorb its new citizens, the city authorities must build roads to the central city. Since speculators own most of the choice real estate within city limits, the resulting relative cheapness of land far from central Phoenix encourages developers to build in the outlying areas. While former Easterners do not want skyscrapers or freeways in their new land, highways are essential there because the city's population is too sparse to support mass transit. Arizonans were not becoming antigrowth in 1974 as Colorado, California, Oregon, New Mexico, and Florida residents were, though they may have become so by the early 1980s. Phoenix would be a good testing ground for the Vermont land gains tax discussed in Chapter 20. Though speculators will bitterly oppose it, imposition of such a tax can reduce real estate prices enough to spark a demand for housing closer to central Phoenix. This demand will enhance Phoenix's growth management efforts.

SAN DIEGO, CALIFORNIA

San Diego has a climate and a booming population similar to those of Phoenix. It also has an active growth management program. Until 1971 sloppy management and scandals plagued San Diego's suburban growth. A series of town meetings in the San Diego area gave citizens a chance to speak about the ways in which they wanted growth managed.

The City Council and the planning commissions began "down zoning" within San Diego's more densely populated areas. Battles erupted between developers and no-growth advocates. The most famous of these was the Friends of Mammoth vs. County of Kern lawsuit. Neither developers nor the overworked planning department helped Mayor Pete Wilson develop his growth management program.[3] He contracted with Robert Freilich, who was involved with Ramapo's growth control plan, to issue position papers.

An Interim Growth Management Ordinance, proposed in late 1976, would have limited building to older areas and selected suburban locations, and eliminated it from environmentally sensitive areas. On July 20, 1977, the city council adopted a residential growth strategy for San Diego, and the planning commission scrapped its interim ordinance one month later. As in Boulder, San Diego planners have had difficulty evaluating growth management's effect on housing supply and prices, except for "single-family lot prices, and prices paid for well-located multi-family properties."

EDMONTON, ALBERTA, CANADA

By the late 1960s, Edmonton, the capital of Canada's Alberta Province, had to develop a plan to deal with its having become the service and refining center for the western Canadian oil industry. It soon made up a General Plan for the Future, which aims to "keep downtown development compact, focusing residential communities of 50,000 and 150,000 around outlying town centers . . . and to keep industrial development downwind of residential and commercial areas" (*Business Week*, 1975, 31).

MERCER COUNTY, NORTH DAKOTA

The region of Mercer County, North Dakota, used the traditional Scottish growth control method of hiring an outside consultant to help the area adjust to open-pit coal mining. Mercer County contracted with a joint venture involving two consulting firms, one French (Société Centrale pour l'Equipement du Territoire, or SCET), and one American (Resource Planning Associates, or RPA) (Peirce and Hagstrom, 1979, 266). The U.S. Department of Energy had originally contracted with RPA to find a European development model useful to American boomtowns, and RPA chose SCET's Société d'Economie Mixte d'Amenagement (SEM) model for Mercer County, an area whose towns faced the usual boomtown problems.

The SEM is a semi-public company controlled by the local government; private industry can also buy part of the SEM's equity. SCET offers technical assistance and the French government offers financing to the French SEMs, which buy and build up land for industrial plants and public infrastructure.

RPA hired two North Dakotans to persuade local leaders to accept the French idea, and they set up the Mercer County Energy Development Board in August 1977, to deal with energy development problems without either the board or the federal government taking decision-making powers from local officials. The board is a monthly forum in which elected officials can discuss common problems. Its planners set up the county's first set of zoning rules for housing and standards for water supply and waste treatment systems. By early 1979 the board had 14 members, including county commissioners, mayors, and school board representatives. The state's Public Service Commission allowed the board to monitor the socioeconomic impact of energy development on Mercer County and the energy firms' cooperation with local residents.

The board also began trying to bring in permanent industries to avoid a later bust, and to encourage energy efficiency among local homeowners and motorists. The board may soon be able to receive coal severance tax revenue directly from the companies, and to persuade the state-owned Bank of North Dakota to finance long-term projects.

This scheme's most intriguing aspect is that private industry is cooperating with local government-level officials, without direct intervention from the state capital or from Washington. This plan also shows that a community need not be large or have sophisticated planners to learn about growth management.

OTHER GROWTH MANAGEMENT APPROACHES

Since 1976 about 25 towns in New Hampshire (mostly in the south) have passed growth management ordinances. Most of them based their laws on limiting housing starts to allow for a 3-5 percent growth rate per year. Typical is the rule of Exeter (population about 11,000) limiting the number of residential building permits that can be granted each year to 96. (Shenon, 1980, 39).

Ellson claimed that most of the growth management approaches so far discussed lead to fixed land supplies and soaring prices. An urban economist with the National Association of Home Builders, he argued that growth management planning can work in practice if

1) an adequate capital improvements and expansion program is planned and implemented to accommodate — not limit — anticipated growth, 2) incentives to draw capital, people and housing to infill (passed-over land) and core areas are used, rather than disincentives levied against suburban development, 3) a sufficient supply of developable land is designated to meet housing and reserve needs, thus moderating speculative and monopolistic influences on land prices, and 4) it is recognized that infilling and redevelopment will provide only marginal increases to housing stock and will not likely appeal to the largest segment of the market. (1979, 4)

Ellson described the use of an econometric model prepared by the N.A.H.B. in helping San Diego planners learn about the economic and fiscal effects of alternative growth control strategies, and about ways to make elected officials more aware of these effects. He also offered the example of Gainesville, Florida, in which the Regional Utilities Board and the Citizens Advisory Committee on Economic Development asked for an econometric study from the University of Florida's Bureau of Business and Economic Research. Ellson claimed that most communities can afford modeling, but Chapter 21's warning against relying too heavily on these models should be kept in mind.

A NATIONAL PERSPECTIVE ON LOCAL GROWTH MANAGEMENT

The federal government has more or less taken both sides in town planning and growth management. While the Environmental Protection Agency has set pollution-reducing standards that "virtually dictate state and local land use in many situations" (Hill, 1974c, 16), Congress has always been reluctant to intrude on state and local freedom of action. This is at a time when towns are limiting growth and states "have done little about rationalizing inevitable community growth," and the federal government is unwilling to set a national growth policy that may be necessary to assure shelter for a population of roughly 250 million people by the year 2000. Hill made it clear that "how to bring some order into this welter of problems is a question that now dominates the councils of urban affairs experts, lawyers, developers, and public officials."

According to Hill (1974c, 16) land use, "the crux of

the growth management problem," has always been governed by 60,000 mostly local units, most of which are so controlled by the towns' business interests that they cannot form plans that go beyond "buttressing established property values and maximizing local tax revenues." This type of haphazard zoning has been judged inadequate by more and more towns that are enacting growth control plans. For towns to have more comprehensive growth management, many experts are saying that residents will have to participate more in planning and have a better idea of the impact of the development choices they make. Of course, this concept runs smack into the keep-the-public-out attitude toward public participation so clearly defined in Chapter 23. Not every town in a state highly in demand can close its doors to development, so growth management may become more a state than a local issue. Even many free-marketeers are starting to advocate state growth management plans, if only as a way to avoid federal growth control.

Land use planning is constitutionally mandated to the states, but they have usually let their communities handle it. By 1974, "30 states were exploring the subject of comprehensive land use planning; . . . 21 states were trying to formulate long-range goals for their population and resources; . . . 10 state legislatures had adopted resolutions on stabilizing their populations; . . . and six states had established population commissions" (Hill, 1974*c*, 16). Hill made it clear, though, that most of these actions are usually "more talk than action."

Since several states have developed growth control sentiments similar to those in Ramapo and Boulder, the problem of a state's deciding what to do when none of its towns want new residents now moves a step up to the national level. However, the highly conservative Reagan White House will be loath even to think of federal growth management. "But whether local and state growth policies can attain coherence in the absence of an overall national policy is . . . conjectural" (Hill, 1974*c*, 16). This problem goes beyond questions of population or housing to the extent to which a state or city can decide what its "fair share" of public nuisances such as mines, refineries, power plants (and of population increase) should be. It is debatable whether or not a state can tell if banning growth or heavy industry, as some states have already done, hurts the national interest unless that interest is clearly stated by a federal growth management policy.

Hill hopes (and many planners have claimed) that the democratic process will ultimately balance out state, local, and national interests in this matter, as a democratic society must always do in many other matters. The level of interstate and inter-regional hostility likely in this process may instead impress all levels of government with the need for a coordinated approach to growth management.

NOTES

1. This is no clear-cut matter. The Supreme Court has always held that U.S. citizens are guaranteed a right to be mobile. The Constitution does not state this clearly, but the Court claims that the pre-1789 Articles of Confederation did (see Hill, 1974*b*).
2. These activists have also attacked towns' growth management rules that ban apartment houses and trailer homes, limit land zones for apartments, and restrict the number of rooms, bedrooms, and floor area in apartments.
3. Wilson was elected to the U.S. Senate in November 1982. As of this writing, the effect of his departure from San Diego on its growth management is unclear. The four candidates hoping to succeed him in May 1983 claimed to support the growth control policies of Mayor Wilson, who dominated San Diego politics for a decade. However,

> he dominated the city government less through the statutory powers than through his political skills and the persuasiveness of his personality . . . . Given the relatively weak powers of the position of Mayor, none of the candidates are expected to be able to run the city, at least initially, as effectively as Mr. Wilson . . . . [Therefore,] despite the candidates' expressions of support, there is a sense . . . that San Diego is at a turning point in its efforts to preserve its character and avoid the freeway culture, congestion and air pollution that bedevil Los Angeles. (Lindsey, 1983, 10)

REFERENCES

Business Week, 1975, "Gateway to the New North," September 1, p. 31.

Cooper, Sandra, 1980, "Growth Control Evolves in Boulder," *Urban Land* **39**(3):13-18.

Ellson, Richard, 1979, "Another Perspective on Growth Management," *Urban Land* **38**(1):3-8.

Fishkind, Henry H., and Peterson, David, 1978-1979, "Growth Management in Florida," *Business and Economic Dimensions* **14**(4):4-12.

Gottschalk, E. C., Jr., 1974, "Boom Town: Phoenix Area's Sprawl Worries City Planners," *Wall Street Journal,* June 18, p. 1.

Hill, Gladwin, 1974a, "Nation's Cities Fighting to Stem Growth," *New York Times,* July 28, p. 2.

Hill, Gladwin, 1974b, "Conflicting Court Actions Perplex Towns Seeking to Curb Growth," *New York Times,* July 29, p. 20.

Hill, Gladwin, 1974c, "National Policy Debate Spurred by Cities' Efforts to Limit Growth," *New York Times,* July 30, p. 16.

Lindsey, Robert, 1983, "San Diego to Change Political Guard After Decade of Battle Over Growth," *New York Times,* January 5, p. 10.

New York Times, 1977, "Boulder, Colo., Moves to Curb Its Growth," September 11, 1977, p. 47.

Peirce, Neal R., and Hagstrom, Jerry, 1979, "Mercer County's French Connection," *National Journal,* February 17, pp. 266-269.

Shenon, Philip W., 1980, "Go-Slow Movement Threatens Development in Growth Spots," *Wall Street Journal,* September 30, p. 39.

26

New Town Developments Today

Government and industry inspire new town construction today as they have for many years. The new towns rising all over the world today have a wide variety of origins. Some are company towns, others are efforts to resettle populations away from large cities, still others are attempts to force a permanent occupation of land considered vital for national security.

COLSTRIP, MONTANA

Colstrip is one of the West's best-known energy boomtowns. It had prospered from 1923 to 1958 as a coal-mining town, but busted after 1958. By 1970 only 60 houses and a few other buildings remained, and the town's population had dwindled to 100. In 1970 Western Energy Co., a subsidiary of the Montana Power Company, declared its intention to open a coal mine to supply MPC's new power plant, both of which are near the town. WEC was to mine the plant's coal, and to rebuild and operate Colstrip itself.

Its population rose from 100 ten years ago to 3,000 in 1980. Few boomtown effects had become apparent by then, but the town's students had to study in a shopping center until 1980. Unlike old company towns, this one provides a much better residential environment for migrants than is available in other boomtowns (Finsterbusch, 1980, 152).

MPCO/WEC knew that the nearest town to the coal mine they planned to open and to the power plant they intended to build was almost 40 miles away. Since construction in Colstrip had to keep up with population increases, future growth was to take place in separate areas near open space. Each area contained one of the three basic types of housing normally sought after by new residents: multifamily housing, single-family homes, and trailers, but the companies wanted only one housing type in each area. They also planned to build a small shopping center with vital health facilities. MPCO contracted out the actual construction work for these projects, and provided funds for them.

MPCO/WEC offered Colstrip's new homes for *217*

rent and for sale. It initially also provided fire protection, sewer and water supply services, parks, streets, and recreational facilities. Rosebud County provided schools, police protection, most health care services, and libraries. Within a few years, WEC planned to offer self-government to the new Colstrip.

WRIGHT, WYOMING

Wright was built to serve the workers and their families at Atlantic Richfield's Black Thunder coal mine, which it began to develop in 1974. "To house its workers, Arco was participating in a subdivision and a townhouse-apartment in . . . Gillette [50 miles away from the Black Thunder mine], along with four other energy companies. But the two developments were not large enough to accommodate the growing influx of workers (Miller, 1979, 54)." The idea of building Wright was considered the alternative to inflicting the boomtown syndrome on Gillette—already a symbol of the disease at its worst—or other nearby towns, and being forced to resort to trailer camps.

In 1974-1975, Atlantic Richfield bought the required land, and planned Wright's development over the next ten years. It never expected Wright itself to produce a profit. Construction began in 1976, with a mobile home park, a waste treatment plant, and a water supply system being among the first features. Housing Services, Inc., a subsidiary of Arco Coal Company (the Atlantic Richfield division developing the mine), was responsible for all Atlantic Richfield's town-building work. Kerr-McGee teamed up with Arco to build a $500 million recreational facility and donated it to Campbell County. Arco built a large enclosed shopping center, to be sold to private investors after full occupation was achieved. By late 1979 it was overseeing the construction of two residential areas, to be sold through developers. Arco planned Wright to have private homes, townhouses, and apartments. The county helped Wright develop, building elementary and junior high schools, a post office, a telephone company center, seven churches, a library, and other necessities and amenities. These were also intended to be available to nearby ranchers, a concerted effort to win their approval not only for Wright itself, but also for Black Thunder and the other mines.

Arco planned for a population between 6,500 and 7,000, based on the expected work force at Black Thunder and at least a dozen other nearby mines. But Wright had only 1,000 residents by late 1979, a population too low to attract a doctor or to enable the town's few merchants to show a profit. Arco admitted that it "missed [its] projections on how long it would take to finish construction. [Arco] didn't fully realize the problems that Wright's remote location would cause (Miller, 1979, 62)." Two consecutive severe winters, a less than ideal soil for construction, faulty shopping mall design, failure to plan for adequate storage space and for enough apartments to make up for soaring home prices all plagued the project.

Two years later, Wright still had only 1,600 residents, and still no "doctor, theater, auto mechanic or pizza parlor."

For a boomtown, Wright is remarkably sedate—dull, even. There is but one bar, but it shares space in the glossy new shopping center with the family-style restaurant. . . . Tennis courts, a modern new school and a country club with an Olympic-size pool have been hacked out of the sage. There is Little League now, and yoga lessons. (Blundell, 1981, 1)

Blundell (1981, 1) called Wright a "refutation of the so-called boomtown syndrome." If this situation is still so, it is due in no small measure to the state's minerals taxes, the increased knowledge of state and local planners, and especially to their insistence that resource companies provide funds to finance town services. "The companies are responding by ladling out cash grants, lending a hand with financing of schools and other facilities, building housing and cooperating in joint planning efforts" (Blundell, 1981, 1). Blundell pointed out that some states and towns today not only insist on but require cooperation. All of this is helping avoid the "Rock Springs syndrome," and companies are learning that it is good business to keep the townspeople happy, thereby reducing employee turnover.

Atlantic Richfield expects the Powder River Basin coal reserves to last 50 years, making the company optimistic about Wright's long-term future, not just as a bedroom town for the miners, but as a center for ranchers and for those engaged in other activities. Arco will incorporate Wright when it reaches 3,000 residents. The town will then have to provide its own services.

Blundell cited other examples in which a large portion of state severance tax income is flowing to boomtowns for infrastructure and service provision, but he also claimed that boomtown problems will occur with varying degrees of intensity regardless of outside aid. They can stem from conflicts between towns and industry, and from unexpected economic slumps, which reduce the flow of revenue from plant operation that the towns need to pay bondholders and other lenders. Blundell offered the example of Rio Blanco County, Colorado, in the heart of the energy-rich Overthrust Belt, that worked out an agreement with Western Fuels, a company wanting to build and operate a mine. Under the plan, taxes levied on present residents will not rise at all to finance construction for the new residents. It is clear, however, that not even this innovative idea can prevent the loss of old-time values among the townspeople and area ranchers.

The future of Wright, however rosy Arco painted it two years ago, and of similar efforts throughout the West is today bedeviled by the plunging demand worldwide for energy, which may have put an untimely end to a similar but far more publicized venture in nearby Colorado.

BATTLEMENT MESA AND THE TROUBLED COLONY PROJECT

Origins

Of all the boomtowns and new towns cited in this book, none so clearly evokes both the good intentions of private industry and the ease with which its plans can go sour as Battlement Mesa, Colorado. A consortium of companies which at one time included Exxon, Tosco, and Atlantic Richfield had planned to build and operate a shale oil plant called the Colony Project.

Shale oil deposits cover 16,000 square miles, not only in Colorado but in Utah and Wyoming. As early as 1955, Union Oil Company had begun testing shale oil extraction methods there. In the late 1970s, all of northwest Colorado was expected to become a beehive of activities similar to Colony. In fact, Union now heads up another major oil shale project in the area near Battlement Mesa. But none of the area's efforts were as controversial from the start as Colony, originally conceived as a joint venture between Atlantic Richfield and Tosco, a large independent oil company. In May 1980, Exxon bought Arco's 60-percent share of Colony. Exxon, the world's largest oil company, had achieved awesome stature even among other oil giants after the oil shocks of the 1970s. In the height of the synfuels fervor then sweeping America, this move convinced many experts that Colony could not fail.[1]

Construction of Battlement Mesa

Prospects looked so good for Colony in the late 1970s that Exxon and Tosco not only undertook the ambitious project of building a new town, Battlement Mesa, "17 miles down the valley, and across the Colorado River from the dusty old town of Parachute" (Schmitz, 1981, 6), but also began to expand Parachute itself. Battlement Mesa, Inc., an Exxon subsidiary under contract to Exxon and Tosco, was given responsibility. Haddow (1981, 20-C) described Battlement Mesa in early 1981 as "a lonely cluster of trailers on a hillside." Across the Colorado River, scores of people lived in campsites, indicative of the inability of new workers to find housing anywhere in the oil shale region of northwest Colorado.

Battlement Mesa itself had only one house completed by late 1981 (Hershey, 1981). Fifteen hundred people had to live in mobile homes. The first 35 of these were rented by early June 1981, and 115 more were waiting for hookup to basic services. Grass was being planted around them. Though the cheapest form of housing (and for most the only kind available even today), trailers were by no means inexpensive. Trailer space cost $200 per month, and a one-family, three-bedroom furnished trailer cost another $600 every month, including utilities (Haddow, 1981, 20-C). Unlike the example of Atlantic Richfield at Wright, Exxon and Tosco therefore planned to make a profit from building and running their town. Other private firms were to build apartment houses, townhouses, and one-family homes during 1981 and 1982. Although Battlement Mesa, Inc. claimed that "this won't be another company town," "the Battlement Mesa of the future may not be able to totally avoid being considered a company town; most of its residents likely [were to be] employees of corporations developing oil shale" (Haddow, 1981, 20-C).

Despite its early problems, the new town was expected to shelter the families of workers not only engaged in Colony but in nearby projects run by Union Oil, Occidental Petroleum, Tenneco, and Gulf. (The latter joined the Colony partners in providing money for ten new Garfield County sheriff's deputies and two new police officers for nearby Parachute.) When the Exxon subsidiary finished Battlement Mesa by 1995, it was to have "churches, schools, supermarkets, recreational facilities and even an 18-hole golf course. Union [was] joining Exxon and Tosco in providing funds for schools and law enforcement" (Haddow, 1981, 20-C). The town builder expected Battlement Mesa to have 10 to 12 thousand residents by the middle of 1984. This town seemed certain to prove Schmitz's assertion that

with soaring housing costs and prohibitive interest rates, corporations are coming to the reluctant realization that if the marketplace isn't providing affordable housing for workers — and in many cases it clearly isn't — they must help out [not just in energy projects, either]. . . . As the head of the [Fluor Corporation] recently told the *Wall Street Journal:* "Corporations are scared to death of the reality that housing is the next fringe benefit for employees. Intuitively, however, they know it's true." (1981, 6)

Collapse

Then, with very little warning, it all came crashing down. Oil prices stopped rising in 1981 in the face of

a worldwide recession bordering on depression and an oil glut. On May 2, 1982, Exxon announced that it was abandoning the Colony project after having predicted that the project's cost would swell to twice the level estimated when Exxon came in. Tosco, backed by federal loans, was willing to stay in, but Exxon, lacking this support, simply doubted that even this oil giant could turn a profit. Tosco agreed reluctantly when its president, Morton M. Winston, said "If [Exxon] cannot see such a project through to the end, . . . it says something about the need for Government participation on a sustained and intelligent basis" (Martin, 1982, D-4). The story suggested that federal price guarantees for synfuel projects may be necessary for this fledgling industry to avoid dying in its cradle.[2] Some analysts, however, have said that crude oil prices had to rise to $50 a barrel when Colony began operation for the project to be profitable. Colony, then, along with other delayed oil shale projects including Occidental Petroleum's Cathedral Bluffs plant and the Gulf-Standard Oil (Indiana) effort at Rio Blanco (both in Colorado), appears to have been doomed by falling crude prices and by an Administration totally opposed to such a massive subsidy.[3]

Strong evidence suggests that bad corporate planning also played a key role in the death of Colony. When Exxon bought into the project in 1980, it wanted higher capital spending to build a more efficient oil extraction plant. But soaring interest rates and construction costs forced the estimated final cost up from the $3.1 billion Tosco used to lure Exxon in to more than $6 billion when Exxon withdrew (Marbach et al., 1982, 75-76). The oil companies' expectations of government backing regardless of the cost collapsed when Ronald Reagan became President.

After the Fall

The sad national aftermath of the synfuels collapse is surely more acute in Parachute. This community, which in two years had sprouted "from a sleepy road junction into a bustling — and often chaotic — community of transient workers and trailer camps"

(Schmidt, 1982a, D-1), may now wither away to a ghost town. One newly laid-off construction supervisor predicted the same fate for Battlement Mesa.[4] Parachute's homeowners, dependent on one project, may never be able to sell their homes. Some of Parachute's workers had come from other mining or lumber areas, where joblessness has been bad for months. Union Oil's project two miles from the Colony site (which as of October 1982 was employing almost 2,500 construction workers and was forecast to employ about 550 operations employees by July 1983) may combine with regional tourism to help the Parachute area survive. Now, however, local merchants have begun laying off workers, "houses barely a year old are vacant, and weeds grow on partly landscaped lots. 'For Sale' signs line the streets. Traffic is but a trickle of what it used to be. . . . About 40 percent of the apartments built for the boom are empty" (*New York Times,* 1982, 337). Nevertheless, with Exxon's decision to "maintain the area as landlord and make an effort to attract families," hope in this area is not quite dead yet.

The entire Rocky Mountain region may soon feel the actue peril confronting Parachute. The Colony failure added to plunging metals and coal prices to bring an abrupt end to the area's boom. Unemployment, while below the U.S. average, was rising all over the area in 1982. But residents of a region whose economy "has historically been dependent on natural resources, ranging from timber cut in the northern Rockies to gold panned from Colorado riverbeds" (Schmidt, 1982b, A-12), and oil, coal, gas, oil shale, uranium, and copper, claimed to be used to booms and busts. They even hoped that out-of-staters have learned not to expect quick and easy riches by coming to the Rockies.

Several areas of the Rockies, however, are in great danger. The shutdown of a nearby Anaconda Company copper smelter and sharp job reductions at its mines have forced the joblessness rate in the Butte, Montana, area well above the national average. Closings of nearly all the mines in Idaho's "Silver Valley" have produced almost 35 percent unemployment there (Sandza and McCormick, 1982, 116).

While the authors illustrate the equally intense pain in another mining area (northern Minnesota), nowhere in the United States had there been such high expectations so recently as in the Rockies. The gloom the area now feels must be more painful than that elsewhere in the recession-plagued United States.

DeBEQUE, COLORADO

Another corporate town-planning effort is noteworthy, even though its fate may be no happier than Parachute's or Battlement Mesa's. In late 1981, Chevron planned to build a shale oil plant at Clear Creek twice the size of Colony. DeBeque, the largest town near the plant site, was expected to "grow from a present population of about 300 to 27,000 within 15 years" (Schmitz, 1981, 7). Unlike the Colony partners, Chevron never had any plan to build a new community, but instead intended to expand DeBeque. Chevron was aware of the political and social difficulties so common to boomtown growth, and its project executives tried hard to portray themselves and their project as different from those of other companies. Perhaps some validity exists for this view. While Battlement Mesa "resembles a slice of suburbia that somehow strayed too far from the city, . . . housing (at the expanded DeBeque) will be clustered and commercial centers will be planned accordingly" (Schmitz, 1981, 7). Unless the entire synfuels industry revives, the question of the relative merit of the two town plans will have become strictly academic.

NEW TOWNS ABROAD

New towns are being built at an increasing rate throughout the industrialized world, including Britain, Scandinavia, Japan, the Soviet Union, France, and Israel. Most are based on the desire to "decongest" their largest cities. These towns appear as satellite towns of larger cities, independent new towns, or twin cities. The latter idea is usually impractical unless geographical limits or the lack of water prevents the old city from growing. Satellite cities, however, are becoming common around Tokyo, Stockholm, and Washington, D.C. (Reston, Virginia, and Columbia, Maryland).

Galantay predicted that "within the next 25 years, several hundred new towns will be founded — designed to contain 20 to 30 million people" (1975, 79), only a fraction of the 1 billion additional people expected in the world by the year 2000. Most of these towns will be traditional industrial centers in the Third World. This area may also have to build parallel cities of 1 to 3 million residents next to Mexico City, Sao Paulo, and other bursting ubran centers. Galantay expects the more advanced countries to specialize in towns in the 100,000 to 300,000-person range, intended to "decongest" their huge cities.

United Kingdom

Britain has been building new towns for decades in its effort to check the mushrooming growth of its major cities, especially London, and to promote more labor-intensive industry nearby. Scotland, for example, built five new towns after World War II. By late 1981, they had combined to account for about 75,000 jobs and 210,000 residents (Meredith, 1981, 35).[5]

Australia

In 1972 Australia began to develop five "growth centers." Scott used this term because "only one [of the new towns] involves from the outset the construction of a new town on a green-fields site, three involve the expansion of existing towns, and one involves the restructuring of metropolitan growth" (1976, 78). Until the 1970s, Australia had been slow to adopt the British new-town concept, Canberra and the Adelaide suburb of Elizabeth having been its only previous efforts. Scott doubted whether or not these new communities[6] could flourish without the massive immigration that helped Canberra and Elizabeth grow in better economic times.

Hong Kong

The exuberant British colony of Hong Kong crammed into a tiny area is undergoing still more population strain, added to a period of economic uncertainty relating to its future colonial status. "Hong Kong has spent billions of dollars to build seven new communities [called the New Territories], with industrial centers and economic independence, for three million people. All are scheduled for completion in 1997, when they could be taken over by China" (Hollie, 1982, 8). These areas, which until 1972 had only a few fishing and farming villages, appear vastly different from the old world-style areas of Hong Kong most familiar to tourists. Public investment has totaled more than $10 billion, and private investment in factories, office structures, and housing has added millions more. Private building, as usual, exceeds the pace of public construction:

The new towns have grown so fast that transportation, schools and medical care have sometimes lagged behind housing development. In Shatin (one of the Territories) 6,000 people a month are being accepted.... Within a short commuting distance from [the] central business district, Shatin is already a city of 200,000.... It has a $20 million race course . . . , a $100 million first-class hotel under construction and a sports club.... Like all towns, Shatin is to be a socially balanced mixture of housing — high-rise housing for former squatters and million-dollar California Spanish houses for the wealthy" (Hollie, 1982, 8)

Hong Kong's real-estate developers, long known for their zealous pursuit of profit, will no doubt make sure that any money they lose on the lower-class housing will be more than offset by the profits from building the homes of the rich.

Israel

New town building may be more extensive elsewhere, but nowhere is it more controversial than in Israel, particularly in the territories occupied since the 1967 war. Even in Israel itself, however, the plans are ambitious.

Israel is a country in which everything appears

either incredibly ancient or brand-new. The proto-type of the Israeli new town is Eilat, for it was not only the first Israeli city built after the 1948 war of independence, but the war in fact made its existence necessary.

As late as World War I, Eilat was nothing more than a series of "mud huts [that] housed a detachment of British policemen" (Clement, 1974, 36). Although the 1947 Palestine partition included the Negev desert and Eilat, the Israelis had to seize and secure the area by force. Not until March 10, 1949—two months after Egypt asked for a ceasefire—did Israeli troops enter the tiny settlement.

Then Prime Minister David Ben-Gurion stated in 1963 that he intended Eilat to be "a big international port, with hundreds of thousands of inhabitants and later with perhaps a million" (Arbel, 1974, 7), a dream so far unfulfilled. Yet it could have been if Israeli planners had been serious about Eilat's purpose from the beginning. Meir Avizohar, once a fisherman and member of the Israeli Parliament, was one of the early settlers there. He and his group of pioneers wanted Eilat to become a center of fishing, shipping, mining, and tourism, but he claimed that they received little government support (Avizohar, 1974, 15-18). The government allegedly thought Eilat too vulnerable to Egyptian attack, and Avizohar argued that the Israeli leadership discouraged Eilat's growth, perhaps avoiding a confrontation with Egypt. The first foreign ship did not dock at Eilat until 1952.

The Israelis then began building Eilat as a port, but even they at first failed to realize the importance of a strong presence there. Only the Egyptian cutoff of all shipping into and out of Eilat in October 1955 shocked the Israeli leadership into this admission of prior neglect. After Israel captured the Sinai peninsula in 1956 and the United Nations placed troops there to assure free passage,

the development of Eilat began in earnest. A port to act as Israel's gateway to the Far East was mapped out and completed nine years later in 1965. Around it, slowly, apartment (blocks) rose from the craggy hillsides that overlooked . . . the gulf (of Aqaba). Miners from the copper works at nearby Timna and construction workers laboring to build the port moved in. (Clement, 1974, 38)

By 1974 Eilat had become Israel's third largest port, but not yet a city to compete with Tel Aviv or Jerusalem. One problem with the effort to settle Eilat was the lack of farmland nearby. After several failures, a farm commune was set up about 25 miles away. Eilat was also a 12-hour trip across a chuckhole-filled path from Beersheba, itself a tiny, raw community, 150 miles away. Air transport was available only twice a week from other Israeli cities. In the 1950s Eilat was a tiny settlement of miners, laborers, soldiers, and a few tourists, subject to severe sandstorms and occasional ambushes of transport by Arab guerrillas. Its "port" had only a small dock. Most ships starting to serve Eilat arrived with cement from Africa and left with Dead Sea potash. Nothing, however, could make up for Eilat's isolation. "It could just as well be a different planet, linked to Israel by two planes and two buses a week, and a hardy little band of truckdrivers who risk[ed] their lives to bring . . . its vital supplies" (Williams, 1974, 24). The arrival of piped drinking water in the early 1950s was a major event.

Eilat's frontier-town era ended with the 1956 war. The arrival of an Israeli gunboat signaled changes to come. After the war, the government made Eilat the terminus of an oil pipeline, and tankers began docking there. At the same time, an all-weather road was built to Beersheba, and trucks could now bring produce from the north to export. Port expansion soon became necessary. Tourists could also come to visit some of the world's most spectacular coral reefs. Eilat became a bonanza for tour operators, including "Club Med." Eilat built its first hospital in 1957. Scientists began building desalination plants.

The 1967 war and the closing of the Suez Canal made Eilat a key oil- and cargo-shipping alternative route to the Cape of Good Hope. The buildup of Eilat spawned even newer towns nearby (Arad, for example, developed as a fertilizer shipping point), and revived the ancient Timna copper mines. By the early 1970s Eilat had 18,000 residents. Tourists now could even go beyond Eilat, into the Israeli-controlled Sinai. Although Eilat suffered from the 1973 war, it had clearly come a long way since 1949. It had shopping centers, several synagogues, an art museum, a zoo, a nearby campsite, a marina, hotels, a modern airport, a sports stadium, and a maritime museum.

Eilat was only the first Israeli attempt at town building. By 1973 Israel had 30 development towns, in which about one-fourth of Israel's roughly three million people live (Sadeh, 1973, 57-58). Newly arrived immigrants nearly make up a majority in most of them.

In the early 1950s Israeli planners realized that as the country was becoming more industrial, it could expect to put fewer and fewer new arrivals on the soil—the old Zionist ideal. Moreover, Israel was incapable of providing enough water to irrigate all potential farmland. Israel did not want to encourage the growth of a coastal urban sprawl from Tel Aviv northward. The answer was

that towns be encouraged to grow throughout the country, around existing small settlements such as Beersheba and Tiberias, and in places where no one had lived for centuries, such as Ashdod and Kiryat Gat and Dimona. Every one of these towns was to become an independent center, serving the agricultural areas around it, but also providing a base for all types of industry. (Sadeh, 1973, 57-58)

Most of them began as "transient camps" for the immigrants arriving in 1949 and 1950, in which life was far from luxurious. By 1973 the towns varied in size from Mitzpe Ramon (population 1,500) to Beersheba (80,000) to Jerusalem (300,000). Twenty-five Israeli communities contain more than 10,000 residents, the population level that planners consider the "minimum for the maintenance of adequate urban services" (Sadeh, 1973, 57-58).

Various industries have grown in and around the towns. Town industries employ one-third of these communities' labor force. Most other workers are in government, education, and other services. Government grants, low-interest loans, and tax concessions make it relatively easy to develop industries. The education-obsessed Israelis have assumed that the towns will have plenty of schools. In Kiryat Gat new apartments and better clinics were being built, playgrounds and parks were being expanded, and street paving and street light improvements were under way in 1973.

The new town planning in Israel has critics, however. Shachar pointed out that

throughout their development, the new towns were plagued by a very high turnover of population and many are still suffering from a considerable negative balance of migration. There are many reasons for this, but it can at least be stated that economic reasons were not the only motive pushing people out of the new towns. Many of those who left were dismayed by the limited opportunities offered in a small town, and by the low level of services, education, and cultural activities. (1974, 86)

Nevertheless, he claimed that "very few countries can equal the size and scale of Israel's national effort in building new towns. The large share of the Israeli population actually living in new towns is clear proof of the remarkable success of the dispersal policy" (Shachar, 1976, 87).

Lithwick and Cohen (1981) were perhaps more critical. They doubt that "population redistribution" can work in Israel without government assistance and without tremendous economic waste. They claimed that during the 1950s and early 1960s, a time of tremendous immigration, people could easily be brought to remote areas. The late 1960s and early 1970s were years of intense economic activity. From 1972 to 1981, the Israeli economy underwent "relative economic stagnation." Lithwick and Cohen argued that only in the first period, one of high immigration, did the "peripheral" areas grow relative to the central region of Israel's population (Haifa-Tel Aviv-Jerusalem). Most new towns expanded during the 1950s and early 1960s, but industrial activity began rising only in the later 1960s. Lithwick and Cohen wondered whether this was a response to growing markets or government intervention.

Moreover, Lithwick and Cohen (1981) claimed that the government planners ignored Israel's geography: Only the Dead Sea area has abundant natural resources, so location near markets, a large labor pool, or a port is vital for a city's industrial growth. Most new towns, however, were set up with the intent either of securing boundaries or opening up new areas. They argued that their statistical analysis "suggest[ed] that without continued public assistance, [the] economic prospects . . . of many of the badly located development towns . . . will deteriorate" (Lithwick and Cohen, 1981, 27).

Equally lacking was a consideration of the type of industry to develop in these towns. Lithwick and Cohen statistically broke down Israeli industry into sectors according to growth potential in production and labor use. Only four of them offered high growth possibilities in both areas.[7] On the other hand, all but four new towns showed many more backward than growth-enhancing sectors. They considered it significant that population growth attracted industry during the period when immigration slowed down and industrial activity picked up, but industrial growth has not attracted more population since the early 1970s. Their reason is that "backward" industries (e.g., mining, food, textiles, leather, wood products) grew rapidly to absorb many unskilled immigrants who would otherwise have become unemployed residents of the development towns. This arbitrary step created a problem of economic stagnation, and population decline has led to socioeconomic problems that have appeared in several towns. Only those new towns near the large cities have seemed able to attract native Israelis. The authors therefore accused the Israeli government of having drawn up population distribution policies without considering their economic implications, a strategy resulting in remote towns' inability to "develop a dynamic industrial base" and their problems of "low incomes, high unemployment, rapid turnover and instability" (p. 31).

If Lithwick and Cohen are correct, these communities are just as badly off as totally unplanned American, South African, and Canadian energy boomtowns.

NOTES

1. Only a behemoth like Exxon could have had even a remote chance of bringing such a huge project to completion. It bascially works as follows: Huge chambers will be carved into 9,000 miles of hills. Out of each room will come more than 1.2 million tons of ore, to be crushed, preheated, and fed into one of six surface retorts. Their heat vaporizes the oil locked into the shale. The vapor is cooled, condensed, and sent through

an upgrading plant, which removes nitrogen, sulfur, and other impurities. The oil is then piped out of the site. The waste shale is wetted down, taken to a mountaintop disposal area, compacted, contoured, and seeded for future vegetation growth (Hershey, 1981, D-1).

2. The survival of Union Oil's nearby project certainly bears this point out. At the beginning, Union signed a long-term contract under which it will sell 20 million barrels of refined diesel and jet fuel over 10 years to the Defense Department at $42.50 a barrel, far higher than the late-1982 world crude price (Marbach et al., 1982, 75-76).

3. Synfuel failures have not been limited to the United States. Only a week before Exxon withdrew from Colony, Shell Canada, Ltd. and Gulf Canada, Ltd. announced their abandonment of the Alsands tar sands project in Alberta, leaving an embarrassed Canadian government as the sole active partner. Five other companies had pulled out earlier in 1982 before Gulf and Shell quit. The two firms had asked the federal and provincial governments to guarantee them a 20 percent return, but were turned down. The province's other oil sands projects (Suncor, begun in 1963, and Syncrude, opened in 1978), although still operating, "have been plagued by continuing mechanical and technical setbacks curbing production and profitability" (Malcolm, 1982, D-1).

4. One week after the Exxon pullout, "a Colony spokesperson said that the status of Battlement Mesa . . . is undetermined at the moment. . . . Nearly all of the basic utilities, streets and public facilities have been constructed" (Pitman, 1982, 65).

5. The five Scottish new towns are East Kilbride, Cumbernauld, Livingston, Irvine, and Glenrothes.

6. The five Australian "growth centers" are Albury/Wodonga, Bathurst/Orange, Geelong, Monarto, and the Holsworthy-Campbelltown-Appin region southwest of Sydney.

7. Chemicals-oil, metal products, electronic and electrical products, transportation equipment.

REFERENCES

Arbel, Naftali, 1974, "Ben-Gurion's Dream," *Israel Magazine* **6**(3):6-7.

Avizohar, Meir, 1974, "Rebirth," *Israel Magazine* **6**(3):15-18.

Blundell, William E., 1981, "Easing the Strain," *Wall Street Journal,* August 12, p. 1.

Clement, Richard, 1974, "The Southern Gateway," *Israel Magazine* **6**(3):33-39.

Finsterbusch, Kurt, 1980, *Understanding Social Impacts,* Sage Publications, Beverly Hills, Calif.

Haddow, Ellen, 1981, "Instant Town Booms in Colorado," *Baton Rouge State-Times,* June 15, p. 20-C.

Hershey, Robert D., Jr., 1981, "Shale Oil is Coming of Age," *New York Times,* November 6, p. D-1.

Hollie, Pamela G., 1982, "Hong Kong Races Ahead Despite Uncertainty," *New York Times,* October 31, p. 8.

Lithwick, N. H., and Cohen, Gad 1981, "Some Economic Aspects of Population Distribution Policies," *Growth and Change* **12**(3):23-31.

Malcolm, Andrew H., 1982, "Alsands Project is Canceled," *New York Times,* May 1, p. D-1.

Marbach, William D.; Cook, William J.; Copeland, Jeff B.; and Lampert, Hope, 1982, "The Death of Synfuels," *Newsweek,* May 17, pp. 75-76.

Martin, Douglas, 1982, "Exxon Abandons Shale Oil Project," *New York Times,* May 3, p. 1ff.

Meredith, Mark, 1981, "New Towns," *Financial Times,* December 9, p. 35.

Miller, William H., 1979, "A New Kind of Company Town," *Industry Week,* November 26, pp. 52-62.

New York Times, 1982, *"Pullout by Exxon Jolts a Boomtown,"* October 10, p. 33.

Pitman, Frank, 1982, "Exxon Pullout is Seen as Deadly for Shale Oil," *Chemical Engineering* **89**(11):63-65.

Pri Gal, Yacov, 1974, "Timna," *Israel Magazine* **6**(3):77-79.

Sadeh, Aryeh, 1973, "Israel's New Frontier," *Israel Magazine* **5**(3-4):56-58.

Sandza, Richard, and McCormick, John, 1982, "Misery in the Minefields," *Newsweek,* December 6, pp. 115-116.

Schmidt, William E., 1982, "Uncertainty in Shale Oil Town," *New York Times,* May 4, p. D-1.

Schmidt, William E., 1982, "Rocky Mountain States Feel Delayed Effect of Recession," *New York Times,* May 11, p. A-12.

Schmitz, Gary, 1981, "Colorado's Rural Suburb," *High Country News,* November 27, pp. 6-7.

Scott, Peter, 1976, "Australia's New Towns," *Town and Country Planning* **44**(2):78-82.

Shachar, Arie, 1976, "New Towns in a National Settlement Policy," *Town and Country Planning* **44**(2):83-87.

Williams, Louis, 1974, "Twenty Five Years," *Israel Magazine* **6**(3):21-28.

PART VI

FORMULATING
AN OVERALL
BOOMTOWN
SOLUTION

27

Suggestions for Boomtown Growth Control

THE ROLE OF NATIONAL PLANNERS

Relatively little advice will be aimed at Washington because the federal government's role in the boomtown solution has to be indirect. One federal contribution, however, can be its upgrading the environmental impact statement preparation process so that it includes social and cultural impacts. Part IV shows that most siting disputes following NEPA's 1969 passage involved the affected area's physical ecology, but rarely considered the more subtle effects on individual residents. One really needs an impact statement to make planners aware of problems that escape most public scrutiny. Most Americans' ecological awareness today exceeds that of 1969, so the United States needs less of a reminder of physical degradation in its environment. It does need to be reminded of the social and emotional problems that accompany the physical problems of energy development.

Baldwin and Baldwin (1974) also remarked that the federal government has to reach some kind of informal agreement with the major energy companies on a long-range U.S. energy policy that will outline those energy sources that Washington and industry consider the most vital to develop. Uncertainty in energy development always begins at the top government level, but it ultimately paralyzes local planning. Reducing this uncertainty at its origin will be Washington's major contribution to solving the boomtown problem.

SUGGESTIONS FOR STATE AND REGIONAL PLANNERS

State leaders have a wider variety of planning improvement methods than those available to national planners, especially in the U.S. Baldwin and Baldwin remarked that the Scottish government has to prevent platform construction towns from going bust later on. "[These] sites can be transformed into marinas for pleasure boats or . . . sewage treatment works." This is more a Scottish than a British task, since London will *229* be less interested in Scottish industry once its oil boom ends. Then the Scottish government will have to prevent the region from sliding back into its pre-1965 depression. The time to plan, however, is before platform work ends forever.

States can convert abandoned military bases to industrial parks. One cannot convert an abandoned coal mine or oil well to other uses as easily, but one can fix up abandoned offices, communications, transportation, and all the other auxiliary services that once helped the energy boom. Attracting new industries to use these auxiliary services, of course, is another state and regional task.

Colorado's Governor Richard Lamm made clear in November 1980 that industry and state government must work together to identify the social and economic effects of the synthetic fuels industry that sooner or later will transform the Rocky Mountain region. He included the possibility of creating new towns, but failed to mention whether industry or the state was to do this. These two groups must also learn how to assemble, train, and keep intact a local energy work force; this, however, could well pose an insurmountable problem.

Unlike Governor Lamm and other Rocky Mountain state leaders, Massachusetts planners had no energy crisis to convince cities and towns of the need for state-local cooperation in land-use planning. Unless an external crisis exists, then, the state may have to let its towns define their own growth management problems, much as Florida appears to have done (see Chapter 24). Once it institutes this "bottoms up" planning scheme, the state will have to respond to local demands and may be forced to reduce the importance of its own views in state land use and growth control efforts. Energy boomtowns, however, will have to accept a major state role in dealing with rapid land development and population growth.

Lee remarked that state governments, particularly in the Rocky Mountain energy belt where boomtown growth is most common, have to understand the need to study the boomtown problem's economic, political, social, and aesthetic elements. The state has to take on much of the responsibility for improving the quality of population and economic forecasting. Part IV indicated the variety of available techniques and models, but warned state planners to check out their preferred model for reliability and accuracy.

Utah planners (Utah State Department of Community and Economic Development, 1980, vol. VI) discussed ways of improving the state's financial response to boomtown growth, insisting that Utah must permit its state and county governments to share royalty (from federal leasing) and other revenues with its towns. More specifically, the state can provide grants directly to boomtowns; increase the permissible level of local sales taxes or impose a severance tax; pass a constitutional amendment to allow revenue sharing; allow more sharing of infrastructure and services among neighboring towns; and improve zoning ordinances, which many small towns have never enacted. Utah, unlike a nonenergy-producing state such as Massachusetts, can use energy as a reason for taking these steps and developing its investment strategy to improve the procedure of local applications for state aid.

These studies, then, suggest that state and regional planners must consider attracting new industry to their towns; cooperate with industry to increase the productivity and quality of life of its workers; learn to predict population growth and service demand; decide the extent to which they can get involved with local planners without creating friction; and improve the flow of funds to towns so that they can receive the aid as they need it.

IDEAS FOR LOCAL DECISION MAKING

Many authors investigating the response of Scottish towns to the North Sea oil boom suggested that American town planners must look for information about the size, location, and type of energy resources nearby, and examine their own planning system and infrastructure if these data suggest an energy boom in their future. They must also give industry advanced notice about those locations in which it may or may not build, let the federal and state governments know the town's preboom needs and interests, and evaluate different ways in which energy revenues can help pay for developing a postboom economy.

Among the ways in which a town's government and residents can influence industry's development decisions are to shape executives' views of the town; enact zoning rules, including health, fire, and building codes that either help or hinder development; and influence the general public's view of the corporation. If they choose to help energy development, towns can also encourage county and state governments to process all their required permits at one time, and help industry acquire land (when most residents favor the energy plant) by using its eminent domain powers. The town also has to inform industry of any ceiling it has on the number of construction workers that its infrastructure can currently care for. In those states in which county governments wield power over energy development, all a county's towns to be affected by an energy project have to cooperate with the county so that none of the towns will have to care for a number of workers and families far above its ceiling.

Part IV covers existing ways in which town leaders can ask industry and state government to help the impacted towns upgrade their financial positions. Lee (1980) and West (1977) summarized them as

awarding outright grants,
guaranteeing town bonds,
providing short-term loans to the towns until they can "sustain standard municipal financing,"
increasing state willingness to share its energy revenues with its boomtowns,
giving the towns full knowledge of industry's plans well before development begins,
helping town officials become more familiar with "grantsmanship,"
and getting local officials more involved with facility planning.

Towns planning growth management strategies have to consider the amount of land left undeveloped (Rick, 1978). The boomtown area's construction industry should support a local growth management strategy that leaves enough land undeveloped by the private sector to allow housing and public infrastructure to be built. Home buyers will also benefit from such a strategy; the lack of foresight in this matter contributed to skyrocketing home prices that crippled postboom industrial growth in so many boomtowns. Towns in early growth stages with large tracts of vacant land (e.g., Phoenix) must realize that allowing construction in these areas will reduce the need to expand public infrastructure; once these lands fill up, however, the suburbs will be the only place left in which to build.

Chapter 23 shows that land speculation must be one key target of local growth control efforts. The comments of Stone and Rosapepe (1982) on nationwide speculation in art, real estate, and precious metals are just as applicable to local land speculation. They made clear that

widespread speculation diverts investment funds. . . . Altering tax, credit and regulatory policies to lower the relative return on nonproductive speculation would be a start. . . . Preferential low rates for capital gains could be limited to investments that actually create more capital for the economy. . . . Another way to limit excessive speculation is control of initial margin, . . . the amount of money that must be put up in cash to enter a . . . venture. . . . As margin levels rise, speculators . . . will start to look elsewhere for extraordinary returns. (Stone and Rosapepe, 1982, A-27)

This idea was the rationale behind the Vermont law discussed in Chapter 24, and unless state law forbids it, boomtowns should consider enacting such laws if they can be shown to help keep land (and therefore all) prices in the towns under control.

The following list of growth-management steps prepared by the Urban Land Institute and the American Planning Association (Utah State Department of Community and Economic Development, 1980, vol. II) contains measures that any boomtown should find useful:

1. aesthetic controls
2. agricultural zoning
3. amenity requirements
4. annexation policies

5. building codes
6. capital budget
7. capital programming
8. carrying capacities
9. compensable regulations
10. comprehensive planning
11. covenants and restrictions
12. dedication or "fees in lieu"
13. district "tiering"
14. down-zoning
15. easements
16. eminent domain
17. environmental controls
18. environmental standards
19. fiscal analysis
20. floating zones
21. greenbelts
22. height restrictions
23. highway/road planning
24. historical preservation
25. holding zones
26. impact zoning
27. large lot zoning
28. performance standards
29. official maps
30. open space
31. rezonings
32. school capacity
33. service areas
34. sewer facilities
35. special districts
36. subdivision controls
37. timing permit issuing
38. urban renewal
39. user fees
40. zoning

INDUSTRY'S ROLE

Industry's major active boomtown control contribution is the provision of timely information about the size and schedule of work force increases that the town and its state can expect. Companies always have to allocate a specific number of workers to any task—either building, operating, relocating, or dismantling facilities. The state and town can then estimate total population growth and service demand. The energy firms must also monitor and analyze boomtown impacts, which includes developing measurements, gathering numerical data and subjective information, and sending reports to important government officials at all levels.

Industry must also consider resource availability. In Scotland, labor was always the scarce resource. Labor and water are both scarce in the Rocky Mountains. Although the North Sea oil firms had to bring in hundreds of non-Scottish employees, there was almost always a nearby town available for expansion. Many Western coal veins and shale oil deposits are miles from existing towns.

Energy firms must obviously carry out their extraction activities at the site, but they need not burn the mined coal, gasified or liquefied coal, or shale oil near the mine. The North Sea oil firms exported most of their crude oil because oil economics dictate refining the crude close to the marketplace. By shipping their coal to (new, if necessary) Western, Midwestern, Southern, and Eastern power plants, these firms not only avoid the environmental disputes that scuttled the Kaiparowits plant but also tap all those areas' skilled work forces. The land-takings problems of laying rail or slurry lines (for coal) merely cancel out those of building electricity transmission lines, and the slurry line's water requirements must be considered against those of a Western power plant. Consumers will ultimately pay regardless of the plant location, either through higher shipping costs to a faraway plant or through paying higher utility bills to cover power plant construction costs.

Labor, however, is the heart of this trade-off. Energy firms planning to extract coal, oil, and shale oil, and the superbuilders (e.g., Fluor, Parsons, and Bechtel) planning to construct huge synthetic fuel plants are already concerned about a looming construction labor shortage. Many unionized American construction workers will refuse relocation to these remote areas (*Business Week,* 1980, 90). The builders' only choice, then, will be to set up company towns similar to Wright, Wyoming, and train the local workers, tasks at which these companies have been adept overseas. Shale oil plants and coal gasification and liquefaction plants, however, need not be built in these remote areas, any more than fossil fuel plants have to be.

Jacobson (1976) provided an industry representative's view of the difficulty these firms will face in dealing with local and state governments. In 1976 he was the community affairs manager of Stauffer Chemical Company's activities in Green River, near Rock Springs, Wyoming. His experience led him to state that "five percent is generally about as much annual growth as a small community can comfortably absorb" (Jacobson, 1976, 288), a much lower figure than Gilmore's 15 percent, and one close to the growth rates of some huge cities whose infrastructures also have been overwhelmed. He showed as much awareness of the boomtown syndrome's components as did Gilmore, particularly housing provision.

Perhaps the most successful housing aid by industry to date was a joint loan of front-end development money by three companies to a small manufacturer of modular houses. This loan enabled the developer to construct a small subdivision of quality single-family houses that enjoyed ready acceptance and enabled the builder to pay off the loan with interest. It had the added advantage of involving industry in the housing business only indirectly. (Jacobson, 1976, 289)

Jacobson cited a 1974 study backing up his own view that most boomtown residents prefer private houses to mobile homes and apartment houses. He also claimed that "one of the few really effective tools for recruiting persons from other mining areas to the West [and producing] a stable, productive work force" (1976, 289) available to the company is the construction of its own groupings of private houses rented for a small fee or "sold at cost, with the companies also willing to apply a portion of the rent to the purchase of the home if the employee elects to buy after renting for a few years" (p. 289).

One of Jacobson's other ideas is the collaboration of company and local government officials in attracting doctors, nurses, social workers, and other medical personnel. They can use professional recruiting firms, but another possibility is

the placement of physicians, dentists, and other health care practitioners by the National Health Service Corps, an arm of the U.S. Department of Health, Education and Welfare. This agency signs up young professionals and places them in medically underserved areas for a two-year commitment period. The community has the responsibility to provide a place for them to practice, as well as anticipate their needs for housing, a job for the spouse if desired, and other similar requirements. . . . [These workers] are salaried and paid directly to the NHSC. The ultimate goal is to retain these individuals in the community on a permanent basis in private practice after their two-year commitment has been fulfilled. . . . [To avoid dashed hopes among the new arrivals,] assignees should be carefully and truthfully counseled beforehand about what to expect in the specific location. (Jacobson, 1976, 303)

The assignees should also get to know each other well before their relocation. One drawback that Jacobson did not mention is that of resentment among the construction or energy workers' spouses (most of whom probably will not be able to find jobs) of the spouses of the new health care workers who have been given assistance toward finding them. Jacobson claimed the best solution is that the energy companies simply hire physicians directly and relocate them to the boomtown as necessary.

Jacobson also backs up this book's many arguments for industry-government cooperation — mainly that industry must give local and state government advanced warning of its plans. Just as local and state governments have formed associations for information-gathering and planning, such as WESTPO, he recommended "the formation of an association by the major firms . . . [which] provides a vehicle for industry to collectively interface with local government, assist officials in securing public funds, supply expertise in various areas such as housing, and make capital available as a last resort" (Jacobson, 1976, 303), all of which helps towns avoid the "front-end financing" dilemma. Such action by Exxon and Tosco, working with Union Oil, would have saved the towns of

Battlement Mesa, Rifle, and Parachute considerable anxiety after the Colony project shutdown.

Unless energy and construction companies can create a highly skilled labor force out of a population almost completely unfamiliar with industrial processes, these firms may have to process all these resources (i.e., burn mined, gasified, or liquefied coal, or burn the extracted shale oil) closer to available skilled work forces. The costs of training new workers, replacing them if they prove unproductive, building new towns, and obtaining plant permits through a maze of red tape, can all be deducted from the cost of building new pipelines and rail lines. Consumers, of course, will bear the remaining costs, just as they would if industry built the new towns. Although the cost of building new rail and slurry lines will be enormous, one must consider this as merely part of an American energy independence effort whose scope and cost will dwarf any project this country has ever undertaken, except perhaps the space program. Moreover, shipping resources out of pristine rural areas removes the environmental problems of processing them.

Energy firms will still have the task of building new towns to serve miners, shale oil extractors, and their families. However, the smaller work force size and its knowledge that they must all leave when extraction ends (or live in the same state of economic depression as that present before the energy boom) make the new town idea more attractive than the alternative of flooding the nearby towns with new workers, and causing all the economic and social problems making up the boomtown syndrome.

THE PROBLEMS OF THIRD-WORLD URBAN PLANNERS

Chapter 12 discussed the runaway growth problems facing cities from Sao Paulo to Mexico City and Cairo. Demko and Fuchs (1980), both geography professors, posed the following questions to national and local urban planners in the Third World:

What determines where people live and want to live?

Which of these can government affect?

How can planners identify population redistribution goals that complement government planning goals?

How and when should government intervene?

What are the best techniques government can adopt to achieve its goals?

How can governments measure the results of their efforts?

What organizations have to be created to design, implement, monitor and evaluate policies and programs?

Demko and Fuchs mentioned various efforts attempted so far to attack population maldistribution. Putting population ceilings on the fastest growing cities has not worked well. Boosting living conditions in the urban slums has been largely successful. Building satellite cities has had a mixed record, though successful in Hong Kong (see Chapter 26), Lima, and Dakar. Promoting the growth of smaller cities has failed because the cost to most Third World governments of infrastructure building exceeds their means, although in countries where this problem does not apply, this method has worked better, as in Ciudad Guyana, Venezuela (mentioned in Chapter 16). Rural development efforts have also had mixed success.

Demko and Fuchs concluded that Third World population planners must begin to think more in economic terms, and its economic planners must start to consider demographics.

REFERENCES

Baldwin, P. L., and Baldwin, M. F., 1975. *Onshore Planning for Offshore Oil*, The Conservation Foundation, Washington, D.C.

Business Week, 1980, "The Construction Boom," September 29, pp. 83-95.

Demko, George J., and Fuchs, Roland J., 1980, "Population Redistribution: Problems and Policies," *Populi* **7**(4):26-35.

Jacobson, Larry G., 1976, "Coping With Growth in the Modern Boom Town," *Personnel Journal* **55**(6):288ff.

Lee, Roger D., 1980, "Energy Development: Socio-Economic Impact Problems and Mitigation Strategies," July, Utah State Department of Community and Economic Development, Salt Lake City.

Oil and Gas Journal, 1980, "Colorado Governor Casts Ideal Oil Shale Scenario," **78**(46):30.

Rick, W. B., 1978, "Growth Management in San Diego," *Urban Land* **37**(4):3-5.

Stone, James M., and Rosapepe, James C., 1982, "Don't Speculate. Invest," *New York Times,* November 5, p. A-27.

Utah State Department of Community and Economic Development, 1980, "Agenda for the Eighties," vols. II and VI, May, UDCED, Salt Lake City.

West, Stanley A., August, 1977, *Opportunities for Company-Community Cooperation in Mitigating Energy Facility Impacts,* Massachusetts Institute of Technology, Cambridge, Mass.

Yaffee, Steven L., 1977, *Municipal Involvement in the Formulation of State Growth Policy,* Massachusetts Institute of Technology, Cambridge, Mass.

28

A Model of the Boomtown Solution

IDEAS BEHIND THE MODEL

This part ties together all the partial solutions to the boomtown problem that are scattered throughout Parts IV and V. This total solution makes up a model, illustrated in Figure 28.1, combining all the participants needed to resolve the boomtown problem. Figure 28.1 (a) shows the extent to which these participants must coordinate their planning efforts, and Figure 28.1 (b) shows the timing of various financial transactions among them. Both show which of these "actors" play major roles, and which are relegated to minor ones—either because they occur early in the solution or their importance diminishes as the solution proceeds.

The model assigns the most notable minor role to the federal government. The previous discussions about foreign siting, compensation, and planning showed the foreign central government's pivotal role in all these activities, from the beginning to the end of a project. The model shows this not to occur in its idea of proper boomtown planning.

The model assigns state and local governments and industry the most important roles because only they are closely enough involved with the boomtown's residents to learn their needs before detailed project planning begins. This provision gives the model a realism (in the Reagan era) that earlier models, such as Gilmore's, with their emphasis on federal planning and help, do not have.

This plan's financial aspect ignores the normal taxing and disbursement systems discussed throughout this book because they were not meant to deal with extremely rapid, unpredictable population growth so common to boomtowns. The model instead concentrates on those financial dealings that must accompany its idea of comprehensive, timely, coordinated boomtown planning.

THE CONCEPT OF COORDINATED PLANNING

Figure 28.1 (a) shows that boomtown planning efforts must begin at the federal government level. No

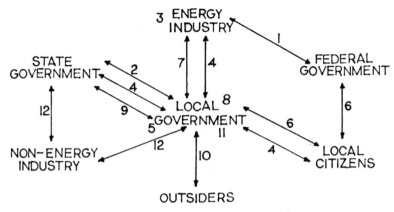

(a) Planning coordination in the boomtown solution.

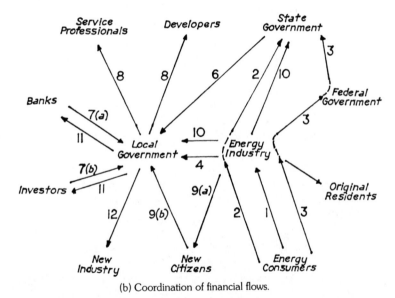

(b) Coordination of financial flows.

Figure 28.1
A model of the boomtown solution (Malamud, 1981).

one will invest in a boomtown unless the investor is assured that industry will be building and operating an energy project there. Industry needs some sort of federal guarantee that developing a particular energy source is in the national interest and will not encounter bureaucratic opposition (step 1).

At this early stage, the state government must enact a severance tax on the resource likely to be extracted, and arrange a general revenue-sharing plan with its towns within the energy exploitation area. The state does not yet know where industry will build or the size of the project. The state should also enact provisions taxing mobile home owners as householders, not vehicle owners, and pass legislation to curb the purchasing of land for purely speculative purposes (step 2).

As the project planning begins, the energy company schedulers and manpower experts determine the dates on which plant construction begins and ends, and the number of workers it will need at each building phase. It also plans these aspects of mine or plant operation. This planning gives the federal government an idea of the royalty money it will earn (if the project site is within federally owned land), and the state then knows how much it will collect from its severance tax and its share of the federal royalties (step 3).

The energy firm and the state government then jointly prepare social and economic impact assessments, using any of the available methodologies discussed in this book and elsewhere, to go along with the federally-mandated environmental impact statement. This step involves extensive public participation, for only the affected area's residents can accurately predict the social and environmental effects of the project on them. This will assure the citizens of several potential project-site towns that their needs and concerns will become part of higher-level planning. The energy firm and the state give the town governments their population predictions and accompanying estimates of service demand (step 4).

Once each of the affected town governments knows that an energy project may be in its future, it examines its infrastructure. The population and service demand estimates will help the town officials determine the additional facilities they will need, their cost, and the compensation level the town government will demand (step 5).

Each town then consults its citizens about the impact they believe they will suffer and the compensation they will need. The federal and local governments then carry out the auctioning process, discussed in Chapter 20. Public participation on the local level is as important here as it was on the state level in the previous step (step 6).

The selected town then negotiates its compensation terms with the energy firm. Among these arrangements should be the prepayment of some of the firm's taxes. With this money, the town can have the necessary housing and infrastructure built (step 7).

The town then devises a growth management plan, containing the laws that will be most useful to its physical layout, present population, and housing patterns. Among the laws should be a provision similar to Vermont's land-gains tax, but on the local level, similar to that passed on the state level in step 2, that will control land speculation, mitigate the housing and land price explosions, and enable new nonenergy industries to move in later (step 8).

Once the state knows its expected revenue from the project, it works out a financial aid plan for the affected town. It can guarantee local bonds, lend directly to the town, or award grants (step 9).

Having received preconstruction payments from industry (and possibly from the state, too), the town builds enough housing and other infrastructure for its expected work force. If the state and town know they will attract new industry after the energy project switches from construction to operation, they put up more permanent housing than mobile housing. Trailer camps are otherwise necessary (step 10).

If the town finds that the cost of building all these new structures and utilities exceeds the tax prepayments and earlier state aid, the state allows the town to raise more funds in a suitable way. If the community's construction costs lag behind prepayments, the town creates a fund for attracting new industry (step 11).

Once energy project operation begins, the town's population declines, and the town faces unused infrastructure and higher unemployment if it has failed to attract a diverse industrial base. If it has done so successfully, some former construction workers will find new local jobs more easily. The state must allow neighboring towns in the same situation to pool their funds to offer incentives to new industries (step 12).

This model offers communities help in avoiding the worst problems of the boomtown syndrome. The town's preenergy industrial base, location, and the skills of its work force will determine its ability to sustain a postenergy economy.

MONETARY FLOWS

Figure 28.1 (b) shows that consumers continue to pay for energy as they always have (step 1). Severance tax dollars will flow from consumers through industry to the state once resource extraction begins (step 2), and royalty payments will follow a more complex path from consumers, through industry and the federal government, to the state, which is now entitled to collect half of federal royalty revenues (step 3). All these payment mechanisms must be planned and ready to operate before any one town becomes the project site.

Once work is about to begin, industry prepays part of its taxes to the town (step 4) and compensates local residents in the amount agreed to by the auctioning process (step 5). State revenue-sharing with the impacted town also begins (step 6). The state allows the town to borrow from the banks (step 7a), and either the state or the energy firm agrees to guarantee local bonds (step 7b). With all these funds contributed before any project work begins, the town now pays developers to build the necessary housing and infrastructure, hires any outside consultants it may need to help town planning efforts, and offers attractive salaries and the certainty of a good quality of life as incentives to doctors, teachers, social workers, and other professionals to attract them to the town (step 8). If the town has the available funds, it also builds whatever additional housing and infrastructure that the townspeople had demanded in the auction and compensation agreement.

The new construction workers and professionals move in, draw wages and salaries from industry (step 9a), and start contributing income, sales, and property taxes to the town (step 9b). Industry itself pays taxes to the local and state governments as its builds and operates its plants or mines (step 10). As these funds

flow in, the town begins liquidating its debt (step 11). These funds also help the town maintain its infrastructure. The town can also afford, both unilaterally and in cooperation with any other neighboring town in a similar condition, to offer financial incentives to new industry to avoid a bust later on (step 12).

Energy consumers have to pay for the energy they use and for any shock that sudden development imposes on impacted towns. This boomtown solution, however, avoids forcing consumers to pay the boomtown residents long after these shocks have worn off. The original residents are compensated for the amount agreed to in the auction, and not a penny more. Consumers pay after that only for the benefits they themselves derive from using the energy extracted from its faraway deposits; severance tax and royalty payments depend, after all, on the amount of coal or oil extracted, not on the demands of boomtown residents.

ANALYSIS OF THE MODEL

This model covers the most common occurrence in rapid energy development—the burden falls on a small, struggling town barely able to keep its population and way of life intact. There are instances, however, when a new town has to be built, or when out-of-town wage and salary earners will not come to the town regardless of the incentives. Many large Western energy sources are miles from civilization, and industry must then build a new town. Furthermore, current industry plans include so many mines, shale oil extraction plants, synthetic fuel plants, and oil wells that it may be unable either to train enough local unskilled workers when one or more towns already exist, or to bring in enough outside employees when nothing exists, to build all its desired projects in the Rocky Mountains. Industry must then consider shipping a large fraction of the extracted resources to processing plants (e.g., coal gasification or liquefaction plants) closer to energy consumers and large numbers of skilled construction workers. Perhaps the 1981-1982 recession put enough of a damper on industry plans so that industry can train enough unskilled workers living near the site or bring in enough outsiders to do the more limited amount of work. Energy, after all, is an industry fraught with uncertainty.

Regardless of economic conditions, however, some projects will be built in the Rocky Mountain region. Industry probably will require both outside managers and engineers and a locally trained labor force. The nonunion status of most engineers and managers enables management to assign them to projects out West if the company's work load is there. Most construction workers, however, are unionized. Their ability to refuse a relocation (so long as work exists for them closer to home) may well force industry to build its projects, wherever possible, near an existing community. The boomtown model then becomes an effective way to show the interdependence of citizens, industry, and all levels of government. Only if they cooperate, by coordinating their planning, decision making, and financial efforts, will they ever solve the boomtown syndrome.

DEALING WITH BOOMTOWN SYNDROME COMPONENTS

This or any model, of course, is useful only if it can attack the symptoms and causes of boomtown growth mentioned throughout the urban-planning literature. This model, however, is the result of a synthesis of the work of hundreds of researchers in urban planning and many other related fields, so a test of the model is really a test of the approaches taken by the authors mentioned in this book. This part of Chapter 28 examines the ability of the model to deal with eight distinct components of the boomtown problem mentioned by Susskind and O'Hare (1977, 8-9).

Social disruption is perhaps the hardest of the eight to attack, since each person's perception of injury or dislocation will be unique. Susskind and O'Hare make clear that "long-time residents are the ones most affected by the disruption," the whole idea of the O'Hare-Sanderson compensation model

discussed in Chapter 20. When the company and state government jointly prepare their social and economic impact assessments, they must concentrate on the project's effects on long-time residents. They in fact have no choice, since the potential newcomers have not even entered the picture. To have any meaning, these assessments have to include the expressed opinions of the residents of several threatened towns near the project if auctioning is to apply, and of those of the single impacted town if the lack of nearby communities makes auctioning impossible. In the model, local government consults its citizens about their perceived impact, regardless of the auction situation. The key to avoiding much of the social disruption among long-time residents, therefore, is public participation on the local level. In small communities such as are likely to be found near a proposed Western energy project, public participation will involve few enough people so as not to evoke government's fear of mob rule. State and national governments can legitimately use this to avoid or control the public participation process, but local governments (unless their domain is of the size of Mexico City) usually cannot. If no town exists near the planned project—a very common situation in the western Rockies—new town construction is the only viable alternative, and environmental impact often becomes a larger concern than the effect on long-time residents.

Public service needs arise along with growth of the private sector, but "during rapid growth these services are often overburdened, or unavailable to some groups. . . . The lead time needed to design and build new facilities means that the costs are borne by those who live in the area before the boomtown population has actually arrived" (Susskind and O'Hare, 1977, 8). The model's remedy of this problem lies in its flow of funds. Once the affected state has severance tax and local revenue-sharing laws before development on a project begins, money can flow to the impacted town in a timely manner. Prepayment of industry taxes will also go a long way to help. Industry, of course, must be confident enough of its own development plans to make this commitment to the town. With all these sources of preboom funds, towns can then pay developers to build housing and other needed infrastructure, attract outside service professionals (see Chapter 27), and prepare plans for luring new industries.

A *shortage of private goods and services* inevitably occurs in boomtowns. Again, Susskind and O'Hare emphasize housing, a concern that better planning and a coordinated flow of funds will be able to address. Once developers are given the funds needed to provide these goods and services, they will have the economic incentive to do so. Of course, this incentive will exist only if the project has been well thought out. Chapter 26, for instance, refers to the Battlement Mesa merchants, whose expectations turned sour almost overnight. Such businesses must be encouraged to begin operation if the new residents' demand for various items is to be satisfied. Chapter 1 shows that preboom merchants may often be unable to deal with the boomtown atmosphere. This is a concern similar to those of any preboom resident, and can be addressed by the model's provisions for consultation and compensation.

Inflation strikes the town's prices, wages, and rents. In any city, land is the controlling commodity. If land prices are allowed to soar, landlords must raise their rents, merchants must hike up their prices, and inflation-ravaged workers will demand higher wages. Of course, the landlords and merchants will initially benefit from inflation; however, local merchants who cannot raise their wages to compete with those offered by the boom-inducing industry will quickly lose their workers, a process shown to have happened throughout Scotland and the Middle East. Chapter 23 makes clear that land speculation must be controlled before a boom strikes an area. Various changes in the local and state tax codes should help reduce the impact of speculators on the area economy. Once this is done, most of the region's land will be owned by people intent on either farming it or building on it. These landowners, therefore, can only help the local food and shelter markets in the long run. One critical item harder to attack is the cost of shipping capital and

consumer goods into remote areas, an item that can severely inflate those items' costs. If the boom industry itself has to ship these goods in and out, these costs become part of the overall project cost, passed on to the consumer. The spread of Western railroads showed the incentive that the new towns created among farmers and new industries, who now had a fairly secure market for their products. One can hope that in certain instances, the development of new farming and industrial economies near the boomtown will help make the area more self-sufficient in various goods, reducing the area's isolation and those goods' cost to the ultimate consumer.

Boomtowns also experience *revenue shortfalls;* "even though growth expands sales and property tax bases, revenues increase more slowly than costs in the short run" (Susskind and O'Hare, 1977, 9). However, this is yet another boomtown syndrome component that a timely flow of funds will help control. The model helps avoid a town's being overwhelmed with new demands on its treasury by spreading out its costly infrastructure provision and giving it far more preboom funds than most boomtowns now enjoy.

A boomtown's *resources lost to other uses* include water, land, and labor.

In some states' energy development regions, groundwater use is unregulated by state permits. Increased consumption by energy development may mean water shortages for cities and agricultural producers. . . . When strip-mining removes land from agricultural production (for at least ten years in most places), local food processing industries fail . . . [and] face a shortage of inexpensive labor. (Susskind and O'Hare, 1977, 9)

The key to controlling this problem, of course, is planning, especially at the state level. Such efforts as Utah's Agenda for the Eighties help state governments become aware of their water supplies and the projected demand for them. Sophisticated mathematical models for predicting population growth should help here. Just as cities, states, and the whole nation have become aware of the limits in their energy supplies and the need to plan allocation of these resources in emergency situations, so should they consider water, land, and labor as finite resources to be distributed under conditions of rapid energy development, certainly an emergency in the impacted area. Any overall boomtown model must consider those industries that cannot match the energy industries' high wages. In most instances, this can be considered part of the impact assessment and compensation-measuring procedures that should take place before the boom.

Boomtowns clearly suffer *aesthetic deterioration,* primarily from mobile-home construction. Providing timely funds to housing builders will give them the time and financing to develop and construct attractive housing, especially single-family dwellings that many studies have shown most boomtown residents to prefer. Old-time residents, who now have to suffer the presence of trailer camps near their own homes, will also benefit. One financial measure can also help here: the raising of taxes on mobile homes to levels applicable to permanent dwellings. If the government makes clear that it does not favor trailers, the chances are they will not be built. Moreover, if enough planning has gone into the project, the knowledge that it will go on for a while should give builders still more incentive to provide houses that will please both new and old-time residents. They will also be encouraged to provide paved streets and landscaping around unavoidable trailer parks.

The final component of boomtown growth is the *fundamental change* itself. "The injury such [disruption] causes is only partly mitigated if the 'new' town is clean and orderly" (Susskind and O'Hare, 1977, 9). Planning, however, it vital too. If long-time residents are given enough warning about impending change, and their government lets them participate in planning needed to deal with the change, these people will feel less alienated from the new reality and have more time to adapt to it.

When industry has no choice but to consider expanding towns already near a large planned project, the application of the ideas summed up in this model will go far toward reducing all these components of the boomtown syndrome. The auction concept may often prove useful in this instance. Even when the existence of only one town eliminates this step, the procedures in the model will still reduce the syndrome's impact. When no town exists at all, the situation is completely different, and new town construction and employee relocation by the boom industry becomes the only viable boomtown solution.

REFERENCE

Susskind, Lawrence, and O'Hare, Michael, 1977, *Managing the Social and Economic Impacts of Energy Development,* Massachusetts Institute of Technology, Cambridge, Mass.

29

Concluding Remarks

Uncontrolled growth can occur in communities of any size because most local governments lack the ability to manage their own growth and to coordinate their efforts with state and national governments and with individuals and industry, and because industry cannot forecast the likelihood of project delays that will make boomtown growth even more chaotic until after the delays occur. Most crucial to solving the boomtown problem is the need to reduce the level of uncertainty of any development project's future. Uncertainty restricts the forecasting of population growth and demand for future goods and services, which in turn inhibits financial and other forms of aid to these towns.

Of all the boomtown research discussed in previous chapters, perhaps no one better described the steps necessary for solution of the syndrome than Ira Robinson, Professor of Urban Planning at the University of Calgary. He was dealing mainly with brand new Canadian resource towns, but his ideas for sensible development are just as accurate in rapidly growing boomtowns all over the world.

It is clear that the days are gone when the . . . company was the sole actor or agent in planning, building, and managing resource communities: when it alone selected the location for the town (as well as for its industrial plant); determined the future amount of employment and population to be accommodated; prepared the town plan; and served as the developer, banker, town council, fireman, and recreation director, as well as major (if not sole employer). In recent years, there has been a growth in involvement of senior governments . . . in resource town developments. I recommend that this involvement increase even further in the future. At the same time, the resource companies themselves will and should continue to play some role in the development of new resource towns. . . .

In addition to continuing to provide needed regional infrastructure, provincial governments (and the federal government, where appropriate) should play a more active role in three key planning-policy decision areas affecting resource town development: (1) the decision to establish a new resource town, including its function and location; (2) the actual development of the town site; and (3) the fate of existing declining or dying communities and future towns faced with the same prospect. . . . (Robinson, 1979, 69-70)

243

In the first area, government should make sure that any necessary new towns be built in areas "where economic [industrial] diversification would be possible and are provided with the necessary facilities and services required to bring this about; and where this is not feasible, to construct nonpermanent communities" (Robinson, 1979, 70). Before building a permanent new town, government should obtain firm commitments from more than one industry to operate there. In town site development, "the appropriate senior government should play a more active role in . . . their planning, the ownership and disposal of land in and around the towns, the provision of housing, the construction and financing of certain town site components, and management of the town affairs, particularly in its early stages" (Robinson, 1979, 71). To prevent a new contagion of ghost towns, Robinson suggested that government help attract other industries to threatened towns and retrain workers for employment in them; this book, however, has shown many times that this step is far easier said than done. Finally, if new towns are deemed absolutely necessary,

resource agreements between government and the company should stipulate that a town will not be built unless and until a sufficient life of the resource is proven. Special legislation [should define] the role of both government and . . . industry . . . to assist in phasing out the community in question, relocating the population, liquidating the assets and rehabilitating the site. Investigation should . . . determine the feasibility of developing mobile-type, nonpermanent communities which can be moved from one site to another. (Robsinson, 1979, 73)

Other steps, outlined in Chapters 27 and 28, are clearly necessary when existing communities undergo extremely rapid growth, but Robinson clearly stated the need for extensive cooperation and coordination of planning efforts among all government levels and industry.

Utah's Agenda for the Eighties made much the same argument from an American standpoint:

Governments are notoriously slow and cumbersome in responding to dramatic growth. . . . The officials who preside over cities, counties and state are frequently changed; the resistance to government action is strong and broad-based within the population, and governments are fragmented, uncoordinated and yet work in environments of shared responsibility among the many levels of government—federal, state and local. Conflicts among the different levels of government are common and the action by any one level of government is often dependent on corresponding action by other units of government. . . . Most will agree that it is government's responsibility to manage growth by careful planning, by designating growth centers, by arranging front-end financing where the existing tax base is inadequate and by providing . . . law and order, protection for the environment and basic services. . . . If government is to function well, better mechanisms are needed to harmonize the actions and policies of federal, state and local governments. . . . A taxing system adequate for a stable or no-growth environment may be inadequate for an environment of rapid growth. (Utah State Department of Community and Economic Development, 1980, 19)

This entire field is wide open to additional research. Numerous theories and ideas have addressed the legal, economic, and social problems of boomtown growth, but future research should look at the extent to which they have successfully been applied to actual boomtowns. This is especially true for the auctioning idea. In certain regions, such as the coastal regions of the United States, where millions of people live in thousands of communities, such a scheme could work very well in determining the future location of ports, oil refineries and storage areas, and other major construction projects. With so many towns and cities near any likely site, industry would probably be foolish even to consider building new towns for its workers, and enough existing towns will be available to hold auctions.

The situation is radically different in the Rocky Mountains and in Scotland, especially the Shetlands, where areas are vast and towns are few and far between. The Rockies, especially, are such a huge area that no town might exist for many miles around a potential oil-shale project or coal mine. If the Battlement Mesa experience has not soured industry on the idea of new town construction and if this study's recommendations for better coordination and planning are at least partly followed, new town construction may be mandatory for successful project operation in uninhabited wilderness areas. The existence of nearby communities may persuade industry to avoid new town building. If only one town is nearby, its planners will just have to work out the best compensation arrangement possible with industry, and the company's officials will have to coordinate their planning and construction schedules with local, regional, and state government. Only in the instance in which several towns are nearby will the auction method be feasible. Additional research, then, must determine the number of times this latter case existed, and of those, the number of occasions auctioning proved a solution to boomtown growth.[1]

Research possibilities exist in other areas, too. Studies should determine

the level of success of the growth management and planning innovations discussed in Part V,

the impact of the early 1980s world recession on boomtown growth in Scotland, the Middle East, the Rockies, and other oil-producing areas mentioned in Part III,

the success of efforts in Houston, Mexico City, and other exploding cities to control rapid population growth,

the development of more sophisticated taxing-disbursement schemes in the Western states and overseas that deal directly with boomtown problems,

and the development of public participation as an essential part of social and environmental impact assessment.

The last chapter in the definitive boomtown syndrome book is still being written.

NOTE

1. The number and size of existing communities will also make a big difference in the success of genuine public participation. Government does have a legitimate concern when this involves thousands of people, each of whom will demand the most for himself or herself with no consideration of everyone else's problems. But in remote areas where only a scattered population is to be affected, public participation should prove far more satisfactory, both to the residents and their local and state governments. The West, after all, pioneered government-by-referendum years ago.

REFERENCES

Robinson, Ira M., 1979, "Planning, Building, and Managing New Towns on the Resource Frontier," in William T. Perks and Ira M. Robinson, eds., *Urban and Regional Planning in a Federal State*, Dowden, Hutchinson & Ross, Stroudsburg, Pa.

Utah State Department of Community and Economic Development, 1980, *Agenda for the Eighties*, UDCED, Salt Lake City.

Index

About the Author

GARY W. MALAMUD earned the M.B.A. degree in management from New York University, after earning the B.S. degree from The Cooper Union and the M.S. degree from Pennsylvania State University, both in chemical engineering. His M.S. work, which included a minor in air pollution control, was financed through a traineeship awarded by the university's Center for Air Environment Studies. He worked for more than eight years in several engineering and design firms as a process and environmental engineer.

Boomtown Communities is an expansion of Malamud's M.B.A. thesis, "A Comprehensive Solution to the Boomtown Syndrome." His M.S. thesis was published in the February 1975 *Journal of the Air Pollution Control Association,* and his M.B.A. thesis appeared in condensed form in the August 22, 1983 edition of *Chemical Engineering.*